Codify

Codify: Parametric and Computational Design in Landscape Architecture provides a series of essays that explore what it means to use, modify, and create computational tools in a contemporary design environment. Landscape architecture has a long history of innovation in the areas of computation and media, particularly in how the discipline represents, analyses, and constructs complex systems. This curated volume spans academic and professional projects to form a snapshot of digital practices that aim to show how computation is a tool that goes beyond methods of representation and media. The book is organized into four sections; syntax, perception, employ, and prospective. The essays are written by leading academics and professionals and the sections examine the role of computational tools in landscape architecture through case studies, historical accounts, theoretical arguments, and nascent propositions.

Bradley Cantrell is a landscape architect and scholar whose work focuses on the role of computation and media in environmental and ecological design. He is currently Professor and Chair of the Department of Landscape Architecture at the University of Virginia School of Architecture and has held academic appointments at the Harvard Graduate School of Design, the Rhode Island School of Design, and the Louisiana State University Robert Reich School of Landscape Architecture. His work in coastal and riverine landscapes forms a series of methodologies that develop modes of modeling, simulation, and embedded computation that express and engage the complexity of overlapping physical, cultural, and economic systems.

Adam Mekies is a licensed landscape architect and planner at Design Workshop in Aspen, Colorado, where he leads many of the firm's computational and interactive technologies in the construction of the public and private realm. He received his Bachelor of Landscape Architecture from Iowa State University, and has applied his interests in advanced construction modeling and computational technology to design projects across the country and overseas. He is the recipient of multiple ASLA design and research awards for his work in community design and implementation of interactive and parametric technologies.

Codify

Parametric and Computational Design in Landscape Architecture

Edited by
Bradley Cantrell and Adam Mekies

Routledge
Taylor & Francis Group

LONDON AND NEW YORK

First published 2018
by Routledge
2 Park Square, Milton Park, Abingdon, Oxon OX14 4RN

and by Routledge
711 Third Avenue, New York, NY 10017

Routledge is an imprint of the Taylor & Francis Group, an informa business

British Library Cataloguing-in-Publication Data
A catalogue record for this book is available from the British Library

Library of Congress Cataloging-in-Publication Data
Names: Cantrell, Bradley, editor. | Mekies, Adam, editor.
Title: Codify : parametric and computational design in landscape architecture / edited by Bradley Cantrell and Adam Mekies.
Description: Milton Park, Abingdon, Oxon ; New York, NY : Routledge, 2018. | Includes bibliographical references and index.
Identifiers: LCCN 2017049527| ISBN 9781138125032 (hbk) | ISBN 9781138125049 (pbk) | ISBN 9781315647791 (ebk)
Subjects: LCSH: Landscape architecture—Computer programs. | Landscape Architecture—Computer-aided design. | Landscape design—Data processing.
Classification: LCC SB475.9.D37 C63 2018 | DDC 712.0285—dc23
LC record available at https://lccn.loc.gov/2017049527

ISBN: 978-1-138-12503-2 (hbk)
ISBN: 978-1-138-12504-9 (pbk)
ISBN: 978-1-315-64779-1 (ebk)

Typeset in DIN
by Florence Production Ltd, Stoodleigh, Devon, UK
Printed and bound in Great Britain by Bell & Bain Ltd, Glasgow

Contents

Notes on contributors

Elizabeth Christoforetti works broadly across scales as a strategic thinker and an architectural and urban designer. She received a Master in Architecture with Distinction from the Harvard Graduate School of Design, where she received the Henry Adams Medal, the school's highest academic honor. Elizabeth also studied religion at Bowdoin College in Maine and grew up in Pittsburgh, Pennsylvania.

Joseph Claghorn is Research and Teaching Fellow at Leibnitz Universität Hannover. His research explores methods of form and space making based on the patterns and processes of landscape, infrastructural and ecological systems, and the application of parametric and generative design tools to landscape architecture projects.

Will Cohen works to integrate technology and quantitative analysis into planning and design. Will is an urban planner specializing in the use of mapping and spatial analysis as part of citywide and neighborhood master plans. He received a Master in Urban Planning from the Harvard Graduate School of Design, and studied sociology and English literature at the University of Chicago.

Kurt Culbertson, FASLA, is the Chairman and CEO of Design Workshop. He is currently pursuing a doctorate from the Edinburgh College of Art. Kurt joined Design Workshop in 1979. He is a full member of the Urban Land Institute, participating in the Recreation Development Council, and served as chapter chair of the Rocky Mountain chapter of the Young Presidents Organization. He has served as a fellow of Dumbarton Oaks, the American Society of Landscape Architects, and the Institute of Urban Design and received a Fulbright Scholarship to the Wirtschaft Universität in Vienna, Austria. He also has served as co-chair of the Cultural Landscape Foundation.

Brian Davis is Assistant Professor in the Department of Landscape Architecture and Director of the Borderlands Research Group. He is also a registered landscape architect and a member of the Dredge Research Collaborative. His research and teaching is part of the emerging field of fluvio-urban morphology: the study of form and process of rivers and cities, and the way they are related.

Stephen M. Ervin is Assistant Dean for Information Technology at Harvard Design School, Director of Computer Resources, and lecturer in the Department of Landscape Architecture, at the Harvard Graduate School of Design. A pioneer in applications of computing in landscape architecture, planning and design, Ervin is the author of numerous articles, including "Digital Landscape Modeling, a Research Agenda" and the book *Landscape Modeling: Digital Techniques for Landscape Visualization* (McGraw-Hill 2001), coauthored with Hope Hasbrouck.

Leif Estrada is an artist, designer, and researcher in the fields of architecture, landscape architecture, urban design, and technology. His interests in utilizing cartographic representations and visualizations in the development of theoretical frameworks earned him an honorable mention at the 2014 National Geographic Award in Mapping administered by the Cartography Specialty Group of the Association of American Geographers, followed by the Howard Fisher Prize in Geographic Information Science awarded by the Center for Geographic Analysis at Harvard University during his first year.

Pete Evans is Senior Lecturer at Iowa State University, where he teaches digital design communications and industrial design CAD/CAM and prototyping. He is the university coordinator for the Forward Learning Experience (FLEx), a K–12 design-focused STEM outreach program delivering twenty-first-century learning through Iowa State Extension and partnered with 4-H.

David Fletcher is an urban designer and landscape architect, professor, and writer. His work addresses process, urbanized watersheds, green infrastructure, and postindustrial urbanism. David has taught urban design and landscape architecture at Harvard Design School, the Southern California Institute of Architecture (sci_Arc), the Centre d'Etude d'Architecture et d'Urbanisme in France, Woodbury University, UCLA, Otis College, and the USC School of Architecture. He was the Assistant Chair of the Architecture/Landscape/ Interiors program at Otis College and the Assistant Director of the Landscape Architecture Department at the University of Southern California.

Luis E. Fraguada investigates critical issues in architecture, design, and urbanism through various modes, including associative design, scripting, and fabrication. Luis is currently member of the Faculty of Architecture at IaaC in Barcelona, Spain, as the principal computation instructor, focusing on the interface between computational processes and fabrication. He is currently developing Iris, a plug-in for McNeel's Rhinoceros that allows users to export their geometry to the web. Luis joined Built by Associative Data as an associate and became the Director of the Barcelona office in 2010.

Anthony Frausto-Robledo AIA, LEED AP, is Associate Architect in Practice at Morehouse MacDonald & Associates, Inc., Architects, a leading regional design firm focused principally on custom single-family residential architecture, interiors, estate master planning, and select commercial architecture (in the areas of hospitality and offices) in the US and select foreign markets. Anthony is also the owner, publisher, and editor-in-chief of Architosh.com, one of the world's leading online CAD and 3D publications, providing unique editorial, information resources, online communities, and market research information to ISVs and more than 200,000 site visitors worldwide annually.

Jared Friedman is a computational designer and licensed architect based in Brooklyn, New York. Jared has a Bachelor in Architecture from Carnegie Mellon University and a Master in Design Studies in Technology from the Harvard Graduate School of Design. Much of his research has focused on thermodynamics, computation, and digital fabrication. Jared enjoys thinking about how to best deploy robots in the construction process and how we can design buildings as heat exchangers rather than giant insulated boxes.

Andrea Hansen Phillips is the principal of Datum Digital Studio, a boutique design studio located Washington, DC that specializes in web design and development, data visualization, community engagement tools, and mapping for landscape, architecture, and urban design projects. In addition to her practice, Andrea is the editor of *Atlas of Visualization*, an online catalog that features compelling maps and visualizations from the past and present.

Justine Holzman is Assistant Professor of Landscape Architecture at the University of Toronto Daniels School of Architecture, teaching visual communication, site technologies, and studio courses. Additionally, Holzman is a member of the Dredge Research Collaborative and coauthor of the book *Responsive Landscapes*.

Nicholas Jacobson of Aspen, Colorado, is recent graduate of the Harvard University Graduate School of Design, where he received a master's degree in design (M.Des Technology). He is a computational designer/digital fabricator/design researcher focusing on creating new techniques to explore new design possibilities. Trained as an architect, mathematician, artist, and chef, he has a particular interest in a technically innovative and logically rigorous approach to form.

Ricardo Jnani Gonzalez has over seven years of design experience, a master's degree from MIT, and a passion for emergent technologies. His work aims to synthesize design, technology, science, and the arts. He is an award-winning designer and published researcher with a deep interest in thoughtful design and meaningful innovations.

James Melsom is a practicing landscape architect collaborating in projects in Switzerland and throughout Europe as a member of the BSLA. Since 2007 he has worked as teacher and research fellow at the Institute of Landscape Architecture, ETH Zurich (girot.arch.ethz.ch) and is co-founder, with Ilmar Hurkxkens, of the research laboratory LANDSKIP.

Brian Osborn is Assistant Professor at the Cal Poly College of Architecture and Environmental Design. His research interests include the use of digital design and production methods in the coupling of constructed form and biological systems. In addition to his teaching and research, Brian is a licensed landscape architect with over 15 years of professional experience across the fields of environmental design.

Brian Phelps is a landscape architect and Senior Associate at Hawkins Partners, Inc. Over the last 18 years, he has been exploring solutions for repairing our cities and improving our urban experience. As a senior associate at Hawkins Partners, Inc., a landscape architecture and urban design office in Nashville, Tennessee, he is involved in wide array of projects ranging from the design/planning of mixed-use developments, public space, and transportation and the integration of green infrastructure. He is also the founder of the

AGILE Landscape Project, a think tank dedicated to exploring urban design solutions that improve cities and public space through adaptive, generative, and intelligent landscape experimentation.

Heike Rahmann is a landscape architect and urban researcher and a lecturer in landscape architecture at the RMIT School of Architecture and Design, Melbourne, Australia. Her research explores the intersection of landscape and contemporary urbanism with a focus on design practice and theory. Her most recent project explores the relationship between digital technologies, landscape architecture design practice and fabrication. She holds a PhD in Architecture from the University of Tokyo where she received awards from the German Academic Exchange Service (DAAD) and the Japanese Government (MEXT).

Chris Reed is Founding Director of Stoss Landscape Urbanism. He is recognized internationally as a leading voice in the transformation of landscapes and cities, and he works alternately as a researcher, strategist, teacher, designer, and advisor. Reed is particularly interested in the relationships between ecology and landscape and infrastructure, social spaces, and cities.

Craig Reschke is an architect and Designer-in-Residence in the Department of Landscape Architecture at the University of Illinois at Urbana-Champaign. He graduated from Harvard's Graduate School of Design where he received the Jacob Weidenmann Prize, and holds a B.Arch from the University of Tennessee. His research focuses on rural American landscapes and how the real-time data streams and mapping technologies of precision agriculture could be applied to change how CRP sites are selected and maintained, allowing a faster response time to conservation needs. He has his own architecture and landscape practice in Chicago with partner Ann Lui: Future Firm.

Alexander Robinson is Director of the USC Landscape Morphologies Lab and principal of the landscape design, research and planning practice at the Office of Outdoor Research, based in Los Angeles. Robinson's research and practice is focused on the means necessary to advance the design and implementation of high-performance landscapes and infrastructures. He is motivated by multiple qualities that synthetic landscape solutions can offer urban life across numerous spectra ranging from experiential to performative.

Christopher J. Seeger is Professor and Extension Specialist in Landscape Architecture and Geospatial Technology at Iowa State University. His work focuses on healthy community design, walkability, and safe routes to school development. He specializes in the use of collaborative community mapping using mobile and online geospatial technology tools, crowdsourcing, and facilitated volunteered geographic information. He also teaches courses in community and regional planning that involve GIS, landscape modeling, and visualization.

Jillian Walliss researches the relationship between theory, culture, and contemporary design practice. Her current focus is on two areas: digital technologies and their application in landscape architecture and evolving notions of civic in the twenty-first century. She is Senior Lecturer in Landscape Architecture at the Melbourne School of Design, Melbourne, Australia. She is the recipient of several awards and has taught landscape theory and design studio at several universities in Australia and New Zealand.

Acknowledgments

01100101 01101101 ++ { It goes without saying that this book is made possible by the generous contributions of my colleagues. Their insightful essays and innovative projects are what made this book possible. I could not have completed this work without the support and love of my partner, Emma Mendel, and my children, Hannah and David. I would like to also thank my co-editor, Adam Mekies, who pushed this process forward and brought a professional perspective that has helped ground the essays and range of contributors. The book also owes itself to the Harvard Graduate School of Design and the University of Virginia School of Architecture, which have supported me during the production and editing process. } ++ 01100010 01100011

Bradley Cantrell, 2018

01111000 01100110 ++ { I am profoundly indebted to all of the mentors and colleagues who offered their scholarly expertise, constant encouragement, and contributed an unparalleled array and breadth of knowledge and experience through their essay contributions. I am thankful to my father, Saul, without whose steady assistance and constant prodding my part of this project would doubtedly have come to fruition. My eternal gratitude goes to Mr. Steve King of Landscape Structures for his vision in creating the Barbara King Scholarship, which provided the initial funding for the project, and to the Iowa State University College of Design for its substantial encouragement of this endeavor. I wish to thank Mr. Dominic Audia, Mr. Brian Martz, and Mr. Nicholas Lorch, along with so many early mentors in the now-blurry technical and design fields of computation, construction, and robotics, which have shaped the background of this book and my career. I am deeply indebted to my co-editor, Bradley Cantrell, who, before anyone else, recognized the potential for this project, encouraged me, and guided this process from its early conception, bringing his academic perspective and theoretical underpinning to the wide range of essay contributions. A significant recognition must go to Gabriel Comstock, and Justin Massey whose many years of conversations, and debates shaped so many questions and conversations surrounding this project. My appreciation goes to Josh Lee for his dedicated assistance with the text's graphic design and layout. The project also owes a great deal to the leadership of Design Workshop for their encouragement and guidance in completing this project. } ++ 01000001 01001101

Adam Mekies, 2018

00.00
About code

Contributor:

Christophe Girot
*Chair of Landscape
Architecture, ETH
Zurich*

When the verb "codify" appeared in the early nineteenth century it stemmed from the thirteenth-century old French word *code*, which originally meant a book compiling together some laws. The word *code* itself came from the Latin word *codex*, which meant a book of laws, and this word originated earlier from the word *caudex*, literally signifying a tree trunk or a rudimentary book made up of wood tablets coated with wax for the purpose of notation.[1] Decoding these early wooden tablets required not only genius but also a strict set of rules to help decipher the signs inscribed and attain full disambiguation. In computer jargon, the word "coding" is much more recent; it appeared in the 1950s, when source codes were punched out of cards and then fed into Univac computers that transcribed them into either words or complex binary numerals. The punch cards were not made of waxed tree bark but of cardboard, a derivative of wood, and it is interesting to note how this original organic link to etched wood prevailed well into the early coding years of the cybernetic age.

The first computerized SYMAP landscape plans were produced by Carl Steinitz and depicted the large-scale territory of the Delmarva Peninsula. The project produced at the Laboratory for Computer Graphics and Spatial Analysis at Harvard University in 1966 made history. The grid-based plans were printed with character types on scrolls of paper and marked the beginning of early GIS planning. Starting in the early 1970s, IBM 3270 mainframe computers began transcribing computational results on monochrome green cathode display terminals. The screens were limited to a maximum display of 80 characters on 24 rows; each character appeared as a phosphorescent green cipher blinking against a black background.[2] We could no longer speak of an organic link to the early wooden tablets of the *caudex* but the color green made a shortcut back to nature as a possible synecdoche. Since these pioneer times on the early Unix mainframe, the cardboard punch cards have become obsolete and been relegated to the archives of early machine language, as have the green blinking type screens of the IBM 3270s, with their ominous magnetic reels and scroll printers. But acknowledging an "organic" evolution of coding into the twenty-first century seems particularly relevant today with respect to how landscape has become codified. This past century saw the launch of cybernetics; will the logic of twenty-first-century landscape coding be robotics?

"Codifying" addresses a question long overdue, as to the place and role parametric design and related modeling activities in landscape architecture through advanced computational design. It bears new meaning and offers a vast spectrum of possible arrays; it is an injunction to creative thinking in a field where old analogue habits of design tend to stall on innovation. Two threads of "coding" run parallel to each other throughout this book. The first, more analytical and deductive, looks at possible rules of conduct in a general context; weighing social factors over cultural aspects, sensing environmental urgency over economic pragmatism, the sum of it is spelled out in a programmatic way. The other thread in the book is more synthetic and inductive. It directly investigates possible applications and implementations of parametric design in the "material practice" through the use of "code," enabling a much broader palette of potential landscape transformations. Several essays deal with the issue of place, and how an enhanced approach to site design can better strengthen qualities that are unique to a particular culture and location. In an age of unilateral ecological systems methods, there seems to be little place left for any critical design thinking at all. Through new approaches to "coding" it becomes possible to repair this missed opportunity, to create a creative dialogue and to link with a technique that is more in tune with terrain. We may no longer be there scratching the waxed surface of a piece of bark to imbed code, but we could very well leave our mark on the land in return for a more significant way to design. The informative yet highly reductive 2D mapping overlay techniques that followed Ian McHarg's and Carl Steinitz's teachings introduced programmatic layering as a ready-made answer to many of our design questions, but it offered no choices in design per se for a very long period of time. This prolonged design amnesia led, more often than not, to out-of-the-box designs based on a single dogmatic methodology. It is my belief that a return to a heuristic approach to terrain discovery and surveying could offer a

more plausible, diversified, creative and open approach that would harness some of the finer possibilities offered by advanced computational methodologies. Such a break in traditional planning methodology could also help diversify design answers and reduce what has become a redundant homogenization of "ecological" planning solutions produced over the past five decades.

The extraordinary palette of possibilities offered by new computational methods through geographically positioned modeling and its attributes will enable designers to access more readily a broader palette of options, questions, and solutions, responding physically and spatially to the specificity and inherent complexity of a place. This will also enable an entirely new form of ecology to arise and succeed, one that is much more imbedded in the cultural and topographical quality of each place. Contrary to conventional wisdom, "coding" does not correspond to some fleeting trend but rather marks a return to a need to inscribe essential meaning in our daily lives on the ground we tread upon. It will help induce a complete change of mind about our world for generations of designers to come, a revolution of sorts, that will wipe out any risk of reduction or homogenization that could linger on. If a real threat exists for landscape architecture in the coming decade it is that of being flattened and packed into a zoned-out 2D abstraction based on scientific methods belonging to another age. Landscapes are being understood and recomposed along a completely new array of sensors that react to a broad range of material properties and signals in the world (visible and not visible), where our reasoning no longer stands on the simple binary relation linking cause and effect but rather on countless sets of stochastic iterations. The change in computer trends is by nature fleeting, but what if these became self-regulating and adaptive? Then, perhaps, the fear of landscape homogenization and 2D standardization will be overthrown by the extraordinary potential that we now see in computers coding our world in an age of landscape remediation guided by intrinsic scientific knowledge. It is my belief that generative design and advanced landscape fabrication will move hand in hand with computational thinking into a new form of intelligence hybridized with clearer operating principles, which will be better suited to terrain modeling, finally reaching a sounder physical response to the materiality and true potential of a place through seamless scaling from object to object across the entire field of design.

Notes

1. Oxford English Dictionary etymology.

2. Brandstäter, Klaus; 3270 *A Brief History*, HOB Techtalk, Documentation Posted on December 9, 2008. Retrieved on December 14, 2016.

00.01
Coding landscape

Contributors:

Bradley Cantrell
*ASLA, FAAR,
Professor and Chair
of Landscape
Architecture,
University of Virginia
School of Architecture*

Adam Mekies
*PLA, Associate,
Design Workshop Inc,
Aspen Colorado*

Developing syntax

Coding: To express in syntax a set of operations so as one or a system of computations may be made.[1]

The discussion and implementation of code is an undeveloped discourse in the profession of landscape architecture, yet that seemingly arcane world of computation may not differ from other disciplines or techniques, at their nascent origins, which ultimately extended the agency of human societies.

The act of coding is like authoring a well-written work of fiction. The organized collection of words, in a particular language, frames the story line and describes the characters, actions, and context.
The algorithm of a computer program is analogous in its reasoning. The relationship of variables, inputs, parameters, and results forms a story based on the sequence of events. Computing or "the computer" is the reader of this story, compiling the words and interpreting the code that forms the narrative. In this vein, change one key action or location, or replace a key character, and the story unfolds in an entirely different way.

Code and algorithms are discussed in the daily milieu of contemporary culture, remotely related to their original computer science definition. This discussion of code can take place in one of two types of languages, as Paul Coates describes "natural" and "artificial" languages.

> Natural languages have developed over the last 100,000 years or so and are, of course, based on the way we inhabit the world with other people. Natural languages have unknown syntax and the lexicon is subject to at least some natural drift and development. Artificial languages have an explicit syntax and well-defined lexicon.
>
> Using these artificial languages, one can define algorithms – one class of algorithms is those written in computer code. Computer code is a very particular kind of text. It is designed to be readable for humans, after training; in this it is much the same as natural languages – no one would expect to be able to read Proust in the original French without learning French beforehand.
>
> Coates[2]

It is therefore important that we establish a theoretical and practical underpinning to guide the shifting syntax of landscape architecture and computation: the discussion of "code" as a syntactical language and heuristic process that we push for computational design to become a subject of thought and common language in landscape architecture, to promote new ecological, social, economic, formal, and material design systems in the built environment.

Early history of computation

Computation and the quest for a machine to facilitate complex calculations can be traced to centuries before the Common Era. Various computational achievements can be attributed to the Chinese,

Babylonians, and Greeks, among others.[3] The first modern mechanical computer, the so-called analytical engine, was developed in 1834 by Charles Babbage, a British mathematician, engineer, and inventor.[4] The analytical engine merited the term "computer" as it adhered (in retrospect) to the basic principles of today's mechanical computers.

The foundation of the modern computer was soundly established by a British mathematician and scientist, Alan Turing, in 1937 in his seminal paper on "Computable Numbers."[5] Apple's Steve Wozniak believed that Turing set the standards for modern computation: in his keynote address to the 2012 Turing Festival, Wozniak said that "Turing came up with what we know about computers today."[6]

FIGURE 0.1.1 **Computers in 1942. For the first half of the twentieth century, finding their roots during the Second World War, "computer" was a job description, not a ubiquitous machine**

Source: Public Release National Archive[9]

The term "computer" has been in use from the early seventeenth century (its first known written reference dates from 1613) and meant "one who computes,"[7] referring to a person executing calculations; this was of course prior to electronic computers becoming widely available. For Turing's contemporaries, computation, or computing, meant getting as many people as necessary to complete a task in as short a space of time as was possible. The use of a machine to complete human tasks was a new concept of the time, one society still struggles with in new ways in contemporary culture. Much of Turing's work investigated the potential of what could be computed by machines in place of their human counterparts.[8]

Around a hundred mechanical computers existed in the world in 1953, capable of making hundreds of calculations a day. We now take for granted that billions of calculations are made per second and that technology is further advancing in exponential strides as we now enter the world of quantum computing and qubits.[10] Gradually the world began to take advantage of inventions and replaced the "human calculator" with the mechanical machine. However, just as with electronic compilers (translators), in landscape architecture we still struggle with the translation and abstraction of thought processes to machine language.

The frustrations we still face to this day were just as salient at the earliest stages of military and top-secret computing. Similarly, these recurring frustrations were dealt with humor, even at the NSA (National Security Agency), as illustrated (below) in the monthly "Techniques and Standards" bulletin.[11]

Emergence of computation in landscape architecture

The origins of computation, from our perspective as designers and planners,

emerged first in the 1960s with new thought processes in analysis and environmental planning. This approach is perhaps best explained in 1967 in the seminal paper "Design with Nature," by Ian McHarg, an approach now referred to as "McHargian Analysis." Mcharg's explanation of an overlay system for land classification, coupled with much of the work done and courses taught by Carl Steinitz at the Harvard Graduate School of Design, established a basis for the development of modern GIS (geographic information systems).[12]

In 1965, Chicago architect and Harvard Graduate School of Design Architecture alum Howard T. Fisher, created the Harvard Laboratory for Computer Graphics and Spatial Analysis. There, supported by a major grant from the Ford Foundation, Fisher further developed GIS, which spun off a number of computer applications and integrated mapping systems, including tools such as SYMAP (Synagraphic Mapping and Analysis Program), with the ability to print contour maps on a line printer.[13]

These initial forays into GIS and related tools were initially speculations in computation and mapping but were eventually developed into commercial software applications and hardware implementations. Hardware purchasers would have access to free software, which the users could also develop for their own specific needs. Fisher's pioneering ideas, in turn, inspired Jack Dangermond, then research assistant at the lab from 1968 to 1969, to put these ideas to practical use. Dangermond's start-up company, ESRI (Environmental Systems Research Institute), was founded in 1969, focusing on software for land use analysis.[14]

In the early 1970s, computation in landscape architecture focused primarily on a two-dimensional understanding of data and mapping overlay. It was not until the late

FIGURE 0.1.2 *Cryptolog* magazine, June 1979 – Cover and Cartoon

Source: Public release, National Security Agency

1970s that three-dimensional computation expanded, gaining more traction not only in research institutions and government agencies but also in the entertainment industry.

The late 1970s saw government entities, such as the National Forest Service, take a deeper interest in nascent landscape architecture computational techniques of visualizing and documenting large landscapes and forest lands.[15] Built originally to monitor forest harvesting and annual forest fire behavior, these simulations encountered many of the same level of detail (LOD) challenges we face today in modeling and visualizing large expanses of vegetation.[16] The entertainment industry, both film and television,[17] explored the capabilities of computer graphics during that period of time. Early projects, however, struggled with budgets and especially story lines that did not expand beyond the "novelty" of computer graphics. Film director George Lucas pierced through those obstacles. In 1979, Lucas created a special computer graphics division for his company. It was in this environment that researchers had access to funding but more importantly guidance from a serious producer with "definitive goals."[18]

> A special effect is a tool, a means of telling a story. People have a tendency to confuse them as an end to themselves. A special effect without a story is a pretty boring thing.
>
> George Lucas, 1983[19]

Accessibility of computation in the private practice of landscape architecture

The first commercially accessible computers for the masses expanded rapidly in the 1980s, and with that hardware expansion software development would soon follow at an ever-increasing rate. In 1982, Autodesk, founded by John Walker, launched its first version of AutoCAD.[20] AutoCAD, to this day, is one of the most heavily used programs for detailed design and drafting in landscape architecture and other design and engineering fields. That same year, Dangermond's ESRI finally launched Arc/INFO, its first commercially available GIS platform. Arc/INFO remains the leader in large-scale planning and analysis work in landscape architecture.[21] Both of these tools, from their early creation, have been dominant in their use in the landscape architecture profession for the last 35 years.

Only recently have the detailed drafting and 3D world of CAD (computer-aided design) and the analysis and large-scale data platform of GIS truly started to merge in the software approach of "geo-design." Perhaps popularized through the first geo-design summit in January 2010, the ideas of geo-design codify the challenges in scale and complexity of landscape computing when shifting scales of models are required from regional ecologies, to civic spaces, to the visual presence of the virtual "wild."[22]

Early innovation in design computation often occurred in specialized studios that focused on the implementation of technology for specific scenarios or for moments within the design process. Overly specialized employees focusing on the development of experimental technology are a strain on the bottom line of traditional design practices when existing outside of two conditions: 1) the development group is increasing efficiency of specific billable tasks within a contract structure that allows for increased profit margins; and 2) the studio is developing marketable products or services that expand the existing scope of services that can be obtained by the design practice. Often the specialized studio exists as a marketing platform, a side hobby of specific design staff, and/or a "think tank" to explore opportunities within a traditional practice.

All are valid approaches in landscape architecture, but owing to the financial draw on firms, this specialization has historically lacked the resources to inflect great change in technological development.

As with the emergence of ESRI and Jack Dangermond from the work at Harvard Laboratories, or contemporary collaborations with labs such as the MIT MediaLAB with Sasaki Associates, applications of new technology often take the form of university collaboration or consulting partnership. Hence, with the concurrent need for both special skills and investment, a historical division in design and landscape architecture developed between the business models of toolmaker and that of tool users.

A case study interview in landscape architecture technology investment and the lessons to be learned

In the 1980s the young firm Design Workshop, led by co-founders Joe Porter and Don Ensign along with partners Richard Shaw and Kurt Culbertson, saw an opportunity for what would become one of the pioneering practices in early environmental simulation technology. These valiant but ultimately failed incursions into the technological market prompted the first crack in a schism between the landscape architect as a "creative" designer, and the landscape architect as a "technician."

> The real reason those efforts failed was the disconnected relationship of the individuals running the simulations. There was too much interest in simulation for simulations sake and not for solving the real-world problems.
>
> Culbertson, pers. comm.

The early 1980s was a time of need for new tools and new methods in landscape architecture. In 1982 Design Workshop reached out to Lucas Films in search of a consultant for assistance in visual simulation. The response included a plan far too expensive for the services required and stakeholders' budget. At the time, the stakeholders consisted primarily of western communities in sensitive ecological and visual contexts, large-scale land developers/resorts developers, and government entities such as the National Park Service or The Federal Bureau of Land Management, which were interested in these large-scale visual resource assessments. Many of these early efforts in natural and visual resource assessment built on the early work by Carl Steinitz and the Delphi process.[23] These early goals of open lands and "natural landscapes" simulations were in stark contrast to the majority of early simulation work being done in architectural or urban contexts, observed Joe Porter, retired principal and co-founder:

> I recall one of the few other groups we could see doing these simulations at the time was SOM, but these were all building focused, not the large-scale simulations we needed help with.
>
> Porter, pers. comm.

The ensuing conversation and recommendation from Lucas Films led Design Workshop to invest in an early Iris computer, which resulted in an investment of roughly $45,000; the Design Workshop Byte Cave was born. Beyond this initial investment, Design Workshop spent nearly $4,000/month on a consulting staff to operate and program the Iris computer system for the firm's ongoing projects. These are significant investments for a young landscape architecture firm, particularly considering that this was in the early 1980s.

> We didn't start the BYTE CAVE for marketing purposes at the time.

We started it because we thought we would be better designers. We were designing large landscapes with complicated forms and relationships; we needed a way of seeing.

Porter, pers. comm.

At this time there were really three paths to invest in, and I recall discussing which one it should be. There was CAD and GIS that we basically could see were going to come anyways, and we would have to incorporate. It was the 3D simulation work that no one in the profession was doing at the time.

Porter, pers. comm.

It was one day in the office someone called "Joe, Joe you need to see this." When I walked over the individual had a dinosaur standing in a street and you could see a car driving by reflecting in the dinosaur's eye, and I realized we were spending money on things we really didn't need. It was at this time (around 1993) that we sold the IRIS computer and began investing in putting individual computers on the designers' desks. It took time but eventually over the years there was a computer on everyone's desk in the office.

Porter, pers. comm.

Complex three-dimensional simulations were integrated in the formation of numerous projects. Artists' renditions were given a new approach for the first time with an accurate geometric base to draw over. With the advent of the 3D computer wire frame, studies could be done combining the best of both worlds: creativity in design and efficiency and precision in visualization. Computational accuracy in digital simulation and artistic composition were now firmly in the hands of skilled landscape architects.

The entire purpose at the outset was accurate representation. The world had changed to a point which demanded the honesty.

Shaw, pers. comm.

Even with great successes in early efforts of simulation at the business level, at the survival level the balancing act between the needs of the landscape architecture studios and the prowess of the computer whizzes was difficult to merge with the need for efficient solutions. The critical nature of landscape architecture and the problems the discipline is addressing are often overshadowed by the computer graphics that gloss over the technical challenges posed by the public and private built environment.

Implementing new technological avenues is always a challenge in established practice. To be "the first" is a common struggle[24] as explored further in the first essay, "Computation in Practice." The investments in technology we make can be a significant pull on a firm's revenue. Therefore, it is imperative that the technical support or innovation staff communicate effectively with the design team and stakeholders. The critical discussion of innovation for innovation's sake on the one hand, and creative design on the other hand, requires a careful balance in business practices according to Kurt Culbertson, CEO of Design Workshop: "This is the choice between being on the leading edge versus the bleeding edge, in practice."

To this day and anticipating the increasing prevalence of machine learning, the need for effective communication between the computational capability and defined human goals will remain paramount.[25] At Design Workshop, it was the Byte Cave "machine" that had a mind of its own; other firms faced similar struggles where the computer specialists and the designer, or seemingly the software itself, had a different understanding of the same challenge at hand.

FIGURE 0.1.3 **Top: 1986 simulation of the Little Nell Hotel in Aspen, Colorado. Bottom: 1986 sketch of regrading – as viewed from the simulated or proposed hotel deck**

Images: Design Workshop

FIGURE 0.1.4 **Top: 1988 computer simulation of Whistler Blackcomb Base Village. Bottom: 1988 sketch of computer simulation of Whistler Blackcomb Base Village**

Images: Design Workshop

FIGURE 0.1.5 **Top: 1989 wire frame computer simulation of Canyon Village (Yellow Stone). Bottom: 1989 sketch of top of wire frame of Canyon Village (Yellow Stone)**

Images: Design Workshop

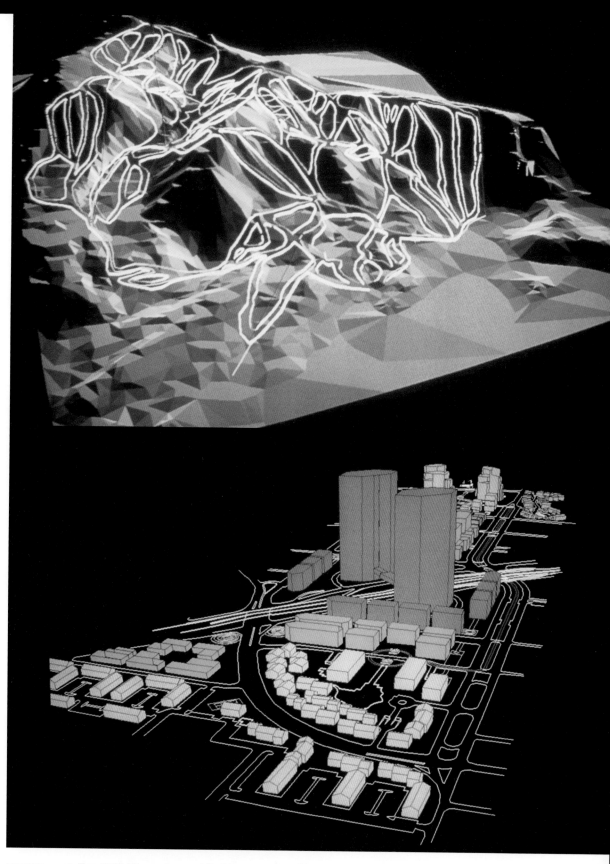

FIGURE 0.1.6 **Top: 1990 3D massing model of Canyon Village (Yellow Stone). Bottom: 1991 screen capture of 3D fly-through video created for HKS Architects of City Place Development Proposal (Dallas)**

Images: Design Workshop

In landscape architecture, the struggle remains one of translation between the tools of computation, with all their prowess, and the creativity of the designers, with all their imagination—whether that struggle implies two separate individuals or one with an inner struggle, the syntax of communication is the bridge to be crossed.

New paradigms

Computation inherently asks us to define elements of landscape architecture: associated characteristics, rules, actions, and relationships that form the model. Landscape architecture strives to understand the interrelationship of multiple, not inherently formal but synthetic models that define methods for designing living systems utilizing data, metrics, and speculation. The inherent relationships and rules that define landscape systems are apparent in contemporary proposals of urban form generation, or even economic regeneration. These relationships surface in practical terms through municipal codes or even climate resiliency planning, which are themselves inherently computational.[26]

The discipline of landscape architecture has been acutely concerned with the simulation of an established set of analog tools in computer software and hardware for the past two decades. Our tool set is comprised primarily of ways to paint, mark, draft, and model digitally in a way that mirrors physical materials that use paper, chipboard, pencils, pens, and markers. What we find is that, rather than claiming that there is a "digital" media, we have instead adopted computation as a simulator and optimizer of analog systems.[27] This state perpetuated a dialog in our discipline that has attempted to justify "computation" or defend "hand-drawing"; that discussion has been wholly unproductive over the past decade.[28] What is important to acknowledge

is that neither methodology, analog or digital, defines the discipline of landscape architecture. To move forward in a contemporary design practice, or academic setting, requires a nimble understanding of how each tool may be deployed and the range of results it may produce.

Computation in landscape architecture provides more than opportunities to expand current design tools, workflows, and methodologies. Instead, the translation of landscape systems from modes of visual representation to relational, numerical, and temporal models provides a new lens that focuses the agency of landscape architects. Within the last decade, with the increase of computational efficiency, we find new models that more directly take advantage of the power of computation to build relationships and form new heuristic models in landscape architecture. This agency provides landscape architects with new territories of influence that thrust design into closer relationships with the exploration of iterative form for aesthetic and performative evaluation, as well as deeper connections with physical landscapes with new methods of construction that both collapse and expand current design processes.

New modes of thinking

Emerging coded environments

The term "code" is used in computation to refer to the instructions that drive software and hardware. Coding, the practice of creating code, implies an active state where software is created through a personal or collaborative syntactical process. Coders single out a group of individuals responsible for the creation of code while also implying an underlying culture built on these processes.

Code also provides a range of other definitions and can be used to describe rules or definitions that propose to delineate use or function. The coding of the environment implies a classification, the abstraction of physical and environmental phenomena to create a model that may be used for representation, analysis, or simulation. Design models, visual and/or numerical, describe the world and are the essential fodder through which designers develop design solutions. The continual construction, evolution, and maintenance of these models mediates and develops our relationships between the physical and virtual, underlying our assumptions of the physical world.

Our methods of abstracting the world, as landscape architects, are primarily computational and therefore generative and alterable in real time. The profession of landscape architecture is being reshaped and this is a calling to be aware of what is to come and how, ultimately, we may indeed reshape the profession in ways that may not currently be predictable. Computational design is woven into the surroundings of our daily lives. It controls the visuals we see on the ever-ubiquitous smart/mobile device, the time we wait at the mundane stop light, what we see first when we do a search on the Internet or send an email. Yet often we are intimidated by the prospects of computation, coding, or computer algorithms governing these daily tasks.

As our world becomes increasingly algorithmic, we must be aware that technological data usage does not simply become a reflection of privatized mobile/social media data mining, which, while a powerful tool and offering exciting new opportunities in urban planning, does have its limitations in data reliability or sample set.

As landscape architects have engaged in the previous decades with GIS, geo-design,

and mobile data, we have garnished great rewards in being accumulators of some rather large data sets of physical topography, sea-level rise, and socioeconomic distribution. However, the gathering of data (the inventory) and understanding the algorithms controlling, sorting, or processing that information (the analysis) present the next stage of untold value for the potential of social, formal, materialistic, and environmental models that are more synthetic and controlled by the designer's intent. This is explored in essay 01.04, "Big Data for Small Places."

> The greatest value of building models is the disciplined way they require us to think about the impact of city policies and infrastructure on residents and visitors.
> Nick Chim and David Ory, Google Sidewalk Labs[29]

Doctoroff (Alphabet's Sidewalk Lab CEO) argues that the great leaps in economic growth and productivity have depended on the interaction and close proximity of the "physical environment," especially urban development and innovation.[30] The advent of a number of innovations and inventions such as electricity, the steam engine, and automobiles, for example, have drastically altered our way of life. However, in terms of architecture and landscape architecture, while a marked contrast exists between 1870 and 1940, Doctoroff asserts that "hardly anything" changed from 1940 to the present. The landscape architect's scope of work, contract structure, and client base remained largely the same in that span of time.

Whether we accept this hyperbolic proposition or not, we do begin to see the manifestation of that proposition. The information age is ushering in the high-tech "campus." The "campus" offers all the amenities of urban life that would appeal to a newer generation of professionals in the high-tech industry, in an attempt to attract the best talent and maximize or, better expressed, inspire productivity and creativity. The high-tech campus movement and the current early efforts, just as many of the pioneering efforts, have their quirks and, as economists are fond to say, have unintended consequences.

In the case of Apple, the quirks for their new "Spaceship" building meant housing problems, whether shortages of or high price of, and transportation problems. Google's "Googleplex" campus faced similar problems in addition to a hostile reaction from San Francisco as a result of the gentrification it brought about. Facebook's Frank Gehry-designed complex boasts of being the largest open-office workplace in the world.[31] However, questions remain about the "open space" concept and its effect on morale and productivity.

By far the most stinging of criticisms is about the role of the edifice in the urban setting, returning to the concept of the symbiotic relationship between innovations and the physical urban environment. All of these "campuses" have earned high marks not only by expert but also in the court of public opinion in the area of architecture, risk-taking, and bold and inspiring leadership in the workplace. While concurring, Louise Mozingo, landscape architect at the University of California, Berkeley, claims that Apple (and probably others) misses the point:

> You can't understand a building without looking at what's around it—its site, as the architects say. From that angle, Apple's new HQ is a retrograde, literally inward-looking building with contempt for the city where it lives and cities in general.[32]

As a landscape architect, Louise Mozingo, observes, in the 1950s and '60s corporate flagship offices fled the "dirty" inner city to the suburbs, building structures architecturally ahead of their time while nurturing and channeling their corporate culture toward productivity; but they did so deliberately. By contrast, Apple, Mozingo argues, fails: "Successful buildings engage with their surroundings."

Today's design culture seems to have a fascination in urban and architectural design with the electronically plastered and seemingly back-lit surfaces of reflectivity. The glorification of an apocalyptic aesthetic extends through our media-driven environment, bringing the worlds of reality and science fiction ever closer together.[33] Whether it be large billboard media or subtle sensor integration, the component makeup of urban landscapes is shifting from a static makeup to a more dynamic/responsive material composition.[34]

> One of the barriers to faster and wider change is a lack of dialogue between the people who live in today's cities and the folks who build tomorrow's technologies.
> Daniel L. Doctoroff, CEO, Sidewalk Labs[35]

The argument could be made that, in addition to those inhabiting the city and building the technology, our cities' future is largely influenced by a third group composed of landscape architects, architects, urban planners, and engineers. These "technocrats" are shaping the physical cities and environments within which future technologies and innovations must be integrated. They must anticipate and create "space" for a future that no one can define.

Our contemporary context romanticizes the technological, the "clean and simple," and the start-up culture, part of which is ephemeral. However, as landscape architects, the tie to urban form and "grit" of urbanity manifests itself on a much broader scale. By definition, the landscape architect must include all inhabitants, residents, and workers alike, in addition to purposefully capturing, or preserving, or creating, or even modifying the nontactile aspects of the city, well beyond the asphalt; those are aspects the technocrats are too often accused of missing.

The technological agenda we seek, as landscape architects, is that of a systemic socioenvironmental connection to technologies (known and unknown). Perhaps already within our reach lies not simply a cultural "Internet of Things" but an "Internet of ecologies," an "Internet of built environments." Presenting itself here is a model that influences not only the creation of day-one active spaces but the temporal dynamics of such environments throughout an evolving lifetime. Landscape architects are already "embracing digital media as a tool with analytic, performative, and representational possibilities." The computer is no longer the rival.[36] In a dramatic shift, the profession is rapidly moving beyond computation as a design representation medium; the tool is now influencing the thinking process of the landscape architect to shape dynamic models for adaptive and responsive landscapes.[37]

The aversion to computation

The human character may harbor an instinctive aversion to computation, coding, computer programing in the planning of our living environment and daily life. Understandably, we may express a fear of these media as manipulated by specialized individuals perceived to be somewhat distant from our world of daily social and physical existence, controlling our destiny.

This aversion may stem from our profession's attempt to reach far beyond the simply observable or gestural in nature. As designers, we struggle primarily with

interface of the traditional syntax of code/computation. These traditional programming interfaces, such as coding in C# or Fortran, or even scripting in Python, have not yet operated at a level of abstraction designers are accustomed to thinking. Designers have had to rely on a team of computational experts attempting to translate the designer's language into computer code (scripting). Much can be lost in the translation. However, with developments in GUI (graphic user interfaces) such as Grasshopper software (plug-ins), a huge barrier has been crossed.

Doctoroff and the Sidewalk Labs team at Alphabet (Google) strive to close the gap between the residents of a city and the developers of future technology and their vision for urban planning: "We believe that when you put technologists and urbanists on the same team you have the potential to transform the urban environment."[38] By bringing together landscape architects, architects, planners, technocrats, and of course city residents, who will live with the changes, we will all be closer to the ideals of urban planning. It is critical that landscape architecture engage with these conversations.

Not all landscape architects will become avid coders. However, it is imperative as a profession agitating for creativity, exploration, innovation, and substantial investment in form generation and alteration of the urban realm that we understand and communicate with those shaping the future components of the synthetic urban construct. The risks of not doing so are very high. There are risks as well for being in the leadership. The business sector is littered with companies that took risks and failed, but also others that did not innovate (or innovated too late or even too soon). The once-revered Eastman Kodak Company comes to mind.[39]

The interface barrier

With the conceptualization of the mouse in 1965 by Douglas Englebart and its popularization with the advent of Apple computers in 1983, we begin to see elements of the hand and first extensions/abstractions of analogue media emerge into the digital realm. However, it is only recently through the GUI of scripting that we observe a widespread use of computational means and methods in landscape architecture and our related disciplines. GUI-based scripting engines such as Grasshopper, Dynamo, Kismet, and Marionette have all become a contemporary phenomenon, opening up new computational vistas to designers who would simply not have bothered to cross the learning barrier to entry in text-based coding editors.

These coding and scripting abstraction/interface platforms have acted as a gateway for many designers, who expanded their reach to numerous problems and data sets in the emerging technological world. Grasshopper, for example, initially launched by McNeel and Associates and created by programmer David Rutten,[40] was built upon, after its creation, by numerous add-ons, plug-ins, or extensions (e.g., Rhinoceros). With the built-in script in the background, designers could now engage in parametric design, skipping over the tedious and discouraging scripting, undeterred by the computational demands of the past. Moreover, designers could now concentrate on their work, instead of spending time learning and acquiring computational tools to get to the task. The simplicity with which Grasshopper and Rhino could be utilized led to widespread use of the software across top architectural firms and eventually landscape architecture offices, opening the computational world.[41]

The success of the software was largely due to Robert McNeel's insight: "Writing code is not something designers really want to get their head into." His "business model" had a two-pronged approach: "designers set up sophisticated relationships between the parts of the design problem" and, in addition, the company would make the software available for free during the development process, benefitting from the input of users worldwide.[42] Although a small firm by comparison, without the deep pockets of a Dassault Systèmes or Autodesk, by 2009 McNeel reported having 250,000 Rhino users worldwide, among them 50,000 in the field of architecture. This number has since bourgeoned further, as Rhino became commonplace in architectural offices and urban design practices.[43]

This continuous improvement is a necessary survival mechanism in the marketplace. Competition, at times driven by monetary rewards and at times by self-motivation or satisfaction of rising to an intellectual challenge, leads to explorations and innovations. Progress in parametric design was not enough. In the field of architecture, the virtual wall beyond software and data-based design has already been pierced, as architect Rivka Oxman declared in 2008: ". . . novel directions for environments that support performance-based design are beginning to emerge."[44] Even five years after Oxman's remark, architect Michael Hensen showed more concern for the profession and the lack of progress, and ominously warned that "architecture is on the brink. It is a discipline in crisis."[45]

Admonitions such as Hensen's, although debatable in their severity, may also increase motivation to leverage technology for performance's sake. We know the field of innovation is littered with failures for a variety of reasons, at times for the better: "creative destructions" is what economists refer to when they mean that an old technology is naturally replaced by a new and better one (e.g., video tape cassettes replaced by CDs, DVDs, and flash drives).[46] The let-down may include at times the failure to keep up with innovation, lack of organizational skills, or lack of insight or any of these combinations.[47] The path to innovation does not follow a scientific course. At times risk-taking is necessary and at other times excessive risk (neither is quantifiable) leads to failure. The Eastman Kodak Company is a case in point. The iconic firm had failed to gauge the digital revolution, ironically a field in which the company was a leader; meanwhile, management decisions on how to cope with the threat from competition were sluggish or not appropriate. The company, listed on the illustrious Dow Jones since 1930, was dropped in 2004. It was founded in 1888 and filed for bankruptcy in 2012.[48]

This is not to say that the profession of landscape architecture as a whole lies at risk or is even impaired owing to the lack of a digital or computational engagement. However, the societal relevancy, particularly in urban contexts, raises a question over the role of technology (particularly start-up) companies in shaping the environments. Whether from direct infusion of investment from the technological sector or from simply a shift in technology available in urban futures, the influence with which computation and the computationally minded will shape our built environment is without question.

It may appear that the complexity of the world around us is increasing in the human ability to interact and control our surrounding everyday objects. In reality, we are seeing an increasing translation from mechanical to digital (coded) language within our daily lives. While perhaps it would be more difficult for the everyday individual or "traditional" car mechanic to work on a 2017 car than it might be to repair/restore a 1960s hot-rod, it might be the very opposite for robotics engineer or computer

programmer, who may now be the most able to "work" on their own car over the weekend. It is the simple algorithms of our daily lives that we are not accustomed to engaging with to control our surroundings – unless we are given that control directly through pre-manufactured application. The barrier to "customization," "jerry rigging," or "fiddling with" lies in the cultural translation of the basic algorithms controlling our surroundings. Not understanding these algorithms, the language (codes) these instructions are written in makes the objects appear more complicated—when in reality they are simply more complicated in a digital sphere than in a physical or mechanical interaction. There are now fewer moving parts and more moving electrons.

Initiatives, risks, successes and failures

Designers' aversion to computational tools, especially for landscape architects, is no longer suitable.

Enormous risks are taken by those who profess to be in the avant-garde of their fields, some with tragic ends, but "the road not taken" may be just as calamitous. Landscape architects may end up as the quaint Norman Rockwell pharmacy pushed aside by the chain stores, in our case by related disciplines and unanticipated neo-disciplines eager to fill in the gap. Landscape architects, by their own design, yearn to be at the cusp of creativity and therefore need the computational tools to remain relevant, if not lead.

The rapidly growing technical and cultural interactions between humans and computers, whether they be touch screens, haptic devices, or virtual or augmented realities, are enabling our return to the gestural and observable interface process at the roots of our profession: free-hand spontaneous drawing and sketching—not coincidently, the word "digit" comes from the Latin word *digitus*, meaning finger or toe.

A new generation of digital natives have been brought up by the new interactive normalcy to live, work, and create abstractly through these virtual media. Machine learning and script definition of software are assisting to fill in the gaps of the executable details of our creative process. The executable interface is now rapidly evolving. It is accessible for designers to "code" problems at the highest levels of abstraction through gesture and real-time feedback, all while designers observe the instantaneous impact of their digital interaction on the built environment.[49]

The inspiration stemming from computation/parametric design manifests itself predominantly through the language of mathematics.[50] The relationship between form and environmental data is often more attuned to the architectonic or geometric nature of the architecture disciplines than those of landscape and the "wild" in nature. However, even though the more geometrically "simple" in design and process are easier to calculate through computational design, why do we see this technology being so often only used and advertised in the most abstract or biomorphic of projects? It is certainly refreshing to see these tools used as an enabler or inspiration for complex and new ways of design thinking. However, we must also take advantage of the day-to-day problem-solving capabilities and practical use of such computation engines.

Is it truly that these tools are used more commonly for esoteric competitions in architecture? Or, yet, that these tools are the "idolizable" graphics that we see published time and time again? Are the day-to-day applications of these tools being misconstrued as a tool for renderings over form generation? Are the forms of competition architecture and "deflated sea creature" starchitecture of our day reflections of computation for computation's sake? Or are these an interpretation of "computation" or "parametric" as an aesthetic even if made through more traditional modeling techniques?[51]

We describe, perhaps in a negative tone, the common perceptions and prevailing uses of Grasshopper and other parametric engines to hopefully draw the reader's attention to a new platform of thinking about computational design and technology in landscape architecture. Software, such as Grasshopper or Dynamo, must be recognized as problem-solving tools and engines of creativity. These tools are not simply engines of graphic communication that perhaps a new generation of design professionals may have mistakenly interpreted and represented as a means to an end in itself. Rather, parametric tools, such as Grasshopper, are practical instruments with the potential to address problems and find solutions while unleashing a vast source of creativity. For example, graduate students used:

> Rhino to create the model and Grasshopper to drive the dynamic inputs; i.e. sensors and their inputs that drive responsive actions. The model focused on the device's formal aesthetic and the transformations the device will make. The Grasshopper components were used to drive actual values within the digital model such as rotation (0–360 degrees), transformations (movement in feet/meters) and/or binary actions (off/on).[52]

Emerging from the most ancient of traditions in design and architecture, our obsession with geometry and form are driven by mathematical relationships that are both discreet and subliminal. Grasshopper, Dynamo, and Python are some of the first conversation openers in computational design today, yet it is specifically their abstraction of and thus accessibility to computation that have driven their remarkable success.

Abstraction and productivity

Abstraction improves productivity. You don't need to worry about the decisions made at the underlying levels. This is why designers are so well suited for large-scale thinking and master planning efforts, as we are trained to think abstractly and focus on the "big idea." The only thing you need to worry about is the interface to the next level. This is what we, as designers, need to begin understanding and interfacing with the systemic models available. Understanding that, we can influence that next level of realism in the tools of what we want them to perform. The higher up you go in this list, the more abstract you are getting with the execution of the problem. When creating your flowchart or algorithm you don't need to know the syntax of a specific computer algorithm. When translating that algorithm to a specific syntax you don't need to know the flow of logic gates or circuits of the hardware that will implement that code. These synthetic models of thinking across scales and variables are beginning to allow landscape architects to test and visualize in real time the implications of macro to micro decisions.

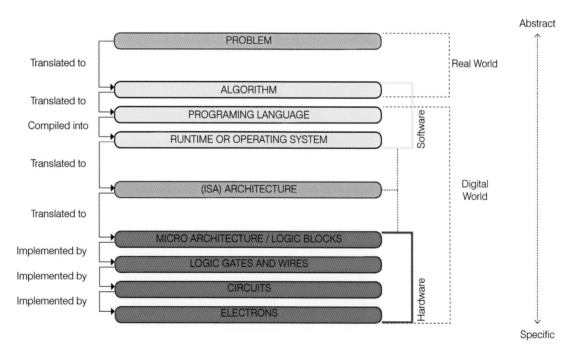

FIGURE 0.1.7 **We solve problems with computers through electrons. You can "program" at all of these levels; you can program at high levels of abstraction in flowchart and problem-solution discussion in everyday language; you can program all the way down so as to physically program the circuit gates or transistors to command a machine to perform a specific task. Some of the first computers required that level of involvement. It is helpful, however, to understand the logic of these lower levels so as to understand why something may not work, or may not work as anticipated**

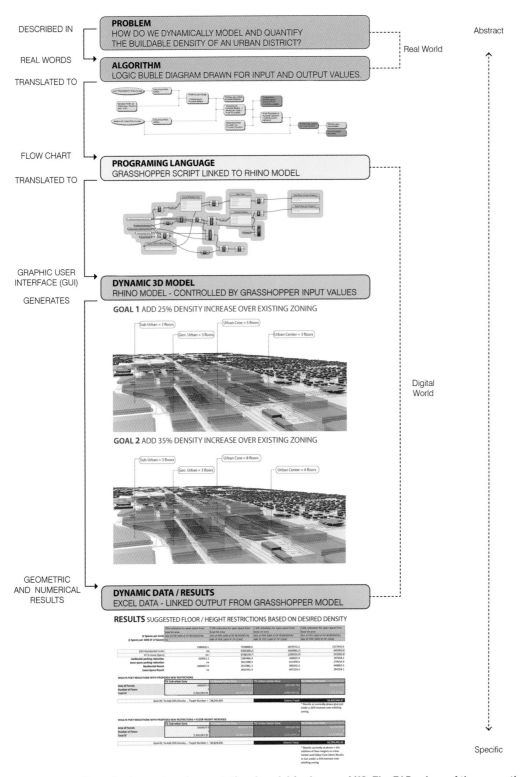

DESCRIBED IN

REAL WORDS

TRANSLATED TO

FLOW CHART

TRANSLATED TO

GRAPHIC USER
INTERFACE (GUI)

GENERATES

GEOMETRIC
AND NUMERICAL
RESULTS

PROBLEM
HOW DO WE DYNAMICALLY MODEL AND QUANTIFY
THE BUILDABLE DENSITY OF AN URBAN DISTRICT?

ALGORITHM
LOGIC BUBLE DIAGRAM DRAWN FOR INPUT AND OUTPUT VALUES.

PROGRAMING LANGUAGE
GRASSHOPPER SCRIPT LINKED TO RHINO MODEL

DYNAMIC 3D MODEL
RHINO MODEL - CONTROLLED BY GRASSHOPPER INPUT VALUES

GOAL 1 ADD 25% DENSITY INCREASE OVER EXISTING ZONING

GOAL 2 ADD 35% DENSITY INCREASE OVER EXISTING ZONING

DYNAMIC DATA / RESULTS
EXCEL DATA - LINKED OUTPUT FROM GRASSHOPPER MODEL

RESULTS SUGGESTED FLOOR / HEIGHT RESTRICTIONS BASED ON DESIRED DENSITY

Abstract

Real World

Digital
World

Specific

FIGURE 0.1.8 **Example abstraction of computational model for Leawood KS. The FAR values of the properties were associated in Grasshopper as dynamic variables among others to test scenarios for the city of altering current zoning regulations to allow for increased urban density**

Image: Design Workshop

Abstraction of code to scripting and the graphic user interface (GUI)

Many designers will not engage at the high level of syntactical knowledge necessary for scripting given time constraints as one of significant barriers. However, Grasshopper, Rhino, other GUI-based scripting allows designers to more readily connect the outcome of code with the formal representation without having to know how to write code.

The world-renowned architect Bjarke Ingels, in his 2013 interview, "Inside the Business of Design," described the impact of Grasshopper and visual scripting on architecture in these simple terms: "Grasshopper is to parametric scripting what Windows and Macintosh were to the graphical interface for personal computing." Ingels describes the essence of GUI-based parametric design as follows: "Scripting came from being this incredibly difficult thing in architecture to, at least, I can understand the principles. You basically construct incredibly complex formulas by graphically combining different variables with little wires almost like a switch board."[53]

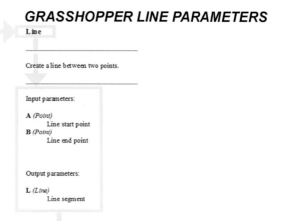

```
PYTHON CODE TO DRAW LINE
canvas.print_figure("line_ex.png")
canvas = FigureCanvasAgg(fig)

ax.add_line(l)
l = Line2D([0,1],[0,1])
fig.add_axes(ax)
ax = Axes(fig, [.1,.1,.8,.8])
fig = Figure(figsize=[4,4])

from matplotlib.backends.backend_agg import FigureCanvasAgg
from matplotlib.lines import Line2D
from matplotlib.axes import Axes
from matplotlib.figure import Figure
"""

""" line_ex.py
```

GRASSHOPPER LINE PARAMETERS

Line

Create a line between two points.

Input parameters:

A *(Point)*
Line start point
B *(Point)*
Line end point

Output parameters:

L *(Line)*
Line segment

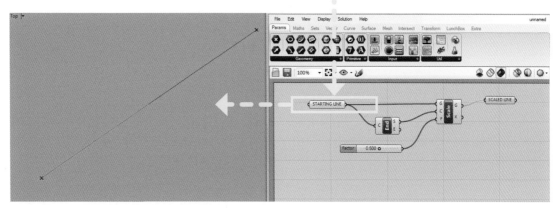

FIGURE 0.1.9 **With a line in Rhino/Grasshopper, the definition at the lower right can be seen as graphic icons representing the syntactical commands of the software. The line in question to be scaled by (.5) is represented by the node at the top left—with the process, variables, and resultant line shown as their own nodes. Within these nodes is a mass of "code"—this is what gives scripting, particularly GUI-based scripting, its efficiency and ease of use: in that background, the code extracts or translates the level of detail/syntax for the designer**

The roots of understanding computational and parametric design do not lie buried beneath complex mathematical formulas or coding syntax. Instead, they reside in the organization of thoughts and a design approach. When designers understand code and computation in this manner, it is possible to then frame design problems through this lens, opening up a dialogue between design intent and computational iteration and generation.

Language of change

The design profession is beginning to see fascinating examples of these new computational approaches and applications. However, the vehicle by which these applications are brought to life remains mysterious. What is not as evident is the logic, the thought process, and the utilization of parametric design that have been applied to bring about the complex execution. Years of efforts dating back to 1967 at the MIT Media Lab succeeded in "civilizing" or "taming" design and computer code. Starting from "Scratch," so aptly named, in 2003, the program began to use graphics interface rather than the cumbersome coding string.[54] At MIT Media Lab, computer scientist Mitch Resnick directs the "Lifelong Kindergarten," where, at a very young age, children learn to program and design. As Resnick explains, "When you learn to read, you can then read to learn."[55]

One entry barrier to that vehicle, the aversion to understanding the potential of computational media and its syntactical interface, has been widely broken down in recent years by young designers through the GUI syntax of scripting. How can we leverage this newly acquired foothold and understand better what we are gaining from parametric modeling/visual programming/coding as a design process and conceptual generator?

Coding is a common language of creation, iteration, logic, communication, exploration, and innovation for the twenty-first century. Just as the tried-and-true graphic conventions of landscape architecture (the heyday of the "EDSA," Mike Lin-style penmanship) have become an international standard for landscape communication, so too have the various languages of coding to the world of technology development.

Computation and parametric design are grounded in the field of mathematics. As such they are by-products that the field of mathematics, in its pioneering age, had not envisioned. Edward Frankel, a mathematician, expresses the practical use of the discipline in much the same way we might broach the subject of computational design:

> One of the key function of mathematics is the ordering of information. This is what distinguishes the brush strokes of Van Gogh from the mere blob of paint. With the advent of 3D printing, the reality we are used to is undergoing a radical transformation: everything is migrating from the sphere of physical objects to the sphere of information and data. We will soon be able to convert information into matter on demand by using 3D printers just as easily as we now convert a PDF file into a book or an MP3 file into a piece of music.[56]

A computer program is not a task that someone who knows how to code goes right into and writes simply because they know the language. The program is dependent on a problem to be solved. A programmer must know the logic and sequence of commands intended to be developed. The code is simply the wording telling the computer what to do. That communication ability is vital.

Similarly, in the design professions the knowledge of how to use a software media is not the same as the knowledge of creating built environments. Our landscape architecture profession understands the language of design, drawing, and planning. We would look at someone rather wearily if they assumed that the ability to use CAD alone is a license to create a master plan for a community.

The development of a computer program is much like the comprehensive master plan for an urban design at different scales. The larger the design challenge, the more complex and comprehensive the design must be, just as the more demands asked of a software program, the more complex and comprehensive the algorithm development must be for that software.

The design itself and the creative development of the key algorithm make the software run and create the city. The letter keys typed into the computer, or the lines drafted onto the plan sheets, are mere translations of the critical thinking that went into the original creation. The vision is what counts. Ideas carry most of the weight.

Computerization vs. computation

One of the greatest struggles we face, as a design profession, is our attempt to overcome what we perceive to be the limitations of technology and computation. That perception is that computation is "only" a tool kit, only a set of operations. We must understand computation as a way of thinking, as a way of linking our thought process and dynamic environments. This is very different from "computerization."

We must make a critical differentiation between the contemporary computerization and the vast potential of computation. The most common mode of using mechanical computers in contemporary landscape architecture is just that: computerization. We input preconceived,

and often predrawn, solutions into their digital format for safekeeping, printing at various scales, or enhancing their graphic presentation. The ideas themselves often do not grow by this means of digitalization but many times lose their clarity of communication in the cumbersome translation of media.

One increases the amount and specificity of information, while the other only contains as much information as is initially supplied. A computer-aided approach assumes an object-based strategy for encapsulating information into symbolic representations – method of organizing information. In contrast, a computational approach enables specific data to be realized out of initial abstraction – in the form of codes which encapsulate values and actions.
Sean Ahlquist and Achim Menges[57]

Computerization is a tool kit of prefabricated software that we accept or use within the bounds of what it allows our landscape to be. What we yearn for as a profession is computation. That concept goes far beyond the tool kit. Computational design is the systematic method for critical thinking that emphasizes thought process and iteration over memorization and duplication. It stresses the linking of ideas, and interaction between the parts of the problem and the solution.

Computational thinking combines the powerful orderly process of algorithmic organization with the equally powerful, but more chaotic, process of iterative design. Computational design is a way of approaching all the challenges in the world around you in a more visionary, creative, far-reaching, and organized way that is more likely to succeed. We engage with computational decisions each day whether we realize it or not. In the design field the passage beyond computational skills, and tools, albeit influenced by computer thinking, is a paradigm shift: "Steps away from 'form making' and toward 'form finding.'"[58]

Of course, the danger with any innovation or innovative techniques is that the ultimate practical goal and problem-solving may be lost. Entertainment and dazzle at times supplant substance. No discipline, however, is immune from such temptations. The entertainment aspect, and even the ostentatious, are an integral part of the creative and inventive mind:

> At present scripters tend to be of the "lone gun" mentality and are justifiably proud of their firepower, usually developed through many late nights of obsessive concentration. There is a danger that if celebration of skills is allowed to obscure and divert from the real design objectives, then scripting degenerates to become an isolated craft rather than developing into an integrated art form.
>
> Hugh Whitehead former head of the Foster + Partners Specialist Modeling Group[59]

It is perhaps this lone gun mentality that has shaped the professional misconception of coding or scripting as a distant task related to but not a part of the design process.

Models for landscape architecture: computation as transitional tool set

A fundamental shift in the design tool set for landscape architects is required to address the hyperscaled issues of climate change, global extraction economies, and megacities, to enable the profession to develop viable synthetic design proposals into the future. The landscape architect must embrace a tool set that is real-time and more fully augments and extends the capabilities of the human mind. This goes beyond simulating analogue media in virtualized environments and beckons for design and construction techniques that are more directly connected to material and biologic systems through responsive technologies.[60]

> Creating new models is difficult and hence the tendency is to work with existing models of thought. In computation this is even more likely due to the reusability of algorithms in the form of code. The path of least resistance has led to a limited set of computational models for design being used over and over again.
>
> Gengnagel, Kilian, Palz, and Scheurer[61]

The transition will be a complex evolution from "static" built/urban environments to "dynamic" self-constructing, living, breathing, and even artificially intelligent (thinking) environments.

These cities are not in such a distant future; our urban environments are rapidly becoming "responsive" habitats, not simply static constructs. For how long will a "set" of static drawings help us to create working and living environments for a dynamic and mobile populace, ecology, and culture?

Computation and technology become ways of testing/experimenting with not only more complex physical but also social systems in the built environment. The scale of our built environment, based on the practicality of contemporary physics, will be built through systems of subcomponents/assemblies. While the vast potential of media such as 3D printing are contemporary "shock and awe"

FIGURE 0.1.10 **Ecopods**

Source: Squared Design Lab/Höweler + Yoon Architecture

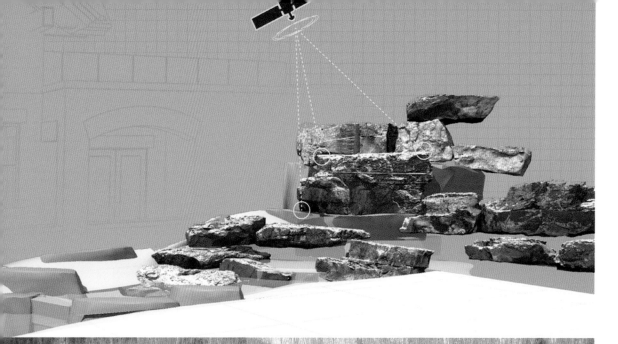

FIGURE 0.1.11 **3D Boulders scanned and assembled in the computer for contractor construction**
Image: Design Workshop

examples forming themselves at life scale/inhabitable environmental scale, these methods are already predominantly integrated as means of component assembly alongside traditional construction trades and typologies.[62] Whether the applicable "codes" involved are in syntax of jurisdictional zoning requirements, mandated decree by an ancient ruler, or Python scripting running a 3D printer, any deviation from the variables at hand is governed by the associated impacts to the project. What our new computational media and new methods of construction allow is a fundamental bridge between design idea and physical reality. The connection of the virtual and physical model in space can now exist in direct mirror or alternate reality of each other, as opposed to the cumbersome two-dimensional abstraction of orthographic drawings and measured scales.

At the core of the essays in this volume is an attempt to place landscape architects at the forefront of discussions and solutions to the future demands of the built environment that are often dominated by the technology industry. Technology companies will continue to extend their reach into the city, providing us with a glimpse of the future workplace and living place as seen in corporate campuses of Facebook, Apple, and Google. However, maintaining the involvement of the designers in that plan for expansion is critical, not only for those outside the industry affected by the design but also for the enterprise itself (employees and technological elites), which may not see "the whole picture." Landscape architects and designers must understand the potential and collaborative nature of these movements. They must insert themselves, not for the sake of it but to help avoid the pitfalls of the past, contribute from the hard-fought lessons of the past, and offer the intellectual capital earned through research and practice.[63]

Our emerging design methodologies mean nothing without the profession understanding its potential and investing in its development. Currently in landscape architecture the profession has achieved for design what Ford achieved in 1913 for his Model T.[64] The profession has created a fundamental industry shift in process and efficiency, with less impact on creativity or new service development, producing a system of creating the same things faster and more cost-effectively rather than utilizing the potential of a new paradigm to think, generate, and analyze.

In 1915, a survey revealed that at Highland Park, in the factories of the Model T, laborers spoke more than 50 languages, very few speaking English.[65] How was it that execution remained so efficient? The assembly line labor of the engine did not join the paint department two days out of the week—they knew their component execution and it did not matter what was to their right or left. It is this seemingly streamlined process that allows specialists within firms to execute a task more rapidly such as 3D rendering, paving details, or specification writing in contemporary landscape architecture. However, it is the massive precut libraries of two-dimensional people copied and pasted from one proposal to another, or Grasshopper definitions of white hex grids over green terrain, which represent the globalization of a design "aesthetic" in contemporary computational models of practice, rather than a complex and adaptable model of shifting local variables.

There is an economy of shapes, anyone who has ever worked all night to create design drawings or models on a deadline is vividly aware of that. Some shapes are quick and easy to construct with available tools, but others are slow and laborious. Since architects (and landscape architects) must always produce designs

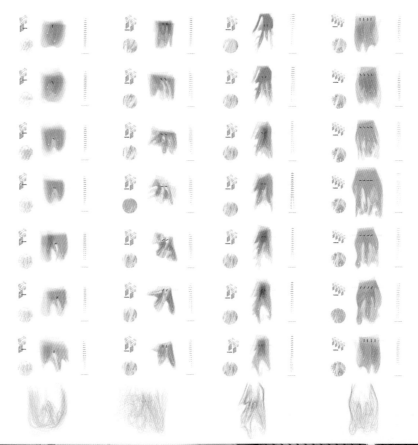

FIGURE 0.1.12
Responsive topography for fluvial landscapes exhibition at Harvard Graduate School of Design, Bradley Cantrell, Leif Estrada, Jeremy Hartley, Tyler Mohr, Andrew Boyd, Cambridge, MA
Image: Keith Scott

within finite time periods, and with limited expenditure of resources, they are always constrained by the current shape economy.

William J. Mitchell, Cambridge[66]

We must look to the new economies surrounding our profession to reshape our own. What the smartphone/mobile device network created as a new market for mobile app development, or what the Wright brothers created for the transportation industry in disruptive technologies, is what our profession must look forward to, not shy away from. When cars fly (as Airbus has already demonstrated) or become automated pods at half their current size, what will happen to our scopes of urban streetscape design? Will there be increases in green space development, or will terrestrial urban land become an undesirable back of house, with high-rise green walls and fifty-story or more green roofs the gentrified public spaces? The opportunities of a future design economy lie not only in new materials and levels of formal complexity in architectural and environmental fabrication but also in opportunities to tackle greater challenges of execution, and influence over the direct relationship between design, ecological systems, and fabrication.

Notes

1. Coates, P. *Programming Architecture*, Routledge, 2010.

2. Coates, P. *Programing Architecture*.

3. Randell, B. "The Origins of Computer Programming," *Annals of the History of Computing IEEE*, 16, 6–14, 1994.

4. Bromley, G. "Charles Babbage's Analytical Engine, 1838," *Annals of the History of Computing*, 4(3), 196–217, July–September 1982. doi:10.1109/MAHC.1982.10028, http://ieeexplore.ieee.org/stamp/stamp.jsp?tp=&arnumber=4640697&isnumber=4640695

5. Turing, A.M. "On Computable Numbers, with an Application to the Entscheidungs problem," *Proceedings of the London Mathematical Society*, s2–42, 230–265, 1937. doi:10.1112/plms/s2–42.1.230

6. Trueman, C.N. "Alan Turing," *The History Learning Site*, April 21, 2015, historylearning site.co.uk, accessed November 24, 2017.

7. "Computer." Oxford English Dictionary (3rd ed.). Oxford University Press.

8. http://european-section-with-lepoutre. blogspot.com/2013/09/memory-wwii-alan-turing.html#!/2013/09/memory-wwii-alan-turing.html

9. www.nsa.gov/about/cryptologic-heritage/ historical-figures-publications/women/ honorees/caracristi.shtml

10. "Quantum Internet Is One Step Closer," *Wall Street Journal*, June 15, 2017, www.wsj. com/articles/quantum-internet-is-one-step-closer-1497550005

11. NSA, *Cryptolog* #54, published June 1979. Released Public Declassified by NSA October 12, 2012, accessed June 25, 2017.

12. Weller, R. "Planning by Design Landscape Architectural Scenarios for a Rapidly Growing City," *Journal of Landscape Architecture*, 3(2), 2008.

13. https://cga-download.hmdc.harvard.edu/ publish_web/Annual_Spring_Workshops/2006_ HRG/Harvard_Chrisman.pdf

14. Chrisman, N. *Charting the Unknown: How Computer Mapping at Harvard Became GIS*, ESRI Press, 2006.

15. Ervin, S. and Hasbrouck, H. *Landscape Modeling: Digital Techniques for Landscape Visualization*, McGraw-Hill, 2001, p. 34.

16. www.foresthistory.org/ASPNET/ Publications/multiple_use/chap5.htm

17. www.danielsevo.com/hocg/hocg_1970.htm

18. Morrison, M. *Becoming a Computer Animator*, Sams, 1994.

19. MLA. *The Phantom Menace Review Quotes*. Quotes.net, www.quotes.net/mquote/1110673, accessed June 27, 2017.

20. http://fourmilab.ch (John Walker's personal website), accessed June 25, 2017.

21. Walliss, J. and Rahmann, H. "Introduction," in *Landscape Architecture and Digital Technologies*, Routledge, 2015.

22. Steinitz, C. *A Framework for Geodesign*, ESRI, 2012.

23. Vargas-Moreno, J.C. *SPATIAL DELPHI: Geo-Collaboration and Participatory GIS in Design and Planning*, Department of Urban Studies and Planning Massachusetts Institute of Technology, 2008.

24. Christensen, C.M. *The Innovators Dilemma*, Harvard Business School Press, 1997.

25. Brodie, M.L., Mylopoulos, J., and Schmidt, J.W. (eds.), "Preface," in *On Conceptual Modelling. Perspectives from Artificial Intelligence, Databases, and Programming Languages*, Springer-Verlag, 1984.

26. Ahlquist, S. and Menges, A. "Computational Design Thinking," in Menges, A. and Ahlquist, S. (eds.), *Computational Design Thinking*, Wiley, 2011.

27. Manovich, L. *Software Takes Command*, unpublished, http://softwarestudies.com/softbook/manovich_softbook_11_20_2008.pdf, accessed October 10, 2012.

28. Treib, M. *Representing Landscape*, Taylor & Francis, 2008.

29. www.sidewalklabs.com/blog/a-key-to-democratizing-urban-solutions-is-building-better-models

30. https://medium.com/sidewalk-talk/reimagining-cities-from-the-internet-up-5923d6be63ba

31. Frankel, T.C. "What These Photos of Facebook's New Headquarters Say About the Future of Work," *The Washington Post*, November 30, 2015; Boorstin, J. "Inside Facebook's Futuristic New Headquarters," ETCNBC.com, May 22, 2015.

32. Rogers, A. "If You Care About Cities, Apple's New Campus Sucks," *Wired*, www.wired.com/story/apple-campus, June 8, 2017.

33. Rappaport, M. "States of Distraction Media Art Strategies Within Public Conditions," in Aneesh, A., Hall, L., and Petro, P. (eds.), *Beyond Globalization. Making New Worlds in Media, Art, and Social Practices*, Rutgers University Press, 2012.

34. Srinivasan, R. "Digital Public Spaces: Implications Toward Cultural Memory and Participation," in the proceedings of CATAC (Cultural Attitudes toward Technology and Communication), 2008.

35. Doctoroff, D.L. *It's Time for Urbanists and Technologists to Start Talking*, https://medium.com/sidewalk-talk/it-s-time-for-urbanists-and-

technologists-to-start-talking-df1b57abfbd1

36. Cantrell, B. and Michaels, W. *Digital Drawing for Landscape Architecture: Contemporary Techniques and Tools for Digital Representation in Site Design*, John Wiley & Sons, 2010.

37. Oxman, R. "Thinking Difference: Theories and Models of Parametric Design Thinking." *Design Studies*, 52, 4–39, 2017.

38. www.sidewalklabs.com/about

39. Deschamps, J.-P. "Classic Root Causes of Innovation Failures—Things We All Know but Sometimes Forget," *Strategy and Communication for Innovation*, 41–60, 2017.

40. Tedeschi, A. *Parametric Architecture with Grasshopper*, Le Penseur, 2011.

41. *AEC Magazine* "Review: Grasshopper ArchiCAD Connection," December 8, 2015.

42. Martyn, D. "Rhino Grasshopper," *AEC Magazine*, 42 (May/June), 14–15, 2009.

43. Martyn, D., "Rhino Grasshopper," *AEC Magazine*, July 1, 2008, and May/June, 2009.

44. Oxman, R. "Performance-Based Design: Current Practices and Research Issues," *International Journal of Architectural Computing*, 6(1), 1–17, 2008.

45. Hensel, M. *Performance-Oriented Architecture: Rethinking Architectural Design and the Built Environment*. John Wiley & Sons, 2013.

46. Schumpeter, J.A. *Capitalism Socialism, and Democracy*. Harper & Row, 1976.

47. Jensen, M.C. "The Modern Industrial Revolution, Exit, and the Failure of Internal Control Systems," *The Journal of Finance*, 48, 831–880, 1993. doi:10.1111/j.1540–6261.1993.tb04022.x

48. Deschamps, J.P. "Classic Root Causes of Innovation Failures—Things We All Know but Sometimes Forget," *Strategy and Communication for Innovation*, 41–60, 2017.

49. Kayser, M., Laucks, J., Duro-Royo, J., Gonzales Uribe, C.D., and Oxman, N. Silk Pavillion, 2013, CNC Deposited Silk Fiber & Silkworm Construction MIT Media Lab; Kayser, M., Duro-Royo, J., Sharma, S., Bader, C., Kolb, D., and Oxman, N. A Perpetual Spring Environment for Bees and Humans, 2016, MIT Media Lab; S.J. Keating, Lelad, J.C., Cai, L., and Oxman, N. Towards Site-Specific and Self-

Sufficient Robotic Fabrication on Architectural Scales, *Science Robotics*, 2, 2017.

50. Burry, J. and Burry, M., *The New Mathematics of Architecture*, Thames and Hudson, 2010.

51. Schumacher, P. *Parametricism as Style – Parametricist Manifesto*, London, 2008.

52. Cantrell, B. and Melendez, F. *Responsive Systems*, Dissertation, Louisiana State University, 2012.

53. Ingels, B. 2013 interview, "Inside the Business of Design," www.youtube.com/watch?v=otsmpjaeHXc&list=PL1IM4xtSxXPPHPYEoR6f-87ccWfOWGfqo

54. Nagle, J. *Getting to Know Scratch*, Rosen, 2014.

55. *Mitch Resnick TED Talk*, November 2012, www.ted.com/talks/mitch_resnick_let_s_teach_kids_to_code

56. Frankel, E. "Love and Math, The Heart of Hidden Reality," *The New York Times*, November 18, 2013.

57. Ahlquist, S. and Menges, A. "Computational Design Thinking," in Menges, A. and Ahlquist, S. (eds.), *Computational Design Thinking*, Wiley, 2011, pp. 10–11.

58. Oxman, R. "Performance-Based Design: Current Practices and Research Issues," *International Journal of Architectural Computing*, 6(1), 1–17, 2008.

59. Burry, M. *Scripting Cultures*, Wiley, 2011, p. 252.

60. Cantrell, B. and Holzman, J. *Responsive Landscapes*, Routledge, 2015.

61. Gengnagel, C., Kilian, A., Palz, N., and Scheurer, F. "Computational Design Modeling," in *Proceedings of the Design Modeling Symposium*, Berlin, p. VII, 2011.

62. Loosemore, M. *Innovation, Strategy and Risk in Construction. Turning Serendipity into Capability*, Routledge, 2014.

63. Sheppard, S.R.J. "Participatory Decision Support for Sustainable Forest Management: A Framework for Planning with Local Communities at the Landscape Level in Canada," *Canadian Journal of Forest Research*, 35(7), 1515–1526, 2005.

64. Womack, J.P., Jones, D.T., and Rood, D. *The Machine That Changed the World*, Harper-Perennial, 1991.

65. Cossons, N. "From Manufacturer to Prosumer in Two Hundred and Fifty Years," in *Transactions of the Newcomen Society*, 74(1), 2004.

66. Terzidis, K. "Foreword," in *Expressive Form: A Conceptual Approach to Computational Design*, Taylor & Francis, 2003.

Syntax 01

Computation in landscape architecture requires that designers extract and abstract rules for landscape performance from an ecological, formal, cultural, and material perspective. Developing the rules, or syntax, of landscape is its own design project, requiring that landscape architects cleverly define how an environment is represented with behaviors and relationships.

01.00

Computation in practice

An inquiry into the business of computational design

Contributors:

Jared Friedman
Computational designer and licensed architect

Nicholas Jacobson
Designer at Davis Partnership Architects

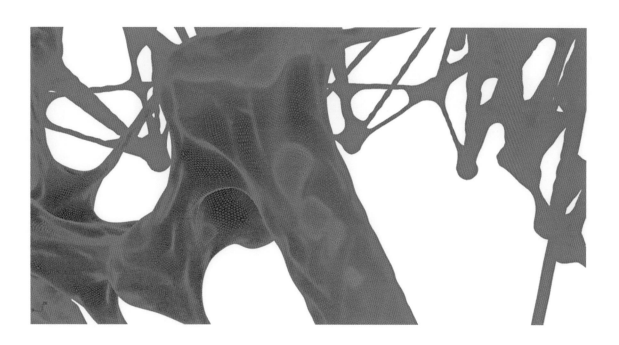

The terms "computational design" and "parametric design" can be defined in many ways. They may bring to mind forms driven by generative algorithms or the ability to design with various types of data sets or simply the use of Building Information Modeling (BIM) software. We can argue that what the fields of computational design and parametric design hold in terms of potential and capability, they lack in clarity and specificity. How do we begin to define these terms to a potential client? And how do we choose which computational juice is worth the squeeze? These are just a couple of the considerations when integrating computational and parametric design strategies into practice.

FIGURE 1.0.1

Image: Paralabs

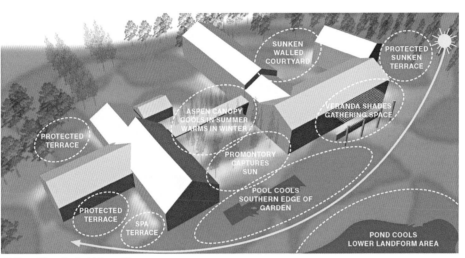

12-Hour Time Period | June 20

Labels within diagram:
- SUNKEN WALLED COURTYARD
- PROTECTED SUNKEN TERRACE
- ASPEN CANOPY COOLS IN SUMMER WARMS IN WINTER
- VERANDA SHADES GATHERING SPACE
- PROTECTED TERRACE
- PROMONTORY CAPTURES SUN
- POOL COOLS SOUTHERN EDGE OF GARDEN
- PROTECTED TERRACE
- SPA TERRACE
- POND COOLS LOWER LANDFORM AREA

Ideal Gathering Areas

12-Hour Time Period | September 20

Ideal Gathering Areas

12-Hour Time Period | December 20

PLANNING FOR ACTIVITIES

 MORNING

Outdoor Dining for Breakfast
Morning Swim
Trail Walk
Master Bedroom Reading Terrace

 NOON

Central Courtyard for Lunch
Mid-Day Swim
Outdoor Reading Terrace
Recreation Lawn

 AFTERNOON

Outdoor Veranda for Reading
Mid-Day Swim
Secondary Terraces for Gathering
Trail Walk

 EVENING

Promontory Gathering Lawn
Central Courtyard for Dinner
Western Fireplace Terrace
Hot Tub

FIGURE 1.0.2 **Landscape radiation and environmental analysis. With the property devoid of vegetation, creating habitable outdoor spaces would be a challenge. Thermal and wind analyses informed critical design decisions – each aimed at the goal of extending the hours and seasons during which the landscape can be used**

Image: Design Workshop Inc and Paralabs

3D BODY SCAN

ROUGH SURFACE OF DRESS AS BREP

PRIMARY CURVATURE FOR FABRICATED STRIPS

PLANARITY ANALYSIS ON BASE SURFACE

CIRCLE SIZE BASED ON PLANARITY AND DESIRED DRAPING

FIGURE 1.0.3 **Process of dress fabrication**
Image: Paralabs

A designer that is working parametrically may be thought of as someone who is flipping the traditional process, an editor of constraints first, and an empirical designer once the constraints are designed. What this means for practice is often far more interesting and innovative than the complex forms that initiate such projects. Inherent in the computational design process is the ability to quickly explore multiple design iterations throughout a project. This process is sometimes referred to as "optioneering," in which consultants and collaborators are brought on early in a design in order to help define the project constraints. As design processes and schedules adapt to emergent modeling and analysis workflows, we find opportunities for new models of practice that simultaneously react to, and influence advances in the field of computational design.

The following interviews were conducted by Paralabs, a small computational design practice, founded in February 2016. Our design lab is built on the notion that quality design emerges from a rigorous approach in which designers are conscious of, and able to work with, more of the parameters at play. We utilize computational thinking and techniques in order to investigate design problems, and ultimately arrive at creative solutions that are informed by the context.

Within the early development of our lab we have found ourselves constantly adjusting our business model to allow for flexibility in exploring the applications of transdisciplinary computational design, where we work to create new intersections with other professions. We have collaborated on projects with fashion designers, medical professionals, and landscape architects.

It is not initially obvious nor easy to explain how a computational way of thinking can be applied to new and unexpected collaborations. Hoping to shed some light on the subject, we have chosen to investigate how other successful computationally focused practices situate themselves, both from a design perspective and a business perspective. All of the questions asked are questions that we have asked ourselves since forming a business. Leaders from four unique design and engineering–based practices have been selected to gather a variety of perspectives and insights on how they integrate computational thinking into practice. We hope that these conversations can also provide a glimpse into the struggles and opportunities for an emerging computational design practice.

The interviewees

Bill Allen (BA)

Computational Designer
Partner and Director of Building Information Management Services at EvolveLAB

Bill has over a decade of experience managing technology for buildings in the AEC industry including managing large, complex BIM workflow mechanisms as a BIM manager for cutting-edge firms. He is an expert in parametric systems and interoperability between different software. EvolveLAB is a full-service BIM consulting firm. As building technology professionals, they influence and mentor engineers, contractors, owners, and architects. Their mission is to make project teams more successful through innovation, progressive workflows, and technology. They provide the tools, the resources, and the knowledge to make project teams more efficient and sustainable.

Hanif Kara (HK)

Structural Engineer
Founding Partner of AKT
Professor of Architectural Technology
Harvard University

AKT is a London-based progressive design-led structural and civil engineering practice. P.ART is their nonprofit in-house parametric research team working to develop bespoke software programs to interrogate and analyze projects at any stage of the project.

Benjamin Koren (BK)

Managing Director of ONE TO ONE

ONE TO ONE is a computational geometry and digital fabrication consultancy on art and architecture projects, offering services in bespoke geometric computation, precision 3D CAD construction, integrative CAM fabrication and innovative R&D at all scales.

Andrew Witt (AW)

Co-Founder of Certain Measures
Lecturer at Harvard University

Certain Measures is an office for design science using geometry, mathematics, data, and new technologies to create new spaces and ways of making. Tapping open-source software and knowledge, embracing a flexible collaboration structure, and building new software and robotic tools for these novel projects, Certain Measures draws on diverse backgrounds in architecture, robotics, computer science, and mathematics, to simplify beautiful complexity and to delight, surprise, and enrich human experience.

Interviews

Paralabs (PL): Computational design is a somewhat new process that can be foreign to clients. How is marketing this process different than a traditional design process? How do you explain this process to potential clients?

AW: In and of itself, computational design is too vague and, to most clients, abstract to be a useful category. First, it becomes this kind of Rorschach test for what potential clients think computational design is, which can be very limiting. Second, it becomes too easy for clients to think computational designers all have the same skills and are simply interchangeable. What matters is the specific domain expertise or your specific communicable perspective, which is extended by computational tools.

We don't think of Certain Measures as a computational design practice but as an office for design science or as an incubator for design technologies. In this sense, we focus on particular domains – such as machine learning, urban optioneering, and of course design geometry – around which we develop our own specific products and technologies. We solve problems which are not computationally defined but which admit computational solutions.

HK: I'm not convinced it's different. It's current and relevant. It's a way of adding value to everything you are thinking about. It could be losing weight, better design, or making something cheaper and quicker. Manufacturing helps to collapse a process down the line. Sadly, some people call it BIM – it is progress, but it's limited. When we didn't have projects, we showed what the potential was, and there is an element of marketing through showing prototypical ideas. Later on we did buildings that proved these concepts.

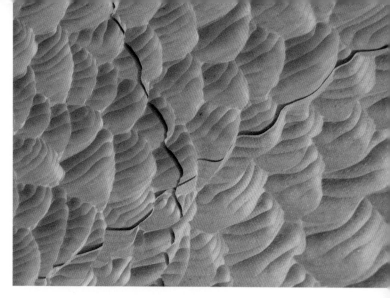

FIGURE 1.0.4 **Close up view of sound panels**
Image: Ben Koren, ONE TO ONE

BK: It depends on the client. To architects and artists, we stress the quality and precision of our work and the potential it offers in enhancing their vision. To workshops and contractors we stress efficiency, speed and cost reduction in using automation and optimization techniques. In the best projects, it is a balance of the two, when working on both ends. However, we tend to avoid the term "computational design" so as not to compete with the creative work provided by the designers. We understand our practice to be a consultancy firm in computational geometry, not a design firm.

PL: Digital tools allow designers to collaborate in new and different ways. How is your business management model and interactions with collaborators different than a traditional design practice?

AW: At Gehry Technologies, I developed a prototype for a product called GTeam (now Trimble Connect), which was all about new modes of digital collaboration. While it was a fascinating process, what I found was that it is a heavy, slow, and heroic effort to try to change business processes, particularly when you are only a consultant. It requires extensive training and a real change in mind-set by many stakeholders. Quantifying the benefits those changes would bring is also a challenge. I'm glad someone is doing it, but I think there are more effective ways to provide value. In short, it is the opposite of the kind of problem around which you can build an efficient business.

Now we try to focus on methods and processes that are "productizable," that is, they can be packaged and consumed with as little friction as possible, and produce impactful results without boiling the ocean. It also makes it much easier for these tools to be sold or spun off later, because there is not a heavy service component.

HK: The business model has not changed. The way we collaborate is through being able to do more work early on. With architecture, we can very quickly send data and optimize before we even present to a client. In the old days an architect would do a presentation and the engineer would respond, then the client would say yes or no. These days we are able to do most of that computationally. So in terms of what is expected of us, early, what we find is that clients are expecting a lot more refinement because they understand the design better. I would separate this from "optioneering" because that is just drawing prototypical ideas for all kinds of types; but when you are engineering properly, and optimizing with an architect, you can actually optimize at many levels because it has to do with light, environment, structure, and architecture – not just structural engineering and architecture.

The business model isn't different and the fees don't go up hugely just because nobody wants to pay any more; they just want more for their money. The difference is this: after building a reputation in it, your initial number for your fee is always higher. So when people call you in the first instance, they know they

are going to pay 10 percent or 15 percent more than calling the guy down the street because they know that the quality of service they are going to get is much higher, and the return that they get in their value – whether that is lighter, quicker, etc. – is worthwhile.

The investments we made in computation were not intended for immediate return. It took time while the culture was being built; and when you see the response that we produce from having built that investment, the value, now over time, is making profits for all of us. The Phaeno Science center could not have been built unless everyone invested hugely. We all lost a lot of money doing that just to prove that it could be done. So that was a massive investment from Zaha Hadid Architects, from AKT II, from the contractors, from the client and everyone involved. But it changed the industry. The software that was developed over the project is now the normal software used in reinforced concrete design in the UK. It wasn't until we did that project that that software improved to where you can analyze as much and as fast and as complexly as you can today.

PL: Do you typically start with a project(s) that has a particular need that leads to the development of tools/scripts or is it more an idea that is developed and then applied to projects? In other words, do you find it more needs-driven or more opportunity-driven?

BK: In the professional work – mostly needs-driven. We usually arrive on the projects at too late a stage to influence fundamentals. More often than not, we have to work with whatever basis is provided to us. In some cases, the most interesting projects are opportunity-driven, such as the work we did on the acoustic panels in the Elbphilharmonie Concert Hall. In that project, the architectural, acoustical, fabrication and coding parameters all influenced each other, and we got involved very early on in the process. It was a feedback loop, where the design drove the code, and the code, in turn, reinfluenced the design.

AW: Our most interesting work has been initiated by research projects we have developed, after which we connect with clients who can use the technology or process that we have researched. Occasionally interesting things will emerge out of a client's needs, but clients pattern-match with what you have already done, so it becomes a chicken-and-egg problem. We thus find the constant up-front investment in new possibilities essential. Of course, some of these self-initiated projects grew out of problems we noticed, but could not address on other projects because of scope limitations. So there is a virtuous cycle between the two.

BA: Our firm typically builds custom tools/scripts in more opportunistic-driven applications. We like to disrupt current and traditional methods of design and building by automating tasks, augmenting efficiencies, and mitigating mundane responsibilities that are repeated over and over. We find ways to streamline processes and avoid data drops. Even for a simple task like designing a façade, you can design the façade using traditional sketching techniques or build the façade in static 3D modeling software. The challenge is that you can only model so many static options of that façade in a day. However, if you are able to parametrize the façade, set rules, and drive the façade parametrically, you are now able to create many more options and much more pragmatically.

PL: When designing computational tools, what are some strategies you use to ensure your tools are robust and not subject to failure, as software, APIs, and projects undergo changes?

AW: It is essential to build a codebase which is fairly independent of specific CAD packages but which can easily be integrated with them. This also circles back to the need for specific domain knowledge distinct from computational expertise: it helps ensure that there will be less impact with these API changes, since your tools are domain-specialized.

BK: There is usually a development phase that focuses on all possible applications of a script – developing and testing the code to make sure it works flawlessly. If there are changes, that process has to be redone. It requires a certain level of rigor and patience to keep things tidy and clean, especially in projects with lots of design changes. Most tools are developed for a specific project and a specific purpose. Once the projects are over, the code never gets used again. Only a handful of scripts and functions get saved and are developed further for broader applications and find their way into collections we continuously develop, which we call the ONE TO ONE TOOL. Since this collection is coded at a very basic level, we hardly ever have issues with updates.

BA: When designing computational tools, some strategies we use to ensure our tools are robust and not subject to failure is to try building them as natively as possible. What do I mean when I say that? There has been this HUGE push to open-source tools (which is amazing), but comes with its own set of challenges. As an example, Dynamo is an open-source program to which the industry can contribute its own custom packages, or add-ins. The challenge when using someone else's open-source package is that you are now subject to the integrity of their tool. If there is a flaw in their tool, or if it no longer works when a new release of Dynamo comes out, you are now subject to that defect. We prefer to use our own custom nodes, as it gives us greater control over the tool and its integrity.

PL: What would you say the breakdown is of research and tools aimed at making existing workflows better versus that which is aimed at opening new possibilities?

AW: The very idea of optimizing existing workflows suggests a services-based activity which is contextually specific and extremely difficult to scale. Our office is more interested in productizing and scaling up new possibilities.

BA: In general, technology really hasn't affected the architecture, engineering, and construction industry all that much. We, as an industry, pretty much execute the same tasks that we have done for hundreds of years, but now electronically on a computer. If you compare our industry to others, you can see how others have increased their efficiencies through technology in contrast to our industry which has pretty much stayed static. There have been quite a few tools that are aimed at making existing workflows better. However, we, at EvolveLAB, believe we as an industry are going to see a huge shift over the next 10–15 years. With advances in generative design, machine learning, and the Internet of Things, the way we design, build, and operate buildings is going to be night and day compared to what we do today.

PL: What caused you to focus on computation? And what was the manifesto when you got started?

HK: The manifesto was very simple. We recognized that the relationship between construction and design was dysfunctional. There weren't enough people doing good design and there were even fewer people making good buildings. So we attacked both ends. One end was to improve the connection between the two and the other end was to sharpen design and sharpen construction systems. So that what we tried to do as a

manifesto was to start with a position of wanting to make good quality buildings. Quality and innovation were the two big targets and then from that: how does that change the process of design?

If you follow the linear process of the AIA or the RIBA, it, by definition, is a productive process, which is very rational and it doesn't always allow you to innovate because it goes from A to B to C to D. It doesn't go from A to Z and back to A. We wanted to improve design quality; we wanted to innovate and apply that to construction, which demonstrates the connection between design and construction that works together. When you add those two things up you are increasing value. No matter which way you look at it, it was an increase in value: better buildings, happier occupants, and architects thought we were the sexiest thing on Earth.

All of those value-adds just came out of that manifesto. And being able to prove that we can make that just because we were designers doesn't mean that we have to hand over the chaotic, dysfunctional construction system. We can engage with it and we can improve that to a point where high-quality construction people often employ us.

Things then can transpire from that manifesto. I often say to clients that you shouldn't give us a simple project, but it's also your mistake if you don't. Because an office that knows how to do complexity does simplicity better. People think that simplicity is the most economical and best thing on Earth and it's just not true. It's just not true and I know that so well.

BA: I remember attending a parametricism conference in 2011, and seeing these amazing buildings that designers were creating using computational design and parametric modeling. I loved the idea of making something that had movement, and could update dynamically. After returning from the conference, I started learning Grasshopper, Dynamo, and other programming tools. From that point, I also found myself obsessed with interoperability, and getting separate software platforms to talk to each other, such as Rhino and Revit. I was able to accomplish this using the add-in Hummingbird.

PL: Is starting a computationally based practice more difficult today compared to when you first began? And do you have advice for someone starting such a practice?

HK: In my opinion, and this is personal, there is no other way to work than computationally. If I was starting a practice in engineering right now, I would be starting out to set the curve, rather than follow the curve. To do that, you have to arm yourself with the best computational tools because if you don't start there, in my opinion, you will not have a difference to show. That does not mean that you don't have an eye for sketching or painting or an eye for the traditional instruments for design; what it means is that you are capable of doing it from a position of knowledge, a position of what is current, and relevant. The next machine age, which everybody talks about, is past the digital; so there is no way society can survive now without a combination of the computational with everything else we do from communication, to transportation; everything has a computational edge to it. So if you try and start, in any discipline, from somewhere else I think you would struggle.

BK: I was first introduced to computation in architecture in 2005 through one of my professors at the Architectural Association, Charles Walker, who led the Advanced Geometry Unit at Arup in London at the time. The work the AGU did in the mid-2000s was groundbreaking, and immediately sparked

my interest in computation. I went on to work at the AGU for a while, and really learned a lot from my co-workers, a mix of architects, engineers, mathematicians and computer scientists. It was a very optimistic period, as most of the techniques were brand new, as was their potential for design and construction. I suppose that optimism has subsided a little over the years, as the industry got overly saturated with increasingly complex designs, for the sake of complexity. I think, in that regard, the manifesto changed a bit from when I first got started. In the beginning, it was all about pushing the boundary, finding NEW potential, I think nowadays there is a push back to fundamentals, finding the INHERENT potential of computational techniques, especially when linked with computer-aided manufacturing tools.

BA: I believe starting a computationally based practice is easier today compared to when I first began. The reason is twofold. One, the industry is more open to these ways of designing and constructing buildings than it ever used to be. Two, there has never been a time such as this with so many advancing technologies.

If I was going to give any advice for someone starting such a practice, I would say, understand that not everyone is going to think like you are. It is going to sometimes take multiple times of explaining to someone and seeing a process before they believe in a new way of design. I would also say there is a balance between disrupting a couple-thousand-year-old process, and playing by the rules that are established in the industry. Sometimes we need to recognize that the industry is not ready for such a paradigm shift, but we should never ever be willing to settle for the status quo.

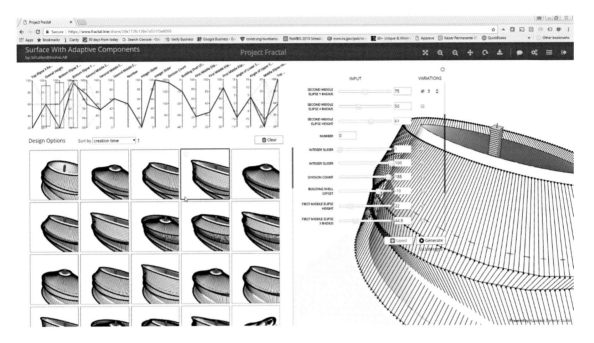

FIGURE 1.0.5 **Option engineering with project fractal**
Image: Bill Allan, Evolve Lab

Synopsis

This series of interviews is intended to present a snapshot of computational design applications in practice today. It highlights a diversity of approaches that diverge from the common practices established across the architecture and engineering industries. If we were to map these practices along a scale from pure consultant to pure designer they would each likely fall at different places on that scale. Differences are also found in the common typologies and scales of the projects that each of these practices works on. Despite these differences, we can begin to extract some common threads, advice, and unexpected challenges that appear across the variety of practices in regard to the business of computational design.

First and foremost, there is a general evasion of all-encompassing terms such as "computational design" owing to their vague and abstract nature. Since computational design comes in so many shapes and sizes it is best to describe more specifically what is being offered by these individual practices. In some cases, the focus is on efficiency and precision. In other cases, the focus may be more about achieving a particular level of complexity or in realizing a unique aesthetic. Computational design in and of itself does not possess a style or even a process, but rather provides a broad characterization of a way of thinking through design issues and realizing a project by simply incorporating more layers of information.

For the practices such as ONE TO ONE and P.ART at AKT that have been around long enough to see clear evolution, we see a shift from a focus on how to achieve new potentials in geometric complexity to a focus on further extracting inherent value from computation techniques. This tends to reflect changes in the industry as a whole over the past decade. While complexity in architecture does not show any signs of going away, we are seeing a maturation in how and where to apply it. It is no longer a question of if we can do it, but what value can be gained from it and the processes that underlie it. The word "value" was used a number of times by interviewees, and it suggests that, while it may be true that computational design strategies open up new paradigms and design opportunities, it is ultimately about adding lasting value and improving performance on projects.

The impact that this nebulous concept of computational design has had on business is, predictably, quickly changing the dynamics of the design profession from the inside out. Numerous subdisciplines have been created and existing areas of expertise are being explored on deeper levels. However, value is socially constructed and most of the practices we interviewed struggle to balance the supply of new possibilities with demand from clients. In this bottleneck we see offices, empowered by access to a vast set of new options, choosing to bypass the traditional scope of work and engaging earlier in the process as a "design assist," becoming a more integral part of the design process. This is also allowing a shift from designers as being mainly intermediaries to become producers with a direct economic stake in the final outcome and more directly dictating the broader stylistic decisions. There is a recurring theme in developing ideas prior to client involvement or by prototyping ideas at a small scale that may then be deployed at a larger scale when the right client comes along. One way to do this is through a "productization" of methods that can be deployed to satisfy the requirements for a variety of project types. The resulting "product" (which is actually a process) can

then be used to find clients who are interested in this type of process. In this way designers are able to foster a better understanding of the criteria that defines a shared value between the profession and clients. Each of the practices interviewed deployed this strategy in one way or another, and each suggested it is a preferred method of working.

Design and its related fields have been notoriously slow at adapting technology in comparison to other industries, such as the automotive and medical industries. There are a variety of reasons for this, and calls in the early 2000s to mimic these other industries have had little traction. Impediments to replicating the efficiencies of these industries have had less to do with technological challenges and more to do with fundamental differences in project delivery methods and business models. The development, application, and education of computational design techniques has taken great strides forward over the last decade. We have seen significant improvements in digital workflows as well as important stylistic impacts from these tools. However, there is certainly still room for further growth. As was noted by several of the interviewees, little has really changed in terms of how we execute projects – particularly at larger scales. In order for the wide range of processes that fall under the umbrella of computational design to continue to advance, it is clear that a multipronged approach is necessary. It is not only about designing better tools, but rethinking the business models and avenues taken when applying such tools.

Contributors:

Chris Reed
*Professor in Practice,
Harvard Graduate
School of Design;
Founder and Director,
Stoss*

01.01

Generative modeling and the making of landscape

Landscape practices have recently been informed by two distinct lines of inquiry. Ecological and environmental concerns have thrust landscape and ecology into the center of design discourse in ways that explore the dynamic, operational, and even physical aspects of ecological systems as a starting point for generating design—whether landscape, building, or urbanism. Simultaneously, advances in software technologies have brought generative and associative modeling tools into the academic design studio and into the professional office, allowing for a new generation of techniques and fabrication technologies to emerge.

This essay argues for the interplay of these lines of inquiry: agendas of responsiveness, flexibility, and adaptability inherent in complex dynamic systems ecology can in many ways be played out through generative and associative modeling tools—allowing for multiplicity and differentiation from the intimate scale of the human body to the wide expanses of the territory. Such modeling techniques, which can be utilized to initiate design inquiry and ultimately generate physical form, allow for a continuous and increasing complexity of inputs to the modeling process, producing a multiplication and elaboration of possibilities that each respond to a slightly different set of priorities or agendas. Thus design is neither static nor compositional, but dynamic; assemblies of forms and components (at any range of scales and serving any number of functions) can be generated from a set of logics that can adapt themselves to circumstances, all the while maintaining their essential characteristics and operational protocols. This is conceptually not so far removed from the work of late twentieth-century ecologists, who emphasized an organism's or ecosystem's adaptability in assessing overall health—with the idea that various inputs could produce shifts and changes in the environment over time, and the final physical form of a healthy organism or ecosystem would change and adapt to these new circumstances.[1] Multiple outcomes are possible here; physical form is malleable—it is more the functioning and operation of systems that are in play. In marrying these two lineages, then, the opportunity and the emphasis is on the *performative* aspects of the physical forms that may emerge—to paraphrase Stan Allen, not so much what they look like but more so what they can do.[2]

This essay will examine three scales of the application of associative and generative modeling techniques in the conceptualization and making of performance-based landscape and urban form. At the scale of the human body, recent applications speak to the translation of associative modeling principles and methods into fabrication and construction processes for furnishings and elements, allowing for the generation of nonstandardized and nonrepetitive units that may better serve diverse body types and shapes and differing agendas for how to use public space. Site scale work explores the ways in which hydrology or social program or even desired experiences or relationships can inform the delineation and hybridization of landform, pathway, and gathering space. Subsequent work in both academia and practice test and push this further, with elaborations across the broader urban field, including landscape and infrastructural systems, and the generation of urban form— instigating multiplication and elaboration across large territories in ways that can adapt and adjust to specific conditions on the ground. Underlying all this is a set of dialogues between academic explorations and applications in practice that continue to reverberate and inform one another as the work advances.

Body

Up until recently, the simple bench had been standardized, in part owing to twentieth-century advances in industrial manufacturing processes that found efficiencies in the production of repetitive, self-same parts and assemblies. The result was that the act of sitting, hanging out, slouching, etc. had all been simplified and standardized into a typical, mass-produced bench whose formal profile was consistent, that was geared toward an average human body, and that invested choice or difference in style or color alone.

While the body is exceptionally versatile and adaptive—and can make a seat out of a wide range of objects (tree stumps, walls, barrels, logs, etc.)—generative and associative modeling software offer opportunities to customize seating that is better adapted to different body sizes and body types—or simply offers choice to suit one's mood— while maintaining production efficiencies through evolutions in digital design, fabrication, and production techniques. The key is to develop prototypes of different sitting profiles—tuned specifically to different body types and different sitting or lounging positions—and script the software to loft or transition between two different profiles. In this way, a bench can begin with three to five different profile positions, as did the benches at the Harvard's Science Center Plaza, but result in an easily reproducible bench, created from CNC machines at the fabricator's shop, that accommodate over a dozen different sitting positions or scales. When this technique is reproduced with different starting profiles for five unique custom benches, the result is a plethora of choices for how one wishes to sit in public: alone or in groups, cross-legged or straight upright, lounging or lying down completely, or with a friend on one's lap. At Harvard, the overall form is assembled from a series of Alaskan Yellow Cedar "ribs," mounted to a steel frame; if one rib is damaged during snow removal or the like, the rib number can be retrieved from the digital file and an identical replacement piece fabricated for reinstallation. This is still a process that allows for replicability and efficient production, but is better tuned to the body and choice.

At the University of Michigan's Eda U. Gerstacker Grove, sitting functions were hybridized with slope retention and drainage strategies, but many of the same generative design and fabrication techniques were in play. Here, path edges were thickened first as concrete curbs to direct water to infiltration gardens. Curbs then transitioned into backless seatwalls that simultaneously retained the higher elevations behind, and eventually into seats with backs, with select runs then finished using polished metal ribs. Eventually the seats transitioned back down to seatwalls and curbs. Variation also occurs here in plan, allowing for sinuous shapes that could articulate both convex and concave moments, which translate in small, more intimate gathering areas and more outwardly focused sitting areas as well. Here, the bench-wall-curb configurations were made from over 40 distinct but repetitive unique modules, which could then be combined and configured in 2,243 linear feet of seatwalls that weave across the four-acre site.

In some ways a response to the highly adaptable nature of people and the human body—and the multiplicity of tasks a simple bench can be asked to take on in a public landscape.

Site

At the scale of the site, generative modeling can take on increasing levels of complexity in terms of function, program, site conditions, and any other set of technical or experiential

criteria. Early studies in the academic design studio explored the various creative relationships between the protocols of remediation technologies, for instance, and the generation of responsive and productive landscape systems. The water treatment process was translated into performative criteria (basin size, flow criteria, duration, and planting and soil conditions) that could then generate a series of clustered basins. These basins could be configured differently in response to existing topographic conditions and underlying drainage patterns, producing a variety of basin configurations that all shared an inherent set of logics and performance protocols. Such early studies were translated in full design studios at Harvard's Graduate School of Design, in which students were asked to create landform systems that would respond to water flows, inundation, and infiltration requirements—and eventually be layered to accommodate various forms of human occupation as well. In all of this, iteration, testing, prototyping, and a level of free and open-ended "play" were all at work; adaptability, and dealing with a level of environmental and human behavioral indeterminacy, came directly into play.

In practice, these same principles and techniques are at work in a range of landscape installations and open spaces. Early tests took the form of a play garden at the Jardins de Metis, where principles of free and creative play were at work—the idea that people, being the curious and sentient creatures that we are, can be prompted to explore and play with intriguing but nonprescriptive physical form. Running, jumping, sitting, and handstanding were all possible here, simply prompted by a series of rolling hillocks covered with varying thicknesses of bouncy rubber, itself installed differentially across the site according to specific safety and technical criteria that were determined from the height of the hillocks it was covering.

At the University of Michigan again, generative modeling techniques produced landforms that were calibrated to drain and retain stormwater and to create wetter growing environments for lush gardens; to set up views and prospects to integrated pathways and openings between the landforms for social gathering; to establish various environmental relationships; and to create shaded and sunny areas and to achieve better cut and fill relationships with existing soils. In and among the landforms, pathways swell and deflect, creating small eddies that are conducive to small gatherings for just a few people, accommodated on hardened edges articulated as the seatwalls and seats described earlier.

Other possibilities abound. In a proposal for renovating Harbour Square Park on the lakefront in Toronto, we studied trees through generative techniques for layout across the site, with an eye toward creating physical, spatial, programmatic, and vegetal gradients that transitioned gradually but dramatically across the site. And in a pair of small public spaces in Cambridge, Massachusetts, we are using the same generative frameworks to create related but radically different spaces such as a public square and plaza on the one hand, and an adventure play park on the other. Both schemes started from a similar point of translating morphed grids into physical landscape and surface, but differing site conditions and relationship and the different performative requirements of the spatial programs (sitting, gathering, watching a movie, etc., versus running, climbing, jumping, and swinging) are input to produce vastly different kinds of spaces and qualities.

City

From here, it's an almost simple leap to complex urban systems—systems that include functional infrastructure, social spaces, dynamic landscapes, even building form developed according to environmental performance criteria. In some ways you could think of these advanced urbanistic and social requirements as additional sets of criteria that are plugged into the software. Here urban infrastructure can be figured to respond to advanced hydrologic agendas and adaptive water and ecological networks in the city. Buildings can be carved in response to environmental conditions and optimal sun angles for better environmental performance within the buildings themselves and better quality of public social spaces in between them. Generative systems take on multiple and diverse architectural, infrastructural, landscape, and social agendas—that allow for an almost infinite combination and recombination, testing, and evaluation—and that set up principles and tactics that can adapt responsively to conditions on the ground, administrative decisions, and evolving circumstances.

At the city scale, and in the playing out of projects that require time and resources and political will to execute, we finally get the relational piece of these opportunities off the screen of the computer and fully enmeshed in the often messy political and bureaucratic processes that result in urban districts and cities. The district project itself, subject to economic cycles and changes in politics, has the ability to adapt and reformulate itself on the fly, both in response to what's already been built but also in response to these changing externalities. What's realized, then, is not a souped-up, swervy version of a form-based (no matter how elegant) master plan but an adaptive framework scenario, always in the process of adjustment, retooling, or elaboration: a generative ecosystem at the scale of the city.

FIGURE 1.1.1 **Custom seating at Science Center Plaza, Harvard University, Cambridge, MA, USA, by Stoss**
Photo: Charles Mayer

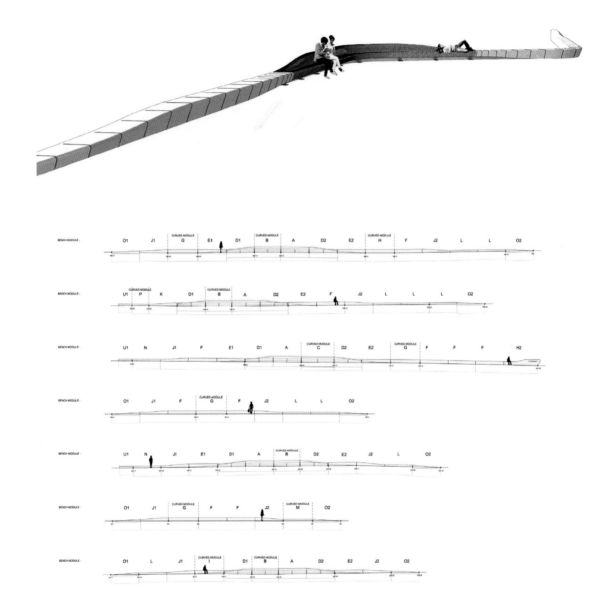

FIGURE 1.1.2 **Custom benches and series of elevations for the Eda U. Gerstacker Grove, University of Michigan, Ann Arbor, MI, USA, by Stoss**

Drawing: Stoss

Eda U. Gerstacker Grove, University of Michigan, Ann Arbor, MI, USA, by Stoss

Photo copyright Michigan Engineering

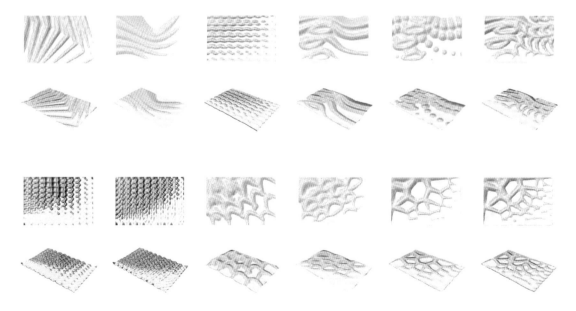

Performative water landscapes, studies

Project and drawing: Sonny Xu, Lanisha Blount, Harvard Graduate School of Design. Chris Reed and Bradley Cantrell, studio instructors

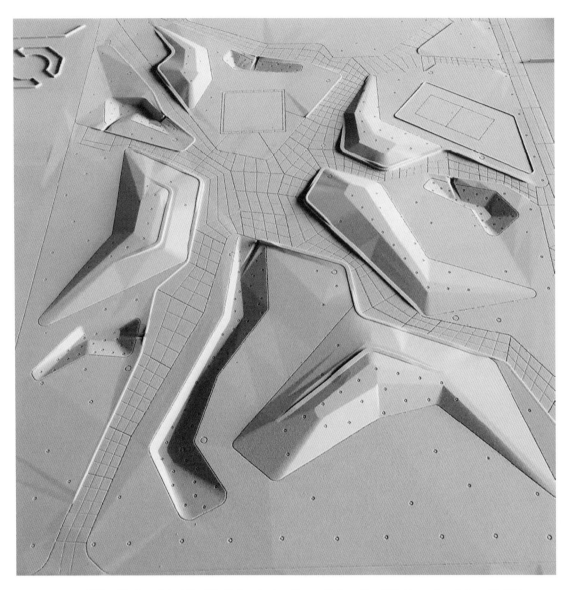

FIGURE 1.1.5 **CNC-milled model of the Eda U. Gerstacker Grove, University of Michigan, Ann Arbor, MI, USA, by Stoss**

Photo: Stoss

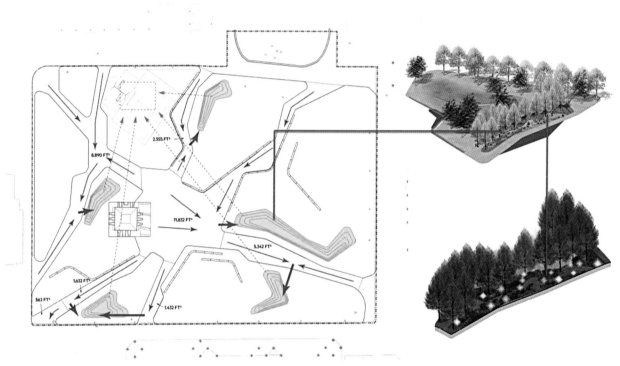

FIGURE 1.1.6 **Drainage and infiltration garden diagrams for the Eda U. Gerstacker Grove, University of Michigan, Ann Arbor, MI, USA, by Stoss**

Drawing: Stoss

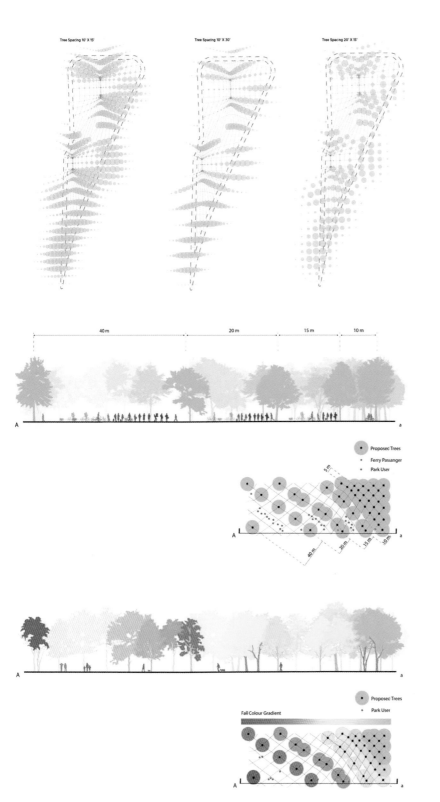

Tree Spacing 10' X 15'   Tree Spacing 10' X 30'   Tree Spacing 20' X 15'

Proposec Trees
Ferry Passanger
Park User

Fall Colour Gradient

Proposec Trees
Park User

FIGURE 1.1.7
Top: Generative grid and intensity studies for Triangle Park, Cambridge, MA, USA, Bottom: Generative grid and intensity studies for Cloud Park, Harbour Square Park, Toronto, Ontario, Canada, by Stoss

Drawing: Stoss

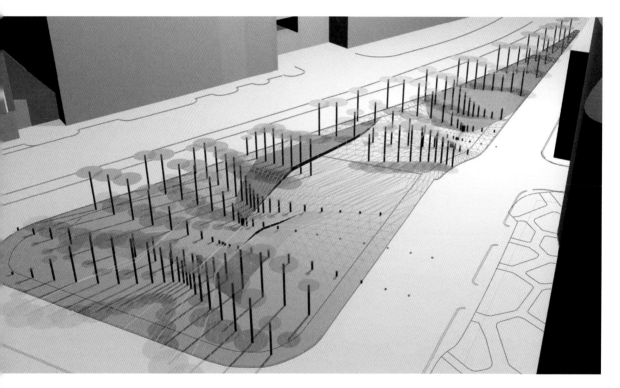

FIGURE 1.1.8 **Three-dimensional model of Triangle Park, Cambridge, MA, USA, by Stoss**

Drawing: Stoss

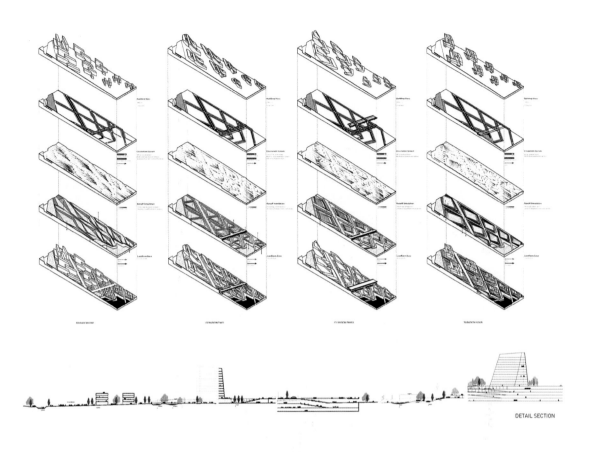

DETAIL SECTION

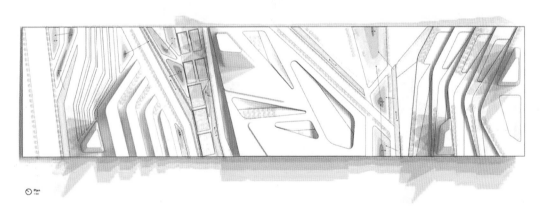

FIGURE 1.1.9 **Landform, infrastructure, building block studies, "Flux City" studio proposal, Allston, Massachusetts**

Project and drawing: Xun Liu, Jianwu Han, Harvard Graduate School of Design. Chris Reed and David Mah, studio instructors

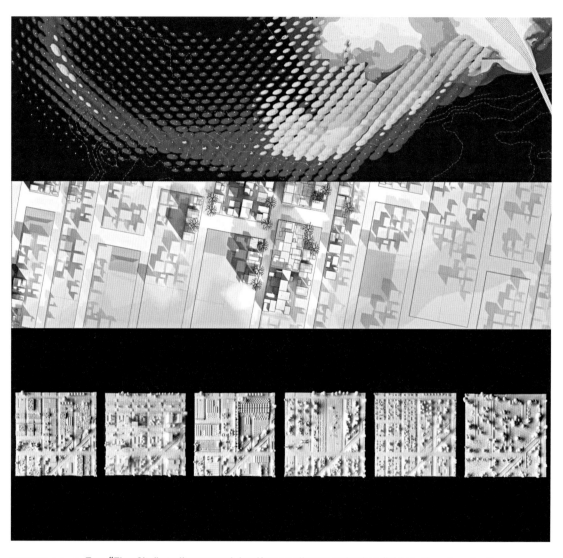

FIGURE 1.1.10 **Top: "Flux City" studio proposal, landform sediment and urban field studies, Jamaica Bay, New York. Project and drawing by Anya Domesky, Justin Jackson, Harvard Graduate School of Design. Chris Reed, studio instructor. Bottom: 3D printed models of neighborhood reuse strategies, Detroit, MI. 3D Rapid Prototyped Digital ABS**

Models: Stoss

Acknowledgments

The author wishes to thank Bradley Cantrell for his advice and input on this work, and for his collaboration in studio work at school; for a host of academic colleagues that contributed to the formulation of the studio work, including David Mah, Leire Ascencio-Villoria, Sergio Lopez-Pinheiro, Eduardo Rico, and Enriquetta Llabres-Valls, and our collective and very talented and energetic students; to Tim Wilson at Stoss, who helped to lead the University of Michigan work and articulate the relationships between the design and fabrication processes; and to all my colleagues at Stoss, who have done the day-to-day work on helping to conceptualize and realize the diverse work of the firm highlighted here.

Notes

1. Reed, C. and Lister, N.-M. *Projective Ecologies*. Harvard University Graduate School of Design, 2014, pp. 15–20.

2. Stan Allen was among the first to link what he called the "material practices" of contemporary ecology (and engineering) to design thinking, culling the research of Harvard Graduate School of Design landscape ecologist Richard T.T. Forman to help shape a performance-based agenda for design inquiry and practices in the mid-1990s. Allen, S. "Infrastructural Urbanism," in Allen, S. *Points + Lines: Diagrams and Projects for the City*, New York, 1999, pp. 46–57.

Contributor:

Pete Evans
*AIA, Senior Lecturer,
Department of
Industrial Design,
Iowa State University*

01.02

Twenty-first-century learning

Introduction

Industrialized education in the twentieth century was envisioned to prepare students for a hierarchical livelihood in either blue-collar or white-collar worlds. One path of education prepared individuals more for factory-oriented work, manual trades and industries (blue-collar). A second strove to prepare thinkers, directors, designers, teachers, planners, and professionals (white-collar). An industrial education was very career-oriented and very specialized even in its foundations toward a specific end.

Today, digital technology is pervasive, with mobile devices and the Internet providing an abundance of information, knowledge, and opportunity. Will Richardson, in his book *Why School: How Education Must Change when Learning and Information Are Everywhere* (2012), points out that by 2020 more than half the US workforce will be "freelancers, consultants and independent workers." This lines up with today's workforce trends, where more and more jobs are part-time, forcing many working individuals to work multiple jobs. Richardson also notes a shift in students needing to master content to being able to master learning. This aligns with a base concept Brown and Thomas put forward, describing "agency" as active participation, creating, and building (2009).

A twenty-first-century strategy for learning by design encourages agency, with each individual actively experiencing new technologies tools for creating and communicating in a combination that supports deeper learning experiences. Activities involve tools that encompass new ways to think, see, make, and do. Today, these tools and ideas are often associated with tinkering, DIY, invention, design, and the maker movement, which are all currently emerging trends. In addition, these tools can be central to design thinking and STEM, where the "T" for technology is a theme involved in all areas of design, science, engineering, and math. The Iowa Core, the Iowa model of the Common Core, has "Universal Constructs," which are: flexibility and adaptability; productivity and accountability; critical thinking; creativity; collaboration; and complex communication (the last four are often referred to as the "4 Cs"), which are "Essential for 21st Century Success" (2016). This becomes a clear entry point where these strategies focus on the connections between design thinking, STEM, and twenty-first-century skills, which holistically define the potentials for a new framework for learning, understanding, and doing.

Currently, there is much energy and support for STEM, especially in secondary schools and in career and technical education, but it is not ideal when defined in a narrow way. Combining design thinking, STEM, and twenty-first-century skills provides a more universal approach to learning that succeeds the twentieth-century model for learning. This strategy realizes a new foundation and paradigm for learning.

SEE and MAKE

Generally there are two types of experiential learning and tools. These experiences and tools overlap in concept and all actively engage the participants individually and directly. The two types of experiences and tools encompass the ideas of "SEE" and "MAKE." These experiences are also described as "visualization" and "fabrication" in design technology education and at the professional level. These two focal points also parallel ideas of "digital prototyping" and "real prototyping," which is also part of STEM and iterative thinking in design.

SEE tools now involve advanced ways of seeing to include augmented and virtual reality. Augmented reality involves ways of incorporating digital information into the real world and virtual reality allows participants an alternate immersive computer-simulated world that replicates a sensory experience. In a sense (seeing), through the mediums of AR and VR ideas can be conveyed and experienced in new ways. It is now possible to see what someone else's perspective is— literally. It is possible to compare and experience iterations of ideas that are not real to ones that are virtual or augmented. This can be done alone or in collaboration with others depending on the type of technology combined with the project and team goals. It can allow a very direct communication—a shared vision of expert ideas to groups of nonexperts for better co-creation and understanding without misinterpretations of representations or translations.

FIGURE 1.2.1
Young student experiencing virtual reality through head mounted display

FIGURE 1.2.2 **Young students experiencing early electronics and programming through circuit bending with littleBits**

This new set of tools to SEE also allows for access into the foundation of the technology through this same immersive experience. Circuit bending allows for users to get an understanding of programming and electronics through physical sets of modules such as littleBits or Snap Circuits. Osmo and Lego Mindstorms take this further by intermixing physical steps with digital ones, with results being visible both ways (digital and physical). VR provides an even richer environment to program with modular blocks in a similar way to visual scripting and is exemplified through a new application for the Oculus and Vive called "SoundStage." Preset instruments can be played in VR or custom ones can be built from the ground up. In a way that combines the scripting of Rhino Grasshopper and modular sliders and seamless interface of Apple Garageband, this new experiential scripting yields a musically creative sandbox—a new way to build sound, experience it, and share it. Eventually, this way of SEEing will connect every foundational scripting medium with new digitally creative and learning opportunities in visually (and acoustically) experiential processes and products.

This is a place where understanding the formalizing nature of the Internet of Things (IoT) in terms of its basic structure is possible to experience and manipulate in virtual reality as if real. This gives the user a sense of presence at the roots (and on up) of this new paradigm in learning tools.

Complementing and overlapping SEE, a MAKE tool set presumes a more physical space of consequence with machines or place. This isn't necessarily required and is likely better understood digitally through virtual reality first in the digital prototyping mode.

This critical overlap cannot be articulated enough. Intermixing these concepts of SEE and MAKE become even richer ground for learning and creating.

For instance, seeing a 3D printer work can be a valuable direct experience to understand the differences in materials and types of 3D printing technologies. It also helps to see the translation of the digital model idea as a design file to a more machine language file for printing—actually seeing the graphic preview of the printed layers going to a fused deposition modeling (FDM) printer and seeing the printer follow the same CNC commands helps to understand the connection to CNC and the direct control of a machine. This can be further extended when considering telepresence and robotics, which are both emerging skills in the marketplace.

Then being able to manipulate physical electronics modules continues this idea of interacting with machines. Again, littleBits, OSMO or Snap Circuits, or other physical circuit-bending technology, provides a physical experience to translate ideas through technology with tangible and sensory-rich results.

These mixed physical/virtual experiences are also powerful for users as they place them in control of interaction, using their body to see things that don't physically exist and share that experience with a group of peers. These new mixed realities are proven to engender creativity (Ritter et al., 2012) and need to be in the hands of future generations.

Importantly, these new technologies are already showing up in the professional design and engineering professions. Today, we can show a client, contractor, or consultant the design intent by moving through the project freely and interrogating the design for many attributes such as a building information model (BIM) that the project provides. Moving through the project—both the materially rich visuals and the essential data—requires much less equipment, investment, and expertise than even five to 10 years ago. In addition to realizing complex forms, advances are also happening through construction, fabrication, and even the operation of facilities where the

FIGURE 1.2.3 **Young students experiencing a collaborative mixed reality wall with physical tools to interact with virtual objects**

01.02 TWENTY-FIRST-CENTURY LEARNING

PAGE 67

transfer of documents is now data-based and real-time and creating new value, opportunities, and deliverables for the professions and stakeholders.

In December 2015, a case study was presented at Autodesk University (AU). Airbus, APWorks, and a generative design team from Autodesk called "The Living" presented a "bionic partition." That "bionic partition" was designed through algorithms, optimizing a micro-lattice structure that was run through thousands of constrained variations, and was ultimately produced in an additive manufacturing process. This amalgam of micro-manufactured parts even required a new metal alloy called Scalmalloy for 3D printing for first/final prototype/production runs.

The rate at which this and similar innovative processes will continue to emerge and develop will only quicken. This requires a rapid change in preparing students to become primed graduates with skills and mind-sets ready to contribute to this new workspace.

Theory

Embodiment and congruence become the connection between the intentions of SEE and MAKE together, which are realized in the this new learning paradigm. One of the best communication platforms created is the one that everyone experiences individually and together every day. The real world as we experience it is one that we all have created knowledge around our entire lives. Alberto Pérez-Gómez makes a case for the inseparability of time and space from a phenomenological perspective, arguing for a perception that involves all senses in a unified whole. His assertion that "meaning is not something merely constructed in the brain" but that it "is given in our normal, bodily engagement with things, things that we recognize [. . .] instantly as the

embodiment of an idea, word, or category" (Pérez-Gómez, 2012) resonates potentially with both the physically and the digitally constructed world surrounding us (Evans and Muecke, 2014). Neurologically, the connections between mental models and the reality of doing through the motor cortex are also very closely tied together (Schegel et al., forthcoming). As novel creative methods are defined across newer mediums such as programming and virtual reality, it is imperative for young minds to be exposed at an early age to new learning opportunities such as embodied programming and virtual prototyping.

Constructivism with seeing and making provides a conduit to real experiences and new digital experiences both individually and together with peers, self-directed to explore and to create their own understandings. These experiences can be observed, shared, and discussed informally. Collaboration can occur through peer help and mentoring. Suggested opportunities and potential outcomes can prompt planning, ideation, and experimentation. Discussion before and following also allows conceptualization and then reflection. This can circle around ideas students have experienced in school such as scientific inquiry and how it compares to other problem-solving methods such as design thinking. They can more easily make the leap from a spreadsheet to a visual construct or from interactive programming to a physical form, and importantly recognize how tools of today are different than tools of the past to recognize opportunities and issues to better solve the complex problems of today and tomorrow.

Simultaneously, society and culture now require more performance-driven solutions. Technologies are advancing rapidly in personal communication devices, consumer computational and visualization solutions, and even parametric controls for new demands that design and engineering must respond, reflect, and inform differently than in past eras. Technology has in some ways now caught and surpassed the theories and learning frameworks that have existed for decades.

New educational opportunities

This framework works with other tools that are emerging with today's digital natives. Programming, which can appear abstract, can be demystified and made meaningful in showing the code and switches through the 3D printing software and even experienced in new visual scripting spaces or in creative lessons in graphics through Processing or Python. There is a lot of learning value with the opportunity to see and experience the steps that go into the user interface decisions to create a 3D print with materials and strength and outcomes in mind, then seeing the machine code, the computer numeric control (CNC) code that will build the 3D print (literally and in a visual preview of the 3D print), and alongside the printer printing the 3D print itself. This experience can become even more robust when the design concepts in the 3D print, or virtual reality concept, are the participant's to create.

This new language of programming and algorithmic thinking connected to physical and active, visual output is already happening at an early age with Lego Mindstorms and Scratch by Mitch Resnick at the Lifelong Kindergarten Group at MIT. Additional software for coding is providing early access into these logic mind-sets such as Codecademy, Tynker, Code.org, and Swift Playgrounds. New fabrication technology uses the same microprocessors that students are getting experience with through Processing and Arduino to control code, graphics, sensors, robots, and milling machines. Creatively knowing this language

can translate directly as a valuable professional skill.

Programs such as PLTW, FIRST Robotics, and Engineering is Elementary are part of a first wave that is more structured as advanced technology integrated curricula. Soon they will begin to be part of something more holistic that will incorporate flexible, adaptable, and both structured and unstructured tool sets and advanced platforms meeting curricular standards, but presenting pathways and scaffolds through new programming, modeling and visualization data-based tools for optimal localized, authentic, and individualized opportunities. Randy Swearer, the former provost and dean of faculty at Philadelphia University and former dean at Parsons School of Design even suggests we are shifting learning to a literal generative learning paradigm—collaboration with intelligent computer systems and active student co-creation as both "problem framer" and "curator" of the solution sets. This is an entirely different future for education.

Conclusion – a forward learning reality

Autodesk CTO Jeff Kowalski presented at AU in December 2015 and discussed four eras of computing: passive, generative, intuitive, and empathic. He suggested that all of these are in the "augmented age" that we are currently entering into: the generative era. This includes such tools as McNeel Rhino3D Grasshopper, Autodesk Dynamo, Dreamcatcher and Fractal, and Vectorworks Marionette. Marionette in particular takes the opportunity to expose and connect the code to its actions through the visual object-oriented interface into the visual scripting node and even to the programming behind the node itself, allowing a dive into and connection between abstract code and concrete action. These are disruptive tools, not just reflecting conventions and methods from earlier days that are affecting many disciplinary fields, professions, and industries.

Maker spaces are becoming seeing spaces (Victor, 2014) that recognize emerging ideas such as mediated spaces, mixed reality, and the Internet of Things. These are all opportunities that today's generation and the next generation onward, the digital natives, will work with and evolve to solve the problems of the day across disciplinary fields we recognize today and into new ones we do not. Emerging tools and opportunities will be challenging to anticipate but a new skill set including programming and mixed realities will be part of the fundamentals. Schools are already allowing computer programming and languages to fulfill foreign language requirements. It is a mind-set, a way of thinking for many already and a growing one for the emerging digital natives in school today. These new skills and mind-sets can be understood, communicated, and experienced from concept to active virtual development and simulation, and to material reality.

Bibliography

Brown, J.S. and Thomas, D. "Learning for a World of Constant Change: Homo Sapiens, Homo Faber & Homo Ludens Revisited," in *Proceedings of the University Research for Innovation: Proceedings of the 7th Glion Colloquium*, 2009.

Iowa Core, https://iowacore.gov/content/universal-constructs-essential-21st-century-success-0, accessed June 13, 2016.

Lau, K.W., and Lee, P.Y. "The Use of Virtual Reality for Creating Unusual Environmental Stimulation to Motivate Students to Explore Creative Ideas," *Interactive Learning Environments*, 23(1), 3–18, 2015. doi:10.1080/10494820.2012.745426

Muecke, M., and Evans, P.M. "Chicken and Egg? Hentagon, Icosa-Coop, and Two Types of Experience," *Architecture Conference Proceedings and Presentations*, 42, 130–136, 2014.

Pérez-Gómez, A. "The Gift of Architecture and Embodied Consciousness," in Jacquet, B. and Giraud, V. (eds.), *From the Things Themselves: Architecture and Phenomenology*, Kyoto University Press and École Française d'Extrême-Orient, 2012, p. 462.

Richardson, W. "Why School? How Education Must Change when Learning and Information are Everywhere," Ted Conferences, 2012.

Ritter, S.M., Damian, R.I., Simonton, D.K., Baaren, R.B., Strick, M., Derks, J., & Dijksterhuis, A. Diversifying Experiences Enhance Cognitive Flexibility. *Journal of Experimental Social Psychology*, 48(4), 961–964, 2012. doi:10.1016/j.jesp.2012.02.009

Schegel, A., Konuthula, D., Alexander, P., Blackwood, E., and Tse, P. "Fundamentally Distributed Information Processing Integrates the Motor Network into the Mental Workspace during Mental Rotation." *Journal of Neuroscience*, forthcoming.

Victor, B. "Seeing Spaces," https://vimeo.com/97903574, accessed June 13, 2014.

http://au.autodesk.com/au-online/classes-on-demand/class-catalog/2015/class-detail/11906#chapter=2, accessed June 13, 2016.

www.core77.com/posts/55470, accessed August 22, 2016.

www.npr.org/sections/ed/2016/03/01/468695376/french-spanish-german-java-making-coding-count-as-a-foreign-language, accessed June 13, 2016.

01.03
The parametric park

Contributor:

David Fletcher
*Founding Principal,
Fletcher Studio*

South Park is the oldest public space in San Francisco, built in 1852. Originally an English picturesque strolling park, it fell into disrepair and has been subject to ad hoc improvements over the years. The South Park Improvement Association hired Fletcher Studio to work with neighbors and community leaders to develop a master plan for the park. The new design may be described as a contemporary interpretation of the picturesque. It provides multiple amenities, arrayed along a meandering programmatic pathway. It also helps to alleviate two major issues, including poor drainage and slopes that exceed ADA limits. The new park includes a custom play area and structure, stages for performance, a large open meadow, and plazas of varying scales. Infrastructural improvements include traffic calming bulb-outs and chicanes, bio-infiltration swales and "flow-through" planters, and a rainwater cistern for irrigation usage.

FIGURE 1.3.1
**Aerial view of
South Park, San
Francisco,
California**

The initial design for the park was developed through iterative analog diagramming, which was then replicated and expanded with the use of parametric software. Systematic urban analysis was performed on the site, evaluating land use, park usage, circulation patterns, tree conditions, and drainage systems. To resolve these interrelated variables, the design team utilized four material systems: an expandable, modular paving system; large sloping meadows; vegetated infiltration basins; and low retaining walls to mediate between paving and planted areas. Site research was also conducted, on multiple days and at different times, to determine both points of entry and desire lines. The design team then mapped these points and movement vectors and created the final design from their interpretation. The points were connected with a central pathway that thickened to support programs and amenities. The design process then proceeded through a hybrid of analog and digital techniques. Utilizing a combination of blend tools, manual adjustments, and hand drawings allowed for idiosyncratic moments while conforming to a robust formal rule set based on environmental, spatial, and material logic. Corrections and adjustments to the design were always performed by hand-drawn overlays. Physical models were created to develop the paving patterns and wall profiles.

The resulting design includes a series of long walls that follow grade and flow through the park, to define spaces, and to provide seating and protection from adjacent streets. The pathway system includes "tablet"-shaped pavers, with rounded edges that are arrayed on the north–south axis throughout the park. The tectonic system for the paths and walls consists of a simply constructed combination of easily-modified components that would allow for a diversity of spatial, programmatic, and topographic solutions. The combination of these two elements

allows for a coherent modulation in the width of the path responding to contextual/external spatial desires, and fine-grain adjustment of vertical and horizontal edge, to respond to site-specific conditions. Both the pathway and wall systems are simple geometric parameters that could be input into parametric modeling, to be used in phases of design and construction documentation.

The primary determinants of the formal design decisions were driven by a hierarchy of circulation patterns, access points, social nodes, existing trees and structures to retain. By linking these points with a single path, the design forms a consistent linear promenade along the length of the park while allowing for lateral crossings across the park. Major and minor plazas are formed at key junctures through the thickening and thinning of the path to accommodate but also to allow for unanticipated appropriation. In the initial design phase, these decisions were made through intuitive understanding of the parameters of the site and embedded in an analog rule set that guided design decisions. In further research we have codified the relationship between the spatial logics of the design and the material logics of the tectonic, in a parametric algorithm.

Initial research was performed in preparation for the Acadia 2014 exhibition, an annual parametric design conference. The central question was: could the design process, the distribution of points and pathways with a distinct tectonic, be replicated? Further, could other contextual influences and conditions be added, and could the tectonic respond to those conditions? Is the use of responsive parametric definitions scalable and can it be applied to larger linear landscapes such as waterfronts, urbanized rivers, etc.? Grasshopper, a parametric plug-in for the 3D modeling program Rhinoceros, was used to further develop the research.

By implementing the design variables into a parametric system, we intended to utilize the system to display the design resiliency of the tectonic and spatial systems. The decision to codify the analog system, developed in the initial phase of design, was driven by the knowledge that future specification of the design in permitting, coordination, and construction documentation would require multiple iterations responding to new constraints and conditions, as they might arise. In the model, a straight line was drawn down the center of the site. A field of weighted attractors was positioned that corresponded to building density, land use, and points of site entry. Each attractor was assigned a different weight (force): on a scale of 1–10, a mid-block entry point might be assigned a 5, while a corner or intersection would be a 10. These individual attractors then deformed the central line, thus modifying it in response to their needs.

Next we introduced a variety of other factors to modify this line and to make it spatial. The line was then converted into the tablet paving tectonic, to establish the spatial distribution of the module. Then repellers were inserted to confine the paving distribution in places where it might conflict with the preservation of existing trees or structures to remain.

Finally, the perimeter of the park was established as an absolute boundary, and served to trim the paver distribution. The use of the parametric software is especially suited to develop multiple design solutions that utilize a coded system and that react to embedded parameters and produces a continuous form in resolving these conflicting constraints. This promising application to sites and to larger-scale linear spaces deserved further study. In response to the observed resiliency of the rule set, we foresee the application of this system to larger-scale linear open spaces. It has the potential to resolve overlapping

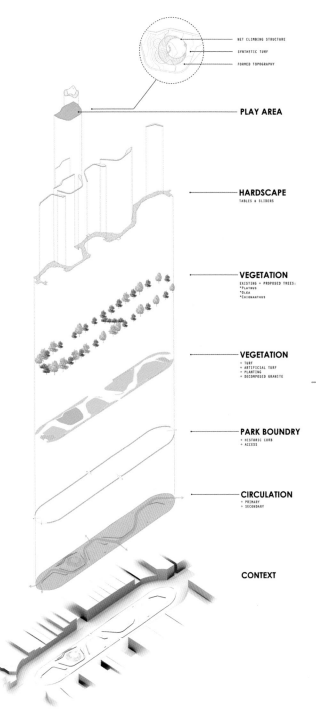

NET CLIMBING STRUCTURE
SYNTHETIC TURF
FORMED TOPOGRAPHY

PLAY AREA

HARDSCAPE
TABLES & SLIDERS

VEGETATION
EXISTING + PROPOSED TREES:
*PLATNUS
*OLEA
*CHIONANTHUS

VEGETATION
+ TURF
+ ARTIFICIAL TURF
+ PLANTING
+ DECOMPOSED GRANITE

PARK BOUNDRY
+ HISTORIC CURB
+ ACCESS

CIRCULATION
+ PRIMARY
+ SECONDARY

CONTEXT

FIGURE 1.3.2 **Landscape components and site performance diagrams**

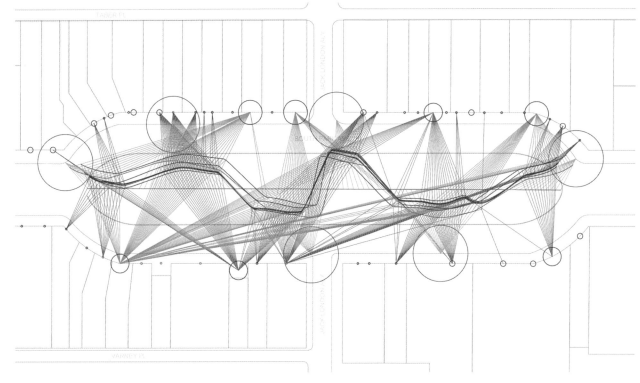

FIGURE 1.3.3 **Site feature prioritization and weighting diagram**

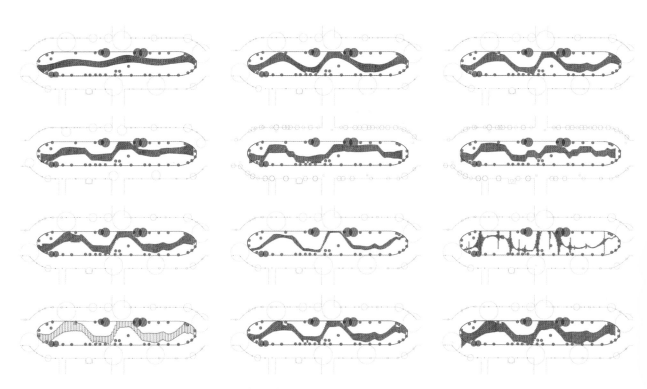

FIGURE 1.3.4 **Pathway generated through prescribed site constraints**

two-dimensional and three-dimensional jurisdictions, circulation patterns, implementation phases, and dynamic processes through a continuous morphologic operation. Potential sites for this application include: urban waterways, waterfronts, corridors, linear open spaces, and rights-of-way.

Many of the same components learned in the Acadia research process were employed in the design development. Grasshopper was further used, to produce the technical documentation for project construction and permitting. A responsive 3D model was prepared, which integrated the site data, including existing utilities and topography. This model was responsive, in the sense that modifications to simple referenced forms would result in universal modifications throughout the master project model. For example, the site walls referenced a single wall profile section drawing. This profile—the radius, batter, thickness, height, etc.—could be modified. The modification of the profile would then automatically apply to the entire park, hundreds of linear feet of walls. Updates to wall profiles, thickness, edge radii and even the distribution and frequency of skateboard deterrents. Paving tablet width, length, and distribution could be adjusted easily, allowing the entry of exact values, or perhaps more intuitive sculpting of vectors. Walls served as trimming forces, and the distribution of the paving field was essentially a simple vector outline that Grasshopper would convert into the modular tablet paver field. This allowed for the clean export of vectors to 2D CAD with minimal trimming and cleanup.

With over 18 feet of grade change on the site, and tight tolerances to achieve and accessible public space, Grasshopper again proved to be a powerful ally. Accurate elevation points from the civil engineer were input into Grasshopper to generate a topo mesh. Civil modifications to the topography

could be checked against the master model for errors or adjustments needed. Drainage invert elevational points could be connected to each other, with the resulting vectors converted into tubes so that the drainage system could be evaluated in model form. Grading and drainage updates from the civil team would then be easily input, and new 3D models of surfaces and drainage infrastructures were automatically generated.

The custom play structure and its groundplane were developed with a similar sequence, analog/hybrid digital, and, finally, parametric modeling. Modeling wire sheathed in vinyl tubing was inserted into holes that were laser-cut into a large pinboard. This allowed the team to iterate multiple routing solutions, which could be documented and lead to the digital modeling. Grasshopper was then used to generate a responsive model for the custom play structure. Like the analog pinboard, this model allowed us to quickly generate multiple versions of the structure. The model would automatically distribute netting, fittings, and play elements, responding to the manipulation of the perimeter and interior tube forms. Running component lists could be generated and output to spreadsheets for cost control and evaluation. Final visualizations of the various iterations could be generated at any time, for community design meetings.

The design of South Park began with ideas, concepts, and impulses that were informed by public process, context, and the many site influences and variables. It is the designer's role to sort through the variables and rules and to pursue a path that leads to a final design proposal. This process, and the design itself, is enhanced with the use of parametric definitions, rule sets, and algorithms. These emerging tools allow the development of an expanded spectrum of possibilities beyond what might be

FIGURE 1.3.5 **View of play structure**

typically achieved with pen and paper.
It also can lead to unanticipated outcomes.
A parametric program can allow for the
generation of infinite iterations, some of
which may never have been conceived.
At times, mistakes made in data entry can
lead a designer onto a new path of
exploration. Yet it is still up to the designer
to make the final call in selecting what is
worth further developent. Great design
often comes from challenging rules and
conventions, from responding to
insurmountable constraints with solutions.
It also comes from human intellect and
experience. Memory, experience, emotion,
and humor are not yet parameters that can
be input into a parametric definition.

01.04

Big data for small places

Systematizing the functional use of complex and sizable data sets in daily practice

Contributors:

Elizabeth Christoforetti

Will Cohen

Yonatan Cohen

Stephen Rife

Jia Zhang

Data, design, and value systems in postdigital practice

On the question of parametric and computational practices, Supernormal sees all practices as parametric and computational. In 2017 designers used computers, and all acts of design contain parameters as constraints that define their limits as quantitative or cultural values. Computation is now an artificial extension of our natural capacity to understand context. It is also a means to reach beyond the digital into the social.[1]

We recognize and embrace the condition of the postdigital cultural context as murky, at best, for the processes of design. We are exploring computation and emerging data sets to broaden our definition, understanding, and translation of context. The goal is a testing and retesting of our intuitions against contextual inputs and the processes we create to translate them into relevant and meaningful design outcomes, and to critically reconnect with our social and natural context.

For us, a move toward increased clarity within the postdigital relies upon defined value systems that guide design during the leap from input to output. Design input – information or "data," cultural baggage and agendas, the natural or postindustrial synthetic context, and sometimes program – can be systematized through computation, but the translation into design remains a product of rigorous cultural criticism and manual logic. How we evaluate and absorb meaningful contextual inputs, how we generate a clear set of spatial and social criteria that define the process of translation from input into design output, and how we generate, catalog, and evaluate outputs, rests upon local cultural intuition and professional skill filtered, modified, and refined by computation.

This is not a fundamentally new design process, but we hope it is a more sensitive one – something like having enhanced taste buds. In a world of endless processes and

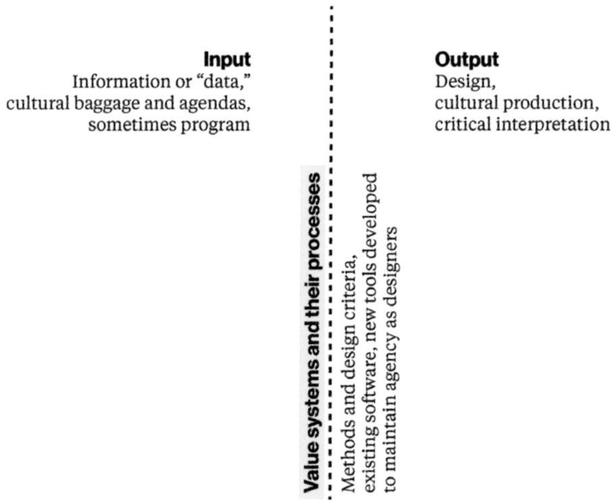

Input	**Output**
Information or "data,"	Design,
cultural baggage and agendas,	cultural production,
sometimes program	critical interpretation

Value systems and their processes
Methods and design criteria,
existing software, new tools developed
to maintain agency as designers

FIGURE 1.4.1 **Input and output. Our translation of meaningful input into design output is not rigid or codified but shaped by clear value systems and tools developed to maintain our agency as designers. As we work through the first year of our practice, defining the process of identifying meaningful data and translating it into critical design output is our most essential creative act**

information,[2] "computation" and new sources of information, generated by the intersection of human activity and emerging technologies, allow us to be more responsive to the continual emergence and remaking of social and cultural context as a product of the same processes and information. We can become connoisseurs of change over time in addition to form, cultural critics with more powerful tools to extend our intuition and our ability to translate information into coherent abstract systems of spatial production.

To be clear, we do not offer (or seek) a direct or linear connection between new forms of input and formal design output. Rather, we advocate for an embrace of new information sources as part of a revised and nuanced design process that opens the door to the construction of more sensitive and relevant value systems. It is the methods and criteria defined by these value systems that generate new formal possibilities for design.

First principles

As practitioners, we embrace careful attention to the type and the constraints of physical development and the material world. However, we prioritize methods of understanding and we project change over time and change over location as first principles in our approach to computation. Below is a set of observations and agendas that we find essential to responsible and progressive contemporary practice but rarely observe in the wild:

1 **The urban block is our first principle in terms of scale.** This is the scale at which human interaction occurs, at which communities grow, and at which we can most strategically generate exceptional design and scalable development patterns. We find that working outward from the block, and balancing bottom-up with top-down planning through a focus on type, encourages fine-grained and highly sensitive development and use patterns.

2 **We engage new forms of granular urban data** that can provide us with quantitative information about this scale to reliably track change over time and change over location. Right now, "smart cities" efforts are largely led by computer programmers and hardware developers who care a lot about cities; we are designers and planners who care a lot about computers. We use these skills to take advantage of new information to make better planning and design decisions. New forms of information (and more of it) trigger new contextual processes.

3 **Our work is replicable, prototypical, or scalable.** On the front end, we build analytic tools that can benchmark conditions across many locations or over periods of time. On the planning and design side, we focus on prototypical planning processes and design products that can be utilized across a variety of conditions, but that have the capability to sensitively negotiate context by location.

4 **We plan and design for change over time.** By embracing rapid changes in culture, technology, and climate as a constant, our goal is to build flexibility into the DNA of our work product. From a planning and design perspective, this requires careful thinking about incremental growth and accommodating shifts in use, land value, or density over time. From an analytic perspective, this means engaging tools to incrementally plan and build, to measure and test interventions iteratively and with tight feedback loops between design and effect in context.

Context, in its fullest possible definition, is our input. In 2017, we see context as a collapse of all moments past and present in a single place. It is a negotiated relationship between a set of actors: physical and digital human experience, history, culture, politics, program, urban form, the natural environment, and time. All sites live a double life in contemporary practice: the physical and digital, the real and imagined, the synthetic and natural, the flat and deep. This complicated stew is rich territory for critical interpretation, particularly with the addition of previously uncollected or nonexistent information.

FIGURE 1.4.2

Exploiting new and old information to produce the contemporary. Design and planning recommendations for the Downtown Boston Business Improvement District. The drawing samples Charles Hubbard's "The National Lancers with the Reviewing Officers on Boston Common," sandwiched between a mapping of the site's digital footprint in 2016 and a proposal for planning and design that balances awareness of previously unobserved patterns of human activity with the rich cultural history of the changing district

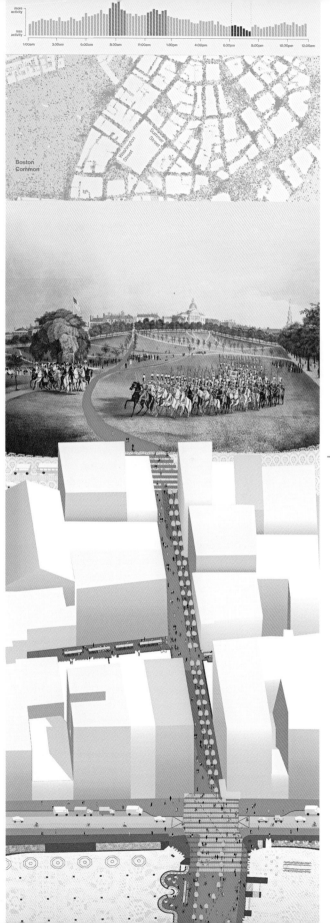

While we use computation to systematize iteration within the design process, as well as optimize processes and prototypes for replication beyond their initial instance by testing enhanced construction delivery processes, this essay will focus upon the more unusual use of computation as it involves the incorporation of emerging urban information sources and "big data" into everyday design and planning practice.

Supernormal in practice

In more specific and practical terms, Supernormal began as a project to develop tools that reflect our collaborative approach to practice more closely than existing software, and to explore meaningful methods for translating new information into locally responsive design and planning outcomes. We felt that improved systematization and greater sensitivity in practice could be best accomplished by pushing together disciplines and skills that would traditionally be siloed.

Supernormal is now an emerging practice that blends architecture, urban design, landscape architecture, and planning into a single process that moves fluidly across a spectrum of skills, rather than dividing disciplines out by phase, scope, or material media. Boundaries of scale, of planning versus design, or of technical versus nontechnical are less relevant to a project like Supernormal, which can only be served by a hybrid approach in terms of both perspective and skill. Our team includes architects, planners, software developers, and data scientists, a mix that we find appropriate for the complex and rapidly changing environment that is the context for our work. However, not one of us has the capacity to execute any single project alone.

Supernormal is also a response to the vast amounts of fine-grained data about our local places that are continuously generated and increasingly available, but not well understood or utilized for the purposes of design and city-making. As a culture, we are now adept at interpreting infrastructural and urban systems data at the scale of municipal boundaries, and energy and material efficiency at the scale of building systems. However, measuring patterns of urban activity and form – and the economic and social processes that drive them – at the scale of the block, the building, and the neighborhood is more challenging. This is where we create our work, fall in love, and live our lives. Humans are complicated and hard to measure. Committing to the scale of human perception and interaction requires us to work with new, and often messy, urban data sets. For example, data from mobile devices and a wide array of sensors can be collected at the site design scale by partnering with new hardware and technology start-ups; informal geo-referenced data can be reliably scraped and repurposed for uses in practice.

We're after access points into something like the emotional landscape of a place to optimize impact and local relevance by reading quality into quantitative information: the stuff that we can't see with our eyes that provides us with a better understanding of the dynamics of time in relationship to design and planning. To service this end, we use each project as a laboratory to develop methods and build tools to maintain agency and accommodate our priorities, including flexibility, replicability, and cultural reinterpretation.

Case studies, methods, and the Downtown Boston pedestrian realm

We currently default to the census to understand the social and economic performance of a specific place across intervals of years. Increasingly, we can understand the life of the street over intervals of hours, and how the age or gender of a place changes between morning and evening. With new methods, we can gain a higher resolution view of the real users of our public realm and how activity patterns shift over time, and in relationship to planning, design, and development. The Downtown Boston project is one of several in our office that leverages granular commercial data, open civic resources, or scraped geo-referenced information – or some combination of the above – to assess a local place and benchmark it across time, and in comparison to other relevant locations. This view, offered by emerging information and technique, exceeds our current capacity for temporal observation, offering a rich supplementary narrative to the relationship between spatial production and human occupation.

The in-progress study tests methods to meaningfully find, analyze, and interpret activity within a defined group of city blocks in Boston's Downtown Crossing. We are actively analyzing a set of continuously collected data within this designated collection boundary to understand the impact of routine block-by-block urban events such as shifts in retail tenancy and the influx of housing units generated by new construction.

FIGURE 1.4.3 **Median age and patterns of concentration. This overall age map shows the median age across all 2014, 2015, and 2016 data at each point within Downtown Crossing. These mapped findings suggest that the Winter–Summer Street corridor functions as a convergence of the young population using the Theater District to the southwest and the older population defining the Financial District to the northeast. There is an opportunity here to pull cultural programming and uses from the Theater District into the underperforming pedestrian zone, which currently hosts a narrow range or daytime retail uses. Capitalizing on the proximity to older users, who tend to leave the district before 7.00 p.m. via public transit, the BID may also promote early evening food and drink opportunities to capture and hold daily commuters as they leave the district**

Median Age
- ■ < 23 (Gen Z)
- ◆ 23 – 38 (Millennial)
- ● > 38 (Gen X +)

BID Boundary

The project began as a piece of research inside the Social Computing Group at the MIT Media Lab, and then spun out as a Supernormal project with the Downtown Boston Business Improvement District (BID) as a client. Although we tested a range of data resources within our research at the Media Lab, at Supernormal we have found mobile device data from the advertising technology industry to be the most effective for the needs of this project and have focused our time and energy on the cleaning, processing, and analysis of this single data source. Data is anonymized and aggregated to respect privacy. While it has not been widely used within planning and design practice, we selected this data source for its high-resolution view of collective demographics and existing use patterns, both of which are geo-referenced and time stamped within our study area.

Demonstrating the value of new data sources such as mobile device and the broader Internet of Things (IoT) to the day-to-day practice of design and planning requires a substantial bank of case studies that show efficient data collection, management, and translation into application. The same is true for industries such as public health, energy, and even the Department of Homeland Security as they develop effective disaster preparedness protocols. The difference is the large volumes of public and private capital behind product development in such industries, in comparison to our own.

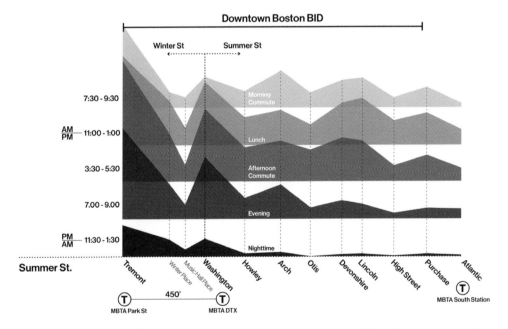

FIGURE 1.4.4 **Activity benchmarked by intersection. Density of mobile activity within 100 feet of sequential Downtown Crossing intersections along Washington Street. Prioritizing action in a complex urban environment is a critical component of any urban design project. Analyzing key intersections based upon activity level allows us to understand the performance of hyperlocal areas in relationship to each other within the district. This benchmarking exercise demonstrates that areas such as Temple Street (near a high level of activity but not currently activated itself) have a great amount of potential, while Winter Street is already very active. From this analysis, we can prioritize design interventions, and programming and use recommendations, in the three most critical zones in Downtown Crossing**

FIGURE 1.4.5 **The reach of Downtown Crossing. For the metropolitan Boston region, areas where devices that appear in Downtown Crossing at least once appear more frequently. In a city, many different variables often show similar patterns either of population density or of inequity and disparity. This activity analysis of Downtown Crossing shows the reach of the neighborhood: what areas of the region and city are places where devices that show up in Downtown Crossing also show up. The map shows a slightly different pattern, and its more active regions are the centers of area neighborhoods, showing that Downtown Crossing is linked to commercial and cultural centers across the city. The diversity in user type and location shows a way forward in terms of district programming and the importance of connectivity and public realm design**

In addition to this work for the BID, Supernormal is partnering with two MIT start-ups – one hardware and one data management – to collect more substantial amounts of sensor data and to develop clear case studies to demonstrate practical applicability. The City of Boston recognizes the need for such efforts and has provided significant support in the form of coordination and staff time to set up Downtown Crossing as a living laboratory for IoT exploration. We hope that this effort will become a resource to designers, engaged citizens, and potential clients that seek new methods to change and improve urban places.

In the meantime, we are finding that our work in this area is primarily valued by clients and groups who are already pushing the boundaries of research and development, for whom the exploration of improved research and development techniques is an essential value. Such clients work with

Supernormal because we are competent at quantitative analysis and the development of clear metrics and systems of urban evaluation; and, as designers, we can translate the results of our analysis into meaningful and effective design or planning outcomes. Newer forms of granular geo-referenced or web-based data become a complementary addition to an already substantial set of services.

Keeping data costs low and analytic techniques efficient is essential. We work with a range of private and public data partners, for some of whom we serve as a tiny laboratory to test the effectiveness of their data in the planning and design industry. These partnerships allow us access to closed data sources at minimal or no cost.

Like many consulting groups before us, using individual projects to systematize these methods, so that we can perform the same analysis over many locations, is also critical for Supernormal. Although we have devoted hours of unpaid time to clean and source, writing good code to analyze key aspects of the urban experience allows us to efficiently observe similar conditions across many places and for many clients. This provides us with a powerful perspective on the relationships between human activity and urban space, and it lets us speculate more broadly about spatial and social conditions.

We strive to ask smart and honest questions of meaningful data sources to reveal a new motivation or rationale leading to culturally relevant and locally specific design, and to do this in a way that is efficient enough to justify our costs; the data is effectively useless unless we ask it clear and targeted questions. Within the Downtown Boston case study, we constructed a set of queries to generate analytic output that is not available using current methods or traditional information sources. We needed to know who the daily users of the BID are and how

they are currently using the poorly performing blocks within the district, the primary focus of our planning and design efforts. We also framed our analysis to understand the impact of several key developments and ground level uses by examining activity levels over a defined period (of weeks and months) in which significant change occurred.

We pulled key indicators such as age and gender, and looked at use patterns based upon data density over average daily and weekly cycles. This is why it has been important for us to combine data analysis with urban planning and geospatial abilities. Urban planning–level mapping and GIS are ways for us to see patterns in space, even if mathematical correlations are less strong, and they let us see how those patterns change over time. Unlike normal GIS mapping, however, these data sets represent millions of points and gigabytes of semistructured data, which requires more sophisticated analysis through relational databases.

We are now applying the analysis that we tested on Boston's Downtown Crossing to a range of cities with different spatial, economic, and social characteristics to iteratively test and refine the methodology. Within each city that we analyze we choose a few areas that we select to represent a range of population, activities, and urban morphologies. As we analyze location types with varying levels of data density we adjust the granularity of the analysis spatially, temporarily, or demographically to preserve anonymity and reach significance thresholds.

For example, the density of mobile activity data at a location such as Manhattan's Times Square allows for studying of a much finer spatial grid with more compact time frames than a suburban residential neighborhood in a less dense area such as ex-urban Phoenix. We use these same spatial density, temporal,

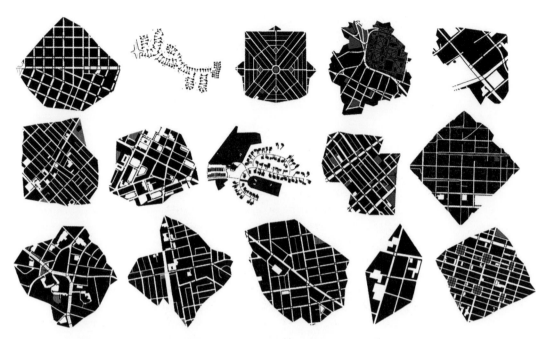

FIGURE 1.4.6 **Developing our own computational tools gives us agency in the design process. We are creating a set of tools to compare urban form and its social performance across many locations by automating data collection within a five-minute walkshed of a given coordinate, a scale we find most indicative of human experience in a place. The analysis utilized to better understand the activity patterns in Downtown Crossing is actively at work across many other locations as we produce a growing atlas of places and corollary set of tools that allows us to automate the analysis of places based upon the very specific value system and criteria that we find most relevant and actionable for future design output**

and other patterns in the mobile activity data to classify locations into area types. We find it useful to target indicators of physical urban form, market indicators, and social opportunity under a single umbrella. As we selectively couple and weight the meaning of this information against layers of data ranging from the physical layout of streets, business and institutional hours of operation to show the presence of third places, or geo-referenced social media data, we refine the data selection, classification, and analytic methods across new location contexts and incrementally improve our ability to scale our analysis and benchmark across locations.

We are currently translating our analysis of the Downtown Boston pedestrian realm into planning, design, and programming

recommendations for the core area of the site, which is centered around a pedestrian zone and sandwiched between two heavily utilized public transit stations. Specific recommendations include bringing managed and regular multimodal traffic back onto Washington Street, which makes up the short, east–west arm of the cruciform pedestrian realm. Currently, use of the pedestrian zone for loading and deliveries is an aspect of the pedestrian experience that leads to confusion and pedestrian danger. Enabling the naturally wider and less utilized Washington Street corridor to host retail loading and deliveries will free up the most promising stretch of the north–south arm of the pedestrian zone along the Summer–Winter Street corridor, which already hosts significant pedestrian traffic (see Figure 1.4.8).

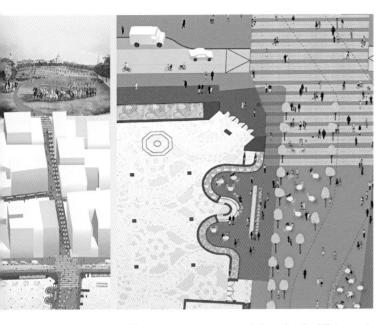

FIGURE 1.4.7 **Diagrammatic recommendations for the Winter and Summer Street pedestrian zone. Based upon the high levels of activity measured along the Winter–Summer Street corridor, but low levels of pause and social space along this same route, we recommend elements that will add friction to help users "stick" along this corridor. In contrast, data shows an absence of activity and heightened safety concerns along Washington Street. We recommend that this street, running perpendicular to the main pedestrian corridor, be revehicularized with the addition of clear street management and way-finding policies**

expanding existing and minimal display windows into street-facing café service (Figure 1.4.7). Within the same area, a more significant display program, and the social infrastructure to support it, will invite public art to enliven the less active Summer Street edges and extend the Theater District into the heart of Downtown Crossing. Analysis of median age throughout the district (Figure 1.4.3) suggests that early evening programs could capture the finance community on weekday evenings and a younger student and theater-going crowd on the weekends.

Understanding the need to create friction within minimal buildable area, we propose a simple allee of trees that frame the corridor while leaving minimum fire lane clearances. The singular architectural intervention, described above, involves the strategic deletion, shaping, and material transformation of existing building envelope to introduce entirely new geometry to punctuate the historic two-block stretch beginning at the Boston Common landscape.

Through temporary testing and implementation, we are working with the Boston Mayor's Office of New Urban Mechanics and the BID to create and measure short-term interventions to test our long-term hypotheses and create tighter and more flexible feedback loops between planning, design, and effect in space. This promising use of continuous data collection during the planning and design process holds potential for more effective long-range planning. Current best practices for analyzing activity involve sending interns out onto the street to observe and collect data on public realm users over the course of several days, or possibly using outdated data sources with fuzzy origins. We can now compliment these impressions with data that is continuously collected and analyzed to show activity patterns over the course of weeks and months in addition to hours and days.

We hypothesize that reconnecting the downtown grid along Washington Street will have an additionally positive effect on activity along the street, which our analysis shows to be almost desolate during the weekends. This Summer–Winter corridor will thus become a more accurately pedestrian-only zone with key design interventions added to increase friction, build upon the area as a natural center of activity, and encourage lingering during and beyond the evening commute, a period that is currently underserved by businesses in the area (see Figure 1.4.8).

For example, one particularly long and blank façade along an introverted department store ground floor can be broken up by

We hope to increase our collaboration with like-minded design and planning practices to make these methods more accessible, and to gradually increase their impact and adoption over time. While it is unlikely (and unnecessary) that designers will all be trained as computer programmers in the coming decades, it is very likely that we will all be called upon to leverage new data resources and use them to make a case for the impact of our work.

A hybrid practice is a challenging business model

From a business perspective, it is worth noting that the multiple disciplines essential to our practice require us to set and sell our own terms over and over again. There is no well-trodden path for a design and planning–led technology practice or scope of work, and we are in a constant state of proving our value above and beyond our essential capacities as designers and planners. We are cheaper than a high-end technology consultancy but more expensive than a traditional design firm.

During corporate formation, we considered several models, and a fundamental question became whether we should structure ourselves as a company that generates income through projects and services or whether we should develop software products and bring on investors and capital. While we do build tools, and create a

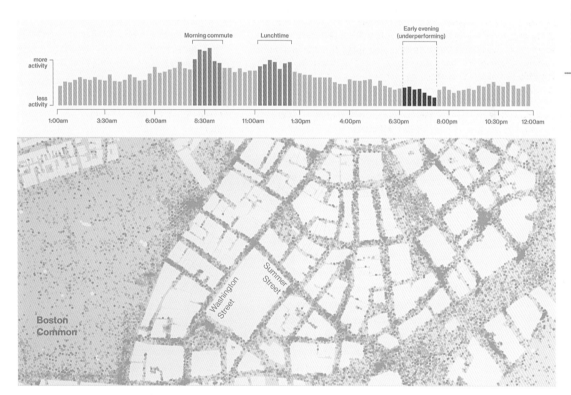

FIGURE 1.4.8 **The invisible footprint of Downtown Boston's digital life. A graph and map of data density shows activity levels during an average 24-hour weekday. The low early evening activity shows potential for new uses while the heavy activity along the Summer Street corridor suggests low hanging fruit for immediate design intervention**

significant amount of code for the purposes of replicating productive design and planning processes and outcomes, we realized that our core competencies are analyzing, planning, and designing the urban environment. This means that we are most useful in the world of projects. We genuinely enjoy collaborating with clients and value the impact we can have on the future of the built and natural environment. We structured our business as a partnership to reflect this, but as our methodologies develop, we may revisit the question of entity structure in the future.

Our goal is to be knowledgeable and productive enough to make sensitive design and planning decisions for many local communities, and to bring the perspective of our city-making disciplines to the urban data and tech conversation, which is now largely dominated by industries that have very different first principles and end goals than our own. More and better criticism of the "smart cities movement" is needed to subvert the drive of private capital to generate endlessly scaled financial (rather than social) returns on their investment in products and the infrastructure that will enable them. Vehicular automation is one among many examples of this push. The current trajectory of our urban futures requires our disciplines to be technologically literate enough as a team to discriminately analyze the continuous flows of information that our cities now produce, and to rigorously explore the moment where this new information translates into planning and design outcomes that will responsibly and critically guide future development.

We hope that our research and practice, in collaboration with others in our own professions and abutting sectors, can increase the relevance of designers as critical players in the physical development and culture of our rapidly expanding built environment. And that the work we produce

will make a case for the value of large, complex, or emerging urban data sources for more than improved infrastructural efficiency and streamlined managerial capacity; that engaging computation to become more sensitive to context in its broadest definition will allow us to look beyond the digital, and into the social in a more systematic and sensitive way.

Notes

All images created by Supernormal.

1. No longer a narrow category of practice or an isolated mode of communication, our digital lives are now unified with our professional practices and personal identities. Consider Dark Sky, iOS, Revit, Grasshopper, Instagram, Photoshop, Mastercam, and Snapchat. Our digital lives exist in a continual feedback loop with our experience of the physical and social world.

2. Researchers at IBM, SINTEF, and elsewhere find that more data has been created in the past two years than in the entire previous history of humanity.

01.05

Turing landscapes

Computational and algorithmic design approaches and futures in landscape architecture

Contributor:

Stephen M. Ervin
Assistant Dean for Information Technology, Harvard Graduate School of Design

1. Introduction

Landscape architecture and landscape architects may have three rather different, although naturally interconnected, modes of interaction with computation (computing hardware, software, displays, peripherals, and the many emergent technologies of telecommunications and electromechanical devices, e.g., mobile phones, drones, robots, 3D scanners, immersive VR headsets, etc.):

1. using software – as a *tool*;

2. writing code – as a *language*;

3. engaging with the Internet of Things – as a *medium*.

The simplest and historically earliest adopted mode of computation for landscape architects is just using commercial software, from word and image processing, to CAD, GIS, video-conferencing, and many, many other sorts. The next mode is writing software, or *coding*, whether simple macros embedded in other software, as freestanding applications for information analysis (more common), or as part of design idea generation and exploration (emergent). The final mode is engaging with connected and computational devices – the ever-expanding

"Internet of Things" (IoT), from sensors, to actuators, to new high-tech building materials and devices – in the real/designed world.

The first mode, using commercial software, caused some upheaval in the 1980s and 1990s as a rapid development and adoption of hardware and software offered new instrumental possibilities to landscape architects, mostly in automation, accuracy, and convenience. However, that development entailed no real challenge to conceptions of landscape or even, for most early adopters, modes of practice, design thinking, or representation. Computer graphics did offer a new and compelling medium for graphic representation, including image processing and digital video; it also generated some instrumental and conceptual reevaluation of and invention of new representational conventions by the turn of this century.

The second mode, "writing code or software," seemed innocuous and mostly instrumental at first, and, again, mostly for automation and convenience, but significantly, also for customization and expressive power – which, once experienced, was captivating for many designers. Today, code is a recognized medium alongside sketchbooks and scale models, and understood to contain rich design potential that has only barely begun to be tapped.

The third mode, engaging with computation via the IoT, not just as aids to conceiving of or representing landscapes composed of the traditional palette of landform, plants, water, and structures but as actual embedded components of new kinds of landscapes, especially "interactive" and "responsive" ones – is the most radical mode of interaction with computation for landscape architects. Coexisting with, and often dependent upon custom coding, this form of "computation-aided-design" (not just "CAD") entails the greatest challenge to conceptions of landscape, of interaction and of design process and representation.

Today, designing with algorithmic approaches and computational tools and embedding electromechanical computer-controlled devices in the landscape are becoming commonplace. Since all these approaches are enabled by computers operating on basic principles now known as "Turing machines," named after the inventor and theorist Alan Turing, I call the landscapes and environments, so imagined and created, "Turing landscapes."

Consider a simple 2 × 2 matrix: Landscapes *designed* with and without computation × landscapes with and without *embedded* computation (digital/electromechanical elements in addition to natural/physical elements) (Figure 1.5.1).

Landscapes designed without computation and without embedded computation (call them "Olmsted landscapes") are very familiar – the vast majority of landscapes designed and built before the year 1990. These traditional landscapes are composed of six essential elements: landform, vegetation, water, infrastructure (including buildings), animals (including people), and atmosphere (including lighting) (Ervin).

Since the advent of sufficiently powerful commercially available software on affordable personal computers, landscapes designed (and, increasingly, built) with computation of some sort are now the vast majority. Landscapes with embedded computation – that is, not just made of plants, paving, structures, etc. but also containing some forms of sensors, processors, and electromechanical actuators controlled by code – are uncommon, or have only primitive computation embedded (for example, increasingly many public and private landscapes have computer-based irrigation or lighting controllers embedded).

Landscapes designed **without** computation, but **with** embedded computation. *rare / simple*	Landscapes designed **with** computation, & **with** embedded computation. *(Turing landscapes)* *the future!*
Landscapes designed **without** computation, & **without** embedded computation. *(Olmsted landscapes)* *pre-year 1990*	Landscapes designed **with** computation, but **without** embedded computation. *current norm*

FIGURE 1.5.1 **2 x 2 matrix locating "Olmsted landscapes" and "Turing landscapes"**

Landscapes designed with computation, and with embedded computation – call them "Turing landscapes" – are emergent, but still rare. A computer-generated landscape scene experienced through completely simulated virtual reality (VR) or overlaid real/simulated augmented reality (AR) is one example of a Turing landscape (the VR headset counts as the embedded computation – even though some might argue that it's not truly a "landscape," a semantic distinction I won't argue with). A modern public park, designed with GIS and CAD software, and possibly custom coding, and containing embedded sensors, Wi-Fi channels delivering custom geo-specific information to visitors, actuators controlling light, water, shade, sound, and other environmental qualities, and other robotic computer-controlled entities, is more fully a Turing landscape (see Figure 1.5.10) – and may well become the norm in this twenty-first century.

Since even before the microcomputer revolution of the late 1970s – and certainly ever since then – the design community has struggled with questions around the nature, value, and implications of "computer-aided design." Early CAD software, originally designed to enable the production of precise and repetitive drawings, focused much of this discussion on representation technologies, and automation, and then on questions of creativity, and the perceived lack thereof in computerized processes.

At the same time, research and developments in artificial intelligence (AI) and robotics fueled a debate about human versus machine-like attributes, sometimes heated and ideological, which sometimes seemed to fit into a larger culture clash between the arts and humanities on the one hand and science, engineering, and technology on the other. Landscape architecture and design always somewhat uncomfortably straddled art and science. Leo Marx's 1964 "Machine in the Garden" (Marx)

trope was reflected as a widespread discomfort with technology in design processes, an expressed preference for "soft pencil sketches on toothy paper" as evidence of "real" creativity, and a dismissal of computation as suitable only for numerical calculations and repetitive operations.

Almost all the digital computers we are familiar with work on some basic principles first laid out in the 1930s and '40s by theorists and inventors John von Neumann and Alan Turing. Both, separately and together, described, in outline, a machine capable of taking in inputs and storing and retrieving values (together "data"), controlled by commands and operations (we might call them "programs and subprograms") capable of producing outputs, as a result of arbitrarily complex calculations, or procedures ("algorithms"). Their work was both abstract and theoretical to begin with, but also practical, as they built early prototypes of modern digital computers. Together, they recognized, early on, the implications of such machines as being capable of reasoning, not just performing calculations. Both inventors articulated many of the earliest ideas and questions about "artificial intelligence." Today, information and communications technology (ICT) is pervasive, and includes microprocessors, mobile devices, drones, sensors, and robotic actuators, among many other technologies.

In 1983, in the seminal text *Microcomputers in Landscape Architecture* (MacDougall) the chapter on "Computer Applications for Landscape Architects" opened with the category "Word Processing." The simple fact that the typewriter could be replaced, with great benefit, by a computer, word processing software, and printer, really was the beginning of the microcomputer revolution.

The very next "killer app" for most professionals, beyond word processing, was "number-crunching" with the proto-spreadsheet software "VisiCalc." That the combination of computation and ICT might be more than just an instrumental amplifier of human eyes, hands, and brains (supporting *techne*) but might indeed be a medium for exploration and expression of ideas and abstract concepts (supporting *poesis*), might, like other media, bring its own characteristics, constraints, and affordances to design processes; and might also, like other fields and disciplines, bring its own ways of knowing, ways of doing, and aesthetics, potentially amenable to fertile hybridization, were not initially obvious, and still are not particularly mainstream ideas, but are increasingly so, as this volume demonstrates.

Whether landscapes were *analog*, meant to be built and visited or appreciated *in situ*, or *virtual*, meant only to be viewed/experienced through audiovisual (and perhaps tactile/kinetic) devices

(e.g., "VR goggles" or "data gloves"), is not a critical distinction. They are both designed, and both invite spatial/sensory experience and appreciation. Perhaps the earliest example of a computer-generated virtual landscape was "The Road to Pt. Reyes," a 1983 composition by Alvy Ray Smith and others (Smith) that featured algorithmic methods to create terrain, plants, road surface materials, reflections, atmospheric haze, and even a rainbow composited in a digital image (see Figure 1.5.2b.)

2. Computer-aided landscape architectural design

Definitions of landscape architecture are necessarily broad. With origins in both the natural sciences, problem-solving, and engineering on the one hand, and visionary imagination, social psychology, and aesthetic

FIGURE 1.5.2 **Early computer-generated virtual landscapes: (a) "Valley Road," Stephen Ervin, 1983; (b) "The Road to Pt Reyes," composition by Alvy Ray Smith et al., 1983**

Copyright PIXAR. Used with permission

composition on the other, the discipline spans many scales and concerns – but all are about design, and about environments, with an emphasis on living and dynamic ones.

The tools of the trade are equally diverse and include notebooks, cameras, drones, computers, and shovels; but many of the tools are primarily concerned with representation, since the design and management of environments are often done with surrogate representations, rather than with full-scale living realities for a mix of convenience, practicality, safety and ethical reasons.

As with any art, or field of human endeavor, a specialized language is also employed. The relationships between art, science, and language are deeply intertwined, and philosophically rich, but, suffice it to say, manipulating sounds or signs (symbols, letters, numbers) as a way of expressing meaning, or emotion, is fundamental to both art and science and part and parcel of design and of problem-solving. Designs and design acts may then be understood as assertions, answers to questions (often more exploratory than definitive) and the language used – whether drawings of circle and arrows, or actual rows of actual trees, or words or equations – certainly have an intimate relationship to, and often a formative influence on, both the creation and experience of the design or designed artifact or process.

Computer-aided design (CAD), in its original conception, was seen as a way to assist designers with graphic symbol manipulation – drawing circles, lines, and arrows more precisely, or more rapidly, or with effortless repetition, rotation, scaling, etc. The very first instance of CAD software, written in 1963 by Ivan Sutherland at MIT (Sutherland) was called "Sketchpad," with a nod to the essential role of sketches and sketchpads for making notes, drawings, and diagrams in design processes. Tellingly, the modern Java-based Processing language (Processing) calls stored programs "sketches." This idea that notations in some language (e.g., graphite on paper, or programs in Java) are essential to design underlies the role and value of computation in landscape architecture.

There are other more immediate/instrumental applications of computation that have led to its general applicability and adoption by so many disciplines and activities, such as speed, accuracy, portability, etc. Some of the earliest computer software introduced to landscape architects came from civil engineering, for such calculations as hydrologic runoff, cut and fill mass balance calculations, and coordinate geometry for horizontal and vertical road alignment. The recent emergence of the landscape architectural practice known as "geo-design" (Steinitz) is based on a combination of computational approaches: GIS-based mapping, spatial analysis, and cartographic representation software, CAD drawing and design tools, simulation-based impact analyses (such as cost, connectivity, biodiversity, energy efficiency, etc.), and online web-based tools for group collaboration, documentation, and video-conferencing, designed to enable groups of design professionals, scientists, engineers, stakeholders, and citizens to collaborate on large problems over extended distance and time, with multiple perspectives and criteria. This development, enabled by satellites, powerful computers, fast networks, and other ICT tools, represents a much more expansive definition of "computer-aided design" than "drawing tool" – even though, at its core, it is still just symbol manipulation.

3. Computation – as technology, and as a medium for design

Many people think of computers as having to do with mathematics, and it is true that many of the earliest practical applications of computation were for calculation, and many still are today. But at their core, computers are much more about logic than they are about math. Alan Turing and John von Neumann, the real inventors of most modern-day computing, were both motivated by the need for rapid and repetitive calculations during the Second World War, but both were drawn immediately into broader and more abstract considerations about "thinking" machines and the nature of human knowledge; both were envisioning "intelligent machines"; the fact that the essential electronic storage was called "memory" was a distinct reference to characteristics of the human brain.

The principal insight that Turing had was that a suitably designed machine could be "general purpose" rather than being designed just to do one thing – say, add two numbers – and this meant that the sequence of instructions about what to do – the "program" – had to be "data," capable of being input to the machine, just like other data such as the numbers to be added together. Thus, although a digital computer could be an adding machine – and the first handheld popular computers were indeed calculators that could perform many mathematical operations other than just addition – it could equally well be a text formatting machine, or a music generating, or a drawing display machine, etc.

An essential characteristic of Turing's universal computing machine design was that processing steps such as entering,

adding, displaying, etc. had to be sequential, one at a time. This reflected both the limitations of electromechanical equipment at the time, and also the basic human notion of a process, or recipe, as a sequence of steps. Although branching and repetition were immediately understood to be essential for many real tasks, they were nonetheless always in sequential order, one at a time. Turing claimed that a single universal machine could be built to perform any process of this sort. He called that process an *algorithm*, using a word first used by a sixth-century Persian mathematician. So pervasive is this idea that computational approaches are often called "algorithmic" approaches, and we often hear of computer-enabled design processes enabled by digital computers (that is, truly "computer-aided design") referred to as "algorithmic design."

Modern-day computer electronics have made possible machines that can do more than one thing at a time, simultaneously; these are usually called "parallel processors." While this inherently makes for faster and more powerful computation, it turns out that algorithms for these non-Turing computers must be noticeably different from those for simple one-step-at-a-time sequential processes. Indeed, a whole world of complications opens up with parallel processing; and, while this is a major study in computer science, suffice it to say that few algorithmic approaches in landscape architecture have yet to be influenced by the demands or capabilities of parallel processing. (One possible exception, the use of so-called "cellular automata" to simulate landscapes and landscape processes, is discussed below. Otherwise, no further mention of parallel processing will be made.)

All modern digital computers and computation have one more salient aspect: they are built on binary representations, and they employ Boolean logic, named after the

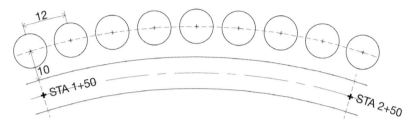

```
(Draw-row-of-trees type=maple
              path=(Get-road-segment start=STA1+50 end=STA2+50)
              alignment=parallel
              offset=10          ;; 10m safety regulation
              spacing=12         ;; 12m arborists recommendation
              number=9)          ;; design decision
```

FIGURE 1.5.3 **Draw-row-of-trees output**

mathematician George Boole, who formalized the ideas of the fundamental binary values TRUE and FALSE, represented as 1 and 0 respectively, and logical operators, such as AND, OR, NOT, and others. In fact, even for mathematical calculations, all numbers are represented in binary (just as letters, colors, and other symbols are). Even processes, such as multiplication or drawing a curved line, are encoded as algorithms involving simple logical operations on individual binary digits, or *bits*. The process of *digitization* – taking measurements in the real, analog world and converting them to bits or pixels (such as a digital camera does) – is fundamental to digital computation, and can give rise to both scientific concerns about accuracy and precision on the one hand, and unintended and intentional aesthetic effects on the other; both are explicit in computational approaches in landscape architecture. For example, the raster cell size of satellite imagery may affect landscape ecological analysis of patterns and processes; and 32-bit vs 8-bit vs 1-bit color makes a huge difference in digital images' appearance.

Building on the foundation of these binary building blocks, the art and science of

expressing algorithms – or "writing code" – has evolved substantially in the nearly 70 years since the first digital computers, when programs needed to specify every individual logical operation on nearly every individual bit of data, in extremely granular detail, in highly specialized code sometimes called "*machine language*." Today, much more high-level aggregations can be expressed in simple code, so that a modern landscape architect could write something like:

This snippet of made-up code shows many of the characteristics of modern high-level programming languages, particularly those called "imperative" and "procedural" languages: named variables (e.g., "type" and "alignment"), named procedures with specific required input parameters (e.g., Draw-row-of-trees . . . and Get-road-segment . . .), access to libraries and databases of values, and plain English language comments to clarify the steps in a process, or the reasons for particular values or calculations. All common programming languages also usually have some ways of expressing repetition (number of times, or until some condition is reached), and conditional tests (IF/THEN statements). Although not seen directly in this snippet, the draw-row-of-trees procedure will likely use some form of repetition, taking the input parameter number=9 into account.

The usual minimum functionality of any programming language includes:

- Some means of taking input, e.g., letters from a keyboard, points from a touchscreen, etc.;

- Stored variables with names and values, often of different types (integers, strings, arrays, etc.);

- Stored procedures (or subroutines, methods, etc.) that take inputs and return values or produce outputs;

- A range of operations on variables, such as logical, mathematical, string-manipulation, etc.;

- Some means of managing repetition (e.g., number of times, or until some condition is reached);

- Some means of conditional branching of control (e.g., testing for true/false, or some condition).

These six simple elements (and usually some other useful programming language functions) can be combined into endless variety and permutation, including every CAD program, GIS program, image processing and speech recognition program, web service, mobile phone app, etc. Algorithms are usually written to serve some particular processing purpose, and then implemented in programs with inputs, outputs, error checking, interfaces, and other usability features. By changing one or more values, say "size" or "spacing," many different variations can be tried out and evaluated in the design process.

Thus the act of writing code is both a technical exercise in appropriate use of specified syntax and a design activity involving intentions, choices, aesthetics,

and ramifications. In this way it is quite similar to making a construction drawing, or a specification sheet. Coding provides yet another language for expressing and exploring design intent in the creative and production processes of imagining and creating landscapes.

Designing procedures and subprocedures that deal with one specialized task, and communicate with procedures – the process of "modular decomposition" (Alexander) – is akin to breaking a large problem into smaller problems that can be combined, or even analogous to the processes in construction of various subcontractors working on different but connected parts of a project. In this way, too, writing code is a design exercise: identifying and naming major procedural modules and specifying their interconnections has direct parallels with spatial and formal design decisions.

When writing code, one must make choices about what is input and what is output (in scientific terms, independent and dependent variables), which is often an important step in determining "what can the designer control" and what are the most important, or effective, control variables. Design, of course, often involves changing these around (e.g., "should the length of the road determine the number of trees?" Or "should the number of trees determine the length of the road?" Or "will the budget determine both?"). Writing code that can take various inputs, and produce outputs that can then be compared and evaluated, is an increasingly useful way of exploring these alternatives – a design process.

Exploring alternatives is a common and essential design activity, and highlights an important point: "What exactly do we mean by exploring?" Exploration is not usually an algorithm, because unforeseen conditions and demands may arise – we can never write down every possible eventuality in an IF/THEN rule in advance. So exploration is more akin to a "heuristic," a general approach, setting out initial steps and general principles but also leaving open the chance of discoveries and opportunities. In this kind of computer-aided design, we most often find a human being exploring in partnership with a computer program. The program may be able to generate alternatives, and even partially evaluate them, but the "flashes of insight" or "inspiration" we often associate with successful design are difficult to explain, much less to program into an algorithm (various attempts have been made, over several decades of artificial intelligence research, but none has been completely convincing, and the AI questions are deep, so we leave this topic out of the rest of this discussion).

Coding in support of design exploration can be understood as a process of:

- Identifying key design aspects, or measurements or characteristics of concern, and giving them names so they can be manipulated as variables;

- Identifying key relationships between design variables that can be computed, perhaps in a simple formula or perhaps in a more complex multistep algorithm;

- Creating procedures (algorithms) to encapsulate necessary or desirable processes (such as "calculate stair dimensions from topographic rise and materials choice," "compute change in biodiversity in $30m^2$ cells for the entire study area," "evaluate likely visual experience given new road alignment," etc.);

- Generating outputs – numeric, textual, graphic, sound, video, 3D, etc.– for human evaluation or for communication or construction.

The last step in this outline characterizes the model of design, proposed by Herbert Simon in 1969, called simply "Generate and Test" (Simon). In this view, two distinct aspects of design thinking – "synthesis" and "analysis" – can be considered (and programmed). Which or how much of each (generating or testing) is done by human or computer hardly matters. Perhaps computation can be used to do the heavy math of a fluid dynamics calculation to evaluate (test) the airflow around a proposed (generated) sculptural shape, or perhaps an algorithm can be used to generate shapes and patterns for evaluation (testing) by the human designer's eye. In this dance between "generate" and "test" there is a continuous feedback loop of iteration and refinement, ultimately leading to some "final" design decision, based on a heuristic approach, not specified by any algorithm.

Some have wondered how any predictable sequence of operations could give rise to invention or design. There are many questions about artificial intelligence, or artificial creativity, and whether any digital computer is even theoretically capable of intelligence or design creativity. But that is not necessary for computer-aided design, in which a human partner provides the design intelligence – at least for now.

One approach to escaping the limitations of predictable algorithms has been to turn to randomness – say, injecting both random numbers and random logical decisions into algorithms, to generate graphics. In general, complete randomness is never satisfactory – it just creates white noise – but "controlled randomness," within some ordered process, can give rise to variations that add interest and diversity. Some computer scientists have explored an approach to programming called *genetic algorithms* that use random processes, akin to genetic mutation, to alter code small steps at a time, using multiple

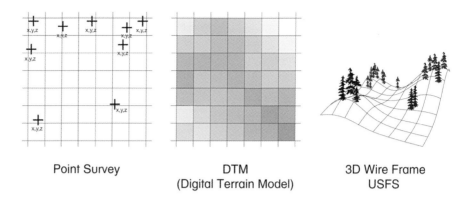

| Point Survey | DTM (Digital Terrain Model) | 3D Wire Frame USFS |

FIGURE 1.5.4 **As tool: from measurement to data structure to graphics**

repeated trials and generations to ultimately make code that is artificially "evolved" to be well suited to some task or goal. Finding applications of genetic programming in landscape architecture is not easy, but the potential for interesting results is there.

Given the capabilities and limitations of computation as discussed, there are three distinct ways, or modes, in which algorithmic/computational approaches are commonly used and valuable to designers:

1. As *tool*: using out-of-the-box commercial software to create graphics, various analyses, and other media/artifacts, used both to "generate" and to "test";

2. As *language*: writing code, in some programming environment, to generate graphics or other output, used both to "generate" and to "test";

3. As *medium*: using computational tools and code to receive input from the physical world (in real time, via sensors) and/or directly control something (display, sound, electromechanical actuator, etc.) in the physical world.

3.1. As tool: out-of-the-box commercial software as tools for helping to create drawings, renderings, calculations, simulations, analyses, etc.

These tools use underlying algorithmic techniques, but these are not exposed; usually little knowledge of them is required to use the software and, in general, the software cannot be modified from its predetermined routine and capabilities, as powerful as they may be. This "using software" mode – the simplest – helps with the convenience and productivity of drawings for the purposes of design and is by far the most common. To the extent that CAD, GIS, and image processing software comprise a multipurpose toolbox, they can be appropriated and used by designers in a wide range of ways. For landscape designers, these are mostly used to make graphic representations, 3D models, videos, and construction documents that describe and prescribe physical interventions in the landscape to be made by people and machines. These tools may, of course, also be employed to create only "virtual landscapes," to be viewed via VR technology for entertainment, artistic, and other design purposes.

3.2. As language: writing code

Writing code may be done either in the context of some graphics or other software, perhaps leveraging an application programmers interface (API) to invoke and control built-in functions of the software, or in a general-purpose programming language (C++, Python, JavaScript, etc.), connected to some hardware capabilities, such as generating graphics, text reports, web content, etc.

Custom-built codes, especially by an amateur, may be more difficult to produce or less effective in performing complex routines for which commercial software has already been perfected; however, it may also be the only way to get exactly the effect desired, if that effect is not included in any commercial software, and it may be more convenient to explore and experiment with in that regard.

Writing code is less common than using software among landscape architects (indeed, most people), but is becoming increasingly normal, as some working knowledge of coding, in some language, is becoming part of everyday training for design professionals. In the US, many high school students now learn coding in some form (there are even proposals to allow learning to code to fulfill a "foreign language" requirement). Consequently, landscape architects and designers in postsecondary education and graduate school are increasingly code-savvy, and are able to incorporate coding as part of the creative and production processes. The proliferation of web-based apps and mash-ups has made the idea of accessible, often custom-built, code-based tools for information-based design purposes a normal expectation of a whole generation of designers.

This "writing code" – requiring different training and knowledge than simply "using software" – can be used to directly express abstract design ideas, and is often used to produce artifacts (e.g., graphics) that can stand alone or be imported into commercial software for production purposes. The "Processing" (Processing) language (built on Java), designed especially for artistic and graphics coding, is one effective approach, which has ease of entry thanks to its clever packaging of essential graphics functions into simple commands, as well as deep expandability, since it is based on the robust and full-featured Java language.

Another popular approach is using graphical user interfaces (GUIs) to CAD software, such as "Rhinoceros" and "Grasshopper" (McNeel), which enables the construction of code by graphical programming, dragging arrows between boxes representing logical/mathematical functions, and built-in capabilities of the underlying Rhino software. Landscapes created by code can be quite abstract, using only mathematical and other parameters determined by the programmer, or through some interactive user interface; or they may be responsive to site information or other base data, such as terrain read-in as a series of elevations, contour lines, etc. Virtual landscapes created by code can be designed to mimic and explore natural processes and forms, such as branching, erosion, flow, etc.; or can be quite fantastic, not meant to reflect any natural systems, or even to be built, but nonetheless to be spatial and to elicit human response, even if only through VR or AR headsets.

An important aspect of writing code for any purpose is to match algorithms with data structures. Certain algorithms work best with regularly spaced grids of values, others with linked tables, others with text strings, and so on.

Sources and methods of capturing digital data (*digitizing*) directly influence this choice: digital cameras and satellite sensors generate raster grids of values; field surveying units lists of (x, y, z) values; and hand sketches may be transcribed as 2D lines and curves. Design algorithms link these inner representations, held in computer memory and operated upon by programming language primitives, with outer representations: 2D line drawings, color raster prints and renderings, 3D fabricated models, and others.

The fundamental landscape medium of topography can be described and manipulated as a collection of 3D points (*point cloud*); a regular grid of z-values (*digital terrain model*); a set of curved lines with associated elevation attributes (*contour* lines); a linked collection of 3D triangles (*triangulated irregular network*); in some cases a mathematical equation, or collection of trigonometric functions (e.g., $x^2+y^2+z^2/2 < 8$); and even a descriptive phrase (e.g., "hemispherical mound 8m in diameter, 4m tall"). Each of these has its best uses and limitations, some set by requirements of construction and, as with poetry and foreign languages, translations from one form of representation (data structure) to another is not always exact. Mismatches introduced by translation may be seen only as errors or undesirable artifacts, or they may become opportunistic design features, appropriated for some aesthetic or abstract purpose, in the crucible of design ideation.

In common procedural programming languages, many individual values are usually involved, and may have names such as {multiply}1, {multiply}2, width, color, type1, type2, type3, etc. An essential part of the art of coding is using variable names that are descriptive, and keeping track of the role that each variable plays in an overall system or algorithm. These variables are typically highly granular, and though they may be used in a collection to represent some physical object, often the overall object is never itself named or individually handled.

In "object-oriented programming," however, the initial emphasis is on creating and naming software "objects" that represent real-world-objects, and that are characterized by having a set of attributes and behaviors that are all bundled together. Thus a "tree" may have a species, height, width, age, growth rate, and condition, and variable names such as tree1.height, tree2.species, etc. In this way, systems, landscapes, environments, and assemblies can be simulated in software, with a very direct correlation between variable names, values, and actual attributes.

In addition, object-oriented systems may often implement a form of class-object attribute inheritance hierarchy, which can simplify coding and give rise to powerful behavioral performance of systems. For example, a tree class may be created with attributes as above, and then "maple-tree" object created as a "kind" of tree, with an additional attribute "sap-production." When reasoning about, or computing with, the maple-tree-1, the code can know that all trees have the attribute "height," and in an addition this maple-tree-1 also has a "sap-production" attribute. The kind of proliferation of objects with special attributes (e.g., even magical powers as found in many video games) is an example of the expressive and flexible nature of this kind of object-oriented programming.

Whether through procedural or object-oriented programming, a common use of both commercial software and custom coding is for the purposes of *analysis* and *simulation*. Designers often need to try to predict future consequences of design proposals and alternatives. The most common form of coding, of course, is visual simulation, which seeks to answer the

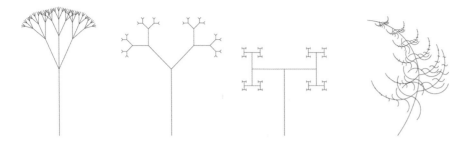

FIGURE 1.5.5 **As language: from logic to code to forms**

qualitative question "What might some change look like?" (from different points of view, in different seasons, in motion, etc.). Visual analysis can be used for more quantitative answers, such as "can this location be seen from some other location?" Or "what percentage of the sky is visible from the plaza?" But simulations of many other kinds of systems and impacts, not just visual, are equally important. Many social and physical phenomena can be simulated, given sufficient scientific understanding of the mechanisms and sufficient inputs. Computational fluid dynamics (CFD) software such as ANSYS Fluent (ANSYS) can be used to simulate the flow of fluids (e.g., air, water, smoke) around and through 3D environments, subjected to gravity, evaporation, turbulence, and other dynamic changes, and used to model the flow of water in a channel or air pollution in a city, given a suitable 3D model to work with. Human behavioral and econometric simulations can model the flow of pedestrians in a plaza, or commuter choices in a multimodel transportation system. These simulations can return a range of kinds of values, from numerical summaries to full-color animations, and, while mostly designed for the "testing" side of computer-aided design, are increasingly being used also as a form of inspiration on the "generation" side as well.

3.3. As medium: the "Internet of Things"

Beyond just producing graphics and artifacts for aesthetic or production purposes, and mathematical and other values via simulation, algorithmic approaches can also be used to gather information from the world, through sensors and "analog-to-digital" converters, expanding the modes of human perception to a wider range of spectra (e.g., infrared) and dimensions (e.g., air or water pollution).

Landscape planners and architects have actively embraced the use of a range of remote sensing technologies, from space satellites with multispectral scanners generating raster images of land cover and weather to handheld LIDAR scanners and unmanned-aerial-vehicles (UAVs) or "drones," creating 3D point clouds representing terrain, vegetation, and built structures. Special purpose software may be needed to collect and decode these data sets, but commercial CAD, GIS and image processing software supply much basic and advanced functionality. The opportunities for custom coding to make creative design use of these sensors and sensed data are many and varied.

For example, using location-based technology embedded in mobile phones or other devices to create web-based adjuncts to physical landscapes, and providing additional information – for either entertainment or education – to visitors depending on their location is an example of sensor-based computation-augmented landscape architecture becoming familiar, much like the audio-guides routinely deployed in art museums. In virtual landscapes, such sensors may themselves be virtual – such as proximity sensors in VR interaction environments, which respond to the presence of the human operator's virtual avatar in the virtual landscape.

Finally, beyond sensing and reacting to the physical world, algorithmic tools can also be used to directly control the physical world, by being connected through "digital-to-analog" converters, to control switches, motors, valves, lights, and other electrical appliances. Motion sensors that automatically open doors sensing an approaching person or controlling water valves in fountains to generate certain choreographic effects are perhaps the most common form of this "digital sensing and control" mode ordinarily experienced, although more and more are becoming familiar, such as controlling lights for functional or decorative purposes, 3D fabrication tools, robotic earthmoving equipment, computer-controlled flood-gates, or other large-scale artifacts.

The "Internet of Things" (IoT) world of connected "smart" objects (thermostats, light fixtures, televisions, houses, cars, cities, etc.) is more fully populated with new devices and new ways of interaction, every day. The Arduino, littleBits, and Particle (Arduino; littleBits; Particle) family of do-it-yourself IoT tinkerers' hardware kits, including computer-controlled motors, lights, and other actuators, as well as sensors, timers, wireless receivers, and a host of other interactive components, have opened up a whole world of analog-to-digital and digital-to-analog experiments and artifacts; they are increasingly evident in schools, science labs, art studios, landscape architecture offices, and digital/interactive landscapes and cityscapes.

This final mode, requiring the deepest and most varied knowledge of digital tools and engineering, is the most complex of the three modes described, and also the most powerful, promising, innovative, and still unfamiliar.

These three modes – "using software," "writing code," and "digital sensing and control" – encompass a broad range of uses and possibilities in design and landscape architecture, both in analog and virtual manifestation.

A special characteristic of landscape architecture, and demand upon landscape

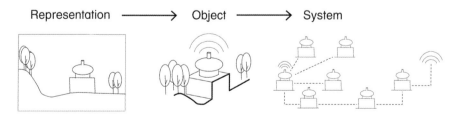

FIGURE 1.5.6 **As medium: from representation to object to system**

design, is the dynamic changing nature of the real-world landscape. Under the influence of ever-changing weather and climate, landscapes and plants grow and die; water flows, wind blows, the sun rises and sets, and people move through landscapes, cities, and buildings. Representing these dynamic processes in drawings and still images has long been a challenge – only the very best painters and artists can draw the wind. But, with algorithmic tools, and computer assistance, we can make models of landscapes and landscape elements that capture dynamics and changing states and can create moving images (video) that represent the dynamics directly. A great power of computational and algorithmic design for landscape architects is this ability to represent, explore, and even design with dynamics. These dynamic landscape animations can represent three fundamentally different points of view:

- Motion *through* landscapes;

- Motion *of* landscapes/landscape elements; and

- Interaction *with* landscapes/landscape elements.

Motion *through*: The prevalence of computer-generated "walk-throughs" in architecture and landscape architecture speaks to the central concern with the visual experience of a viewer, or camera, moving along a path taking in a scene. The choreography of visitor experience is an important aspect of landscape and architectural design, and the generation of video animations through a park, landscape, or building is a familiar application of computational tools in landscape architecture. For the most part these are done with commercial software and built-in functions – few designers code their own viewing or camera animation algorithms – though the effects of doing so can be quite dramatic. "Virtual reality" visualization tools that immersively engage the visual field, presenting true stereoscopic perspective and responding to head movements and other controls to change views and simulate motion, have for several decades been the domain of video gamers and some adventurous designers. These are mostly used in the "test" mode, rather than "generate," but the potential for the latter is intriguing.

Motion *of*: Landscapes and public spaces, of course, are not just static constructions with viewers moving through them (as the simpler walk-throughs would have it!). Wind ruffles leaves and blows clouds across the sky, blocking the sun, sometimes bringing rain, and other people in the scene are moving, too. So, both for more realism and for engaging more expressive components of landscape, digital designs can also be made to imbue motion, as of people walking, wind blowing, rivers flooding, lights moving, etc. These visual simulations are necessarily substantially

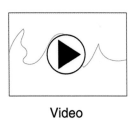
Video

CFD

Interaction

FIGURE 1.5.7 **Representing dynamics**

more complicated than the simpler walk-throughs, and again are mostly made using off-the-shelf software and their built-in dynamics, motion, and animation functions. Many have built-in support for physical simulation of material properties such as elasticity and rigidity that can affect computer-generated motion. An enormous and powerful set of tools for computer graphics and image rendering, so well developed by the movie special effects industry, is available to landscape architects today for visual simulations and design explorations.

Interaction *with*: Finally, people inhabiting or visiting a landscape work not only through a camera lens, viewing motion; they can directly interact with, and influence, the landscape and landscape elements. Whether through touch screens and VR goggles, interacting with a digital model, or via sensors interacting with the real world, the potential for engaging user interaction – beyond just viewing – is one of the most powerful potentials for computer-aided design in the landscape. Working with real landscape elements and digital models of landscape elements that respond to interaction, and algorithms that model behavior and not just dynamics but reactions and interactions – creating "responsive

environments" (Cantrell and Holzman) – represents another much expanded definition of "computer-aided design." Algorithmic design that combines computer-based sensing, acting, and custom-written code creating landscapes, buildings, and even cities epitomizes the impact of computation on landscape architecture, as seen and imagined in the various examples throughout this volume.

4. Algorithmic design

As suggested by Turing's definition of the "Universal Machine" that can perform any algorithmic process suitably described, computer-aided landscape architectural design can produce a wide variety of forms and landscapes, both analog and virtual – theoretically, any that can be suitably described. Rather than try to find a theoretical or ideological limit to the expressive/descriptive power of algorithms, let us consider a range of approaches, by way of illustrating a broad universe of possibilities. This list is neither exhaustive nor derived from any theory but serves to illustrate a range of approaches, from simpler to more complex.

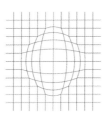

Warped Grids

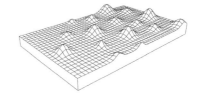
3D Landform

FIGURE 1.5.8 **Warped grids to 3D landform**

4.1. Pattern generation by repetition and variation

Perhaps the first industrial example of a pattern-producing programmable machine was the Jacquard loom. Invented around 1801, this was a mechanical way of encoding complex woven patterns in a series of holes punched in cards that were used to mechanically control the operation of individual warp- and weft-lifting hooks in the manufacture of textiles. The simplest woven fabric is just one color of thread and an "over/under" pattern repeated in both axes. Adding multicolored threads and varying the pattern of over and under can generate geometric patterns in the fabric, as seen in brocades, plaids, etc. These can be made to look floral, abstract, etc. – any pattern that can be described as a repeating arrangement of colored dots (in a "raster") can be made to appear in the fabric. Similarly, just by the use of repetition and conditionals, in logical structures, a digital computer can do the same, and can generate either raster graphics or vector (line-based) representations of grids, now often called "warped grids" since they need not be consistently or simply rectangular. The use of grids (1D, in a line; or 2D, in an array; or even 3D, in a lattice) are pervasive in landscape design, from paving patterns to planting plans and vegetative structures, to lighting, furniture, and other objects. Simple mathematical measurements, counts, and ratios may, in the landscape, become interpreted as "rhythmic" or "repetitive," or given other qualitative experiential and design intent–related descriptors.

4.2. Parametric generation

A parameter is just a number, often one of several, that can define the state or behavior of a system (or, in computer coding, a value given as input into a procedure; other resulting values or behavior are determined by this parameter). Usually, other values are also determined by some relationship – logical, mathematical, or other – to the parameter, and parameters are chosen to be critical or characteristic of the system being described or computed. So, for a road, a key parameter might be "width" (expressed in meters, lanes, etc.), and this parameter will cause a change not only in one dimension but in other values as well (paving material, structural systems, planting details, curve radii, maximum slopes, and many other details may be determined by width).

The ability to write code that changes many values as the result of one input parameter makes possible "parametric exploration" and "parametric generation" (Schumacher). In some cases, a single "slider" may be used to set a value somewhere between a predetermined minimum and maximum value; changing the slider slightly can sometimes generate a wide variety of changes in the result. In other parametric systems there may be number of parameters that are separate, not determined by any other, and serve as the key defining input variables that distinguish the results. So code for parametric variation may be understood as a generating system for a whole family of related designs that all contain similar elements and relationships; these may be used as input in a separate algorithmic testing process, or perhaps just evaluated, by eye or intuition, by a human judge.

The powerful ability and attraction of writing algorithmic parametric design code is the ability to customize a generic process for specific conditions, as with an overall width, density, height restriction, etc., and the ability to also build in logic for responding to unique site conditions, so that different values and logic can be embedded at potentially every location (however defined, e.g., location on a grid) throughout a site. This enables the hybridization of site-specific response with algorithmic form, with a potentially infinite range of variability based on user input, random variation, site conditions, etc. With the incorporation of sensors and actuators, then the design can itself be continually responsive to varying conditions (weather, occupancy, and other local or remote observations. Imagine a garden/installation that uses sensors and computer-controlled irrigation and fans to mirror the rainfall and wind conditions of some distant locale, for example).

4.3. Fractal recursion

A particular form of repetition and variation that gives rise to intriguing pattern is the "fractal" geometry (Mandelbrot) produced by a process of "recursion," an algorithmic approach in which the output of a process is fed back into the same process but with some regular variation (e.g., larger, or smaller, or with a change in angle) each time. Mathematically, this gives rise to something called the "Julia Set." Fractal formulas have been used to model the structure of many natural forms, such as coastlines, leaf edges, tree structures, stream networks, and others. Especially when a small amount of randomness is introduced, mimicking the natural worlds of variation, these patterns can become extremely lifelike.

4.4. Rule-based generation – shape grammars and L-systems

In most algorithmic coding, there is a very clear but potentially complex sequence of operations, from beginning to end (with repetition and branching as required). In rule-based programming, by contrast, there is a very simple structure: a set of rules, expressed as IF/THEN conditions, some starting condition, and a simple sequence: at each time step, check through all rules to see if any conditions for any rule have been meet and, if so, apply that rule, potentially transforming the original condition; then

repeat until no more rules are firing. This approach, developed originally for attempting to encode rules of behavior for complex tasks, so as to enable robotic performance, for example, can also be applied to graphical and three-dimensional conditions. The so-called "shape grammars" and "L-systems" are algorithmic ways of generating shapes and forms by the repeated application of spatial rules. These have been applied to the generation of buildings and gardens in plan (Stiny) and to the generation of biologically inspired plant and animal forms (Prusinkiewicz and Lindenmayer).

4.5. Agent-based simulations

Carrying the "object-oriented" paradigm a step further gives rise to the "agent-based" approach, in which objects represent animated "beings" that have both attributes and relationships to other objects but are imbued with behavior and a "point of view," or motivation, and are usually considered autonomous and mobile. Thus, software "agents" representing shoppers in a commercial marketplace, or hikers or wildlife species in a wilderness landscape, can be "let loose" in a simulated 3D environment, or terrain. Based on their programmed behavior, these "agents" will interact with the landscape and each other, leaving an electronic trail of locations and corresponding attributes. This trail can then be analyzed to discover likely patterns of behavior, preferred paths, bottlenecks, and other characteristics of the designed landscape.

4.6. Cellular automata, particle systems and swarms

Finally, carrying agent-based approach a bit further, the agents may be relatively simple in their individual makeup, but when deployed in sufficient numbers – thousands or tens of thousands, for example – can constitute a system whose overall emergent behavior and resulting forms can be informative. An "automaton" is a term originally applied to a physical mechanical device that could be programmed to produce repetitive simple behavior, switching between two or more states based on some inputs. A *cellular automaton* ("CA") is usually a relatively simple bit of code, which can take several inputs and based on those inputs take on one of several states (on/off, red/blue/green, etc.); it is usually deployed in a regular 2D grid where each cellular automaton is connected to all of its eight neighbors; at each step of a time clock, each CA takes all of its neighbors' states and input, and potentially changes its own state as a result; this proceeds through multiple time steps. Conway's "Game of Life" (Gardner) is a well-known example of this kind of logical system. CA models have been used to simulate the growth of settlements over time, with each CA representing a patch of land, with states of development proceeding over time according to certain rules of individual behavior, which, together in interaction, end up creating a landscape as a mosaic of states, or land uses (Generative Landscapes).

Various CA systems have been used to analyze and model "swarm" behavior, in which emergent properties of structure, motion, and apparent global intelligence appear from a large enough number of connected very simple agents, much like a school of fish or flock of birds (Blum and Merkle). If the CA agents are freed from the 2D plane, and simulated in 3D space, they may be called a "particle system." Each particle in such a system is coded with 3D location, and other parameters such as direction, speed, size, etc., and these are programmed to change over time following some algorithmic rules. These algorithms may simulate physical processes such as gravity, wind-resistance, erosion, flames, or smoke, and the resulting trajectories of the interacting particles give to rise to 2D and 3D forms representing a waterfall, wave, fireball, cloud, etc. These techniques are extensively used in science and for film special effects; their role in landscape design is relatively unexplored but intriguing.

As alluded to earlier, cellular automata and particle systems are examples of computational approaches that can benefit from parallel computing; each CA or particle can be computed by one processor in an array of thousands of processors, and simulations on relatively large arrays can be computed in relatively less time in a parallel

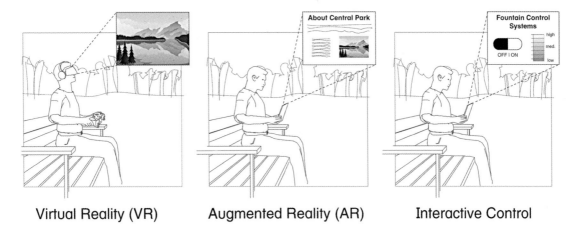

Virtual Reality (VR) Augmented Reality (AR) Interactive Control

FIGURE 1.5.9 **Three ways of being in a park with a computer**

computing environment than otherwise, making larger and more complex landscape simulations possible. Parallel processing in landscape architecture is not well known, applied, or studied, but the potential is obvious.

4.7. Big data, machine learning

All of the design generation methods described above assume that the steps of the recipe are written in code and are applied unchanged unless the human designer/author changes the code. But modern computer scientists have become very interested in the proposition that, with a sufficiently general approach and access to large amounts of memory, computer programs can be written that both can learn from experience and from training samples and can over time self-modify, in effect rewriting the code they run. This is an advanced topic in AI research, but an increasingly well-reported one, and the potential for self-modifying code in the hands of computational designers is not far off. One factor driving this development is the increasing availability of very large data sets, collected by sensors all over the world and gathered from all across the Internet.

This "big data" can represent hundreds of thousands of samples and observations, which can be analyzed and categorized by software and form the basis for "machine learning." This development raises the possibility that computer code can enter more and more fully into the complete "generate" and "test" cycle; it is not too futuristic to imagine a computer program that could be set to monitoring global environmental conditions, at many scales, and that could begin to make design proposals, for improved conditions, at many scales and many locations, based on correlations and observations across a sufficiently large global sample. This raises the specter of "computer-initiated design,"

not just computer-aided design, and of the logical extreme case of the "Turing landscape": landscapes designed *with* computation, with *embedded* computation, and *by* computation.

5. Turing landscapes

In 1950, theorist and inventor Alan Turing, realizing that a "universal computing machine" such as he had begun developing could produce output in the form of language (e.g., typed on a mechanical typewriter), famously proposed a test of the question "Can machines think?": if a human being, in communication with such a device, could not reliably tell whether she was communicating with another human being or with a machine, the answer would be "yes" (Turing). This, he predicted, would be true in not so many years. (It has not yet been unequivocally demonstrated, although his prediction from that same time that "computers will be able to play great chess" has been.)

From "can machines think?" to "can machines design?" is not a great leap. What are some equivalent tests for "Turing landscapes"? The "Turing test" ("mimic a human being, in conversation, well enough to fool one") applied to landscape architecture, and to design, might be understood in three successively more challenging versions:

Landscape Turing test v.1 (representation): "Does a picture of a landscape look so real a human being can't tell if it's computer-generated?" – We are already there! Photorealism in computer graphics, even of complex scenes such as dew on moss in a rainforest, or seafoam on a sandy beach, has been fairly well conquered by the special effects industry in Hollywood, and to some extent supported by developments in the military. It is no longer really feasible for most people to know if a digital scene has been simulated by computation or captured by a camera in the wild.

An early approach to landscape visualization used carefully cropped photographs of real plants, digitally composited together to form a scene, whose underlying geometry was simple planes and cylinders; but because of the texture-mapped photographs the scene was sufficiently realistic for applications such as flight simulators and video games. However, it would not stand up to close inspection, such as enabled by more advanced VR applications. More complex 3D geometry can be created with sufficient processing power and powerful graphics capability; mathematically defined algorithms for plant form (such as Figure 1.5.4) coupled with botanically correct plant growth simulations, including such effects as phototropism and phyllotaxis, augmented with advanced image processing and texture mapping, can produce startlingly lifelike high-resolution images.

Landscape Turing test v.2 (process): "Does a built landscape behave so well we can't tell if it is 'designed' or 'natural?'" – We are almost there. Using lighting, irrigation, and ventilation systems, coupled with high sensitivity sensors and high-tech building materials and techniques, we can now create landscapes that rival natural ones. Of course, we can't replace natural evolution of plants and animals, nor do we know if these synthetic landscapes could last hundreds of years. Working with all-natural materials, just relocated, rearranged and possibly re-formed by pruning or chiseling, Olmsted landscapes, as defined earlier, already blur the distinction between "designed" and "natural," especially over time. How much more can this distinction be blurred with digitally manufactured and enhanced materials, digitally aided engineering of landform and water features, and mechatronic engineering of digitally designed and controlled structures and

fixtures of all sorts? These designed/digital artifacts may be obvious, high-contrast, stainless steel and plastic, and obviously synthetic, or they may be subtle, embedded, integrated and hidden, serving to direct and corral natural forces, water flows, plant growth, patterns of light and shade, and landscape forms.

Landscape Turing test v.3 (design thinking): "Can you tell if a design has been generated by a computer or a person?" – Simply looking at a single instance, drawing, or model it would be very hard indeed. Many landscape designs can be characterized by a few simple paving and planting motifs (e.g., "double allee of trees (or of bagels!)," "checkerboard paving," "concentric rings") and geometric patterns or mathematical ratios, which could, in principle, be programmed into a "design machine." How such a machine would respond to context and unique site conditions would be an immediate issue, where algorithmic approaches might fail, for there is little consensus on any rules or even general principles (e.g., "fit in" vs. "stand out") that might really distinguish a human designer versus a programmed response.

In an extended design conversation – in which we would expect a human designer to know about human psychology and behavior as well as material properties and conceptual design ideas – likely a computer program today would still be identifiable by a certain lack of knowledge of these matters, and a lack of humanness in its responses. But these requirements go back to the original Turing test – and in large part depend on a sufficiently large repertoire of human conversational gambits and an encyclopedia of design knowledge and precedents.

Current AI research into the topic of "deep machine learning" may hold promise for enabling a computer to model high-level design abstractions, and so engage in a design conversation, but no such example has yet been developed or demonstrated, and there is currently little economic or other incentive to pursue this goal – there are so many other pressing areas where computer-based intelligence may fruitfully be applied (autonomous vehicles, smart energy systems, medical diagnosis, and others). Digital landscape architecture is truly still in its infancy; there is still very much to be discovered about the kind and qualities of landscapes made possible just by the combination of human designers, computer code, and electromechanical sensors and actuators.

In a less competitive approach than a "test," thinking about the potential and characteristics of Turing landscapes is intriguing. The hybridization of human–machine, and analog–digital, at each of several scales in the landscape – from regional and climatic (*ecto*), through local/site (*meso*), to human body scale (*endo*) – will bring all new kinds of landscapes and landscape experiences:

- Sensors at the regional scale that respond to weather, rainfall, and wind conditions seasonally and daily, and communicate with actuators at the local scale, to adjust dams, gates, sunshades, and windscreens to promote comfort and safety and deter erosion and plant damage; and deliver information, messages, and images to wearable digital devices on your body, in your autonomous vehicle, in your knapsack or tent, or at your café table;

- Geo-design software systems that enable landscape architects and collaborating disciplines to design interventions from wildlife reserves to parks, housing developments, power stations, transportation hubs, and individual buildings and courtyards, with integration

of simulation tools that aid in identifying impacts (energy costs, carbon footprint, socioeconomic costs, crowding, visual impacts, gain/loss of biodiversity and habitat, and others); and, in information-enabled generate–test cycles, design ever more fitting and carefully adjusted designs, proposals and projects;

- Computer-controlled fabrication and GPS-enabled construction tools on site that enable precise site measurements and locations, material placement, for increased cost-effectiveness and adherence to precise design specifications;

- Digitally augmented materials that can provide sensors, information, lighting, sound and other effects under interactive algorithmic control, such as pavement materials that provide lighting and navigational signage, hand railings that sense individuals' grips to respond and communicate, overhead adjustable canopies that provide shade and rain protection, lighting and informational graphics interacting with both regional weather sensors and individuals' digital devices and control systems . . .

- Wearable digital devices providing location-enabled, customized navigation, access to information and entertainment to augment human experiences, from solitary to collaborative.

These possibilities, and others as yet unimagined, make it clear that the six traditional elements of Olmsted landscapes (landform, vegetation, water, infrastructure, animals, and atmosphere), the conception of the "landscape experience," associated design practices and conventions, and even of "landscape" itself, will all necessarily be redefined in this Turing landscape era. All of the six essential elements of landscape are transformed by digital technologies and the possibilities of coding, in different ways to different degrees.

Turing landscape elements in brief

Landform

Sensors embedded in the earth are already used to inform seismic, geological, hydrologic and agricultural processes. Autonomous bulldozers with only digital input and control are already in use in extractive and construction industries. Movable dikes, walls and barriers at the landform scale are already an element of flood control in some environments; in the coming era of sea-level rise many new such constructions will doubtless be required, coupled with complex sensor and control networks. Paving in roads and paths can have traffic and activity sensors embedded; new paving materials allow for integral lighting, digital signage, and interactive way-finding aids directly embedded.

Water

Sensors of water level, quality, velocity, and temperature are already a part of hydrologic engineering for flood control, recreational, municipal, and agricultural processes. Digitally controlled irrigation systems and fountains and waterworks in public open spaces are already part of the designer's palette. As water from surface channels, underground springs, residential waste systems, rainfall on roofs, and runoff from surrounding mountains and fields is better integrated into ecological and urban networks, enabling better aquifer recharge and reduced waste, pollution, and erosion, the demands and opportunities for intelligent hydraulic control systems, designed for both beauty and function, will only increase, especially in the many water-stressed areas of the planet.

Vegetation

Plants are one area where it is least easy to imagine the hybridization of analog and digital materials and techniques: What exactly might a "cyborg tree" or forest look like? Still, digitally managed irrigation systems for horticulture are commonplace, as are ornamentation and illumination schemes involving plants. Perhaps a structure providing bird habitat, with digitally controlled overhead shading devices and solar panels, might be a new kind of "Turing tree" in the landscape.

Infrastructure

Algorithmically designed smart buildings with sensors, controls, and actuators (automatic doors and elevators and windows, for example) are already commonplace. In the landscape, hardscape elements (paving) and furniture (benches, lights, etc.) offer the greatest opportunity for new hybridized digital forms. Sidewalks with embedded lighting, sensors and information channels are already appearing in modern environments. More multipurpose furniture incorporating Wi-Fi networks and many kinds of sensors are also appearing. These elements, coupled with weather control innovations, will continue to help blur the distinction between inside (building) and outside (landscape) as landscape architecture, architecture, and urban design continue to coevolve.

Animals

Like plants, because they are also living, animals (including humans) are the least easy of all the elements to imagine as hybridized analog/digital beings (cyborgs). And, yet, arguably, the modern landscape architect, and modern park/garden visitor, already come digitally augmented, with CAD/GIS software and laser surveying tools on the one hand and portable telecommunication devices, display systems, and personal sensors on the other. Landscape ecologists and wildlife managers are learning that animals outfitted with simple lightweight sensors can perform important functions as sensor agents in the landscape, and the opportunities for systems design incorporating sensor-bearing animals in public parks are fascinating.

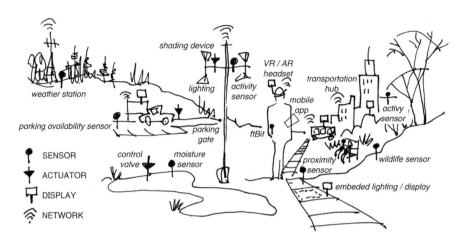

FIGURE 1.5.10 **Elements in a Turing landscape**

Atmosphere

Landscape architects have long had the opportunity to design with "landscape lighting" but these designs have for the most part been rather simple and their controls mostly limited to "on-at-dusk, off-at-dawn." In an environment with multiple sources of sensor input, including presence and activities of people, other activities, and ambient weather conditions, how much more complex, expressive, and potentially informative can these become? As controllable multihue LEDs make possible all the colors of the rainbow for no extra expense, and LED/LCD display technologies broadly expand the range of shapes, sizes, and structural possibilities for illumination systems, including embedded lighting in many kinds of materials, the possibilities for integrated control of atmospheric lighting – and, indeed, other water-based and sonic dimensions of atmosphere, as well – are much expanded for landscape architecture. Climate and seasonal effects also have great impact on landscape perception, use, and enjoyment, and climate data and sensors are now regularly a part of the landscape designer's toolkit, as illustrated in Figure 1.5.10.

6. Conclusion

Landscape architecture and landscape architects have three distinct modes of interaction with computation:

1. Using software – as a *tool*, for *automation*: from numbers to lines to graphics/objects;

2. Writing code – as a *language*, for *algorithms*: from logic to code to forms/landscapes;

3. Engaging with the Internet of Things – as a *medium*, for *augmentation*: from static to dynamic to interactive/alive?

And "Turing landscapes" of the twenty-first century have three salient characteristics:

1. They are designed using software, algorithmic approaches, and simulation;

2. They incorporate embedded sensors, actuators, and digital/algorithmic control of electromechanical elements;

3. They provide information exchange between people and environment, in digitally mediated responsive interactions and behavior.

Clearly, digital computation and information technology and communications (ITC) *tools* can be instrumental amplifiers of human eyes, enabling us to see and capture wavelengths and time frames impossible for the unaided eye; hands, enabling us to achieve strength and precision and resistance to environmental conditions that would be impossible for unaided human hands; and brains, enabling us to perform rapid calculations, store and retrieve enormous amounts of information, and explore chains of reasoning and trees of consequences impossible for the unaided human mind. These tools are in extensive use and of real value to designers. Satellites, digital image processing, laser printers, 3D fabrication tools, mobile devices, crowdsourced data, complex simulations, searchable databases, and so on are all essential tools of the trade, enabled by ITC developments.

However, coding and algorithmic thinking – the essential information processing components of computation – are in their own right a rich design *language* for exploration and expression of design ideas, providing as much value to meaning and value–laden experience and expression (*poesis*) as to purely instrumental manipulation (*techne*).

Like other media, computation and algorithmic thinking bring their own characteristics, constraints and affordances, ways of knowing, ways of doing, and aesthetics. Coding is a language and a representational medium and coding is, itself, a kind of designing, requiring abstraction, naming, modularization, and generate-and-test methods ("debugging"); code can reflect and respond to real-world conditions as inputs, as well as express abstract ideas and intents. Digital representations (data) and processes (algorithms) are as rich and productive as analog ones (earth, water, wood, plants,

metal, paint, etc.) are; in their ability to either mimic the characteristics and limitations of those analogs or to transcend/transform them, digital/algorithmic/computational media are powerful design enablers.

These tools of code and embedded computational intelligence and behavior are particularly effective in representing, manipulating, and manifesting dynamics and responsive interaction, as other essays in this volume demonstrate. Such dynamic/interactive/responsive landscapes make possible many new kinds of landscapes, landscape experiences, and landscape design approaches.

Digital techniques can enable dynamics, plasticity, mutability, and responsiveness of varying types, at different frequencies and with finer control in virtual landscapes than with analog/living materials (earth, water, plants, etc.) in real landscapes, and so are of great value and interest to landscape architecture. This does not mean that a day spent in a VR viewing tank experiencing a simulated oceanside beach will be as rich and nourishing to human body and spirit as a day spent at a real, unpolluted beach – but the former may be as intellectually and even aesthetically rewarding as time spent in a museum or at a movie. There are of course deep human evolutionary bonds to the "real/natural" landscape, and its primitive elements of landform, vegetation, water, and atmosphere – there may even be as-yet-undiscovered psychological and health benefits from human exposure to and interaction with these natural elements – and landscape architects and others will surely continue to celebrate and enable these contacts with nature.

The great promise of augmented reality (AR) is in the hybridization of these real environments (both "natural" and "built") with digital and information-based

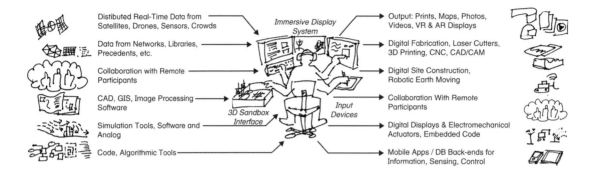

FIGURE 1.5.11 **Turing landscape designer**

processes. With these new techniques, materials, and technologies, landscape architects can fully embrace the potential for people to be not just "visitors" in a landscape but "participants" in it, and buildings and other mechanical infrastructure to be not just static/dead elements in the landscape but dynamic, responsive, interactive (and "alive?") elements of the landscape design palette.

The intellectual challenge of AI and that of imagining and devising autonomous design algorithms and agents with artificial design intelligence (ADI) and capable of passing the "design thinking" variant of the Turing test, as described above, will remain a fertile area of research and development into the indefinite future. For now, however, the real challenge is to deeply explore and develop a complex and productive hybridization and collaboration between algorithmic/ computational approaches – as tools, as language, and as medium – and human designers, as illustrated in Figure 1.5.11.

References

Alexander, C. *Notes on the Synthesis of Form*, Harvard University Press, 1964.

ANSYS, www.ansys.com, accessed May 20, 2016.

Arduino, www.arduino.cc, accessed May 20, 2016.

Blum, C. and Merkle, D. *Swarm Intelligence: Introduction and Applications*, Springer, 2008.

Cantrell, B. and Holzman, J. *Responsive Environments: Strategies for Responsive Technologies in Landscape Architecture*, Routledge, 2015.

Ervin, S. and Hasbrouck, H. *Landscape Modeling: Digital Techniques for Landscape Visualization*, McGraw-Hill, 2001.

Gardner, M. "Mathematical Games – The fantastic Combinations of John Conway's New Solitaire Game 'Life,'" *Scientific American*, 223, pp. 120–123, October 1970.

Generative Landscapes, https://generativelandscapes.wordpress.com/ 2015/06/26/disturbance-cellular-automata-example-12–2, accessed May 20, 2016.

Grasshopper, www.grasshopper3d.com, accessed May 20, 2016.

littleBits, www.littlebits.cc, accessed May 20, 2016.

MacDougall, E.B. *Microcomputers in Landscape Architecture*, Elsevier, 1984.

McNeel R. Grasshopper (generative modeling for Rhino), www.grasshopper3d.com, accessed November 28, 2017; Grasshopper3D – Speed Modeling – Generative Architectural Patterns, https://youtu.be/oCfpy8gdATo, accessed November 28, 2017.

Mandelbrot, B.B. *The Fractal Geometry of Nature*, Freeman, 1982.

Marx, L. *The Machine in the Garden: Technology and the Pastoral Ideal in America.* Oxford University Press, 1964.

Particle, www.particle.io/prototype, accessed May 20, 2016.

Processing, https://processing.org, accessed May 20, 2016.

Prusinkiewicz, P. and Lindenmayer, A. *The Algorithmic Beauty of Plants*, Springer-Verlag, 1990.

Rhinoceros, www.rhino3d.com, accessed May 20, 2016.

Schumacher, P. "Parametricism – A New Global Style for Architecture and Urban Design," *AD Architectural Design – Digital Cities*, 79(4), July/August 2009.

Simon, H. *Sciences of the Artificial*, MIT Press, 1969.

Smith, www.alvyray.com/Art/PtReyes.htm, accessed May 20, 2016.

Steinitz, C. *A Framework for Geodesign: Changing Geography by Design*, ESRI Press, 2012.

Stiny, G. "Introduction to Shape and Shape Grammars," *Environment and Planning B*, 7, 343–351, 1980.

Sutherland, I. *Sketchpad: A Man–Machine Graphical Communication System*, Garland, 1961.

Turing, A. "Can Automatic Calculating Machines be Said to Think?" in Copeland, B.J. *The Essential Turing: The Ideas that Gave Birth to the Computer Age*, Oxford University Press, 1952.

Perception 02

The perception of landscape systems formulates an approach to defining the scope of addressable issues and their relationships. This perception in turn provides the generative potential and project trajectory for a design problem. Computation and the abstraction of landscape systems have the capability to generate complete new perceptions of landscape through models, simulations, narratives, and interfaces.

02.00

Landscape models of the scientific imaginary

A visual textual précis

Contributor:

Justine Holzman
*Assistant Professor,
University of Toronto*

From early explorations by naturalists to the classic sciences to the current interdisciplinary science and modeling of climate change, methods of codifying within practices of scientific modeling have mediated our understanding, manipulation, and management of the landscape. A reading of codification within landscape architecture quickly turns toward debates about the transition and hybridization of analog and digital methodologies for design—however, an expanded reading of codification of the environment exposes long histories of structuring and formatting the landscape to become computational. Attempts to measure and predict landscape phenomena has simultaneously led to the production of digital simulation tools as well as highly surveilled and sensed physical landscapes. In her recent text, *Program Earth: Environmental Sensing Technology and the Making of a Computational Planet*, Jennifer Gabrys describes the continual concretization of techno-social relations between the ecologies of environmental sensors and the environments they monitor as "becoming environmental" in a "project of instrumenting or programming earth."[1] Gabrys (after Whitehead) argues that, if the expectation of expanding networks of environmental sensors and sources of data is to better understand the management of the environment, then careful attention must be paid toward the reality, "that sense data are less descriptive simply of pre-existing conditions and more productive of new environments, entities, and occasions of sense that come to stabilize as environmental conditions of concern."[2]

The foundations of scientific knowledge come from the observation of the physical, material world[3]—within which, the physical instantiations of experimentation have a way of reifying techno-social relations. Of interest is how the organization and articulation of the material world might take the form of a model through processes of analysis and augmentation. The role of physical modeling and, more importantly to this collection of texts, the role of physical computation in the history of simulation and the production of knowledge about landscape systems should augment any discussion of computational design, particularly as it relates to the modification of large-scale dynamic landscapes.

In the history of scientific modeling, methods of modeling originally developed to discern the past evolved as theory progressed to be predictive—morphing the scientific inquiry of how a particular condition came to be to what that condition might become. In her chapter, "From Scaling to Simulation: Changing Meanings and Ambitions of Models in Geology," Naomi Oreskes tracks the evolution from explanatory modeling to simulation through a careful study of scientific models in the earth sciences starting with the early eighteenth-century physical analogues used in geology and concluding with climate change simulations. The necessity of her historical analysis was to state that the development and application of simulation for prediction is far from the primary task of knowledge production:

> A significant share of the demand for credible prediction in the earth sciences was generated by the social and political context of nuclear waste disposal and other policy issues. The task of geologists was to build predictive models that could be used to say yea or nay to a proposed repository site. Similarly, the task of much climate modeling, hydrological modeling, geochemical modeling, etc., has been to generate predictions to inform policy decisions.[4]

Within the time frame of this multi-century evolution of scientific modeling is the totalizing reformation of the earth and its atmosphere. As analogues, fictions, simulacra, and simulations, models hold significant power to shape reality.

What follows is a glimpse of the scientific imaginary, the sites and material assemblages that mediate the conception and construction of the landscape through practices of scientific modeling. Embedded within these specific histories of epistemic formation are stories of power, persuasion, and failure. The selection of cases presented call attention to the codification—the systems of ordering and organization—of the physical landscape for the production of knowledge. It is at this intersection between what we know of the landscape and how we intervene that models and design have agency. In their argument that "[models] mediate between theory and the world,"[5] Margaret Morrison and Mary S. Morgan describe the agency of models for design and experiment:

> the power of the model as a design instrument comes not from the fact that it is a replica (in certain respects) of the object to be built; instead the capacity of mathematical/theoretical models to function as design instruments stems from the fact that they provide the kind of information that allows us to intervene in the world.[6]

While there has been much discussion of computation as it relates to simulation and modeling as design methodology, it often falls short in accounting for the multitude of cases in which practices of scientific inquiry and modeling have led to the codification of the landscape across scales and media—already shaping the physical landscape through tools, methodologies, and policies.

Harvard University's Arnold Arboretum

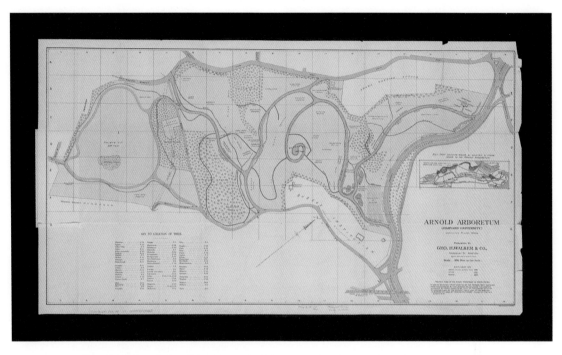

FIGURE 2.0.1 **Geo. H. Walker & Co., "Map of Arnold Arboretum showing location of the trees and shrubs"**
Source: G.H. Walker & Co., 1900[7]

> Every year the destruction of the American forests threatens us with new dangers. Every year renders it more imperative to provide some measures to check the evils which our predecessors in their ignorance have left us as a legacy with which to begin the second century of the Republic.[8]
>
> Charles S. Sargent

The Arnold Arboretum is a collaboration between the *father* of landscape architecture, Frederick Law Olmsted, and Charles S. Sargent, a prominent author, explorer, and silviculturist who specialized in the forests and woods of North America and more broadly the northern hemisphere. Imagined as part of the emerald necklace,

the Arnold Arboretum was devised as "the tree museum of Harvard University . . . in which the University undertook to grow a specimen of every tree and shrub able to support the climate of eastern Massachusetts."[9] In its making, through careful organization and global accessions, the arboretum can be interpreted as a model of the trees of the northern hemisphere within a similar climatic range. Sargent and Olmsted agreed upon the arboretum as a didactic public place, devoted to serving the public alongside scientific endeavors. With careful attention to perceptual and experiential qualities of landscape, as well the potential for scientific study, the Living Collections were planted according to a systematic ordering: "The historic interplay

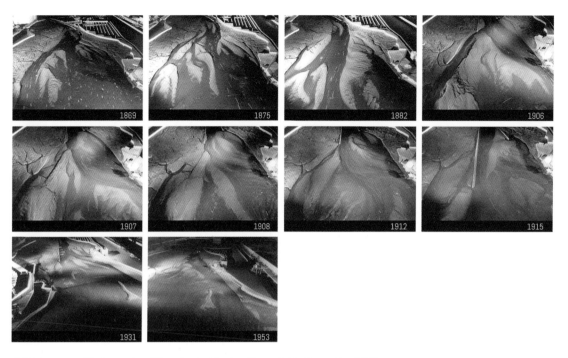

FIGURE 2.0.2 **Photographs of the physical hydraulic model in Grenoble, 1955**
Source: Courtesy of Artelia, formerly SOGRÉAH

between taxonomic, floristic, and cultivated diversities has resulted in one of the most comprehensive and heavily documented collections of temperate woody plants in the world."[10] As one of the longest lasting records of temperate woody plants, the arboretum has unprecedented potential as an experimental landscape.

In addition to his role as director, Sargent published often about the state and future of American forests. As the founding editor of the journal *Garden and Forest: A Journal of Horticulture, Landscape Art and Forestry*, he states that "In no other civilized nation of the world are forests so recklessly managed."[11] In the introduction of "A Few Suggestions On Tree-Planting," a piece Sargent wrote for the Massachusetts State Board of Agriculture urging farmers to plant trees across the agricultural landscape to offset the loss of American forests, he quotes

George P. Marsh's *The Earth as Modified by Human Action*: "it is impossible to suppose that a dense cloud, a sea of vapor, can pass over miles of surface bristling with good conductors without undergoing and producing some change of electrical condition."[12] Through his writings and political position as US Congressman, Marsh proliferated the theory that if forests were removed from the landscape the local climate would dry, leaving an arid, inhospitable landscape. Without a foundation in scientific knowledge, *desiccation theory* had profound effects on local and global forest management.[13] Sargent's advocacy and intent for the Arnold Arboretum to contextually inform scientific and political discourse on the large-scale management of the landscape is apparent in its legacy and current trajectory. Beginning again in the 1970s, the Arnold Arboretum has continued to collect plants from across the world to facilitate and advance research about climate change. While not explicitly stated in the arboretum's current campaign for the living collections, the arboretum is actively being retooled as a living laboratory for both predicting the effects of climate change and planning for the inevitable northern migration of species. This is evident in the arboretum's hope to acquire plants for the purpose of researching "ex situ conservation and study of endangered temperate woody plant taxa" as well as the "successful cultivation of taxa currently or historically perceived as marginally hardy in Boston."[14] A multitude of studies conducted at the arboretum are researching the specificity of climate change effects and adaptation. As the collection continues to grow and diversify, current scientific experimentation will continue to ground itself in archives of scientific observation and physical specimens.

SOGRÉAH's physical hydraulic model of the Seine Estuary

. . . establishing metrics to describe a river's geomorphology is notoriously difficult.[15]

T.J. Coulthard and
M.J. Van De Wiel

One of the earliest, longest lasting, and most significant contributions to the field of physical hydraulic modeling is the modeling of the Seine Estuary. Over a century of annual hydrographic studies, movable bed scaled models, and digital computational models created in Grenoble, France, a hub for hydraulic research, were critical to informing engineering modeling practices across the world.[16] The Seine Estuary is part of the French navigational route for ships

headed upstream to the port of Rouen. In the nineteenth century, intensive siltation, the formation of sills, and shifting channels posed serious navigational challenges along the route and significantly limited ship draft. After the failure of several projects to improve the navigability of the channel, the authorities recognized the potential value that a scaled model might bring. Early hydrographic studies were executed in the area in 1834, "preliminary tests and calibration tests were numerous and complex," and the first scaled movable bed model was built between 1885 and 1895.[17] The original scaled model experiments were conducted with the actual sediments of the Seine Estuary and the infrastructures built based on these early modeling investigations failed owing to the limited body of theory surrounding sediment transport and model similitude. The visual and/or behavioral similarities perceived in the analogue model supported by the transference of materiality and scaled topographic representation ultimately did not achieve the algebraic similarity necessary to reproduce the conditions of the model within the landscape. Although processes observed in controlled laboratory experiments often resemble those in the field, it requires a precise algebraic conversion between prototype and model that has yet to be accomplished for such complex nonlinear systems. While these tests (within the model and the estuary) were considered failures, they provided a foundational framework for physical hydraulic modeling by establishing some of the basic theories of hydraulic movement and sediment transport that have allowed engineers to come close to establishing similitude with later models. In the 1950s, Société Grenobloise d'Études et d'Applications Hydrauliques (SOGRÉAH)[18] used these former studies to pursue a period of trial modeling of the period between 1875 to 1953. The series of trials captured the natural evolution of the estuary (1875 and 1895), infrastructural work on the estuary

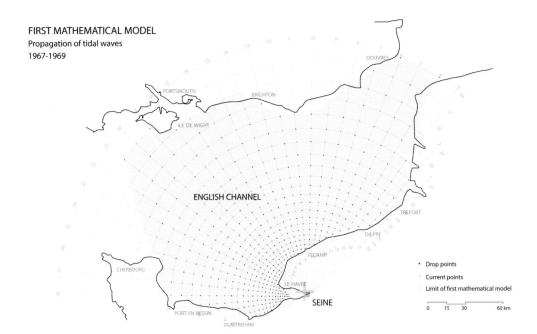

FIRST MATHEMATICAL MODEL
Propagation of tidal waves
1967-1969

SECOND MATHEMATICAL MODEL AND PHYSICAL MODEL
Scope of implications of infrastructure work on the Seine estuary
1967-1969

FIGURE 2.0.3 **Diagrams showing the scope and limitations of the numerical (digital) models**

Drawn by Justine Holzman and Marianne Lafontaine-Chica

(1895–1925), and the effects of the infrastructure on the continued evolution of the estuary (1925–1953). The first trials effectively proved the model to be capable of reproducing the cyclic evolution of the natural process through channel variations which included accurate representation of both global and micro evolutions of the channel systems.[19] The ability to reproduce historical circumstances in a scale model advanced the efficacy of the practice as well as the mathematical theory required for numerical modeling.

International Institute for Sustainable Development's Experimental Lakes Area

There is every reason to believe that the use of small isolated lakes for experimental purposes will immeasurably enhance our knowledge of lakes and the efficacy of specific pollution abatement measures.[20]

Wally E. Johnson and Jack R. Vallentyne

In response to the increasing pollution of the Great Lakes, a pristine area of Kenora District, Ontario, Canada, encompassing 58 freshwater lakes and their respective watersheds, was set aside in 1968 by the Province of Ontario and the Government of

FIGURE 2.0.4 An aerial view of an algal bloom in Lake 227 (Lake 305 in the background) in the Experimental Lakes Area, Kenora District Ontario, Canada

FIGURE 2.0.5 An aerial view of an algal bloom in Lake 226 divided by a curtain in the Experimental Lakes Area, Kenora District Ontario, Canada (right)

Photos courtesy of the IISD Experimental Lakes Area

Canada for the scientific study of anthropogenic influences to freshwater lakes. Designated as the Experimental Lakes Area (ELA), the collection of lakes was parsed and systematically polluted under controlled conditions to measure and better understand the effects of agricultural runoff, household chemicals, industrial pollutants, and other causes of water pollution. The purposeful pollution of the lakes was considered necessary to conduct ecosystem-scale experimentation as well as to develop long-term monitoring of ecosystem processes. Operated by the Fisheries Research Board of Canada, Dr. John Reubec Vallentyne and Dr. W.E. Johnson coordinated and directed the initial experiments at the ELA.[21]

Dr. David W. Schindler, an early hire and long-time director of the ELA, is responsible (among others) for one of the largest contributions to science originating from the ELA—phosphorous as the leading cause of freshwater lake eutrophication over carbon and nitrogen. The first study was undertaken on Lake 227, a lake with naturally low amounts of carbon, in which phosphorous could be identified as the contributing factor. After pushback from industry, the hourglass-shaped Lake 226 was divided into two sections with a thick nylon curtain across its narrows in which controlled amounts of nitrogen and carbon were released in both sides and phosphorous only in the northern section— the bright green algal bloom visibly apparent in Lake 226N unequivocally exposed phosphates as the leading contributor to eutrophication:

> An aerial photograph of this experiment was to become world-renowned. It had more impact on policy making than hours of testimony based on scientific data, helping to convince them that controlling the phosphorous was the key to controlling the eutrophication problem in lakes.[22]

Despite their long track record of scientific inquiry, global recognition in the field of limnology, and tremendous support from the scientific community, the ELA was defunded by Bill C-38[23] in 2012. Activists and scientists questioned the lack of funding as the primary reason for decommissioning the ELA—in addition to implicating various industrial activities in the pollution of the Great Lakes, Dr. David W. Schindler had been conducting experiments starting in 1970 (during the first oil crisis), implicating the contaminated and altered hydrology of the Oil Sands region in Alberta, the effects of acid rain, the increased release of methane from flooded peatlands, and methylmercury in fish (to name a few).[24] The movement to cut funding of the ELA and force its closure or hand off to an organization outside of government was far more likely a political avoidance to accept the policy implications of the scientific findings. After heated public protest and debate, the ELA was handed over to the nongovernmental organization, the International Institute of Sustainable Design (IISD). After their first year of operation, the chair of the IISD-ELA, Scott Vaughan stated the importance of the ongoing experimentation: "Over almost 50 years of lake monitoring, IISD-ELA has been researching the effects of climate change before it even realized its results were attributable to climate change. And what we have discovered is significant."[25]

The South Florida Water Management District's Loxahatchee Impoundment Landscape Assessment (LILA)

Never before in the history of biology has landscape modeling been applied at this scale of restoration.[28]

Fred Sklar et al.

The Loxahatchee Impoundment Landscape Assessment (LILA) is an eco-hydrological landscape scale physical model. Described as a living laboratory, LILA is designed to simulate the water flow and ecological function of the Florida Everglades within the actual landscape for the purpose of scientific experimentation to inform the adaptive management of the Everglades system. Located in the Arthur R. Marshall Loxahatchee National Wildlife Refuge, two 17-hectare (ha) impoundment cells contain various landscape features including tree islands, ridges, sloughs, and deep-water refugia (simulated alligator holes).[29] LILA is part of the Comprehensive Everglades Restoration Plan (CERP), developed by the South Florida Water Management District,

FIGURE 2.0.6 **Aerial image of the Loxahatchee Impoundment Landscape Assessment**

FIGURE 2.0.7 **An aerial view of a mesocosm flume experiment with four dosing channels, a walled control and an unwalled control in an unenriched slough in southern WCA-2A**

Photo by Curtis J. Richardson[26]

the US Army Corps of Engineers, and many other state and federal partners to reengineer more natural variation within hydrologic processes by strategically manipulating the hydroperiod (length of time the marsh is inundated with water), flow rates, and water depths. LILA is used to conduct highly controlled experiments while understanding responses from natural wildlife communities that intersect the model boundaries including free-ranging wading birds, native fish, and invertebrate communities.

As part of the comprehensive Everglades system's ongoing adaptive management activities, the site serves to demonstrate landscape performance as both laboratory and didactic landscape. Using landforms and actual biologic materials, scientists are able to model the Everglades system in incredible detail. The planning and design for LILA began in 2000; construction was completed in 2003, in which 5,736 native trees were established on the land and in the water; and in 2005 scientific studies began. Studies have included "the effect of water depth on wading bird foraging and the effect of water flow on the transport of sediments."[30] Individual landscape features can be studied according to the configuration and installation of sensing devices and practices (which the team refers to as toolboxes), separating tree island projects, ridge and slough projects, and wildlife projects. Specific projects look at tree species survival and growth,[31] the foraging success of wading birds,[32] and habitat selection and movement of fish.

FIGURE 2.0.8 **Fertilizer experiment plots in a slough site in WCA-2B were dosed with nitrogen and phosphorous**

Photo by Curtis J. Richardson[27]

The four leveed containment areas with pumps can be manipulated so as to reflect the current operative capacity of the system of levees and control structures orchestrating the federally mandated flow of water through STAs and water containment areas (WCA).

Conclusion

The brief narrative descriptions of exemplary cases illustrate the breadth of spatial and temporal scales across a range of landscape models. While these descriptions are necessarily provisional, the use of physical computational modeling for the pursuit of landscape knowledge and the application of said knowledge requires closer study. Although methods of scientific modeling in the formation and transformation of the physical environment are significant, Morgan and Morrison have identified a lack of historical documentation in the design and construction of scientific models: "There appear to be no general rules for model construction in the way that we can find detailed guidance on principles of experimental design or on methods of measurement."[33] They attribute this gap to "the creative element involved in model building, it is, some argue, not only a craft but also an art, and thus not susceptible to rules."[34] In addition, the lack of evidence might also be attributed to the autonomy required for the model to both inform theory and the real world. This distance, perhaps craft, is most certainly a project of design. Housed within the sciences, the power and persuasion of models will undoubtedly continue to shape policies, approaches, and opportunities of concern to landscape architecture.

Notes

1. Gabrys, J. *Program Earth: Environmental Sensing Technology and the Making of a Computational Planet*, University of Minnesota Press, 2016, p. 36.

2. Ibid.

3. Smith, P.H. "The History of Science as a Cultural History of the Material World," in Miller, P.N. (ed.) *Cultural Histories of the Material World*, University of Michigan Press, 2013, pp. 210–225.

4. Oreskes, N. "From Scaling to Simulation: Changing Meanings and Ambitions of Models in Geology," in Creager, A.N.H., Lunbeck, E., and Norton Wise, M. (eds.) *Science Without Laws: Model Systems, Cases, Exemplary Narratives*, Duke University Press, 2007, p. 119.

5. Morgan, M.S. and Morrison, M. (eds.) "Models as Mediating Instruments," in *Models as Mediators: Perspectives on Natural and Social Science*, Cambridge University Press, 1999, p. 11.

6. Ibid., p. 23.

7. Digital Commonwealth, http://ark.digitalcommonwealth.org/ark:/50959/3f4636752, accessed April 23, 2017.

8. Sargent, C.S. *A Few Suggestions On Tree-Planting, The Report of the Massachusetts State Board of Agriculture for 1875*.

9. Sargent, C.S. *A Guide to The Arnold Arboretum*, Riverside, 1911.

10. Friedman, W.E., Dosmann, M.S., Boland, T.M., Boufford, D.E., Donoghue, M.J., Gapinski, A., Hufford, L., Meyer, P.W., and Pfister, D.H. "Developing an Exemplary Collection: A Vision for the Next Century at the Arnold Arboretum of Harvard University," *Arnoldia*, 73(3), 1, 2016.

11. Sargent, C.S. "The Future of Our Forests," *Garden and Forest: A Journal of Horticulture, Landscape Art and Forestry*, 1, 25, 1888.

12. Marsh, G.P. *The Earth as Modified by Human Action*, New York, 1874. Quoted by Sargent, C.S. in *A Few Suggestions On Tree-Planting, The Report of the Massachusetts State Board of Agriculture for 1875*.

13. Bennett, B. *Plantations and Protected Areas: A Global History of Forest Management*, MIT Press, 2015.

14. Friedman, W.E., Dosmann, M.S., Boland, T.M., Boufford, D.E., Donoghue, M.J., Gapinski, A., Hufford, L., Meyer, P.W., and Pfister, D.H. "Developing an Exemplary Collection: A Vision for the Next Century at the Arnold Arboretum of Harvard University," *Arnoldia*, 73(3), 1–18, 2016.

15. Coulthard, T.J. and Van De Wiel, M.J. "Modelling River History and Evolution," *Philosophical Transactions of the Royal Society*, A 370, 2123–2142, 2012.

16. Dalmasso, A. "SOGRÉAH (Société Grenobloise D'études et D'applications Hydrauliques) : Du Laboratoire à L'ingénierie Indépendante (1923 – 2010)," *Entreprises et Histoire*, 71, 23–38, 2013.

17. Parthiot, F. "Development of the River Seine Estuary: Case Study," *Journal of Hydraulics Division*, 107, 1283–1301, 1981.

18. SOGRÉAH was formed from the Laboratoire Dauphinois d'Hydraulique of Neyrpic and is now Artelia.

19. Chapon, J. "Intérêt de la Méthode Historique pour les Modèles Réduits à Fond Mobile – Application à l'Estuaire de la Seine," *La Houille Blanche*, special B, 784–792, 1960.

20. Johnson, W.E. and Vallentyne, J.R. "Rationale, Background, and Development of Experimental Lake Studies in Northwestern Ontario," *Journal of the Fisheries Research Board of Canada*, 28, 123–128, 1971.

21. Stokstad, E. "Canada's Experimental Lakes," *Science*, 322(5906), 1316–1319, 2008.

22. Schindler, D.W. "A Personal History of the Experimental Lakes Project," *Canadian Journal of Fisheries and Aquatic Sciences*, 66, 1840, 2009.

23. Bill C-38 is short for "Bill C-38 Jobs, Growth and Long-Term Prosperity Act Cutbacks to Science."

24. Schindler, "A Personal History of the Experimental Lakes Project," 1840.

25. Vaughan, S. *IISD Experimental Lakes Area 2015–2016 Annual Report*, International Institute for Sustainable Development, 2016, www.iisd.org/sites/default/files/publications/iisd-ela-annual-report-2015-2016-spread.pdf

26. Richardson, C.J. "The Everglades Experiments: Lessons for Ecosystem Restoration," *Ecological Studies*, 201, Plate 7, Springer, 2008.

27. Richardson, C.J. "The Everglades Experiments: Lessons for Ecosystem Restoration," *Ecological Studies*, 201, Plate 8, Springer, 2008.

28. This quote relates to a study of the many environmental models being developed for the Everglades and the need for a model like LILA. Sklar, F.H., Fitz, H.C., Wu, Y., Van Zee, R., and McVoy, C. "South Florida: The Reality of Change and the Prospects for Sustainability: The Design of Ecological Landscape Models for Everglades Restoration," *Ecological Economics*, 37, 380, 2001.

29. *Everglades Project – Loxahatchee Impounded Landscape Assessment (LILA)*, South Florida Water Management District.

30. *LILA: Loxahatchee Impoundment Landscape Assessment: An Everglades Living Laboratory Student Booklet*, South Florida Water Management District, October 2008.

31. Stoffella, S.L., Ross, M.S., Sah, J.P., Price, M.P., Sullivan, P.L., Cline, A.E., and Scinto, L.J. "Survival and Growth Responses of Eight Tree Species along a Hydrologic Gradient on Two Tree Island Types," *Applied Vegetation Science*, 13, 439–449, 2010.

32. Lantz, S.M. et al., "The Effects of Water Depth and SAV on the Foraging Success of Wading Birds," *The Condor*, 112(3), 460–469, 2010.

33. Morgan and Morrison (eds.), *Models as Mediators*, p. 12.

34. Ibid.

An enquiry into atmosphere

Contributors:

Jillian Walliss
Senior Lecturer in Landscape Architecture, the University of Melbourne

Heike Rahmann
Lecturer, RMIT University

02.01
Computational design methodologies

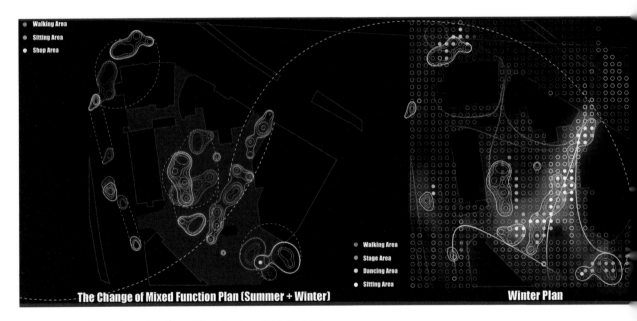

FIGURE 2.1.1 *New atmospheric conditions for inserting program*
Source: Tengxiao Liu, Yaxi Ye, Yingxuan Huang, Zheichen Tang

Unprecedented temperatures have occurred regularly over the past three years, with the global temperatures experienced in the northern and southern hemispheres during 2016 declared the hottest on record. While the longer-term effects of climate changes remain largely undiscernible to human perception and senses, the magnitude of these changes manifest noticeably in data that highlight temperature peaks and intensities. Vast volumes of real-time temperature readings are increasingly informing the future planning and design of our cities, central to both understanding the implications of climate change and establishing the solution. This climatic information contributes to what is considered big data, an extensive collection of dynamic information that is continuously being generated.

Accompanying the production of big data are new epistemological approaches for analysing data and defining problems. Big data offers landscape architecture great potential for engaging with dynamic systems and processes, supplementing the limitations of representational techniques such as mapping and the diagram. However, to work effectively with data requires an interrogation of how this unprecedented access to information shifts design processes and methodologies. While landscape architecture has a long history of spatial analysis, it is less positioned to work effectively with systems and data.

With a focus on heat and atmosphere, this essay discusses the potential of big and small data explored through the computational to inform transformative research-driven design techniques for engaging with climate change. This is demonstrated through the outcomes of design studios run at the University of Melbourne and RMIT University over the summer of 2015–2016, which challenged students to move beyond the application of generic mediation techniques to produce novel material, spatial and programmatic interventions.

Drawing on selected work, we highlight the value of computational design methodologies in offering time-based investigations in which change is implicit through the active composition of behaviours and relationships. In this new context, the designer adopts an experimental process, establishing

interdependencies and relationships between information, phenomena and systems across micro and macro scales. Rather than prescribe solutions, these research-driven design methodologies present 'a controlled discovery,' offering productive techniques for engaging with the unpredictability of climate change.[1]

A new data-driven epistemology for landscape architecture

Considered a 'disruptive innovation', the era of big data has radically altered epistemologies across all disciplines. Big data refers to rapidly evolving data sets characterised by volume, velocity and variety,[2] which have been made possible through technological innovations such as cameras, the Internet and remote sensing. Big data, often generated in real time, offers a variety of medium such as images, text and statistics, and most importantly is unfiltered. Access to this volume of information is unprecedented, and therefore demands new ways of thinking about data.

In his insightful 2014 essay 'Big Data, new epistemologies and paradigm shifts', Kitchin offers a valuable critique of how this new form of empiricism, driven by big data and data analytics, is reconfiguring research within science and the humanities.[3] For science, the phenomenon of big data has inspired some to declare the emergence of a fourth science paradigm, premised on the potential of data to reveal new knowledge free of theory. In a challenge to the traditions of scientific deduction, this paradigm claims that empiricism highlights patterns and relationships beyond the prior knowledge of the researcher, thereby producing new knowledge without guidance from theory,

hypothesis or domain specific expertise.[4]
In a less radical interpretation, a data-driven science maintains a scientific method but is more responsive to:

> a hybrid combination of abductive, inductive and deductive approaches to advance the understanding of a phenomena, extracting new insights that 'knowledge-driven science' fails to produce.[5]

The influence of big data within humanities and social science, observes Kitchin, is less clear. Certainly big data offers the possibilities to develop more detailed and nuanced analysis that can be valuable in refining theoretical knowledge concerning the spatial and social world.[6] However, emerging critique of the digital humanities and computational social science highlights the danger of an overly reductionist surface analysis that may identify new patterns but lacks an ability to explain them if approached without theoretical grounding.

Given this response from science and humanities, how might big data influence the analytical processes and creative practices of design, and landscape architecture more particularly?

The extensive research and design policy generated by the urban heat island (UHI) phenomenon offers a cautionary tale on the potentials and dangers of using big data to inform mediation strategies. Mitigation strategies, which have emerged across numerous global cities, emphasize general recommendations such as increasing vegetation within the city through green walls, roofs and urban forestry, along with the use of high albedo surfaces. However, research suggests that many of these design guidelines may not achieve the desired large-scale outcomes[7] as interventions have far greater consequence on microclimatic conditions: roof top plantings may increase night-time temperatures; 'cool' roofs can slow wind and limit rain precipitation; green infrastructure on buildings has minimal impact on thermal comfort at street level; while extensive tree-planting can actually increase humidity. Consequently researchers are beginning to warn against a 'one size fits all' approach to climate change mediation.

We argue that these generalisations owe much to the scale of data used to understand and define the UHI problem, which in turn influences the subsequent mediation strategies. These recommendations are often established at the scale of the city – frequently through the consideration of a single factor. For example, a recent Melbourne study focusing on the cooling potential of vegetation found that average summer temperatures could be reduced up to 0.5 degrees Celsius by increasing the vegetation cover in Melbourne's existing urban fabric, and up to two degrees Celsius if the entire city were replaced by forest parkland.[8] The clearly defined outcomes of these single factor studies make them highly influential in determining subsequent policy and design guidelines. However, in this case they offer a very broad understanding of heat, with modelling developed for an uninhabited city. For example, reducing the heat of a city is a different question to that of improving the thermal comfort of people, which instead requires the consideration of related factors such as humidity, wind and shade. An increase in vegetation might decrease some aspects of urban heat but may also contribute to higher humidity levels or decrease wind movement, thereby affecting the thermal comfort at street level.

Some of these limitations can be traced to the considerable challenges of running complex simulation at the scale of the city. Nonetheless, given the future impact of climate change and our increasing levels of urbanisation, it is important to move beyond generalised outcomes to instead engage more comprehensively with the complex spatial and ecological realities of the city. It is here that research-driven design methodologies, which can interrogate and engage with multiple scales of big and small data fluidly (non-hierarchically), along with the relationships between multiple factors, become important.

So how might we construct data-driven design methodologies that engage with the complex issue of heat?

For designers it becomes useful to shift emphasis from a specialised focus on data analytics as explored in science to a broader interrogation of the behaviours of systems informed by a combination of simulation, design theory, and existing scientific research.

From analytics to behaviour

Working with computational fluid dynamics, simulation, and real-time data, designers can now engage with largely invisible climatic phenomena such as heat, humidity, and wind. A new generation of designers inspired by the critical writing by scholars such as Latour, De Landa, and Sloterdijk are departing from an architectural focus on surface to question the environmental and social politics of air quality, the bio-politics of atmosphere, the individual's relationship to modified environments, and the fundamental premise of space as bounded territory or surface.[9]

Designers such as Philippe Rahm and Sean Lally provide important precedents for how landscape architects might engage with atmospheric behaviour, challenging the separation of external and internal boundaries to instead redefine spaces as intensities of phenomena and energy.

These concepts shift from comfort and efficiency as the indicator of success to the consideration of the amplification of material energies.[10] 'Material energies,' states Lally, 'are defined by waves and particles, producing boundary edges that behave more like a gradient of intensities and fallouts, and less like lines, points or surfaces.'[11] Accordingly, concepts of climate mediation are replaced by the ambition to strengthen and augment climatic phenomena such as solar radiation, pressure, and humidity.[12] No longer viewed as constraints, these phenomena are transformed into the very material of design.

The consideration of atmospheric behaviours directly within design processes is made possible through the computational, which offers a major shift from the site investigation techniques of maps or diagrams favoured in landscape architecture. Mapping offers 'a visual representation of information and position the designer to respond to what is already known or what can be visually discerned'.[13] In contrast, computational simulations model knowledge based on measurable data, 'requiring the active identification of specific parameters or conditions and an understanding of their relations to each other'.[14]

The value of simulations in engaging with relationships and behaviours is clearly demonstrated in a landscape architecture master's project, which aimed to modify the extremely humid streetscape of Singapore's premier shopping street, Orchard Road.[15] Research sourced from scientific journals highlighted the negative effect of traditional linear street tree-planting in increasing air temperature (owing to the reduced wind speed), as well as the potential for tree coverage to raise humidity levels.

Working parametrically with Rhino, Grasshopper, and small and big data, it was possible to optimize tree placement for

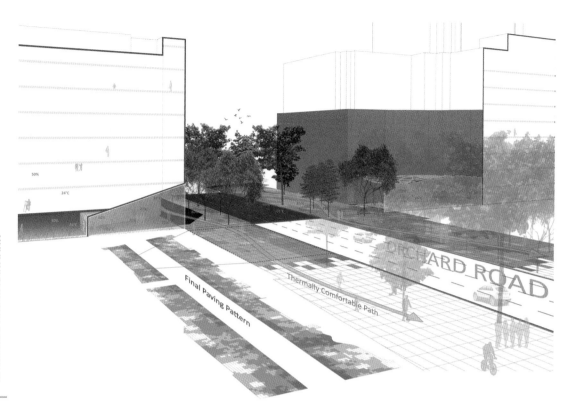

Final Paving Pattern

Thermally Comfortable Path

ORCHARD ROAD

FIGURE 2.1.2 **Defining a thermally comfortable path for pedestrians along Orchard Road, Singapore**
Source: Jason Toh

maximum shade but with minimum tree coverage to allow uninterrupted airflow. In a second phase, this new street tree-planting scheme was reconsidered in conjunction with the different albedo effects of paving colour to further increase air circulation along the street. Central to the Grasshopper definition was a matrix of weightage that placed more value on certain effects over others in different locations. For example, lighter coloured pavers were placed under trees to achieve the effect of drawing air away from the trees, while darker shades of pavers were placed nearer to the road to encourage air movement towards the centre, aiding in its dispersal.

Through simulation and parametric tools, it is now possible to derive the most thermally comfortable path that emerges from the aggregates of these design strategies. Adopted as the foundation for street design, further design interventions can be introduced to enhance pedestrian comfort along this optimum path (shown in Figure 2.1.2) such as the programmatic use of the space and the location of street furniture and gathering points.

In a further example, this time engaging with Melbourne's hot Mediterranean climate, students used Grasshopper and real-time data (wind speed data and radiant temperature) to develop a dynamic simulation, which translates temperature data into zones of thermal comfort levels – a parameter of more relevance to designers.[16] Altering the different parameters within the simulation facilitates the identification of strategic points, where the designer had most potential to achieve maximum effect. The design develops through the manipulation of these specific climatic points, resulting in a new atmospheric condition in which to then consider questions of program and other aspects of experience and function (Figure 2.1.1).

Common to both of these design methodologies is the understanding of dynamic climatic site behaviours, and most importantly the identification of the greatest potential for manipulation and effect. This approach is best articulated by Keith VanDerSys, who uses modelling to reveal shifts in the magnitude and speed of systems that are 'representative of processes that have material consequences'.[17] Influenced by ecologist Gregory Bateson, simulations aid VanDerSys to uncover 'a difference that makes a difference', identifying conditions, behaviours, and forces of greatest degree of change in which to intervene.[18]

Returning to the question of epistemologies, data, and design, we can start to see how landscape architects might respond to big data – not to declare new knowledge but instead to develop more complex understandings of dynamic site conditions. For example, all of the simulations discussed so far draw on the review of related scientific literature to establish the parameters for simulation, i.e. thermal comfort index, research on tree performance, or the albedo effect of paving. This approach represents a shift from implicit to explicit knowledge facilitating the incorporation of scientific knowledge directly within design processes. The dynamic nature of the system is then tested drawing on big and small data, combined with particular software. This process is somewhat aligned with Kitchin's conclusions regarding the use of big data within social science, where he states:

it is possible to think of new epistemologies that do not dismiss or reject Big Data analytics, but rather employ the methodological approach of data-driven science within a different epistemological framing that enables social scientists to draw valuable insights from Big Data that are situated and reflexive.[19]

For designers, the possibility of drawing on data crossing micro and macro scales offers an unprecedented ability to understand site as part of much larger forces, continuum, and dynamic influences. This fundamentally expands the discipline's conceptualisation of context, temporally and spatially. However, what becomes critical in engaging with this broader realm is the identification of what computer scientist Chris Leckie defines as a 'high value' problem. He comments that our unprecedented access to data demands a high level of critical thinking, requiring us to move from a vast amount of data to 'pick out the interesting or unusual events that are worth exploring and then filter them down to high value problems'.[20] Big data and simulation therefore only become useful to a designer at the point when data is transformed into valuable knowledge.

An explicit intent is central to this ability to find value in these computationally driven design methodologies. This is highlighted further in the following discussion, where we introduce design approaches shaped by the health imperatives to protect vulnerable members of society from heat and other atmospheric conditions such as pollution.

Designing for the vulnerable

In 2003, a heat wave across Europe accounted for a total 35,000 deaths from causes attributed to prolonged exposure to extreme heat, with the largest casualties among the elderly population reported in France, Germany and Italy. While many places are better adapted to hotter temperatures and frequent occurrence of heat waves, unusual extremes nevertheless pay a toll. For example, the record-breaking four-day heat wave in January 2014 severely affected Melbourne's population and economy, with an estimated 167 excess deaths[21] and an estimated loss of revenue of AUD 37 million from businesses in the Melbourne Metropolitan area.[22] These events are set to become increasingly common in Melbourne, prompting demands for the design of urban heat refuges for the young and the elderly.

To engage with our rapidly evolving atmosphere, understood as a 'result of complex interaction between natural and anthropogenic environmental conditions',[23] designers are required to work with meteorological and chemical aspects that link spatial with material performances. These material studies can be applied across a range of scales from the exploration of environmental patterns at a city level, climatic simulations within a neighbourhood, to material explorations at site scale. In the case of heat-related deaths, high

temperatures alone are not as important as the length of the heat wave and extreme night temperatures. These later factors relate to the manner in which material interacts with heat, influenced by 'different radiation and heat budget due to the physical properties of construction material, like heat capacity and thermal conductivity'.[24]

Within architecture, the investigation into material behaviour and effect has a long tradition, driven by the notion of purging hot air at night to cool the building. Investigations into the physical properties of construction material such as thermal mass and heat transfer also provide a vital opportunity for landscape architecture to respond to the UHI phenomena, expanding the repertoire beyond the addition of green infrastructure such as green roofs and street trees. Instead, an engagement with thermodynamics and materiality offers new approaches for future-proofing the design of the public domain in hot climates, as demonstrated in the following design speculation located in the outer suburbs of Melbourne.

Through the analysis of real-time data collected on site through i-button sensors, students discovered an anomaly in climatic

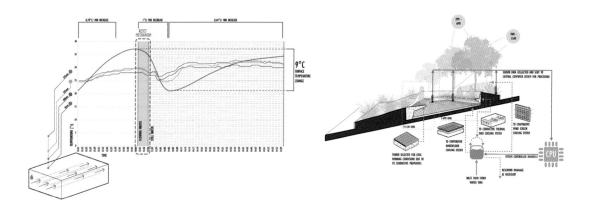

FIGURE 2.1.3 **'Reset Pods', testing material behaviour and system**
Source: Ravi Bessabava and Lillian Szumer

behaviours, where the air temperature at certain locations would significantly drop for an extended period of time despite the overall trend of rising temperatures. The cause of this temperature drop was never fully established. However this observation prompted further investigations into the potential for material effects to interrupt the building up of heat, acting to 'reset the external spaces' and thereby preventing spaces reaching maximum temperatures.[25]

Starting with an investigation into the thermal mass of different surface materials such as concrete, brick, steel, timber and vegetation, a series of physical experiments was developed to explore passive cooling techniques by altering the material performance in regard to conduction, convection and radiation. CFD simulation and parametric environmental modeling facilitated the testing of a design intervention capability (Figure 2.1.2) to enhance comfort levels at strategic locations within the site, without the need to cool down the entire outdoor space.

The relationship between material performance and the body remains one of the most interesting factors in the design of outdoor spaces as surfaces with high surface temperatures emit long wave radiation, while the human body absorbs 'nearly all long wave radiation'.[26] As such, surface temperature has a direct impact on the heat gain in the human body, which, regulated to 37 degrees Celsius, allows for only very little deviation. Thus heat gain in the body is of special concern when designing places for the vulnerable members of the community, including the elderly and people with medical or mental health conditions. For example, research shows that people with dementia face an increased risk of temperature-related death during heat waves owing to the impairment of cognitive, mental, and physical capability to process information and to regulate body temperatures.

Moving between various scales at which these atmospheres can be experienced, a 2016 landscape architecture design studio at RMIT University explored the link between climatic experience and the design of urban landscapes responding to the aging population, which will see a doubling of dementia sufferers in Australia between now and 2040.

Many of the symptoms commonly experienced by people with early onset dementia such as short-term memory loss, a decline in the ability to retrace steps, and confusion with time or place directly affect a person's ability to navigate spatially. Working with these conditions, students explored new morphologies for a 20ha urban development site in Melbourne, which would improve spatial navigation, offer multiple sensorial stimulations, heighten comfort levels and support independent movement. In the second phase, these morphological explorations were paired with considerations of urban density and spatial orientation along the cardinal directions to investigate the impact of the new urban fabric on the climatic experience of outdoor spaces.

Utilizing computational modelling and simulation techniques, including CFD modelling and Grasshopper plug-ins, projects foregrounded the understanding of atmosphere as perceived space, experienced through 'material energies' that diversify the climatic experience to a multitude of 'stimuli and information'[27] the human body can respond to. Informed by scientific and human research, the projects exposed serious limitations in the repetitive street layout of Melbourne's current urban grid, which proves to be disorientating and discomforting to people experiencing early onset dementia. In addition, the central grid facilitates extreme heat build-up in the summer months, as hot air remains trapped at street level.[28] Simulations further highlighted the ineffectiveness of street trees in providing relief from heat stress, with little shade

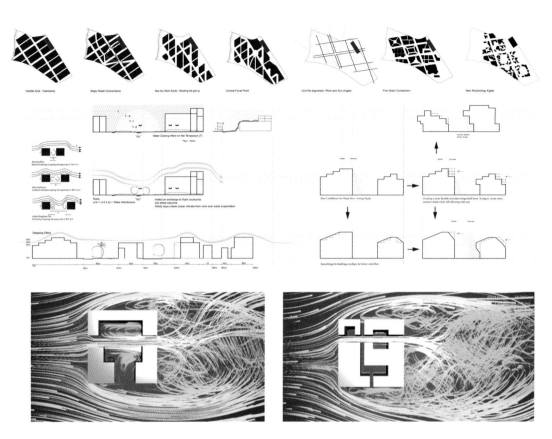

FIGURE 2.1.4 **Using data, scientific research and simulation to test the link between outdoor climate and built form across scales**

Sources: top: Joshua Groenewald, bottom: Luong Xuan Khoi

provided during the late afternoon hours when temperatures reach their peak in the city.

Expanding the performance of atmospheric qualities through a data-driven design process guided the development of diverse densities and block configurations to facilitate better airflow conditions and differentiated spatial and climatic experiences. This more climatically responsive urban fabric shown in Figure 2.1.3 also allowed for an intensification of green spaces to create additional climatic buffers (e.g. by retaining moisture, providing shade and changing wind patterns), recreational facilities, and

opportunities to enhance the overall way-finding and legibility of the urban environment.

These design explorations highlight the potential of the computational and real-time data to encourage novel design responses that extend beyond the application of standard design guidelines proposed for our urban spaces. Drawing directly on the research that informs guidelines, the designer can explore site-specific responses that bridge the urban morphological scale with the experience of inhabitation. This potential is further demonstrated in our final example, which focuses on the major issue of air pollution in China.

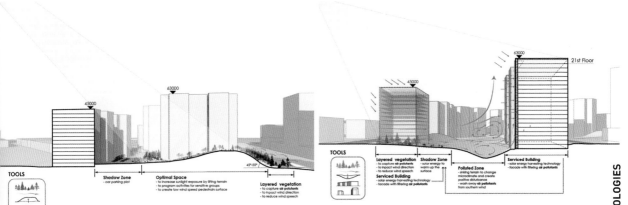

FIGURE 2.1.5 **"Polluted City: A Meteorological Driven Design Approach for Beijing"**
Source: Junya Yu

Air pollution is challenging the design of healthier cities, especially in developing countries. In the case of China, rapid industrial growth over the past decades has accelerated the increase in air pollution in almost every major city, affecting now over 700 million people. With pollution reaching unprecedented levels that dwarfed ambitions to meet environmental standards, Premier Li Kequiang declared in 2014 a 'war on pollution',[29] bringing the discussion to parliament following fears that environmental crisis could lead to social unrest.[30] One year later, Chinese journalist Jing Cai's compelling documentary *Under the Dome* exposed publicly the devastating health consequences of pollution in China, particularly for the young.[31]

This documentary formed the provocation for a recent University of Melbourne master's thesis in design, which explored the potential to reduce pollution exposure in a new residential suburb planned for the Daxing district of southern Beijing.[32] Focusing on the everyday residential environment, the project aims to work across multiple scales to leverage the combined effects of site planning, open space design and materiality

to reduce resident exposure to pollution. Beginning with GIS, the plug-in Airflow Analyst and data accessed from a Beijing monitoring station (made available by a visiting Chinese professor), the optimum configuration and heights for standard Chinese residential buildings was explored. Decisions were premised on encouraging favourable pollution dispersing northern wind speeds maintained between 7–10 m/s, minimising the problematic southern winds that funnel pollution into the site and maximising solar access for residential buildings.

Importantly, the move into more detailed design investigations was not a linear progression. Once the configuration of the buildings was established, a different question drove the next set of design decisions, beginning with an investigation into which times of year and times of day result in the highest pollution exposure. This bringing together of two temporal scales – that of the yearly pollution fluctuations with the 24-hour cycle of Chinese life – revealed that, while air pollution levels reach their highest levels during winter nights (when people are largely inside), the daytime pollution levels are much lower during the day in summer. Here we see the difference between making a decision around maximums versus understanding the relationship between pollution levels and people's day-to-day behaviours. This observation formed the basis for establishing an open space strategy shown in Figure 2.1.4 based on 'warming' winter spaces primarily through the insertion of a large mound to maximise exposure to winter sun. This space was also designed to function well in summer. Functional uses such as car parking were placed in less healthy areas of the site, while in the most polluted areas spaces were designed for no inhabitation and acted as pollution traps incorporating smart pollution diminishing materials in the facades.

Conclusion

Pressing issues of climate change and air pollution provide an increasing demand for landscape architects to engage with the complex and challenging environmental conditions of the next millennium. Computational design methods capable of linking big and small data to spatial settings offer exciting new opportunities for design, moving away from broad-brush problem-solving approaches to instead facilitating a more experimental and data-driven design process. This highly creative process is underpinned by a critical analytics, requiring designers to define where they can make a difference.

The projects discussed in this essay highlight how this process evolves through the constant redefinition of the problem, gained through the use of simulation, data and supporting scientific research. In no way are simulations offering the solution. Instead the designers are curating the process, developing greater insights through each exploration and gaining more knowledge about where they can have agency and

impact. This ability to define the point of intervention (spatially and temporally) is particularly important when engaging with atmospheric conditions such as heat waves and pollution. Given the complexity of climate change, it is impossible to directly affect the extremes of these phenomena, which are tied into broader global concerns such as global emissions and deforestation. However, as designers it is possible to tactically interrupt, heighten, or minimise different aspects of these conditions as they play out at the scale of site. Through the abstraction of environmental processes, behaviours, and relationships, computational tools afford a seamless transition between the macro and the micro scales, transforming the notion of atmosphere as constraint to instead a perceivable material space.

Notes

1. Walliss, J. and Rahmann, H. 'The Experimental Nature of Simulation', *LA+ Simulations*, Fall 2016, 41.

2. Ward, J.S. and Barker, A. *Undefined By Data: A Survey of Big Data Definitions*, http://arxiv.org/abs/1309.5821

3. Kitchin, R. 'Big Data, New Epistomologies and Paradigm Shifts', *Big Data & Society*, 1, 1–15, 2014.

4. Ibid., pp. 3–5.

5. Ibid., pp. 5–6.

6. Ibid., p. 7.

7. Hoag, H. 'How Cities Can Beat the Heat', *Nature: International Weekly Journal of Science*, August, 2015.

8. Chen, D., Thatcher, M, Wang, X., Barnett, G., Kachenko, A., and Prince, R. 'Summer Cooling Pontial of Urban Vegetation – A Modeling Study for Melbourne, Australia', *Environmental Science*, 2(3), 656, 2015.

9. Velikov, K., Thun, G., and Ripley, C. 'Thick Air', *Journal of Architectural Education*, 65(2), 71, 2012.

10. Lally, S. *The Air from Other Planets: A Brief History of Architecture to Come*, Lars Muller, 2014, p. 105.

11. Ibid., p. 9.

12. Ibid., p. 108.

13. Walliss and Rahmann, 'The Experimental Nature of Simulation', p. 42.

14. Ibid.

15. Toh, J. *A New Thermal Condition for Orchard Road, Singapore*, Faculty of Architecture, Building and Planning: University of Melbourne, 2015.

16. Liu, T., Ye, Y, Huang, Y, and Tang, Z. 'New Atmospheres', in *MSD Summer Heat Elective*, University of Melbourne, 2015.

17. VanDerSys, K. *Interview at the University of Pennsylvania Philadelphia*, 2014.

18. Ibid.

19. Kitchin, 'Big Data, New Epistomologies and Paradigm Shifts', pp. 9–10.

20. Leckie, C. 'The "Big Data" Gold Rush: Mining Data for a Smarter Melbourne', http://eng.unimelb.edu.au/events/professorial/chris-leckie/

21. Victorian Auditor General, *Heatwave Management: Reducing the Risk to Public Health*, 2014.

22. Jones, L. and MacLachlan, B. *2014 Heatwave Business Impacts – Social Research. C. O. Melbourne*, City of Melbourne, 2014.

23. Parlow, E. 'Urban Climate', in Niemelä, J. (ed.) *Urban Ecology: Patterns, Processes, and Applications*, Oxford University Press, 2011, p. 42.

24. Ibid. p. 31.

25. Bessabava, R. and Szumer, L. 'Reset Pods', in *MSD Summer Heat Elective*, University of Melbourne, 2015.

26. Parlow, 'Urban Climate', p. 42.

27. Lally, *The Air from Other Planets*, p. 96.

28. Groenewald, J. and Khoi, L.X. 'E-Gate: Inclusive City of the Future', in *Upper Pool Landscape Architecture Design Research Studio 'Hot to Cold'*, RMIT University, 2016.

29. Stutts, J. 'Smog is the Enemy #1 in China's "War on Pollution"', http://foreignpolicyblogs.com/2014/03/25/smog-is-enemy-1-in-chinas-war-on-pollution/

30. Martina, M. Hui, L., Stanway, D., Reklev, S., Blanchard, B., Stanway, D., Gopalakrishnan, R., and Birsel, R. *China to 'Declare War' on Pollution, Premier Says*, www.reuters.com/article/us-china-parliament-pollution-idUSBREA2405W20140305, accessed November 28, 2017.

31. Jing, C. *Under the Dome*, 2015.

32. Yu, J. *Polluted City: A Meterological Driven Design Approach for a Beijing*, Faculty of Architecture, Building and Planning, University of Melbourne, 2016.

Contributor:

Joseph Claghorn
*Leibniz University
Hannover*

02.02

Agent-based models to reveal underlying landscape structure

Agent-based modeling background

The design of sequences and systems of movement is one of the key tasks of landscape architectural design. The pattern of walks and ways is often, at least in plan view, the most distinctive and characteristic element of a landscape composition or style—the meandering paths of the English garden vs. the axial geometries of the Baroque being well-known examples of this. The imposition of an incompatible system of geometries onto a site, however, can often lead to problems, especially when the subtle structures of the existing landscape are not adequately accounted for. Paths going through low-lying areas often fall victim to chronic drainage problems. In other landscapes, the system of paths as envisioned by the designer fails to correspond to how users actually navigate the landscape, as evidenced by the emergence of "desire paths" in many parks, gardens, campuses, and urban spaces. On steeper sites, it is also possible that the intended composition of the landscape architect does not allow for accessible paths of movement, and when considered late in the design process the problem can sometimes only be resolved with zigzagging ramps with unsightly and expensive railings.

Many of these problems can be productively addressed with a relatively recent approach to analyze and reveal subtle and underlying landscape structures and patterns: the computational paradigm known as agent-based modeling. This paradigm, closely tied to the computational development of artificial intelligence, has become quite popular in disciplines throughout the natural and social sciences. In general, agent-based models seek to reveal underlying and complex bottom-up patterns and structures based on the interaction of agents among themselves and with their environment. An early proponent for the use of agent-based models in the spatial design disciplines was the architect Stan Allen, who described the emergent patterns created by some of the first simple computer agents—Craig Reynolds' "Boids"—in his influential essay "From Object to Field" (1997), although he gave no specific examples of adapting this process to an actual design problem. A small handful of architectural theorists have, from time to time, revisited the use of agents for understanding complex urban and landscape dynamics, but their application to site scale design problems remains limited.

The problem and process

In this example, a simple agent-based approach is used to analyze the topography of a site to reveal potential paths of movement that do not exceed a maximum allowable slope. The most practical use of

such an analysis is for the design of a network of paths that meets jurisdictional requirements for accessibility, but such an approach also can ensure that the greatest number of users can traverse a path network comfortably. In general, any agent-based model is comprised of three elements: first, the agents themselves have a series of defined attributes and behaviors; second, the agents have a series of relationships that define how and with whom they interact; and, third, the model has an environment with which the agents interact (Macal, 152). In this example, the environment is a 3D topographical surface modeled in Rhino. In this particular case, the agents do not interact with other agents but only with their environment based on a few rules defined using the scripting engine Grasshopper together with the looping plug-in Anemone.

Three very simple parameters will govern the agent's movement. The first is the maximum vertical rise or slope for a specific horizontal run that the agent is allowed to travel. To study accessible paths, for example, this value could be set at 1:20 but other values could be tested to explore other phenomena. The second parameter is the amount of random deviation the agent will be allowed from its current heading. A third parameter is the step size or distance the agent travels with each iteration of the loop. Smaller step sizes will increase the accuracy of the simulation but will also increase the time needed to run.

At the start of the simulation, a predefined number of agents are randomly populated on the terrain, although these can be placed at specific points as well. The simulation then draws a cylinder with a radius equal to the step size, and with a height equal to the maximum allowable slope (rise) in both an up and down direction. The simulation then performs a Boolean intersect operation between the terrain surface modeled in Rhino and the cylinder. The resulting intersection arc (or arcs) represents possible directions of movement for the agent. The simulation prioritizes movement in the current direction with a bit of randomness by tentatively moving the agent one-half of the step size with a vector determined by the agent's current position and previous position, with an optional random deviation slightly to the left or right.

The agent movement for each round is then fixed by taking the closest point on the arcs of possible movement to this tentative movement point (Figures 2.2.2 and 2.2.3). The process is then repeated as many times as desired, with an optional curve drawn between the agent locations at each time step to show the overall path (Figure 2.2.4).

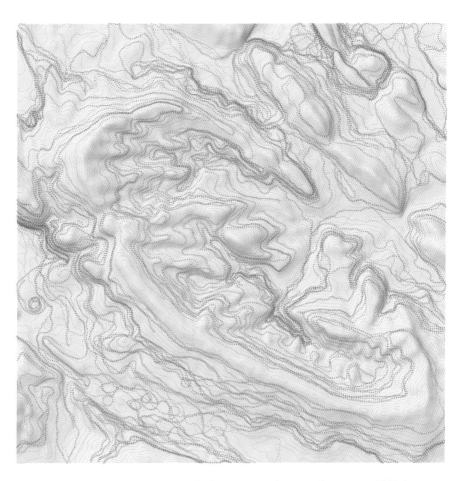

FIGURE 2.2.1 **Traces of a population of 100 agents moving over the course of 300 time steps. More recent traces are colored with a larger plus sign, while older traces gradually fade and get smaller. The amount of movement in each step represents 0.5 percent of the total width of the simulation. This simulation is run on an area derived from the topography of a 16x16km area near Delligsen, Germany**

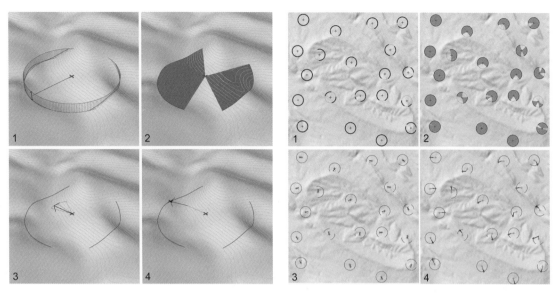

FIGURE 2.2.2 **The basic steps of the algorithm. 1) Cylinder is drawn based on step size and rise/run parameter. 2) Boolean intersection between cylinder edge and surface represents the range of possible movement. 3) A preliminary step is determined based on the previous heading, with an allowed random deviation. 4) The next agent step is determined by finding the nearest point on the curve or curves associated with the agent point**

FIGURE 2.2.3 **Results in plan view of one step of the algorithm run for 20 agents. Here the step size is set to a high value for clarity**

Results and reflection

In the flatter areas of the site, no ideal or preferred structure may be evident, but other areas reveal clear preferred corridors of movement. Depending on the topographical surface as well as the boundaries of the site, it may also be apparent that certain parts of the site cannot be easily or practically connected with an accessible path (Figure 2.2.1). These may point to areas of the site where some topographical manipulation could be desirable. Additionally, the tests were run with a random population of agents, but it may also be desirable to start the agents at key points on the site, such as near existing or proposed entries to the site, or at key points on the site that need to be accessed. More complex rules can refine and improve the process further. Combined with a simulation of the water network on the site, for example, the agents could be programmed to avoid areas of excess water accumulation. In general, however, such models do not "design" the path network of the site—they only point to possibilities, and it is then up to the designer to incorporate this understanding into an understanding of the project's goals.

Such a simple process, however, can reveal underlying structures in a meaningful way. As a small test of a landscape that is familiar to many, the script was run on a topographical model of the Iberian Peninsula and the south of France to speculate as to

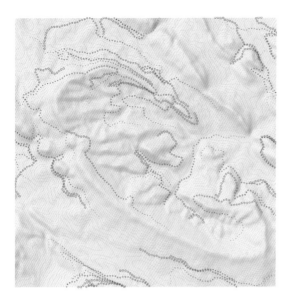

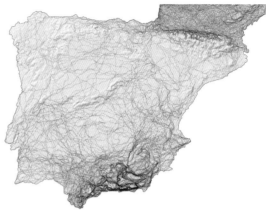

FIGURE 2.2.4 **Traces of the 20 agents after 60 iterations of the algorithm. Smaller circles represent older traces**

FIGURE 2.2.5 **Results of a quick study on a topography derived from the Iberian Peninsula: 150 agents are populated in southern France, while 150 agents are populated along the coast of southern Spain closest to North Africa. The dominant agents in each region correspond very closely to the regions of control after the initial Islamic conquest and before the period of the Reconquista**

how historical corridors of movement may have formed (Figure 2.2.5). Interestingly, a clear corridor of movement emerges along the northern coast of the peninsula, linking it to the south of France. Those familiar with the history of the peninsula will recognize this emergent path as the Way of Saint James, a popular pilgrimage route in the Middle Ages. This, along with Barcelona, was also the only part of the peninsula that retained strong cultural links to the rest of Western Europe, while the southern and central parts of the peninsula were under Moorish rule with strong links to North Africa. Such models, developed to a more advanced degree, have been influential in the historical study of landscapes and effects of the collective acts of actors through time (Mlekuz, 7–8). Perhaps such models will also be helpful as to how we understand and design the landscapes of the future.

References

Allen, S. "From Object to Field," *AD (Architectural Design)*, 67 (May–June), 24–31, 1997.

Macal, C.M. and North, M.J. "Tutorial on Agent-Based Modeling and Simulation," *Journal of Simulation*, 4, 151–162, 2010.

Mlekuz, D. "Exploring the Topography of Movement," in Polla, S. and Verhagen, P. (eds.), *Computational Approaches to the Study of Movement in Archaeology. Theory, Practice and Interpretation of Factors and Effects of Long Term Landscape Formation and Transformation*, De Gruyter, 2014, pp. 5–22.

02.03

Open-source mapping

Landscape perception, participatory design and user-generated content; collecting user-generated walking and biking route preference data through repurposed apps, custom coding, and open-source mapping tools

Contributor:

Christopher J. Seeger, PLA, GISP
Professor and Extension Specialist, Department of Landscape Architecture, Iowa State University

How a user perceives or participates in a landscape or particular environment, engages in participatory design practices, and shares their personal perspectives are all issues that designers, planners, and researchers need to consider.

This is of particular importance when working on projects related to transportation and the built environment in which the walking and biking route preferences and desires of the local users are critical for community buy-in and informed decision-making in policy and design planning.

Landscape architects, planners, and health researchers working on built environment or projects related to nonmotorized transportation often have need for both detailed infrastructure and user data. Unfortunately, these data are often not readily available. A solution to this lack of data is to utilize participatory and crowdsourcing techniques to collect the users' perceptions and interactions. This case study presents the process the author employed in identifying and developing technologies and techniques to meet the immediate data needs and participation of users in a transportation route-mapping project. The processes consist of a mixture of coding, repurposed commercial phone apps, and open-source mapping tools using a methodology that can be replicated for future use.

Background

The precedents and frameworks identifying the capacity and value of user perception, participation, and information sharing are not new. In fact, many of the first papers and essays discussing the topics were written several decades ago. The half-century-old writings of J.B. Jackson identified the vernacular landscape and an individual's "sense of place," while Appleyard, Lynch, and Myer's *The View from the Road* and Ervin H. Zube's environment–behavior research involved landscape perception and assessment. These and several other writings of the time allude to the notion that a user's perception and action within the environment can be characterized as a "feature" of the environment. In *Site Planning* (1984, 3rd ed.), Lynch states that site planning requires that two things be understood: "the nature of the site" and "how its users will act in it and value it." Participatory design and its role in landscape planning and design have its roots in Arnstein's 1969 "A Ladder of Citizen Participation," in which eight levels of participation were identified. Author and planner Henry Sanoff stated, "When people participate in the creation of their environment, they need the feeling of control" (Sanoff, 1988). Various forms of user-generated content (specifically geospatial data), information sharing enabled through electronic media, and interests in crowdsourcing have led to what Michael Goodchild termed volunteered geographic information (VGI) in his paper "Citizens as Sensors: The World of Volunteered Geography" (Goodchild, 2007).

While these frameworks each have a purpose and have been implemented broadly over the past several decades, the adoption of app-supported cellular devices, advances in data sharing, and improved integration of geospatial technology provide an opportunity to integrate the frameworks in an unprecedented way. What Benjamin Kuipers described as an "unobservable structure of information that represents spatial knowledge" in his 1976 paper "Modeling Spatial Knowledge" (Kuipers, 1976) can now be easily captured and visualized using today's accessible and affordable technology.

The problem

Using traditional methods, user preference and interaction data can be collected by asking workshop participants to draw the routes they use on a large-format paper map. Unfortunately, this approach is limited in that an individual user's routes are not identifiable, making it difficult to identify the start and end points of the route. An analog solution to this participatory mapping

provides each workshop participant with their own copy of the map on which to draw their routes. While this solves the problem with overlapping routes, it creates a new burden when trying to filter and quantify the routes. For example, identifying the most popular street segments biked by women vs. men or by residents over the age of 55 could take considerable time to filter. Converting the routes to digital data would provide benefits when querying the data; however, the data would first have to be digitized and attributed – a task that could also be time-consuming if there is a large data set.

GPS-enabled smartphones and tablets and various open-source mapping technologies to facilitate the collection, management, and visualization of the data have been used over the past several years to overcome the limitations presented from analog methods and to allow for digital crowdsourcing methods to be implemented (Surowieck, 2005; Haklay and P. Weber, 2008; Brabham, 2009; Misra et al., 2014; Badenhope and Seeger, 2014). However, finding software that meets the project's needs can often be a real challenge. A solution is to identify what gaps exist in the available software and to determine if multiple applications could be utilized together to meet the needs of the project.

Project history

The author had completed several previous transportation workshops in which 12–20 participants utilized the provided GPS smartphones and applications to map routes. However, the challenge was how to scale-up the data collection activity to include 50+ simultaneous participants recording route data within their community while completing the activity in under one month.

Working under the paradigm of participants utilizing their own devices, several parameters were established to help identify the type of apps that might support the project.

1 Cost: Ideally there would be no cost to purchase the application and the bandwidth requirements would be very minimal.

2 Privacy: The app could not be used to track the current location of a user. Thus, live streaming of data would not be necessary, but the user would need to somehow manually share the data to the design team after the route was mapped.

3 Usability: The app would need to function on multiple platforms (Android and Apple iOS).

4 Ease of use: A limited number of steps would be required to collect and share the data and the need to create redundant user accounts would be eliminated.

5 Functionality: The user would be able to record the route with sufficient accuracy using a phone's built-in GPS.

While collecting the data was the most important part of the project, a second component of the project required that the collected data could be queried, analyzed, and visualized.

1 Data format: Collected data had to be in an accessible and recognizable format that if necessary could be parsed or converted. Thus, collection of data into a propriety database was not desirable.

2 Data quality: Bogus or repetitious GPS data points collected by a user who stopped at a location for a long period of time should be able to be filtered.

3 Data attributes: Identification of the route type, user information, and other data

features should be linked to the route geometry to support data queries.

4 Data analysis: Calculating the speed of travel and other spatial analysis of route networks should be considered as a derived data feature.

5 Data visualization: The data format should allow for the routes to be easily mapped and visualized to illustrate areas where use was the greatest.
A search of existing applications made it clear that there was none that met all the needs of the project, but a few different apps on each platform did provide the ability to record and share a GPS-derived route for free using minimal steps, providing GPS accuracy and preserving user privacy.
The apps identified provided a multitude of features, some of which required purchase. However, the most basic feature available for free was the ability to record a route and save the data in a file that could be shared later. This small feature is all that was necessary for the project to proceed.

Collecting the data

In the initial sharing method, users emailed the GPS files to a project team member, who would then process the file and add it to the project database. While this method was acceptable for a limited number of users, it was difficult to collect the necessary metadata. The solution was the development of a simple web form with which a user could upload their collected data after emailing or otherwise sharing with themselves the collected GPS file. Utilizing basic front-end and back-end web technologies such as HTML, PHP and MySQL, the web form facilitated opportunities for increased functionality and allowed for a broader group of applications to be used to collect data.

The first of these functionalities was that the user could fill in a basic form that attributed the route data with information such as the user's gender, age, and mode of travel [walk | bike], among other details. Once the data had been uploaded, server code developed by the author parsed the data from CSV, KML, GPX, or JSON format into a standardized format that could be easily analyzed or queried and later visualized.

The coding necessary for this part of the project was minimal and made use of existing classes and functions shared by other developers on GitHub to help parse and clean the data.

Visualizing the data

The visualization of data was accomplished through the implementation of the Leaflet.js open-source JavaScript library. This library works much like the Google Maps API by allowing developers to easily configure the display of base maps and to draw data layers derived from the developer's database. The initial development of the map visualization allowed the display of biking or walking layers containing all the individual routes collected in the project (Figure 2.3.1). Displaying data using this method can have several problems. First, the data are 'messy' because the GPS route lines do not match up exactly, making it difficult to quantify the

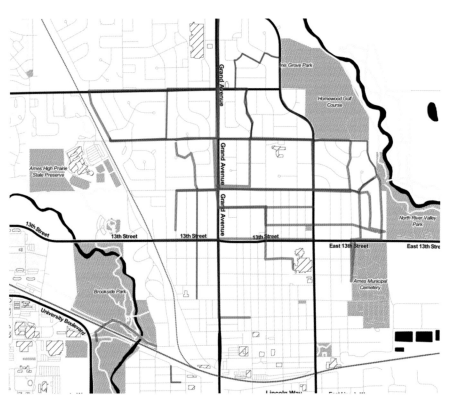

FIGURE 2.3.1 **Mockup of routes collected from users drawing on a map or submitting data via a GPS tracker. Privacy issues would be a concern as it is easy to trace a single line back to a residence**

FIGURE 2.3.2 **Converting line segments drawn by users through an online map into evenly spaced points provided a method to combine the line data with GPS-derived data. To protect user privacy, this point data could then be displayed on a heat map that was configured to mask out the areas where a limited number of participants used the route**

number of users. A second issue is one of confidentiality, because a user's route may lead directly from their residence to the destination in question. To solve this problem, the data lines were converted to a heat map visualization that only showed the routes where more than a set threshold of users walked or biked (Figure 2.3.2).

While the focus of the project was on GPS-derived routes, future project needs necessitated the ability to incorporate data that were collected through an interface in which the user simply drew their route over a web map instead of collecting it in the field. While these data were already in the required format, they did not have the temporal qualities that GPS data have, nor

did it have the number of data points GPS data would. For example, a route that traversed six blocks and then made a right turn for two blocks could be drawn as three clicks or points on the map. Because heat maps are created from point data, the lines between the points had to be segmented. Again, a search of existing technologies identified a JavaScript class called Turf.js that would add points along a line at a specified distance, making a data set that was compatible with GPS data collected in the field.

Conclusions

Utilizing existing applications and writing basic code snippets to parse and manage the collection and display of route data proved to be much easier and more feasible than creating a custom data collection application. It also allowed the team to start applying the methods to various scenarios, make adjustments as necessary to the code to accommodate data anomalies, and focus on the analysis and presentation of the data.

While several data collection apps are available on the market today, it is unlikely that a free tool will provide all the functionality necessary for any given project. Applications that provide an API may be able to be harnessed as data collection tools if combined with locally developed tools that automate data conversion, parsing, or cleaning. Often the costs for testing this capability is minimal but the opportunities are great when one considers the control they have over the data.

Finally, the ability to provide users with technologies that can be easily implemented and utilized cannot be overstated. Removing technological barriers by linking easy-to-use apps and data sharing mechanisms is one of the many things that a designer can do to ensure that the public can participate to their fullest potential in the project.

Acknowledgments

The author wishes to thank Avinash Radhakrishnan, graduate student in computer science, for his assistance with this project.

References

Appleyard, D., Lynch, K., and Myer, J.R. *The View from the Road*, Joint Center for Urban Studies of the Massachusetts Institute of Technology and Harvard University, 1964.

Arnstein, S.R. "A Ladder of Citizen Participation," *Journal of the American Planning Association*, 35(4), 216–224, 1969.

Badenhope, J. and Seeger, C. "Emplaced Mapping and Narratives within the Participatory Planning Process," in *International Digital Landscape Conference for Landscape Architecture and Planning: Developing Digital Methods in GeoDesign*, Swiss Federal Institute of Technology, 2014, pp. 180–186.

Brabham, D.C. "Crowdsourcing the Public Participation Process for Planning Projects," *Planning Theory*, 8(3), 242–262, 2009.

Goodchild, M.F. "Citizens as voluntary sensors: spatial data infrastructure in the world of Web 2.0," *International Journal of Spatial Data Infrastructures Research*, 2, 24–32 (437), 2007. doi:10.1007/s10708-007-9111-y

Haklay, M. and Weber, P. "OpenStreetMap: User-Generated Street Maps," *IEEE Pervasive Computing*, 7(4) (Oct–Dec), 12–18, 2008. doi:10.1109/MPRV.2008.80

Kuipers, B. "Modeling Spatial Knowledge," *Cognitive Science*, 2, 129–153, 1976.

Lynch, K. and Hack, G. *Site Planning*, MIT Press, 3rd edition, 1984.

Misra, A, Gooze, A., Watkins, K., Asad, M., and Le Dantec, C. "Crowdsourcing and Its Application to Transportation Data Collection and Management," *Transportation Research Record: Journal of the Transportation Research Board*, 2014, 1–8, 2014. doi:10.3141/2414-01

Sanoff, H. "Participatory Design in Focus," *Architecture and Behaviour*, 4(1), 27–42, 1988.

Surowiecki, J. *The Wisdom of Crowds: Why the Many Are Smarter and How Collective Wisdom Shapes Business, Economies, Societies, and Nations*, Random House, 2005.

02.04

From solution space to interface

Six actions for landscape infrastructure design

Contributors:

Alexander Robinson
Assistant Professor of Landscape Architecture, University of Southern California

Brian Davis
Assistant Professor of Landscape Architecture, Cornell University

Over the last decade there have been tremendous conceptual and technical advances related to landscape infrastructure.[1] Like all landscape-related fields of work, landscape infrastructure ranges across scales from streetside bioswale systems to regional logistics networks[2] and coastal defenses.[3] The work of Alexander Robinson at the Landscape Morphologies Lab (LML) is a particularly interesting development in this vein. The technical sophistication brought to bear on projects through both physical fabrication and digital modeling at the LML suggest a form of landscape research particularly attuned to large, complex landscapes typically dominated by civil engineering and the values of efficiency and control.[4] The projects developed through the LML call for a finely tuned form of modeling, a move from the engineered solution space to an *interface*.[5] The two projects presented and discussed here – *Greetings from Owens Lake* and the *Los Angeles River Integrated Design Lab* (LA-RIDL) – outline a framework for operating in ways that promise to figure

cultural agency, memory, and human experience on equal footing with technical and engineering considerations, whether civil or ecological.[6] The intent is to augment and complement the goals of engineering approaches, which aim to characterize situations in terms of their problems and solutions.

Historically, concepts and approaches for the Owens Lake and the LA River were developed in an engineering *solution space*[7] – a modeling environment (today these might be programs such as Autodesk Civil 3D or HecRas) with implicit assumptions and where goals are worked toward deductively. While current designs for the Owens Lake[8] and the Los Angeles River[9] propose to expand their performance profiles beyond their primary goals of dust control and flood control respectively, standard tooling is poorly suited to integrate other values. Instead, values such as aesthetics, recreation, and habitat become points of design conflict and are considered as value-adds or extraneous, not integral aspects of the central performance approach.[10] The engineering methodologies that produce these designs rely on synoptic representations that efficiently facilitate primary goals but poorly represent the wide range of agendas and contingencies that are inevitably imbricated with any large-scale landscape system.[11]

Such an approach to design is insidiously powerful. Not only is it effective as a means to achieve prescribed ends; the ability to objectively measure the efficiency of performance goals satisfies governance requirements for sound public investment. To insist that subjectivity or "humanness"

(such as serving an on-the-ground aesthetic reading) become an intimate part of these processes is to potentially undermine their source of power. But these subaltern considerations – including the needs of migratory birds and desires of local communities and tourists – persist in making themselves known.[12] In this context, what is design to do?

To positively consider the diverse milieu of agents that infrastructures operate within[13] (regardless of their original intention) requires entanglement with human cognition and elements that cannot be readily contained by metrics. In such cases a

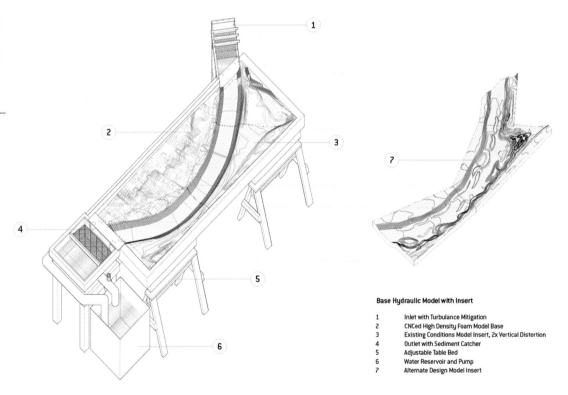

Base Hydraulic Model with Insert

1	Inlet with Turbulance Mitigation
2	CNCed High Density Foam Model Base
3	Existing Conditions Model Insert, 2x Vertical Distortion
4	Outlet with Sediment Catcher
5	Adjustable Table Bed
6	Water Reservoir and Pump
7	Alternate Design Model Insert

FIGURE 2.4.1 **Create a methodological common ground. Diagram of Landscape Morphologies Lab's 2011 hydraulic model system for the Los Angeles River "Bowtie" site with example design insert. Vertical scale is exaggerated three times to improve hydraulic accuracy**

Source: Designed and developed as part of USC Landscape Architecture and Urbanism graduate studio with assistance from the Los Angeles Bureau of Engineering, USC Viterbi School of Engineering, United States Army Corps of Engineers, and USC School of Architecture. Funded by the Los Angeles Department of Water and Power through the Los Angeles Bureau of Engineering

specialized interface can be useful. It can serve as a means to relate human cognition with quantitative processes that bound and spatially determine an infrastructure design. An interface, as Branden Hookway declares, "describes the ways in which humanness is implicated in relation with technology."[14] An interface distinguishes itself from standard design practices by its externalized and transparent architecture of heuristic and metric analysis. It creates a hybrid modeling environment, one that allows the disparate determinacy of each representation to engage in a robust and calibrated back-and-forth. Its fundamental interest in human ergonomics has potential to assess the degree to which nondiscursive values are aligned with engineering performance goals.

The following proposes six actions that distinguish the interface's position in LML's practice that emerged in its work on the Owens Lake Dust Control Project and the Los Angeles River. Each segment – a dialogue between Alexander and Brian – describes, distills, and suggests actions for an infrastructure design interface. The actions are not design per se, but rather a catalog of interface devices and strategies; they are select crucibles by which the problem of landscape infrastructure design is reformulated and actively addressed.

Action 1. Create a methodological common ground (Figure 2.4.1). Even as its urban and ecological "revitalization" are now of paramount interest, the Los Angeles River, above all else, must protect the city's citizens and property from floods. Its radical reconfiguration into a featureless reinforced concrete channel reflects this need, a design that was validated and attuned by mid-twentieth-century physical hydraulic modeling of a "clean" (nonvegetated) condition. The design's success at transporting water at near highways speeds successfully protected the city from flooding and with time practically erased public

consciousness of what was once a major regional concern. This has allowed public attention to shift to ameliorating the collateral damages of this severe solution.

However, the agencies mandated to manage the river remain justifiably fixated on its original performance design. They remain custodians to its original function of flood protection and the methodologies that measure its respective performance. Any attempt to amend the channel must satisfy an equivalency to its current antiquated performance paradigm, as overseen by its custodial entities, while also engaging new paradigms of synthetic design.

Our river design interface developed through the Los Angeles River Integrated Design Lab (LA-RIDL) aspires to bridge this gap by constructing a methodological common ground. Modern versions of the hydraulic physical modeling that originally optimized the river's flood protection are employed to satisfy the interests of the custodians but are modified to better represent and engage with other landscape qualities. The hybrid models adjust modeling parameters, such as eliminating extreme model vertical distortions, to judiciously trade hydraulic accuracy with the representational of other landscape values (such as realistic spatial conditions). While the system is not as hydraulically accurate as the final U.S. Army Corps of Engineering models, they allow designs to be "sketched" in a forum that better relates with the multiplicity of landscape factors contingent on the form of flood protection.

The first action is clear: establish common ground. Action One begins from a place of profound respect for the efficacy of earlier approaches that emphasized flood control through an understanding of river systems as plumbing problems.[15] Rather than simply trying to resist or undo the results of flood control projects that were so hard-won and have come to be relied upon, Action One instead reframes the problem. This is done with an emphasis on methodology and values. This action establishes a set of techniques, protocols, rituals, and concepts that can serve as instruments in identifying and exploring multiple forms of value.

The period just before and after the Second World War saw the simultaneous rise of environmentalism and technocratic approaches to engineering and planning. While the methods of these movements were similar, with an emphasis on increasing quantification and justifiable measurements, they tended to be rooted in radically different, equally ancient world views – humans as destroyers of nature whose actions must be ameliorated or remediated, and humans as improvers of nature. This situation usually resulted in standoffs and power plays: the EPA versus industry, the DOT versus the Sierra Club.

It was a dialectic that played out on public lands and media, with uneasy battles and partial truces.

But Action One is not dialectical; rather, it is pluralistic. Instead of a serve-and-volley between opposing world views and working methods, it is a practice in which multiple states, frameworks, or approaches can be represented, even if only partially, or imperfectly. It rightly begins from a place of respect for the work that has already happened, even if the results have often been found wanting. It proposes to achieve the pluralistic condition not through revolution – throwing out earlier means and replacing them with the new – but by keeping the older ways and augmenting them. Ironically, it is an approach that is inherently pragmatic and historically grounded, even if its tools are primarily digital, virtual, and technological.

FIGURE 2.4.2 **Address subjective and objective concerns. Screenshot of custom visualization and analysis software developed for Landscape Morphologies Lab's "Greetings from Owens Lake" design interface for the Los Angeles's Owens Lake Dust Control Project. During interface operation, perspectival visualization (left) of new dust control design is displayed on a screen, while the rendered planimetric view (right) is projected onto a sand model (or vacuum-formed mold of sand). The planimetric view includes real-time analysis of experiential and engineering parameters. The perspectival view is linked to controls that allow a viewer to move about the landscape and adjust design and analysis conditions, ranging from temporal lighting conditions to the distribution of dust control surface treatments**

Action 2. Address subjective and objective concerns (Figure 2.4.2). Like many land-intensive, ostensibly single-purpose infrastructures, managing the driving performance goals of the Owens Lake Dust Control Project is best done through quantitative and planimetric representations of surface. At the Owens Lake all the currently implemented dust control methods are contingent on the coverage of a nearly flat and dry lake bed, making aerial or GIS representations fundamental for planning, construction, and monitoring.

In contrast, perspective views, as one might experience visiting the lake, are less obviously useful or significant. As subjective representations, they inherently contain distortions and limited vantages, both spatially and in judgment, giving them little obvious utility in logical planning decisions. Furthermore, perspectival representations of utilitarian systems are regularly aesthetically displeasing and can politically obstruct the project's objective performance goals and interests. This has helped cultivate a general suspicion and disinterest in a view that can elicit and empower nondiscursive criticisms of supremely rational and – by the project's synoptic metrics of success – optimal constructions.

While such a perspective view is the most apt representation of experience and "place" for visitors and constituents – often serving as the only placeholder for such concerns – it is regularly excluded from infrastructural design until major logistical decisions have been resolved. Such an approach has proven perilous.[16] By restricting the role of the perspectival representation to either public outreach "visualizations" or the actual experience of the built infrastructure the process cedes design entirely to engineering concerns and aesthetic judgment to volatile public entities and populations to judge postpartum. In such circumstances, aesthetic failure is common and its influence becomes more disruptive than productive. Aesthetics appear to be an erosive influence on effective plans and undermine large, otherwise successful, built projects.[17]

The LML design interface for the Owens Lake acknowledges the agency of perspective and its representations of place. It proposes that such an influence must be accounted for and can yield acceptable compromises. In this example from the LML's Owens Lake design interface, the perspectival, subjective view is given a prominent position with the planimetric and other metric measurements of performance and value. Analysis such as real-time viewshed analysis enrich and even directly map the relationship between different vantages. The arrangement serves to produce a dialogue that may minimize conflict scenarios and pent up reckonings between the disparate vantages. The system places the subjective in a position to redefine itself as a productive view, one that become an integrated or even equal point of reference, representative of its implicit agency and influence within infrastructural landscapes.

Action Two puts into practice György Kepes's exhortation that "we need to map the word's new configurations with our senses . . . discover in it potentialities for a richer, more orderly and secure human life. The sensed, the emotional, are of vital importance in transforming its chaos into order."[18] After common ground is established, Action Two emphasizes perspectival representation as an approximation of embodied human experience. It lets us consider what it could be like to be out there. Essential to this is the necessity of calibrating the simulated experience with field observations: can one really see the ridge in the distance? Do you really not notice the freeway to the left?

The emphasis on perspective as a device rather than, say, collage or video, establishes

FIGURE 2.4.3 **Structure disparate representations in a pluralistic format. Diagrams describe an unsequenced multimedia design engagement with the professional "Greetings from Owens Lake" interface, developed for the Owens Lake Dust Control Project. From left to right: Subtraction – establishing existing site conditions using a vacuum tube mounted on a robot arm. Sand deposition – site modeling using a robot arm to create deposition. Sand manipulation – a digital arm aggregates and erodes depositions. Laser scan – a digital means of measuring and recording the effects of manipulation. Analysis – software uses digital scan for analysis of performance parameters, design, and rendered visualization. Hand manipulation – the modeling medium can be manipulated by hand, allowing for a more intuitive engagement with the site, rather than the more purely deductive interaction necessitated by digital modeling**

the landscape that is within infrastructure system control as a sort of middle ground between the surrounding area and the place one is standing. At first glance this seems trivial: how many people really want to drive to see the Owens Lake? But the implications matter. Action Two emphasizes this intermediate zone and reconstructs it as a modern Second Nature.[19] No longer simply a place of utility and production, outside the precious designed landscapes of the garden and between us and the wilderness this landscape becomes a cultural product and

source of inspiration in its own right. It is here in this pluralistic intermediate landscape that not only are our livelihoods are won but our cultural values are formed and expressed.

Action Two promises the opportunity to genuinely consider experience, not instead of but alongside of other values. Integrating forms of representation that characterize the human experience of a place within the modeling process considers experience in reconstructing these landscapes.

Action 3. Structure disparate representations in a pluralistic format (Figure 2.4.3). The art of designing an interface for the Owens Lake is in the careful structuring of disparate representations. The "Greetings from Owens Lake" interface finds valence through its arrangement of multiple and disparate modes of site and problem representation. These include qualitative and quantitative: calculations of cost, water use, predictive habitat scores, and material spatiotemporal simulations. As is the nature of landscape, each representation of value or form is interconnected and interdependent with others. If habitat value diminishes or increases it impacts many other values and qualities. Few significant relations are linear (e.g., even water use and landscape quality is an irregular relationship) and no element can be assessed by a single measurement. Furthermore, metricized concerns and values, such as infrastructural performance or cost, lie in real, yet difficult to explicate, relations with qualitative concerns. Even as this suggests a kind of impossible solution space, there is a real need for some relation, however imperfect, between these different measurements of landscape, many of which cannot be assessed by some simple metric equivalency. My interfaces seek to place them in a dialogue to generate assessments to match the complex quality and paradox of landscape "problems."

In LML's Owens Lake design interface, physical sand models, software analysis, and algorithmic inputs are structured to spoil standard design problem hierarchies with a multiplicity of representations and vantages. The system creates a prismatic solution space indicative of landscape; it both diffracts parameters and presents itself as a multifaceted whole. It places the operator within an enriched milieu of landscape representations that overlap and interact with consequence and effect – making a design terrain textured with

critical and project-defining objective parameters and qualitative, nondiscursive, representations of place. The power of the interface comes through an arrangement that does not merely repackage our systematic biases for a "problem" approach but stimulates a new open-ended and integrated avenue for design exploration and judgment. The diagram illustrates the multiple tools and vantages, digital, physical and hybrid that structure a enriched engagement with the design conditions.

Every form of representation carries its own blind spots and assumptions. Certain representations are good at capturing specific things but always leave out other considerations. In this case, a digital model works with assumptions or norms related to sand and water – shear coefficients, wind patterns, and water volumes. Of course, this can never capture what happens when a hose clogs or when a slope gives way.

There is a tendency toward determinism when working with one type of representation: "of course the proposal should be this way; just look at the model outputs." Pairing digital parametric models with another form of representation, in this case physical modeling – real piles of sand, produced using processes that replicate important parts of the environmental operations and context – introduces another, different set of assumptions and brings other mechanisms to the foreground. This is the great but often-overlooked lesson of pairing the section and plan – each is a method for understanding specific things about an object or place; each is related to the other, but different.

Tension and friction become desired and necessary components in the process as a means of figuring competing values. As an engineered solution, any given project

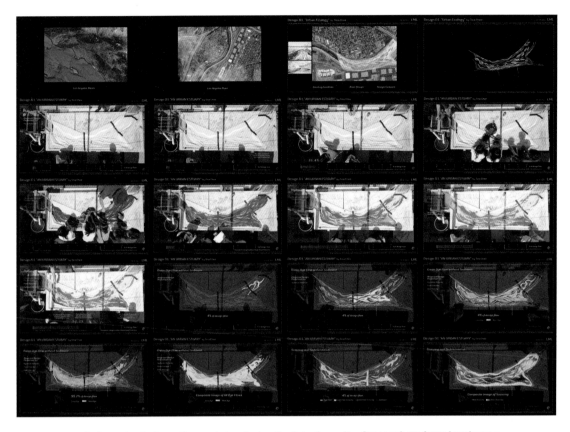

FIGURE 2.4.4 **Induce play by bounding and structuring the interface site. Screenshots from Landscape Morphologies Lab augmented time-lapse video of hydraulic modeling Los Angeles River "Bowtie" site designs developed by USC graduate landscape architecture students**

Insert created by Tina Chee

eventually falls apart because our knowledge is imperfect or values shift. But conceived as a landscape using multiple forms of representation, the project has the potential to maintain integrity and shift through time and space in response to multiple inputs, changing desires, or new context. The job is not to solve a problem but to exercise judgment to decide what constitutes the integrity of the project and just how it should be maintained, rather than projecting a synoptic or totalizing solution.

Action 4. Induce play by bounding and structuring the interface site (Figure 2.4.4). The flood protection system of the Los Angeles River is taut. There is a limited amount of "slack" by which one can deviate from the most efficient method of moving storm water. Design in these circumstances is highly restricted, defined by performance parameters only discernible through complex engineering analysis. Thus the problem of design is confounded by a contingency of challenges: draconian performance requirements ask for extraordinary innovation, a practice that is proportional to precisely representing complex and dynamic site phenomena. To proceed requires an awkward marriage of unorthodox thinking and systematic, highly technical representation of constraints; it is a challenge that begs for an advanced interface.

Fortuitously, the established methodology of hydraulic physical modeling works well in addressing this conundrum. With minor modifications it can become an effective medium to creatively explore taut design constraints. It both measures the controlling parameters of flood protection and operates as a spatial medium for exploring multivalent landscape characteristics. The system's most appealing attribute is its real-time spatial material representation of hydraulic performance. In this example on the Los Angeles River, the model's simultaneous computation and display of complex dynamic flood protection performance engenders an excited cognitive space. The sensuality and speed of the system becomes an invitation to *play* at the edges of what is hydraulically possible and to explore the limits of potential and suitable tangential values.[20] Rather than being inert abstract constraints, the performance boundaries are represented in a fabric and flux whose inherent meter, material, and phenomenality invite exploration. The material quality of these boundary representations cultivates playful human cognitive states where the constraints of an acutely complex and constrained territory demand it most.

Given the general difficulty of engineering analysis and the incompatibility of methods, the easiest approach is to allocate geographical areas outside performance territories, where subjective design and other not readily compatible values can occur more or less freely. Despite claims of objectivity, any engineering problem inevitably offers many possible solutions. Values are needed in order to develop and select from among these possibilities. In typical public projects these have for a long time been efficiency and control in the service of achieving the cheapest option. Through the interface approach, multiple forms of value are figured, cultural significance (through aesthetic effects) and

ecological performance move from mere epiphenomenon to primary drivers alongside efficient solutions to the problem.

Play – a powerful human cognitive method for exploration within bounded space[21] – is an ideal nondiscursive means for studying modeled space through intricate work and calibration. The objective of this approach is to understand without destroying wonder, to discover patterns without reducing the complexity. In the words of polymath Herbert Simon, "the aesthetics of natural science and mathematics is at one with the aesthetics of music and painting – both inhere in the discovery of a partially concealed pattern."[22] This is the task of design, though it is often reduced to sophisticated problem-solving alone. The potential of an interface that emphasizes the concept of play is to explore the range of the possible from a set of givens. It moves modeling from a solution space, founded on deductive logic where the built-in assumptions fundamentally shape the outcomes, to a new type of formation space that is generative in nature, encouraging the production and analysis of novelty.

Action 5. Engage stakeholders with the interface (Figure 2.4.5). To engage a broader socio-political realm, LML's specialized design interface and design output for the Owens Lake Dust Control Project were refashioned within a custom stand-up arcade machine for public use and outreach. Users can select between a variety of vacuum-formed landscape sand models representing possible dust control designs, slide them onto the arcade tabletop, and then utilize buttons and a joystick to dress them with a selection of dust control technologies, modulate water use, and adjust experiential parameters, such as time of day and viewer position.

The system software simultaneously projects the surface treatments onto the plastic topographic model and presents a perspective simulation of the new dust control landscape. The interface is further augmented with instant analysis for a variety of engineering, habitat, and experiential considerations. The system gameplay broadly encourages users to employ *play* to find design configurations of their preference by rewarding them with a postcard depicting their selected design and its performance attributes. A public, constituent-based *Homo ludens* is let loose within the utilitarian solution space of *Homo economicus*.[23] The system keeps record of this interaction and collects the playful impulses and subjective judgments of constituents into a data set that better represents the nondiscursive values within the rational design frameworks. The interface becomes an important means by which we instrumentalize, measure, engage, and inform the social imagination in the strange hybrids of function and beauty that are infrastructure landscapes.

Place-based activism as a generative means in the design process has been popular in landscape architecture at least since the 1960s, with Lawrence and Anna Halprin's groundbreaking RSVP Cycles.[24] By adapting this ethos and approach to digital modeling capabilities, more people can be reached and a wider, perhaps stranger, set of possibilities can be explored. Such an engagement can help popularize and activate the suggested approach in multiple ways. First, by engaging a multitude of constituents in the nondiscursive assessments the results are legitimized by data quantity and provenance. Second, by engaging people within an

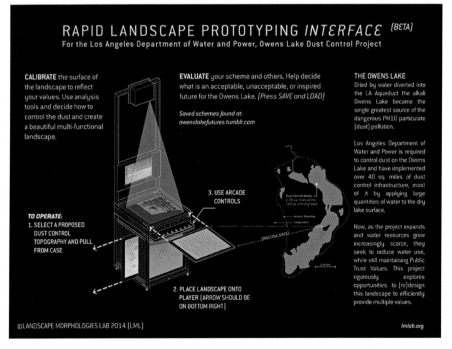

FIGURE 2.4.5 **Engage stakeholders with the interface. Instructions for operating Landscape Morphologies Lab's "Greetings from Owens Lake" public interface. Players are encouraged to arrange and assess dust control surface treatments for a variety of prefabricated topographical treatments. The system records their preferences and rewards them with a postcard souvenir of their preferred design**

FIGURE 2.4.6 **Disseminate pluralistic rhetorical representations. Postcards generated by the "Greetings from Owens Lake" public interface at the Los Angeles Contemporary Exhibition (L.A.C.E.) in April 2016**

enriched spatio-experiential simulation, coupled with design and environmental controls, the system fashions a well-informed social imagination, a fundamental force in the societal relevance, investments, and ultimately transformation of design practices.

Action 6. Disseminate pluralistic rhetorical representations (Figure 2.4.6). The postcards from the "Greetings from Owens Lake" public design and outreach interface depict a perspectival image of the users' preferred dust control configuration, bordered by a set of critical performance measurements such as water use, capital cost, habitat value, and distribution of various dust control methods. The arcade system prints a souvenir postcard as a reward for each user's turn "playing" the game and contributing a public data set of preference and design. As a familiar frame of landscape, place, and resilient social

talisman, the postcard is a useful endpoint for each user interaction; it motivates their "play" toward a personal, yet proud agency of landscape value and experience that may not be otherwise an active goal with this landscape. The postcards strategically operate as hybrid representation, combining objective and subjective representations into a single value object/endpoint. Furthermore they are both projective and an auto-influential record of the social imagination, effectively elevating its agency and attempting to acclimate it to a more pluralistic dialectic.

The interface demystifies abstract, specialized knowledge projects. By making the outcomes of proposals legible in three dimensions and accessible in a vernacular form – in this case, the postcard is literally one of the most popular and banal forms of place representation ever – the potential futures of the landscape become more intelligible to more people. What is more, the interface allows for individuals to have some control over the appearance and experience of the landscape representation, enabling them to pose questions not just through critique (or response) but by making their own versions – "what would Owens Lake be like if the mounds were this high and not that high . . . "

To some degree, specific parameters are set (the height of mounds, volumes of water) to create a bounded space within which to ask those questions. At this stage, rather than the final forms, the designer is most concerned with the boundaries themselves. Are they the right ones, and are they well-tuned? Craft and judgment come to the foreground alongside measuring, which is reconfigured as just one mode of valuation together with narrative and experience. The effect is similar to Repton's Redbooks; a calibrated understanding of what is changeable helps people understand what is significant. The output becomes a decision-making tool that accounts for both a more expansive and more nuanced understanding of the project.

Conclusion

The interfaces developed at the LML are a means of structuring human perception and cognition within a design process normally driven by nonsubjective, quantitative design methodologies alone. They are a technology that mediates between individual human experience and the projected landscape. The interfaces presented here restructure the design process of these systems to include other considerations without compromising or disregarding the infrastructure's original performance benchmarks. This ability to simultaneously figure the particular *and* the synoptic accesses a productive tension that enriches

the conceptualization of the project. It creates a new context within which multiple forms of value can be figured and considered by different invested actors.

This back-and-forth dialogue (in the interface and article) implies a move from a nondiscursive, largely deductive way of modeling and toward a new paradigm, or at least a fuller range of practices and considerations. The interface approach being developed through the LML promises a range of new possibilities and values through alternative modalities such as *play*. Importantly, it puts these forth not only as a critique or alternative to conventional, tried-and-true approaches from engineering, but as a way to augment or extend those. The idea of an interface builds from a deep respect for the validity of engineering approaches, and admits their necessity while also affirming that *engineering is not enough*. The interface also offers a real pathway for considering a range of values including human perception and experience accessible to many different people that is critical in these public infrastructural landscapes.

Notes

1. For early examples see Blood, J. and Raxworthy, J. (eds.) *Mesh Book: Landscape/ Infrastructure*, RMIT Press, 2005; Strang, G. "Infrastructure as Landscape," *Places Journal*, 10(3), 1996; this discussion picked up steam over the last decade through the work of Pierre Belanger, among many others.

2. LeCavalier, J. *The Rule of Logistics: Walmart and the Architecture of Fulfillment*, University of Minnesota Press, 2016. See also, Lyster, C. *Learning from Logistics: How Networks Change our Cities*, Birkhauser, 2016.

3. Rosati, J.D., Carlson, B., Davis, J.E., and Smith, T.D. *The Corps of Engineers National Regional Sediment Management Demonstration Program*, US Army Corps of Engineers, ERCD/CHL CHETN XIV-1, 2001, www.dtic.mil/ get-tr-doc/pdf?AD=ADA604701

4. See Mount, J. *California Rivers and Streams: The Conflict Between Fluvial Process and Land Use*, University of California Press, 1995, p. 302. See also Belanger, P. *Landscape Infrastructure: Urbanism Beyond Engineering*. PhD thesis, Wageningen University, 2013, pp. 276–284.

5. For a detailed discussion and description of the idea and implementation of an interface for "Greetings from Owens Lake," see: Robinson, A. "An Interface for Instrumental Reconciliation," in Anderson, J.R. and Ortega, D.H. (eds.) *Innovations in Landscape Architecture*, Routledge, 2016.

6. It seems fair to characterize the construction and maintenance of complex ecological systems within infrastructures as a form of ecological engineering, rather than a holistic "restoration" of a qualitative landscape condition. Success is no longer pinned to returning to a known model of nature but rather is measured in terms of metricized equivalent, such as bird counts and complex, carefully calibrated, habitat models. Examples of this in the Los Angeles region include both the 2013 US Army Corps of Engineers, *Los Angeles River Ecosystem Restoration Integrated Feasibility Report*, whose design options were largely predicated on an incremental analysis of habitat value and cost, and the Los Angeles Department of Water and Power's Owens Lake Dust Control Project, where a habitat model of the lake's dust controls is the most critical benchmark of success following air pollution compliance measurements. See Los Angeles Department of Water and Power, *Habitat Suitability Model for Species Guilds that Occur on Owens Lake*, December 1, 2011.

7. Cross, N. "On Estimating the Feasible Solution Space of Design," *Computer Aided Design*, 29(9), 649–655, 1997.

8. The Los Angeles Department of Water and Power is currently working with landscape architects to simultaneously improve the water efficiency and public value of their 48.62 square mile dust control project on the Owens Lake in Inyo County, California. Los Angeles Department of Water and Power, Nuvis Landscape Architecture and Planning, *Owens Lake Master Project: Transitioning to waterless and water-wise solutions*, April 2013.

9. The City of Los Angeles and US Army Corps of Engineers are embarking upon a multi-billion-dollar project to improve the Los Angeles River in terms of ecosystem and recreational

value. US Army Corps of Engineers, *Los Angeles River Ecosystem Restoration Integrated Feasibility Report*, 2013.

10. For instance, language in the LADWP's 2010 Habitat Management Plan on the Owens Lake reveals the agency's growing anxiety about having to maintain all the habitats that " . . . water-based dust control *inadvertently* created." Los Angeles Department of Water and Power, *Owens Lake Habitat Management Plan*, 2010, p. 1.

11. The US Army Corps of Engineers proposal to restore the Los Angeles River ecosystem heavily favors metrics of habitat and cost over all other considerations besides flood protection. US Army Corps of Engineers, *Los Angeles River Ecosystem Restoration Integrated Feasibility Report*, 2013.

12. "This was never supposed to happen," begins a website describing the new focus on aesthetics and ecology at Los Angeles's Owens Lake Dust Control Project. "Owens Lake Project," www.owenslakeproject.com

13. Carse, A. "Drought as Infrastructural Event," *Limn: Public Infrastructures/Infrastructural Publics*, 7, 77–82, 2016.

14. Hookway, B. *Interface*, MIT Press, 2014, p. 1.

15. Dixit, A. *Going Beyond Engineering Solutions to Water Problems*, www.thethirdpole.net/2017/02/27/going-beyond-engineering-solutions-to-water-problems/, February 27, 2017, accessed April 20, 2017.

16. The Los Angeles Department of Water and Power produced no perspectival or other aesthetic representations of their dust control project on the Owens Lake until nearly a decade into the project. Up until that point they relied entirely on the inherent aesthetic value of open water and made no other aesthetic considerations. However, owing to public trust doctrine, to reduce their massive water expenditures on the lake they needed to compensate the loss of its value with other aesthetic and public value. By dumbly using water as a kind of aesthetic balm for their otherwise strictly utilitarian landscape, it would put them in a difficult position to rewind their fundamental disinterest in the subjective now manifest in over a billion of dollars of built landscape and infrastructure.

17. For example, the eventual near universal rejection of the Los Angeles River current utilitarian design is product of its aesthetic, programmatic, and ecological failures. Its record of flood protection has been stellar.

18. Kepes, G. *The New Landscape in Art and Science*, Paul Theobald, 1956, pp. 18–19.

19. Hunt, J.D. *Greater Perfections: The Practice of Garden Theory*, University of Pennsylvania Press, 2000, pp. 32–39.

20. In Huizinga's influential formulation of play set boundaries are integral to the activity – dogs play fight with the agreement that no one will draw blood. Huizinga, J. *Homo Ludens: A Study of the Play-Element in Culture*, Beacon, 1955.

21. Hookway, B. *Interface*, MIT Press, 2014, pp. 33–34.

22. Simon, H. 1996. *The Sciences of the Artificial*, MIT Press, 1969, p. 2.

23. Simon, H. *Administrative Behavior*, University of Pittsburgh Press, 1984.

24. Halprin, L. *The RSVP Cycles: Creative Processes in the Human Environment*, George Braziller, 1970.

Employ **03**

The mediated and virtualized space of computation requires that designers find connections to the physical world with new methods of construction, interface, and spatial response. The use of computation to more fully develop these connections requires that code be employed in ways that can redefine the material qualities of landscapes.

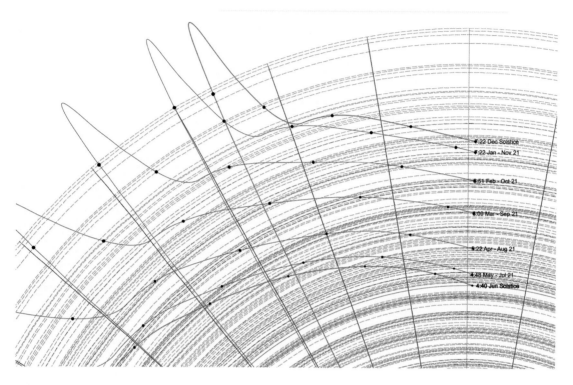

FIGURE 3.0.1

03.00

The role of query and convergence in next-generation toolsets

Contributor:

Anthony Frausto-Robledo, AIA, LEED AP
Architect, and Editor-in-Chief, Architosh

The evolution of next-generation software tools for AEC design professionals will continue to take the user deeper into simulation, optimization and problem definition as mere representational concerns fall away from their preeminent position. Within this context, algorithmic modeling and visual programming software tools have risen from the shadows of academic and early adopters into a professional, cultural awareness that is starting to take the shape of a movement, if not a true shift in the architect or landscape architect's workflows. From conferences such as SmartGeometry—which is now many years old—to a proliferation of online courses, to a recent rise in competitive alternatives in algorithmic design tools, it is now clear that algorithmic design is not a short-term fad.

The expectations behind algorithmic design tools are far-reaching and expanding. Their core value lies in a design premise change: instead of manual and semi-automated design modeling to iteratively test against a design problem's constraints, a recipe (algorithm or algorithms) can be written specifically to address those constraints. By linking the recipe to a design or modeling tool, the user's recipe can be applied to form fitting done by the computer software itself.[1] The advantage to the designer is changing variables in the recipe is far faster than manually changing 3D models or complex 2D design information.

Another expectation of algorithmic design tools is they offer massive execution speed-ups of iterative design workflows. By leveraging the power of today's computing resources, algorithms can govern a computational set of possibilities that can easily number in the many millions. But being able to generate millions of design iterations quickly isn't especially useful if another software solution can't help designers evaluate them. Today, sophisticated "evaluators" are in the works, and the future AI (artificial intelligence) software systems will help algorithmic design tools eventually pass a type of design Turing test—the solution *actually* will look like a human designed it.[2] From the earliest days of parametric modeling tools being linked to advanced scripts (proto-algorithmic) to a notion of a Turing test for design, today's advancing algorithmic and visual coding design tools emerge in front of a backdrop of larger disruptions and their attendant anxieties in the AEC context.

The rise of next-generational software tools inevitably mirrors and reflects the larger context of computer science and technological transformation, while at the same time struggles against—and for—seams of continuity with traditional and existent methods of design teaching and practice. The two key threads of technological transformation in AEC pertain to the "techniques" of the built world and the "digital tools" used by the professionals who design that world. At the heart of the AEC digital tools, disruption has been the BIM transformation, which fundamentally drives

at a new type of collaboration model that challenges notions of expertise, disciplinary turf, the standard of care, intellectual property and the way the Academy prepares future practitioners. Yale professor and former VP of Autodesk Phil Bernstein says that "the next decade will see the convergence of these two distinct threads," referring to two distinct technology realms: building techniques and digital tools.[3]

What the BIM movement promises us under its full development is the ability to systematically and efficiently design, simulate, and optimize before we ever lay shovel to ground. BIM progress continues unabated because no other model better enables the built world and those responsible for it to address and indeed help solve larger world problems. These include our environmental crisis through carbon reduction, the preservation and conservation of natural resources such as water, urban plight, and socioeconomic imbalance issues, and short- and long-term shifts in human transportation systems and their impact on cities. Against this pressing and demanding backdrop, architects and landscape architects must negotiate the most valuable paths forward.

While this transformation unfolds in the AEC world, a far larger shifting backdrop adds new anxieties. As the world becomes both more complex and dynamic, the interrelationship between knowledge, expertise, and value changes. As Warren Berger notes in his thought-provoking book *A More Beautiful Question: The Power of Inquiry to Spark Breakthroughs*, "If we begin to think of 'questions' and 'answers' as stocks on the market, then we could say that, in this current environment, questions are rising in value while answers are declining."[4] Not only has knowledge become a commodity, but in a fast-moving or shifting context expertise loses its "shelf life" in the face of knowledge revision and obsolescence. In this new reality, the value is now being placed on what one "can do with knowledge in pursuit of a query."

Perhaps no better example of value creation in pursuit of a query, as it relates to the future state of the AEC industry, can be found in MIT professor and Israeli-born architect Neri Oxman. Oxman's work centers on the development of single-material systems for constructs at varying scales.[5] A fundamental question in her work is: *what would design be like if objects were made of a single part?* Notably, to attack that core query, Oxman employs the convergence of four relatively new domains of knowledge and expertise:

> computation design, allowing us to design complex designs with simple code; additive manufacturing, letting us produce parts by adding material rather than carving it out; material engineering, which lets us design the behavior of materials in high-resolution; and synthetic biology, enabling us to design new biological functionality by editing DNA.

Oxman's value creation lies in her work's capacity for further innovation, breakthroughs, and industry stimulus for change.

It's equally important to note that, while Oxman's work, for example, begins with a fundamentally powerful question, algorithmic thinking, and the tools that power it can embrace smaller and less ambitious queries that are more germane to everyday processes for both architects and landscape architects alike, creating immense value just the same. In fact, an area where algorithmic design tools have long found usefulness is in the creation of bespoke digital tools that address gaps and shortcomings in off-the-shelf computer applications.

One such example is a set of site analysis plug-in objects built using Vectorworks's Marionette algorithmic scripting environment. Marionette is not an application but rather a technology stack that brings visual scripting and algorithmic design capability to the Vectorworks CAD and BIM line of applications. While many design professionals are familiar, at least in concept, with the notion of complex 3D models being powered by algorithms—such as with Rhino and Grasshopper—the ability to program specific tools that perform queries on data and spit out actionable information is an excellent example of the rising use of algorithmic design.

Take for example the dynamics of our current weather patterns globally. For both landscape and building architects, weather plays a large role in design decisions, and such data helps professionals make decisions about orientation, size, height, material selection, vegetation, drainage, and system design. It is imperative that designers make use of accurate weather data to address core questions such as: what orientation is best on a given site for designing with passive ventilation? The Marionette object, shown above (Figure 3.0.2), is an example of a bespoke tool developed specifically to query accurate and up-to-date weather data collected from weather stations around the world—to help design professionals drive at that query above.

The tool, named Wind Rose—and a part of a set of site analysis algorithmic tools that query weather data such as wind speed and direction, rain and snowfall, temperature data, solar data, and psychrometric data— enables a designer to query wind data for a given location (e.g., Bar Harbor, ME). The tool solves several things at once. First, it queries for data—out on the Internet—impacting design without leaving the designer's application environment.

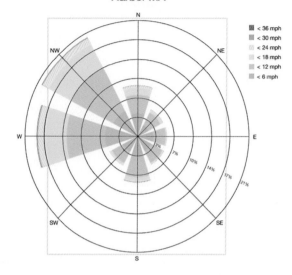

Wind Data for January 2007 - 2016 in Bar Harbor MA

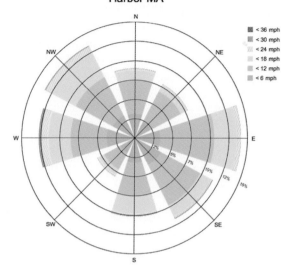

Wind Data for April 2007 - 2016 in Bar Harbor MA

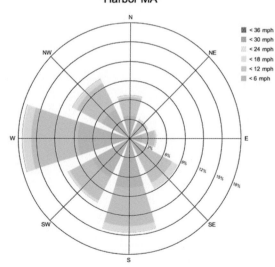

Wind Data for July 2006 - 2016 in Bar Harbor MA

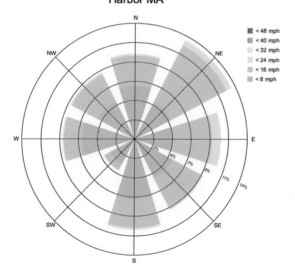

Wind Data for September 2007 - 2016 in Bar Harbor MA

FIGURE 3.0.2 **The Marionette object, Wind Rose, is an algorithmically driven diagram showing wind speed and direction data for a given location on Earth, at a particular point in time. As such, it provides rapid decision support for designers making a range of decisions about environments and structures**

Image: Vectorworks 2017 screenshot. Copyright Anthony Frausto-Robledo, AIA, LEED AP and Vectorworks, Inc.

Second, it presents the results of the data graphically within seconds. And, third, it allows the designer to modify the means by which the graphics are presented.

The Marionette object, as Vectorworks, Inc. refers to it, consists of three components and aspects of the tool. The first component is a saved set of algorithmic scripts arranged via a visual scripting node-based paradigm. Whether we are looking at Grasshopper, Dynamo, Marionette, or some other visual scripting environment, these node-based environments all function roughly the same (see Figure 3.0.3). The second core component of the Marionette object is the Python programming language behind each node. Each node can be edited by right-clicking on the node in the visual scripting view, revealing the line-by-line Python

scripting behind the node's functionality (see Figure 3.0.4). The third major component of the Marionette object is the end user interface presented to the designer. In the case of Marionette inside of Vectorworks products, access to algorithmic design tools can be brought up to the level of the main user interface.

The Wind Rose Marionette object allows an architect to query for prevailing wind direction and speed data for a given site. A landscape architect can simply enter an address or a town name into a field in a dialog palette. They can also search for data across a range of years or simply the current year. They can truncate the results by season or month and customize the units. The result is meaningfully displayed into a 360-degree graph with color-coded arcs showing wind

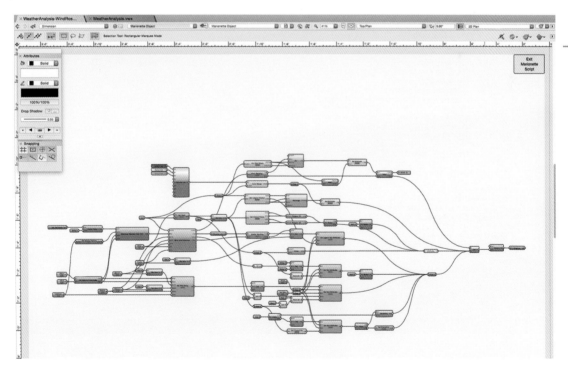

FIGURE 3.0.3 **The Marionette object, Wind Rose, is shown here at the level of its algorithmic visual script. Double-clicking the diagram object itself, seen in Figure 3.0.2, brings the user to this visual node layout. Nodes provide unique functions and are "wired together" to provide data and logic flow**

Image: Vectorworks 2017 screenshot. Copyright Anthony Frausto-Robledo, AIA, LEED AP and Vectorworks, Inc.

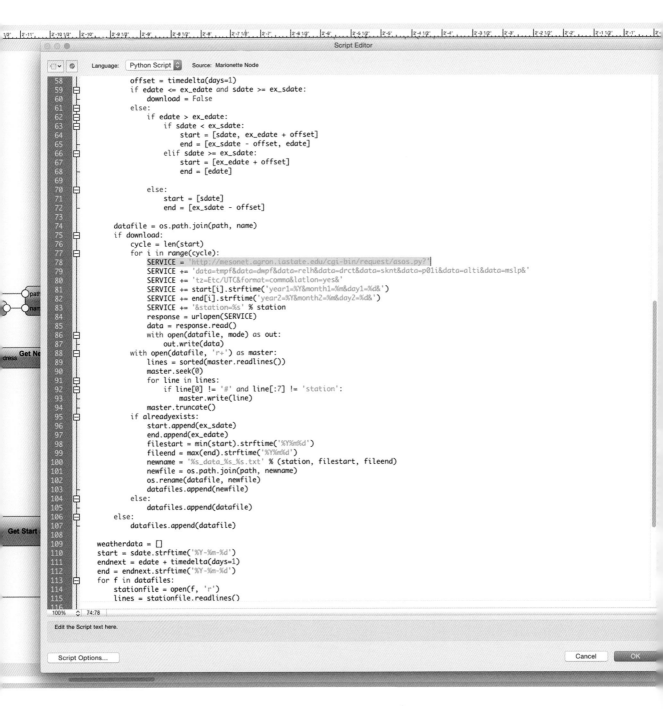

```
58      offset = timedelta(days=1)
59      if edate <= ex_edate and sdate >= ex_sdate:
60          download = False
61      else:
62          if edate > ex_edate:
63              if sdate < ex_sdate:
64                  start = [sdate, ex_edate + offset]
65                  end = [ex_sdate - offset, edate]
66              elif sdate >= ex_sdate:
67                  start = [ex_edate + offset]
68                  end = [edate]
69
70          else:
71              start = [sdate]
72              end = [ex_sdate - offset]
73
74      datafile = os.path.join(path, name)
75      if download:
76          cycle = len(start)
77          for i in range(cycle):
78              SERVICE = 'http://mesonet.agron.iastate.edu/cgi-bin/request/asos.py?'
79              SERVICE += 'data=tmpf&data=dwpf&data=relh&data=drct&data=sknt&data=p01i&data=alti&data=mslp&'
80              SERVICE += 'tz=Etc/UTC&format=comma&latlon=yes&'
81              SERVICE += start[i].strftime('year1=%Y&month1=%m&day1=%d&')
82              SERVICE += end[i].strftime('year2=%Y&month2=%m&day2=%d&')
83              SERVICE += '&station=%s' % station
84              response = urlopen(SERVICE)
85              data = response.read()
86              with open(datafile, mode) as out:
87                  out.write(data)
88          with open(datafile, 'r+') as master:
89              lines = sorted(master.readlines())
90              master.seek(0)
91              for line in lines:
92                  if line[0] != '#' and line[:7] != 'station':
93                      master.write(line)
94              master.truncate()
95          if alreadyexists:
96              start.append(ex_sdate)
97              end.append(ex_edate)
98              filestart = min(start).strftime('%Y%m%d')
99              fileend = max(end).strftime('%Y%m%d')
100             newname = '%s_data_%s_%s.txt' % (station, filestart, fileend)
101             newfile = os.path.join(path, newname)
102             os.rename(datafile, newfile)
103             datafiles.append(newfile)
104         else:
105             datafiles.append(datafile)
106     else:
107         datafiles.append(datafile)
108
109 weatherdata = []
110 start = sdate.strftime('%Y-%m-%d')
111 endnext = edate + timedelta(days=1)
112 end = endnext.strftime('%Y-%m-%d')
113 for f in datafiles:
114     stationfile = open(f, 'r')
115     lines = stationfile.readlines()
116
```

FIGURE 3.0.4 **In Vectorworks, the Marionette technology enables the user to right-click on an individual node revealing the actual Python programming code controlling the function of that node. In this image, we can see the external Internet service, providing the weather data for the overall functioning of the Wind Rose algorithmic object**

Image: Vectorworks 2017 screenshot. Copyright Anthony Frausto-Robledo, AIA, LEED AP and Vectorworks, Inc.

speed, orientation, and percentage of incidence. One can graphically see at an instant, from the resulting chart, the direction of dominant winds and how they change across various times of the year (see the Bar Harbor samples for four seasons of the year, Figure 3.0.2).

Other Marionette objects included in the site analysis algorithmic tools, such as the precipitation tool, can provide a visual display of global warming and environmental change (Figure 3.0.5 below). Duplicating the object, say three times, and then altering the years in sequence can provide a visual array of data as seen over time. The initial query "what orientation is best on a given site for designing with passive design?" can lead the designer to explore the way the climate data is changing over time—simply by experimenting with the site analysis tools themselves. In short, the creation and use of bespoke algorithmic tools can indeed foster deeper queries, in this case, about the global environment or a specific site changing environmentally over time.

If knowledge and answers are declining in value while questions and formulaic queries are rising, where do the new digital tools sit within that spectrum as compared to the older digital tools AEC professionals are well versed in? One may think about the digital tools AEC professionals use today as being multivalent across two interrelated poles. One pole references "answers," the other pole references "questions." CAD systems largely focus on the "representation" of explicit geometric information. BIM systems are laden with metadata and feature the capacity to serve as vehicles for virtual-building "simulations." As such, they are richer instruments to query. Tools such as Grasshopper, Dynamo, Marionette, and others take the query process further in several ways. While they still feature the capacity to be wired to BIM tools and the metadata attached therein, they can be—as seen in the example above—wired to other data outside the realm of the BIM application. These visual scripts on-ramp designers into the world of computer programming, which furthers the nature and

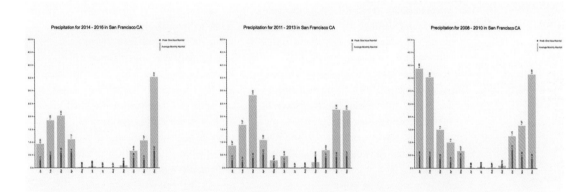

FIGURE 3.0.5 **Another Marionette object in the site analysis algorithmic tools is the Precipitation object. This tool also obtains up-to-date weather station data from around the world and feeds that data into this graphic object. Like the Wind Rose, the user inputs a location (e.g., the town in which the site is in) and the algorithm goes to work at once. In this image, data for precipitation in San Francisco, California, is shown over ranges of years during California's recent drought decades. The most current period is on the left, showing decreased levels of precipitation**
Image: Vectorworks 2017 screenshot. Copyright Anthony Frausto-Robledo, AIA, LEED AP and Vectorworks, Inc.

capacity for designers to ponder and ask *deeper* types of questions—questions that can revolutionize our environments, even if just one project at a time. As Daniel Belcher, of Robert McNeel & Associates, says, when asked what skills coding teaches beyond the world of being a software developer, "the understandings of algorithm, process, flow, and logic that underpin the creative act of programming are critical to agency in the modern world."

Belcher's comment brings up the critical question of how to act. Specifically, in relationship to the coding and algorithmic design process, what are the options and roles possible for AEC design professionals? Architect Randy Deutch, a professor at the University of Illinois at Urbana-Champaign, believes that in the future many architects will sit side-by-side with coders.[6] If so, how will designers talk to these professionals? Will coders learn to speak like designers or will designers learn to speak like coders? Taliesin students were taught how to swing a hammer, use a saw, and erect structures not merely to be self-reliant but because that knowledge acquisition meant they would know how to communicate in the language of the builder. This history finds its echo in the present-day "maker movement," and even Neri Oxman, yet these new tools are digitally driven. Knowing the "maker's language" today—digital tools that are increasingly driven by code—imbues the design professional with capacity beyond design skills that live only in the world of representational systems; the second machine age designer establishes a conversation (and relationship) with and within the fabrication world.

To summarize, there are two primary forces at play shaping the AEC designer's interest in algorithmic or computational design systems. The first is the convergence of realms of building techniques and digital tools, while the second is the rising value of

the power of the query and the diminishing value and commoditization of explicit knowledge. The following quote from Professor Phil Bernstein literally touches on both: "So for the first time since I have been with the company [Autodesk] we have been treating the 'design process' and the 'build process' as a single problem."[7] This statement itself is evidence of the power of questions, particularly questions that challenge the status quo in big initial ways. What happens to AEC design professionals in a near future scenario when, as Bernstein says, the designer's world and the fabricator's world combine into one? How do design professionals enter into that context when the professional competence measure—standard of care—has historically demanded not just separation of responsibility for these two realms but general distaste for experimentation?

This is where Bernstein, a former vice-president at Autodesk and one of the company's chief visionaries in AEC, says the value of next-generational tools come into play. Such tools, Bernstein argues—and particularly their future versions—will "dramatically lower the barriers-to-entry for experimenters while simultaneously reducing the risk of new ideas." Computational software systems when connected to BIM systems, physical fabrication systems (such as 3D printers and additive manufacturing) and data pipelines will enable AEC design professionals to digitally prototype and test with far less expense and risks than with physical installations. This trajectory change for AEC designers is emerging with some visible force, but change is slow in AEC.

When "risk-averse thinking" is supplanted by true "innovation thinking," AEC designers will both embrace next-generation tools and start asking probing questions that break down barriers and assumptions. As such, the value in algorithmic thinking will become clearer to the whole profession—as will the nature of computation-based questions. Today, the architecture industry, for example, still contains its Bible of knowledge: Architectural Graphic Standards. It is, quite literally, a book of answers. What hasn't been written yet is the equivalent book of questions. In this nascent stage of development, algorithmic thinking isn't a mainstay of the AEC design professional; however, progress continues and future computational design software, such as beta-stage Autodesk Project Fractal, seek to create environments that both enable and encourage designers to utilize packaged algorithms that both "generate" and "evaluate" intensively computational heavy design problems via new types of interfaces that elevate the importance of the query.

Notes

1. BIM software maker Graphisoft, the maker of ARCHICAD, has, in particular, related the metaphor of the kitchen recipe to that of algorithmic design. This was first seen in a marketing video where the company says "algorithmic design is like cooking" (*Algorithmic Design Meets BIM*, 2016, www.youtube.com/watch?v=UhCdFa1LpoQ).

2. The Turing test refers to a test of "a machine's ability to exhibit intelligent behavior equivalent to, or indistinguishable from, that of a human," says a Wikipedia entry. The test was developed by Alan Turing in 1950 (https://en.wikipedia.org/wiki/Turing_test).

3. Friedman, D. (ed.) *Goat Rodeo: Practicing Built Environments*, Fried Fish, 2016.

4. Warren, B. *A More Beautiful Question: The Power of Inquiry to Spark Breakthrough Ideas*, Bloomsbury, 2014.

5. Oxman, N. *Design at the Intersection of Technology and Biology*, 2015, www.ted.com/talks/neri_oxman_design_at_the_intersection_of_technology_and_biology

6. Architosh. *Perspectives on BEST of SHOW 2016: From Edge of Market to Maturing BIM, Framing a New Lens*, June 3, 2016. Deutch's talk was at the 2016 National AIA Conference and was titled: "21st Century Skill Sets: Assuring Architects and Emerging Professionals Stay Ahead," https://architosh.com/2016/06/perspectives-on-best-of-show-2016-from-edge-of-market-to-maturing-bim-framing-a-new-lens

7. Architosh. *Phil Bernstein on the Changing Role of the 21st Century Architect—The Interview (Part 2)*, April 17, 2016, https://architosh.com/2016/04/phil-bernstein-on-the-changing-role-of-the-21st-century-architect-the-interview-part-2

The agency of material in landscape architecture

Contributor:

Brian Osborn
Assistant Professor of Architecture, California Polytechnic State University

03.01
Coding behavior

The figure to the right shows temperatures recorded by German meteorologist Rudolf Geiger "at 2.00 p.m. on October 22, 1931, above an asphalt street near the Meteorological Office in Poona, using an Assman aspiration psychrometer"[1] from a height just above the boundary layer, about 1mm, and up to 20cm. The plotted temperatures demonstrate the transfer of heat from the constructed surface upwards into the atmosphere through processes of radiation, conduction, and eddy diffusion respectively as height increases.

FIGURE 3.1.1 **TECMAT material decomposition**

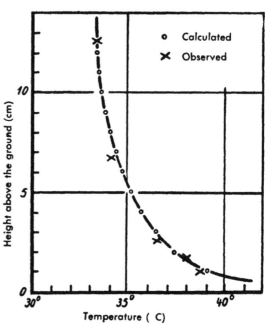

FIGURE 3.1.2 **Theoretically calculated and observed temperatures above an asphalt street**
Source: Courtesy of Blue Hill Meteorological Observatory

Operating in a zone of disturbance

As Geiger describes, at the start of modern meteorological observation in the mid-nineteenth century, measurements were typically taken from a height of two meters and upwards above the surface of the ground, "because at a lower position the variations of the ground, the physiographic peculiarities, and the nearby surroundings, were too evident. The air layer adjacent to the ground was a zone of disturbance which should be avoided."[2] *The Climate Near the Ground* only became a special concern to meteorologists after a realization that agricultural commodities—grapes on the vine, for instance—exist entirely in this zone, leaving their conditions misunderstood through established scientific protocols. A new branch of meteorology, the science of the microclimate, of which Geiger is considered a pioneer, took up the questions of this zone with particular emphasis on its significance to agriculture and botany. Published in its first edition in 1927, the *Climate Near the Ground* was an attempt at "a first survey of microclimatological problems"[3] and includes nearly 200 figures similar to the one included here—carefully, and in their way beautifully, illustrating observations of the dynamic influence of surface materials on the conditions within the first two meters.

Of course, the observation and design of microclimatic conditions is not an uncommon consideration for environmental designers today. In fact, microclimate manipulation may be one of the earliest landscape technologies[4]—found for instance in the gardens of Versailles, where citrus trees were espaliered over south-facing masonry walls in the king's kitchen gardens in order to heroically extend hardiness and fruiting periods. What is useful in revisiting Geiger's survey now, though, is that it catalogs the myriad ways in which materials, both living and nonliving, interact with their surroundings to shape both physical form and sensory experience. In the design of landscapes, where a primary concern is the articulation of the *physiographic peculiarities* of the ground and the space we occupy just above it, material assemblies and the methods they are constructed through are inexorably linked to biophysical processes such as the heating and cooling of the atmosphere, as is the focus of *The Climate Near the Ground*, but also the flow of water, the growth and decay of organic matter, and the erosion and deposition of soil, just to begin a list. Through computation and digital workflows our capacity to see, understand, and work with these complex phenomena continues to increase. Along with this comes a growing potential to consider built form relative to unstable conditions and subsequently, a prompt toward alternate frameworks for considering materials and making in landscape applications.

Growing access to computer-aided design and manufacturing tools has undoubtedly altered the material practices of allied disciplines. The 25-year-long catalog of work and writing on this subject within architecture, for instance, clearly demonstrates the possibility to produce complex, high-performance, and emotive form. Use of computation as a generative tool, rather than for purposes of analysis and or representation, in landscape architecture, however, has begun much more recently and, with some exceptions, has not yet demonstrated fundamental differences in approach or result from precedents in building architecture and engineering. This essay moves forward under the suspicion that they should—that newly accessible technologies provide an opportunity to think differently about materials and methods of making in the landscape, and that doing so may also initiate transformative contributions to the larger discourse of computational design. Specifically, when considered in landscape applications computation provides the opportunity to couple constructed form with ongoing material and environmental processes. Bringing this to fruition requires an examination of the working protocols within the discipline, especially in two critical areas. The first of these is made most clear to me through Michelle Addington's call for a more "fluid medium between knowledge and application."[5] I argue that digital tools prompt a deeper understanding of the underlying physical and chemical processes at work within sites while also providing a venue for those processes to directly inform decisions about materials and methods. The second requires an alignment of materials-first design methods, initiated in architecture and engineering, to the inherently unstable character of landscape. A shift in focus from intrinsic properties to extrinsic behavior reveals materials' agency in the production of form and experience.

B. OSBORN

PAGE 182

Expanding the digital continuum

Technology, as has always been the case, lies at the core of the examination of new working protocols in architecture and building.[6]

In *Manufacturing/Material/Effects*, Kevin Klinger and Branko Kolarevic recount transformations in manufacturing protocols and frameworks for considering materials in architecture as a result of a disciplinary engagement with computation. Central to their argument is the provision of a digital exchange of information. Previously described by Kolarevic as the *Digital Continuum*,[7] this exchange includes the possibility for geometric data generated within a digital model to be developed

simultaneously through modes of analysis and optimization, representation and communication, and manufacturing and assembly. The sharing of data has allowed greater collaboration among professionals of diverse expertise and linkages across previously distinct design phases, from design conception to engineering to fabrication. The impact that this blurring of disciplinary and procedural boundaries has had on practice extends far beyond efficiencies in the design process. More fundamentally, as a digital model is shared, the criteria used by each participant to evaluate that model are shared as well and specific disciplinary concerns, i.e., function, appearance, structure, material, and manufacturing, are made common. This has put areas of knowledge previously not the focus of architectural inquiry into play as generative starting points for design. More specifically, it has prompted the parameterization of intrinsic material properties and manufacturing logics in order to deploy them toward particular effect.[8] These *materials-first* design methodologies have ushered a productive interest in both the performance and the expressivity of material and craft in architecture over the past 25 years.

Latent, I believe, in Kolarevic's account is the possibility that the digital continuum can expand to also engage the input of dynamic site and material processes already underway at the start of design inquiry. Over the last 10 years, several technological developments have drastically increased landscape architects' access to environmental sensing tools, methods of linking the values collected from these devices directly into design models, and the ability to parametrically drive digital geometries with continuous streams of data. Low-cost micro-controllers, such as Arduino and Raspberry Pi, with open-source programming environments supported by

FIGURE 3.1.3 **Environmental sensing device, Surveillance Practices Studio, 2015**

large communities of users, have enabled designers to enter the world of *do-it-yourself* electronics. With as little as $30 and a few hours on one of many blogs, it is possible to build a custom environmental sensing device continuously reporting information about air temperature, humidity, and pressure; visible and ultra violet light levels; wind speed, direction, and dust content; soil moisture and nutrient levels; and even complex processes such as photosynthesis. The data from these sensors can be imported into management and visualization tools, such as Excel, or streamed directly into digital modeling environments, such as Rhinoceros, using add-ons to Grasshopper. Programs such as Firefly allow a real-time connection between sensors, an Arduino microcontroller, and Grasshopper, while others such as Bumblebee allow connections to Excel such that prerecorded sets of data can be called when needed. With Wi-Fi or by logging data

to external memory these devices become remote sensing stations that supply an automated and continuous feed of contextual data into the exchange that is informing our contemporary material practices.

Two examples demonstrate this workflow while looking at very different processes on the same site.[9] The first follows directly from Rudolf Geiger's observations of temperatures above an asphalt street. In this example we were interested in understanding variations of ambient air temperature as a sequence of spatial conditions that are controlled indirectly through the formal and material articulation of the ground. In order to anticipate thermal boundaries that might result from various surface configurations, Grasshopper was used to simulate air temperatures relative to those on existing surfaces measured through a combination of remote sensors and handheld measuring devices. It is important to note that a variety of energy modeling software are available that might provide accurate results through algorithms that are more commonly accepted in the sciences. In this case, however, the development of the simulation was understood to be a creative endeavor in itself, and a critical act of design inquiry.[10] It was also important that the simulation be linked directly to the design model rather than being performed in a separate software. Barring the use of premade algorithms, providing for fidelity in the model, required that the designer become educated in the processes of heat transfer, then apply and refine that knowledge over time through physical prototyping. The designer made iterative adjustments to the form and materiality of the existing ground while recording the resulting changes in air temperature and comparing them to results from the digital simulation. The model was then used to project possible results from more complex imagined surface assemblies. The resulting design armature depicts the site as an ongoing cycle of thermal energy and works to understand proposed material assemblies as strategic interventions within it. Working in this way prompted a deeper understanding of site physics than is typically put to use in design inquiry and depended on that knowledge to directly inform design decisions.

A second project looks at a strategy for organizing the ground plane by intervening in the continuous production of organic matter that follows leaf litter decomposition. Combined research and field observation allowed us to become familiar with abscission periods, leaf qualities, and decomposition rates based on species and to create a digital model of the site represented by a field of particles with differing properties. The designer explored a variety of methods for manipulating the field with the

intention of composing areas with varying intensities of decomposition. She came to imagine the organic layer of the soil as an underlying structure from which a range of future programming might emerge and was especially interested in new patterns of human use that could be found from the logics of soil making. She ultimately developed combined tactics of plant addition and culling—in order to establish a field of decaying plant parts, and interventions with air movement—to control the distribution of that material. Remote sensing devices recorded information about wind speed and direction from several networked locations across the site. The data was imported into the digital model as translation vectors and was used to direct a simulated movement of debris. A catalog of windbreaks, dams, and clearings was developed and deployed strategically to distribute the material toward intended spatial and programmatic effects.

These surveillance practices[11] reinforce our understanding that landscape form cannot be adequately measured through a survey of fixed geometries alone but also requires an attention to the dynamic *behavior* of materials relative to their surrounding environment and embedded processes. Learning about and working with these behaviors requires linked efforts of serial observation, research, digital simulation, and iterative material experimentation. An expanded exchange of information— from ongoing energy cycle through the manufacture of material assemblies— provides the opportunity for novel form to emerge through a parameterization of the temporal and dynamic logics embedded in materials and sites. An example that has come to shape ambitions of the studio work compares two approaches to making a path. In one scenario the designer asks how organic matter could be distributed over a site in order to differentiate paths of human

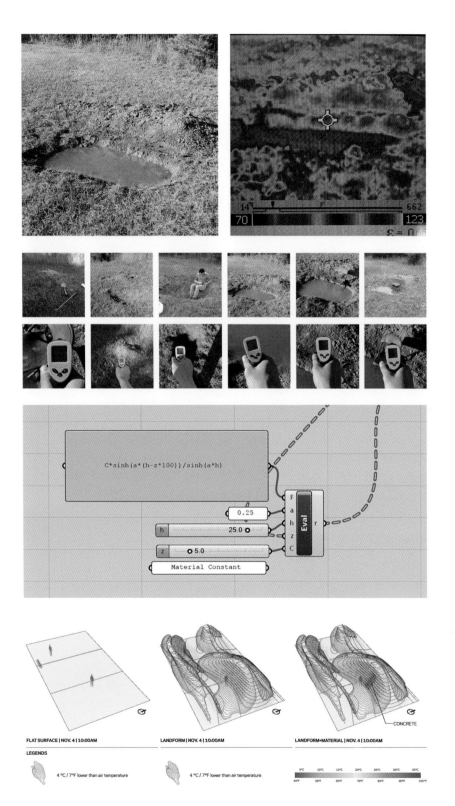

$$C*sinh(a*(h-z*100))/sinh(a*h)$$

0.25

h 25.0

z 5.0

Material Constant

F
a
h
z
C

Eval

r

FLAT SURFACE | NOV. 4 | 10:00AM

LEGENDS

4 °C / 7°F lower than air temperature

LANDFORM | NOV. 4 | 10:00AM

4 °C / 7°F lower than air temperature

LANDFORM+MATERIAL | NOV. 4 | 10:00AM

CONCRETE

5°C   10°C   15°C   20°C   25°C   30°C   35°C
40°F   50°F   60°F   70°F   80°F   90°F   100°F

FIGURE 3.1.4
Combined simulation and testing of thermal conditions over varied surface configurations, Series Zihao Zhang

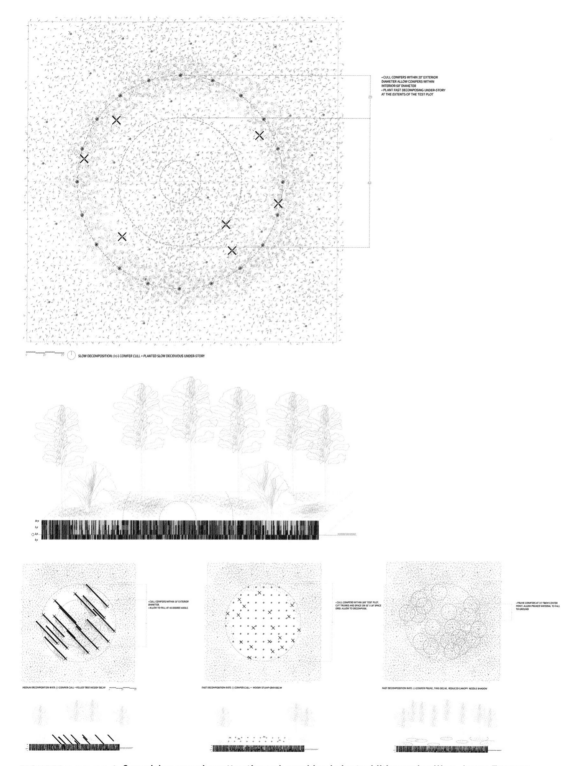

FIGURES 3.1.5–3.1.6 **Organizing organic matter through combined plant addition and culling, Jenna Frances Harris**

circulation from planting areas. In a second scenario the designer asks how people might occupy a ground plane organized to take advantage of the interactions between the decomposition rates of various materials and the availability of sunlight, moisture, and other contextual factors. The first scenario takes an application-based approach to material and works to create what is understood to be a path, including the dimensions and criteria provided for by existing codes and standards but ignoring the dynamic behavior of the material itself. The second allows new forms of human use to emerge from a focus on that behavior.[12]

Coding material behavior

Breaking the paradigm of the hegemonic "material as visual artifact" requires that we invert our thinking; rather than simply visualizing the end result, we need to imagine the transformative actions and interactions.[13]

In *Smart Materials and Technologies for the Architecture and Design Professions*, Michelle Addington and Daniel Schodek distinguish smart materials as "dynamic in that they behave in response to energy fields,"[14] from normative building materials, which are "static in that they are intended to *withstand* building forces."[15] Their text elaborates the misalignments in approaching such dynamic materials through the traditional classification systems used by the design professions, which tend to characterize materials and technologies according to "*what they are and where they are used*."[16] In other words, they focus on nominal descriptions of material type and provide acceptable applications based on existing codes and standards. This application-based characterization leaves

architects primarily concerned with fixed descriptions of geometry and appearance: *how big is it and what does it look like*, as Addington and Schodek say.[17] The text goes on to outline an alternate framework, which instead characterizes smart materials according to "what they do"[18] and prompts designers to consider the behaviors of these materials relative to their surrounding contexts and the formal or sensorial results of those behaviors. Their use of *behavior*, rather than *property*, to classify materials is important. Behavior is generally defined as the range of actions and mannerisms made by organisms, systems, or artificial entities in conjunction with their environment, which includes the other systems or organisms around as well as the physical environment. It is the response of the system or organism to various stimuli or inputs, whether internal or external.[19] Where a material's intrinsic *properties* depend on its internal molecular and atomic arrangements, a focus on *behavior* prioritizes the tendencies of material relative to its environment, and, similarly, acknowledges outputs from the material back to these surroundings. It's about variable interactions rather than discrete properties. While Addington's and Schodek's references to *smart* are most often aimed at "highly engineered" materials and technologies, such as photochromic glass, shape memory alloys or polymers, piezoelectric surfaces, or systems that utilize sensors and actuators, I argue that the term, as well as the focus on behavior that follows, is also appropriate for so-called normative materials when put to use in landscape applications, where an inexorable link to environmental process confuses distinctions between dynamic and static.

One such distinction holds hegemony within the discipline of landscape architecture, where two methodologies for considering materials operate simultaneously: one for organic, or living, materials, and a second for inorganic, seemingly inert, materials. Knowledge for each is organized very differently. For instance, undergraduate landscape architectural education in the United States often requires courses in introductory botany and or biology, plant identification, and planting design. The intention of this sequence is that students enter the discipline with a comprehensive understanding of plants from science to application—including anatomy and physiology, preferences and tendencies in various contexts, and finally their use in design projects. Looking at curricula related to nonliving materials in comparison, one might expect to see college-level physics or material science; both, however, are absent from most programs. Instead, instruction on materials usually falls under the category of landscape construction, where the focus is placed on "best practices" for their application toward the making of known assemblies such as paving systems, site walls, decks, and bridges. As a result of this organization, landscape architects have become comfortable and it seems increasingly adept at working with ideas such as emergence and probability with respect to living material but tend to think of nonliving materials as static. That is, with respect to nonliving materials, we do not consider their staged development in the way that we think of succession in plant communities or morphology in landforms, nor do we quantitatively evaluate how they mediate larger energy cycles. We tend to design with these materials in ways that ensure they withstand environmental processes rather than accommodate, let alone instrumentalize, their roles within them.

Maintaining the binary between living and nonliving materials is neither necessary nor productive. In fact, all matter, organic and inorganic, is quite *alive* in many ways; and each can exist as active and interactive participants in their environments. What's more, ignoring this possibility limits the potential to truly realize the temporal and dynamic conceptions of space promised within the discourse of digital design, where form is understood as variable, capable of responding to external inputs that change over time and distance.

To help dislodge this binary, I would like to invoke the work of political philosopher Jane Bennett, whose *thing-power* version of materialism works to disrupt the common *life-matter* hierarchy that characterizes humans as *active subjects* over all other matter, which exists merely as *passive objects*. Instead, Bennett explores the possibility that matter may have agency[20] on its own, "in excess of human meanings, designs, and purposes."[21] This depends on a more distributed understanding of agency, wherein "the efficacy to which [the] term has traditionally referred becomes distributed across an ontologically heterogeneous field, rather than being a capacity localized in a human body or in a collective produced (only) by human efforts."[22] In other words, agency, or the capacity to actively *make things happen*, is the result of the variable interactions of many things including, but surely not limited to, the behavior of living and nonliving materials, biophysical forces and processes, events, regulatory structures, and social norms. TECMAT[23] is an attempt to develop this type of *agentic assemblage*[24] in an environmental design context, producing form through a staged development and the coordination of multiple material processes. The project includes a shaped surface that is applied to hillsides in order to control erosion. Rather than trying to stop erosion altogether, as is the typical approach, the surface involves processes of erosion and deposition as integral steps in what is understood as the extended fabrication of the assembly. The project works under the premise that, on uniformly shaped slopes, erosion increases indefinitely with slope length. Alternatively, complex slopes, or those that alternate between convex and concave shapes, erode materials from the convex segments and deposit them over the concave with the possibility of balancing soil displacement along the length of the slope. A computer numerical control (CNC) machine equipped with an oscillating knife aggregate is used to perforate 5'x10' sheets of material so that they can be folded into a series of ridge and valley modules. The folded sheets are then transported, expanded to fit, and fixed to the hillside, where they act as mold-tools against the eroding soil. Over time, the hillside inherits the reverse shape of the folded surface— recontouring the hillside to form a series micro-terraces. The sheet material is made up of custom paper-based pulps that are embedded with a variety of additives including mineral grains and plant seeds. As the surface degrades the additives are sown into the soil below. By including specific minerals known to be missing from the existing soil, the breakdown of the paper surface initiates a process of soil improvement aimed at stabilizing loose material. Meanwhile, as seeds germinate and plants establish they begin to bind the soil within their roots while also slowing the velocity of water moving over the hillside. The planting strategy takes advantage of the modular fabrication unit with an alternating grid of shallow and deep rooting plant types that create a multilayered structure below the surface. TECMAT imagines a fabrication process that extends beyond the CNC machine to also include in-time molding, material degradation, and even recomposition. The final assembly represents a coupling of living and nonliving materials and processes.

The LAG bench[25] exemplifies a second manifestation of agency in materials: the capacity to mediate larger energy cycles in order to shape local experiences. The prototypical bench interrogates the transfer of thermal energy through varied thicknesses of concrete in order to produce

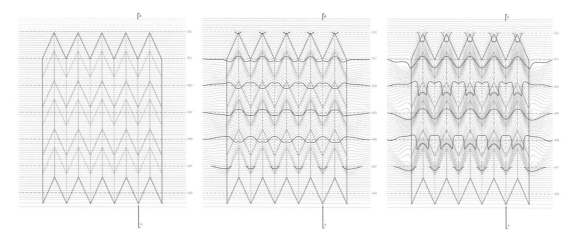

FIGURE 3.1.7
TECMAT Micro-topographical adjustment, Brian Osborn

FIGURES 3.1.8 **TECMAT Soil erosion test: an egg carton was placed on an 80-degree slope and photographed each day. By day 75 the entire upper portion of carton and much of the lower portion is completely engulfed in deposited material**

TECMAT installation, a paper mold-tool re-contours a slope through erosion and deposition, Brian Osborn

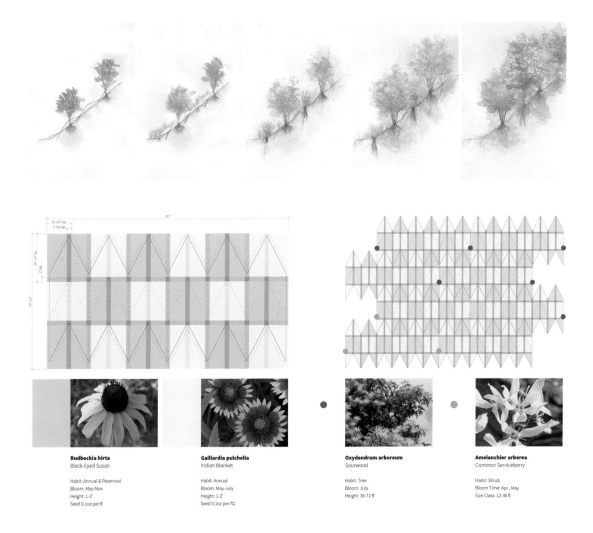

Rudbeckia hirta
Black-Eyed Susan

Habit: Annual & Perennial
Bloom: May-Nov
Height: 1-3'
Seed 0.1oz per ft

Gaillardia pulchella
Indian Blanket

Habit: Annual
Bloom: May-July
Height: 1-2'
Seed 0.1oz per ft2

Oxydendrum arboreum
Sourwood

Habit: Tree
Bloom: July
Height: 36-72 ft'

Amelanchier arborea
Common Serviceberry

Habit: Shrub
Bloom Time: Apr , May
Size Class: 12-36 ft

FIGURES 3.1.11–3.1.12 **TECMAT planting strategy, Brian Osborn**

an always-changing range of ambient conditions along its length. The project has a *fast end* and a *slow end*. The slow end forms a thickened thermal mass, making it slow to respond to fluctuations in solar radiation. As the sun rises on warm summer days, for instance, the slow end remains cool relative to increasing ambient air temperatures and provides a potential relief for overheated occupants. The fast end forms the thinnest possible profile while still providing the necessary structural support. Here the

material responds more quickly to changing temperatures—allowing it to feel warm to the touch on a cool morning just after the sun has risen. A gradient from slow to fast over the length of the bench allows users to populate it based on their individual comfort at any given time. The LAG bench is fabricated from concrete that is precast into formwork tooled with a CNC router. Prototypes were analyzed using thermal imagery in order to understand how adjustments to the form of the bench would

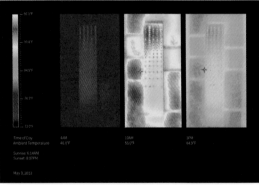

FIGURES 3.1.13–3.1.14
LAG Bench prototype, and thermal behaviour, Chris Woods

affect its behavior toward surrounding energy fields.

While explorations with digital design and fabrication techniques in architecture have inspired an interrogation of intrinsic material properties, the examples described here work to align materials-first design methodologies with the unstable character of landscape. They demonstrate how the extrinsic behavior of materials can be parameterized and deployed toward

particular effect. As Rudolf Geiger observed in 1927, environmental phenomena, such as climate, cannot be understood without accounting for the formal and material qualities of the ground. Likewise, in contemporary practice, landscape materials and assemblies should not be considered separate from the range of environmental and cultural processes that surround them. Instead, alternate frameworks are required that prioritize the potential for materials and assemblies to develop formally over time and or to mediate larger energy flows as a result of their interactions with their surroundings. Landscapes are continuously shaped by micro-topographic change, material migration, transfers of thermal energy, and the emerging and fading of local water and weather-related events, as well as the functions of organic materials. Understanding, drawing, and working with this behavior exposes the agency of material in the production of both form and experience.

Notes

1. Geiger, R. *The Climate Near the Ground*, Harvard University Press, 1950, pp. 60–61.

2. Ibid., p. xvii.

3. Ibid., p. xi.

4. Landscape historian Michael Lee researches and lectures on topics related to the history of technology in landscape architecture. This example of citrus planting in Versailles was included in a course lecture from his seminar *History of Landscape Technology* at the University of Virginia.

5. Michelle Addington and Daniel Shodek use this phrase to describe the need for better transfer of knowledge between disciplines that develop new technologies—science and engineering—and those that apply them—architecture and design (*Smart Materials and Technologies for the Architecture and Design Professions*, Elsevier, 2005, p. xiii).

6. Klinger, K. and Kolarevic, B. *Manufacturing/Material/Effects*. Manufacturing Material Effects: Rethinking Design and Making in Architecture, Routledge, 2008, p. 6.

7. Branko Kolarevic describes the digital continuum in more detail in: "Information Master Builders," in Architecture in the Digital Age: Design and Manufacturing, Spon, 2003, pp. 56–62.

8. Klinger and Kolarevic discuss the use of material-first design methods toward the production of both performative effect and experiential affect (Manufacturing/Material/Effects, pp. 6–7).

9. These examples represent student work from the Surveillance Practices studio led by the author at the University of Virginia from 2014–2015. The thermal boundary example was contributed by Zihao Zhang and the soil production example was provided by Jenna Francis Harris.

10. Eric Winsburg argues that "simulations are a process of knowledge creation" and "a deeply creative source of scientific knowledge" as a result of the large number of choices that are made in order to construct them. For instance, these choices include the identification of controls and variables, selecting sampling size and rate, and determining the appropriate algorithms to be used in computing (*Science in the Age of Computer Simulation*, University of Chicago Press, 2010).

11. I have written previously about the need for a methodological shift from surveying to surveillance ("Surveillance Practices: Drawing the Nature of Sites," in Amoroso, N. (ed.), *Representing Landscapes: Hybrid*, Routledge, 2016, pp. 220–234.

12. Thanks to Teresa Gali Izard for helping to form this comparison through her thoughtful critique of Surveillance Practices studio work at the University of Virginia.

13. Addington, M. and Schodek, D. *Smart Materials and Technologies for the Architecture and Design Professions*, Elsevier, 2005, p. 7.

14. Ibid., p. 4.

15. Ibid.

16. Ibid., p. 26.

17. Ibid., p. viii.

18. Ibid., p. 29.

19. https://en.wikipedia.org/wiki/Behavior#cite_note-1

20. I am grateful to Elizabeth Meyer, who introduced me to the idea of agency in material through her commentary during a review of Surveillance Practices studio work at the University of Virginia.

21. Bennett, J. *Vibrant Matter: A Political Ecology of Things*, Duke University Press, 2010, p. 20.

22. Ibid., p. 23.

23. TECMAT was developed by the author with the help of research assistants Gwendolyn McGinn and Katherine Jenkins.

24. Bennett uses the term agentic assemblage to describe an electrical power grid and outlines

the distinct role that each entity within the assemblage played in the emergence of a widespread power outage on August 14, 2003. Her account includes human, nonhuman, material, and political entities that all operate independently but rub against and affect each other as they do. These, which she calls agential loci, include: the phenomenon of electricity and its properties, the management of several power plants, the capacity and resistance of transmission wires, a spontaneous brush fire, the consumers that create demand on the grid, and the regulatory structures that govern how that demand is met and commodified. See *Vibrant Matter*, p. 26.

25. The LAG bench was developed by Chris Woods as part of the *SurfaceFX* seminar led by the author at UVA, Spring 2013.

Contributor:

Brian Phelps, ASLA
*The AGILE Landscape
Project*

03.02

Beyond heuristic design

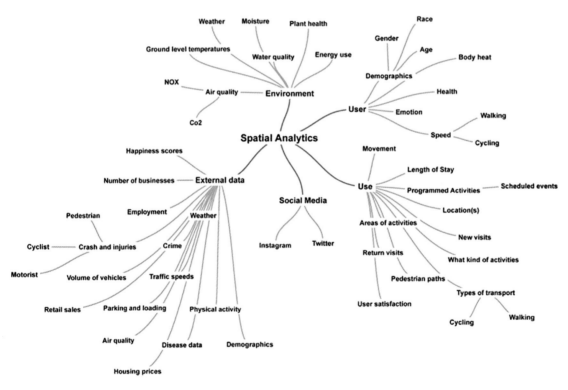

FIGURE 3.2.1

As the world demands evidence-based solutions and the digital world merges with the physical, it becomes an imperative for landscape architects to harness these technologies to develop a greater understanding of their work. The availability of tools to test solutions and document impacts of design decisions enables designers to move beyond heuristics. The AGILE Landscape Project's experimentation serves as an example of the research and development potential of DIY electronics as a means of demonstrating how sensor technology and autonomous data collection can strengthen the profession.

The confluence of the digital and physical world is redefining the landscape. It isn't only about atoms anymore. It's also about bits. Our online interactions and site-specific data generated by our mobile devices have created a new contextual and cultural layer within the landscape. Adding to this unprecedented flow of data is a growing network of sensors embedded within the environment continually gathering information.[1] These systems are augmenting the built environment with new sensing capabilities that extend far beyond our five senses. The wireless network speeds and cloud computing have enabled this evolution into the physical world. Every day new sensors are being developed and deployed. Accessible analytic tools are reducing the complexities of managing this data flow. All these building blocks and insights are shaping the new landscape and opening up new possibilities for landscape architecture.

Technology companies such as Alphabet's Sidewalk Labs[2] and Intel's Collaborative Research Institute (ICRI) are leading this transformation.[3] Many of these initiatives are early in their development. They are experimenting with how these new technologies and data can address issues facing cities. Landscape architects or other design professionals are often not a part of these tech-based solutions. The motivation for many of these initiatives is the demand for evidence-based solutions, and algorithms that help us find new solutions.

The availability of data and its promise to unlock answers to difficult problems have accelerated the adoption of this evidence-based outlook that relies heavily on metrics.[4] Relying solely on heuristics to address issues is no longer acceptable. Daniel Kahneman's publication of *Thinking Fast and Slow* in 2013 argued algorithms performed better than experts in many situations.[5] The book has influenced leadership from the boardroom to city hall. Former New York City Mayor Michael Bloomberg exemplified the use of big data and metrics during his tenure.[6] The city's ambitious Hudson Yards project will become one of the first quantified communities in the United States where many aspects of the built environment are measured and analyzed.[7] It will become a living lab for scaling these data-rich technologies.

The promise of data and our ability to mine it for answers to the problems facing society has accelerated this drive for information. Cities are opening up the vast amounts of data they collect and making it available online.[8] It is not uncommon now for cities large and small to have open data portals. In 2017, Chicago went even further and began installing a real-time network of over 500 sensor nodes.[9] Each node has a combination of sensors measuring a wide array of data points ranging from pedestrian and vehicular traffic to air quality. In the hope of finding uses, the data collected will be open to the public's use.

Experimentation is a common thread found in many of these initiatives. We are at an inflection point where these sensor networks are only beginning to scale. It is an opportune time for landscape architects to be at the table.

Inspired by the trend toward The Lean Start Up proposed in 2008 by Eric Ries[10] and design thinking methodologies popularized by IDEO,[11] the design community has embraced the iterative and human-centered design process. Most notably this was manifested in the tactical urbanism movement. This approach appropriated the use of minimum viable product (MVP), whereby product design and technology companies tested new products and services by building them with just enough features to gather valuable data. By providing real nonpermanent improvements that users could experience for themselves without the commitment, tactical urbanism was able to motivate changes within the community. As noted by MIT's Department of Urban Studies in 2013, few tactical urbanism projects "actively and honestly assessed their successes and failures."[12]

Tactical urbanism is not alone in this data and reflection vacuum. The lack of data is typical of permanent projects as well. Postoccupancy evaluation (POE) is a methodology for evaluating a project's effectiveness in meeting its design goals. Despite the value of POEs to strengthen landscape architecture's knowledge base, POEs are often not a part of the design process. Their exclusion is a result of limited resources, designers' hubris, or, worse, plausible deniability. Designers conduct anecdotal and ad hoc evaluation of a project's success or failures when they are visiting the space or addressing construction issues. The information gathered may not be documented and disseminated within the organization. The Landscape Architecture Foundation (LAF) Performance Series has emphasized the importance of performance measures and data to build a body knowledge legitimizing landscape architectural solutions.[13]

This convergence of the digital and physical world offers an opportunity to enrich landscape architecture's knowledge base by learning more about people and a design's influence on their behavior. It also provides the tools necessary to move beyond heuristic design and ensures postoccupancy evaluation is integral to the design process. Over the last two decades, the profession's core competencies have aligned with the new focus on sustainability and resilience of cities. As a result, its profile experienced an unprecedented renaissance in shaping cities and addressing the problems facing society. Heuristics are useful. They have served the profession well. However, as demand for evidence-based solutions continues to grow, this convergence and the available tools are essential to demonstrating landscape architecture's value and where it can be most potent.

As these networks grow, it is important for landscape architects to harness these technologies to ensure their place at the table. The profession's strength has always been its ability to orchestrate the expertise required to design and build a cohesive project. In short, landscape architects see the larger picture. They will need to have a firm understanding of the possibilities and the language to communicate their vision within this new context. While the profession needs to be critical where these technologies fall short, they also need to be there to help shape the solutions to support their work, or risk marginalization. Landscape architecture's unique focus on environmental stewardship, sustainable buildings practices, the human experience, and the importance of aesthetics will continue to make it well suited to address many of the issues society faces. Incorporating these new tools within landscape architecture's knowledge base can generate unique solutions others wouldn't otherwise address. These new technologies can strengthen the profession.

FIGURE 3.2.2 **Chair as Sensor parklet on Park(ing) Day 2015**
Photo: Brian Phelps

Collecting data for data's sake should not be a goal. Rather, landscape architects need to be discerning about the information for improving the management and design of their projects. By selectively incorporating sensors into the design of physical space, the data collection system offers real-time information about the use of spaces. Like website analytic applications, the network can provide useful information about the number of people using the space, where they congregate, how long they occupy a space, as well as other meaningful measures of public life. The data gathered can then be combined with an array of environmental data such as temperature, humidity, sun/shade patterns, rainfall, water quality, and air quality. In addition, other available data sets such as sales tax collections, building permits, real estate transactions, and programming/event schedules can be overlaid with data to make relationships

between the use of the public space and its context visible.

These trends and the desire to learn about these new technologies inspired the "Chair as Sensor," a proof of concept developed by the AGILE Landscape Project. The project demonstrates how design objects could provide meaningful anonymous information about the use of space. It consists of movable seating grouped in a parklet along an active streetscape. A pressure sensor and microcontroller embedded in each chair transmits the occupancy data to an online database for analysis. A companion website plotted the data received from the devices in real time. The project was developed using the Arduino DIY microcontroller platform. While not its primary goal, Chair as Sensor served as a real-world application of the usefulness of DIY platforms such as Arduino and Raspberry Pi.

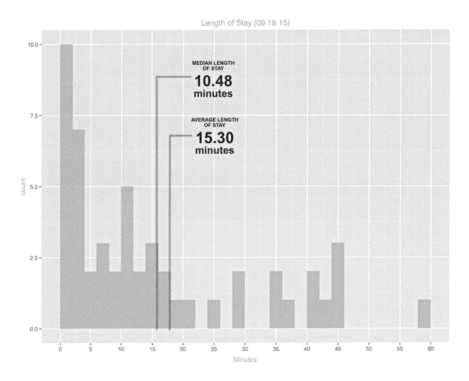

FIGURE 3.2.3 **Utilization capacity for Chair as Sensor parklet during Park(ing) Day 2015**

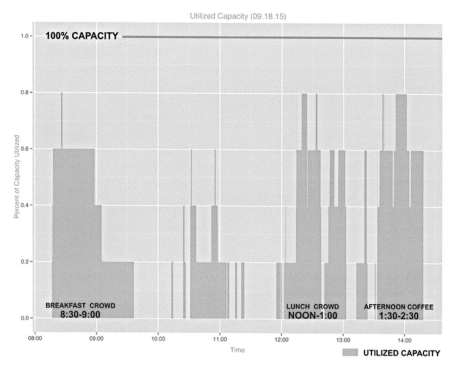

FIGURE 3.2.4 **Length of stay for Chair as Sensor parklet during Park(ing) Day 2015**

The chair was the focus of the experiment because it is an object commonly found within public space and its use represents a relevant and measurable means of quantifying individual user engagement with the space. The project focused on collecting information about the number of people sitting in the parklet, its utilization capacity, and the length of stay of individual visitors.

Capturing the total number of users occupying seating throughout the day provided a quick overview of parklets' daily use patterns. The metric also offered insight into the effectiveness of the design and location of the project. Like a website's daily traffic statistics, plotting the use pattern over an extended period indicates the space's use over the days of the week, months, years, and seasons. This longitudinal view of the ebb and flow offers early indicators of growth or decline in use. This insight allows managers and designers to intervene much earlier through design or programmatic changes. The real-time feedback is well suited to test tactical urbanism installations quickly and with fewer resources.

A closer look at the daily data collection points and slope of the pedestrian counts can offer additional insight. Steep trajectories in use through the day illustrate bursts of activity where groups are sitting down at once over short time periods. Overlaying this data with various programming strategies such as time of events or addition of vendors can help evaluate their level of effectiveness in attracting people. Additionally, one can observe how moving the location of the project can alter the shape of the trajectory, and counts can help calibrate the best locations within a site or district.

Utilization of capacity depicts peak demand throughout the day and pinpoints times when there is excess capacity. Managers can use this data to experiment with various programming changes to exploit these periods and increase the demand when use is low. This ability to target specific times can facilitate the efficient use of limited resources. Conversely, times of peak demand signals the need for expanded seating options within the area. This metric can arm public space advocates with concrete data that demonstrate the need for new spaces and the effectiveness of investments in public space.

The median length of stay signifies a level of connection with a project. The premise is that the more someone is enjoying and is actively engaged with a space, the longer one will stay within it. The longer a person is present, the greater the chance the person is engaged or will likely engage with others. This "stickiness factor" borrows heavily from the online marketing industry. The industry often measures users' interest and a website's effectiveness for maintaining a user's attention by documenting how long users stay on a page.

These metrics and the ability to efficiently capture them over extended periods of time have shown great promise for developing public space analytics methodology that enables designers and managers to make more informed decisions rather than anecdotal observations and assumptions. The ability to cost-effectively and efficiently scale-up the data collection offers the opportunity to study sites over long periods with fewer resources. New insights and discovery will emerge as larger data sets from a wide array of locations are amassed. These new building blocks can also be combined with contextual, environmental, and qualitative data sets to create an even richer picture and deeper insights.

The Chair as Sensor project demonstrates the usefulness of accessible DIY electronics such as the Arduino and Raspberry Pi platforms. The project also emphasizes the necessity of data analytic tools that can help practitioners draw value from the data collected and apply it to landscape architecture. For landscape architects who want to understand their project's impacts and benefits, it will become increasingly important for them to be able to analyze this flow of geo-referenced data to gain useful insights.

Durability and scalability were clear hurdles in the development of the prototypes used. The built environment, particularly the public realm, must be durable enough to withstand the abuses of the public. This reality is an important consideration when designing these systems. They must last. The built environment cannot be replaced every few years. The ability to upgrade the system without fully replacing it is essential to ensuring it can continue to offer value in the future. Exploring systems that can augment physical objects rather than being integral to the object itself is helpful in achieving this. Future iterations of the Chair as Sensor will explore separate units that can be removed and attached to any chair.

The methodology of using sensors to gather data passively without the consent of the users raises concerns about privacy. It is one of the major hurdles when deploying technologies such as computer vision (CV) and Wi-Fi detection. These strategies have the potential to identify individuals and connect data to them.[14] These types of systems, especially CV, coupled with artificial intelligence offer the capability to collect more quantitative activity data.[15] When considering these approaches to data collection, users' privacy is crucial to maintaining the public's trust. In an effort to ensure transparency, new policies and organizations are being developed by cities across the country.[16] Developers can anonymize their data as a means of protecting the individuals from being identified. By using the simplicity of the pressure sensor, the Chair as Sensor project specifically experiments with technologies that maintain the anonymity of citizens while collecting as much useful information as possible.

The data acquired by Chair as Sensor provided an enormous amount of quantitative data. It provides a clear picture of levels of activity. It falls short in providing qualitative data describing what people are doing and the levels of interaction between individuals. Adding the capabilities of sensing the proximity of seating to one another, chair's microclimate data, the direction they are facing, and levels of movement of the seating should be explored in future iterations of the project. These data points would offer another level of understanding of the space and still maintain the goal of anonymity.

The fusion of data and the physical world also opens up more possibilities for the built environment to respond to the user and the activities within it. Design elements such as lighting, shade structures, water features, and others can respond to the use of space. With the growth of mixed reality systems that visually overlay images and text, new information and experiences will become a part of the purview of landscape architecture. Landscape architects need to be in the forefront of these changes and use them to create more engaging experiences.

Understanding the work of landscape architects and the ability to effectively manage projects begs the profession to pursue these technologies. As there is a greater focus on evidence-based solutions, research and development for firms will become essential to maintaining their leadership in the twenty-first century. As Buckminster Fuller has been quoted as saying, "The best way to predict the future is to design it." Landscape architects need to continue to shape the future of landscape instead letting it shaped their practice.

Notes

1. Hosain, S.Z. "50B IoT Devices Connected by 2020 – beyond the Hype and into Reality," *RCR Wireless News*, June 28, 2016, www.rcr wireless.com/20160628/opinion/reality-check-50b-iot-devices-connected-2020-beyond-hype-reality-tag10

2. Doctoroff, D.L. "Reimagining Cities from the Internet up," *Sidewalk Talk*, November 30, 2016, https://medium.com/sidewalk-talk/reimagining-cities-from-the-internet-up-5923d6be63ba#.ubj2h5kdb

3. *Sensing the Park – the Internet of Things*, www.london.gov.uk//what-we-do/business-and-economy/science-and-technology/smart-london/mayor-and-smart/sensing-park

4. Henke, N, Bughin, J., Chui, M., Manyika, J., Saleh, T., Wiseman, B., and Sethupathy, G. *The Age of Analytics: Competing in a Data-Driven World*, McKinsey & Company, www.mckinsey.com/business-functions/mckinsey-analytics/our-insights/the-age-of-analytics-competing-in-a-data-driven-world

5. Kahneman, D. *Thinking, Fast and Slow*, Farrar, Straus and Giroux, 1st ed., 2013.

6. Feuer, A. "Mayor Bloomberg's Geek Squad," *The New York Times*, March 23, 2013, www.nytimes.com/2013/03/24/nyregion/mayor-bloombergs-geek-squad.html

7. Lohr, S. "Huge New York Development Project Becomes a Data Science Lab," *Bits Blog*, 1397473211, https://bits.blogs.nytimes.com/2014/04/14/huge-new-york-development-project-becomes-a-data-science-lab

8. Gurin, J. "How Open Data Is Transforming City Life," *Techonomy*, September 12, 2014, www.forbes.com/sites/techonomy/2014/09/12/how-open-data-is-transforming-city-life/#72b3ae3b4104

9. Moser, W. "The Array of Things Is Coming to Chicago (and the World)," *Chicago Magazine*, September 2, 2016, www.chicagomag.com/city-life/September-2016/The-Array-of-Things-Is-Coming-to-Chicago-and-the-World

10. Ries, E. *The Lean Startup: How Today's Entrepreneurs Use Continuous Innovation to Create Radically Successful Businesses*, Crown Business, 1st ed., 2011.

11. Tjendra, J. "The Origins of Design Thinking," *Wired*, www.wired.com/insights/2014/04/origins-design-thinking

12. Silberberg, S. and Lorah, K. *Places in the Making: How Placemaking Builds Places and Communities*, DUSP MIT, 2013, https://dusp.mit.edu/sites/dusp.mit.edu/files/attachments/project/mit-dusp-places-in-the-making.pdf

13. Landscape Performance Series, https://landscapeperformance.org

14. Dormehl, L. "Facial Recognition: Is the Technology Taking Away Your Identity?" *The Observer*, May 4, 2014, www.theguardian.com/technology/2014/may/04/facial-recognition-technology-identity-tesco-ethical-issues

15. Clifford, S. and Hardy, Q. "Attention, Shoppers: Store Is Tracking Your Cell," *The New York Times*, July 14, 2013, www.nytimes.com/2013/07/15/business/attention-shopper-stores-are-tracking-your-cell.html

16. Elahi, A. "City Needs More Detail in Array of Things Privacy Policy, Experts Say," *Chicago Tribune*, June 20, 2016, www.chicagotribune.com/bluesky/originals/ct-expert-array-of-things-privacy-policy-bsi-20160621-story.html

03.03

The new maker culture

Computation and participation in design

Contributor:

Andrea Hansen Phillips
Founder and Principal, Datum Digital Studio and Assistant Professor of Landscape Architecture, University of Virginia

Within the discipline of landscape architecture, in both academia and in practice, scripting and coding are increasingly prevalent as tools for analysis, design, and communication. While some forms of scripting and parametric design have worked their way into the mainstream for both analysis and design purposes, most landscape architects do not actually code. However, those who do have used computer programming for a range of innovative applications that have the potential to expand the scope and reach of landscape architecture quite dramatically beyond site design into the realm of community engagement and participation tools, web-based site analysis and mapping platforms, mobile and web apps, video games, and more.

This essay represents a significant departure from the current dialogue on coding and scripting in landscape architecture, which tends to consider how such technology is used in site design—for instance, GIS for site analysis, Grasshopper for parametric design, and digital fabrication tools such as laser cutting and 3D milling for topographic representation. While such relational and computational thinking has reached a level of critical saturation in some sectors of the profession, in no small part owing to these tools having become nearly ubiquitous in landscape architecture education over the past decade, most landscape architects are, as Caroline Westort of Iowa State University puts it, tool users rather than toolmakers. She explains: "I actually think we do lose something by not training or teaching students the basic building blocks of what's behind the black box, what's behind the software. . . . We are an information technology discipline, whether we like it or not."[1]

With this provocation in mind, this essay focuses on how landscape architects and affiliated professionals are beginning to assert their role as information technology professionals. Landscape architects are trained to look at complex problems with a critical eye—to digest large amounts of environmental and socioeconomic data and translate that data into landscape designs that are sustainable and socially performative. However, many of the issues landscape architects are trained to care deeply about—climate change, sea-level rise, rapid urbanization, gentrification, sustainability, etc.—will require more than physical design to address. We need policy change, and fast, which requires capital and buy-in at a massive scale. With 3.7 billion users, representing more than half of the global population,[2] there is no better platform than the Internet for facilitating consensus and fundraising of the scope and scale needed to tackle the problems of the twenty-first century. The case studies described in this essay demonstrate how landscape architects have seized on the potential of the Internet, using code and scripting to create software and web applications to facilitate smarter, more efficient approaches to landscape architecture.

A brief history of computation in landscape architecture

Carl Sagan wrote, "You have to know the past to understand the present."[3] Thus, in envisioning a future in which landscape architects become technologists, it is useful to review past examples. It comes as no surprise that the history of computational technology in landscape architecture closely follows the history of the computer itself: as computers became more powerful and more easily available, their use increased, as did the ways in which they were used. In architecture, computation can be strongly traced to computer-aided drafting, which was first used in earnest when Ivan Sutherland at MIT's Lincoln Laboratory released SKETCHPAD in 1960.[4] This technology catalyzed a lineage of formal

micro-movements in which improvements in 2D and 3D modeling software enabled greater formal complexity and a move toward nonorthogonal geometries. We can trace this lineage from postmodernism in the '80s and '90s to Gehry's work with CATIA in the '90s and early 2000s, to "blobitecture" and the embrace of Maya and 3D Studio MAX in the 2000s, and, finally, to parametric architecture as embraced by Patrick Schumacher at Zaha Hadid, the AA, and elsewhere in the late 2000s to present.

While the formal outcomes of each of these architectural movements have been vastly different from one another, the common thread has been a primary focus on formalism. In landscape architecture, on the other hand, while CAD and its successors have certainly been instrumental in the evolution of contemporary landscape form, it can be argued that computation of a different sort has been equally if not more influential: geographic information systems (GIS).

The twentieth century witnessed rapid developments in cartography. In the first half of the century, improved surveying methods allowed many countries to complete comprehensive national surveys. By the 1960s, space-age satellite technology enabled high-quality aerial imagery with full-Earth coverage. These advancements produced enormous quantities of geodata, and governments soon realized they needed powerful software tools to manage this data. One of the earliest forays into the creation of such software happened in Canada. Vast reaches of unoccupied territory in Canada's sub-Arctic zone had increasingly led to land use conflicts and misuse in the 1950s, and, to understand why, the Canadian government established the Canada Land Inventory (CLI) in 1961 in order to produce a federal survey for use in regional land use planning.[5] The CLI commissioned maps of the country's agriculture, forestry, outdoor recreation, and wildlife below the Arctic, and to manage this data a team led by Roger Tomlinson created the Canadian Geographic System (CGIS), which is considered by many to be the model on which contemporary GIS systems are based.[6] Around the same time period, the US Census Bureau developed the first digital geodata format, the GBF-DIME (Geographic Base File – Dual Independent Map Encoding), which allowed the Census Bureau to input and geocode the results of the 1970 Census.[7]

Landscape architects played a central role in developing GIS technologies and establishing their widespread use. At the Laboratory for Computer Graphics and Spatial Analysis at Harvard University, which was founded by architect and urban planner Howard T. Fisher, several landscape architects were instrumental in developing SYMAP and ODYSSEY, the mapping software upon which today's most popular GIS platform is based.[8] Much of the conceptual framing for these tools emerged from ideas set forth by Ian McHarg, a Professor of Landscape Architecture at the University of Pennsylvania, who was brought on as an advisor at the Harvard Laboratory in 1967.[9] McHarg's influential 1969 book *Design with Nature* described an innovative method for environmental land use planning, developed and refined in the early and mid-1960s through projects at McHarg's firm Wallace McHarg Roberts & Todd (WMRT, now WRT), which involved overlaying different types of geographic data using clear transparencies.

Carl Steinitz, a professor in the Department of Landscape Architecture at the GSD, was the first to translate this analog method into a digital one when he and his team used SYMAP for an environmental planning study of the Delmarva Peninsula located at the intersection of Delaware, Maryland, and Virginia (1967). As part of the Delmarva project, Steinitz and his team developed a cartographic decision-making tool in which

grid cells could be rendered in grayscale to represent their land use potential. This tool, called GRID, was later rewritten as the Tomlin Subsystem of IMGRID as part of Dana Tomlin's master's thesis at Harvard. Tomlin, now a professor in the Landscape Architecture program at the University of Pennsylvania, continued work on the use of computer algorithms to process raster data, and his MAP (Map Analysis Package), developed in the 1980s, became the basis for geoprocessing functionality in a long list of present-day GIS tools including Mapbox and ESRI's Spatial Analyst toolkit for ArcMap.[10]

One of Steinitz' students, Jack Dangermond, graduated with a Master of Landscape Architecture degree from the GSD in 1969,[11] and in the same year Dangermond and his wife, Laura, founded the Environmental Systems Research Institute (ESRI). Founded as an environmental planning consulting firm, ESRI utilized cartographic technology Dangermond had learned during his time at Harvard for commercial and government contracts at the local, state, and federal levels. After developing several customized GIS solutions for clients including the City of Los Angeles and the state of Maryland, in 1981 ESRI launched ARC/INFO, the first commercial GIS application.[12] ARC/INFO, which was built on the technical framework of SYMAP and ODYSSEY, introduced a database management tool for assigning attributes to geographic features, and this convenience allowed it to quickly became the preferred GIS system, evolving over time into a robust set of proprietary GIS tools. Today, ESRI's annual revenue exceeds $1 billion.[13]

CAD and GIS remained the primary computational tools used by landscape architects until the late 1990s and early 2000s, when parametric design software, newly championed by architects, opened up the potential for linking geospatial data to formal output. James Corner, in his canonical essay "Eidetic Operations and New Landscapes" (1999), while not explicitly speaking of parametrics, describes the potential of these emerging workflows, calling them "datascapes":

> These are revisions of conventional analytical and quantitative maps and charts that both reveal and construct the shape-forms of forces and processes operating across a given site. Not only are these imagings constructive and suggestive of new spatial formations but also they are so "objectively" constructed—derived from numbers, quantities, facts, and pure data—that they have great persuasive force in the hugely bureaucratic decision-making and management aspects of contemporary city design. Where they differ from the quantitative maps of conventional planning is in their imaging of data in knowingly rhetorical and generatively instrumental ways.

Today, Grasshopper, a visual programming editor for the 3D modeling software Rhino3D, is the primary tool used by landscape architects for both parametric site analysis and parametric design. Conceived in 2007 by David Rutten at Robert McNeel and Associates,[14][15] Grasshopper uses draggable blocks of data and functions (called "components") connected by wires, thus allowing users who do not know anything about computer programming to use computational logic to manipulate Rhino and generate highly complex 3D models. In landscape architecture, Grasshopper is used in both academic projects and increasingly in professional projects as well. For instance, the firm Fletcher Studio used Grasshopper extensively to simulate conditions and create both conceptual design packages and construction documentation for the $2.8 million renovation of San Francisco's South Park.[16] According to Fletcher Studio's

founder, David Fletcher, "Quite literally everything that is in the plans was generated in Grasshopper at one time."[17]

While scripting using Grasshopper and, to a lesser extent, other tools such as RhinoScript and Processing has been employed to generate landscape architecture projects for at least 10 years, the following case studies represent what is essentially uncharted territory: active use of computer programming by landscape architects to create new tools for design and planning—tool users becoming toolmakers. As stated in the introduction, this kind of project, which is often siteless or involving an ambiguous definition of site, represents a significant departure from the traditional role of landscape architecture. In some cases, while the individuals leading these projects are trained in landscape architecture, architecture, or urban design, their careers have taken parallel trajectories into technology, as happened with Jack Dangermond. In other cases, the projects are experimental research or consulting projects performed by practicing or academic landscape architects who are still largely engaged in physical site design on a day-to-day basis.

Regardless of the preferred affiliation of the practitioners themselves, these case studies can be broadly classified into four different categories: design tools, planning and decision tools, community participation tools, and evaluation and assessment tools. For each category, the following case studies may take the form of mobile or web applications, desktop software, scripts, or, in certain cases, prototypes for such software. The commonality between each of the case studies is that the landscape architects and affiliated design professionals involved with each project are actively engaged in *writing code* rather than simply applying parametric or relational principles.

Scripted landscapes: code as design tool

As already discussed, landscape architects are becoming increasingly reliant on parametric design tools such as Grasshopper. As sites have become larger and projects have become more complex, design trends have also shifted further away from the formal, axial landscapes of the early twentieth century into complex, nonorthogonal landscapes with hybridized, flexible programs. To each of these ends, parametric and scripting tools have become huge time-savers. During analysis and conceptual design, these tools allow designers to input environmental and socioeconomic data in various formats and quickly generate design alternatives that have the potential to dynamically adapt to changing conditions.

Architects Eduardo Rico and Enriqueta Llabres have created both tools and methodology for relational urban design as part of their practice, Relational Urbanism. In partnership with the engineering firm Arup, Rico and Llabres have developed software designed to make decisions about land use planning for new towns and communities in developing countries. This software interface, called the Relational Urban Model (RUM), is not a single piece of software but rather a workflow that

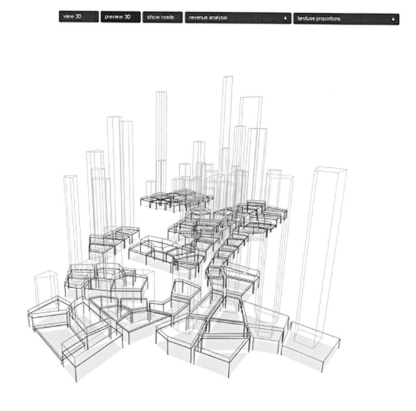

FIGURE 3.3.1 **Baishizhou Relational Urban Model, Arup Global Challenge 2013 First Prize**
Image: Relational Urbanism Ltd[18]

integrates design software such as Grasshopper and Rhino with data in the form of Microsoft Excel spreadsheets.[19] The RUM allows the team to import details of existing urban fabric and environmental constraints such as topography and vegetation, then uses this data to determine block configurations, building typologies, and building heights. The RUM allows for changes on the fly and quick previewing, meaning that many different configurations and scenarios can be created at a highly granular level simply by changing different input parameters.

Nicholas de Monchaux, an associate professor of architecture and urban design at the University of California, Berkeley, has worked since 2009 on Local Code, a project that seeks to design socially and ecologically active landscapes using abandoned urban sites in various cities throughout the United States and abroad. Many of these metropolitan areas have hundreds if not thousands of these sites, thus de Monchaux and his team have sought to find a method for systematically generating designs based on local contexts rather than designing each site one by one. To facilitate this process, de Monchaux's team developed a set of Grasshopper components, collectively called "Finches," which build connections between geospatial data and Rhino geometry.[20] Finches includes components for importing, batch processing, and exporting shapefiles (.shp) within Rhino, meaning that different types of geodata such as parcel boundaries and topography can be combined with Grasshopper's existing parametric modeling tools to generate 3D designs for many sites at once.

The Streetmix project was developed by a team of fellows at Code for America led by Lou Huang, an architect and urban planner turned front-end web developer, and software developer Marcin Wichary. Streetmix is an interactive, web-based tool

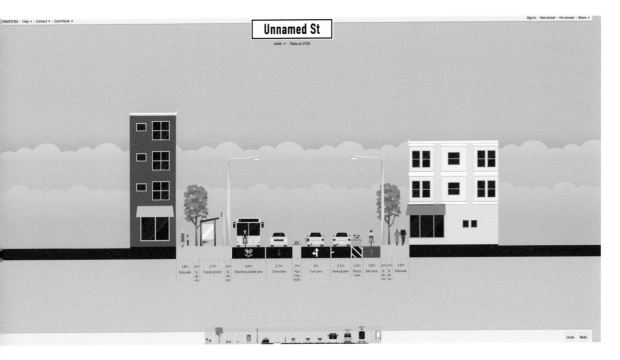

FIGURE 3.3.2 **The Streetmix interface http://streetmix.net**

developed using JavaScript (node.js and Yarn) and MongoDB,[21] which lets anyone create a scaled visual layout for their ideal street. With a simple drag-and-drop interface, Streetmix allows even nondesigners to create sophisticated street sections complete with bike paths, street trees, benches, bus shelters, lighting, and more. Once the user is satisfied with a street section, the section can be shared using email, Twitter, or Facebook, or downloaded as an image.

The company Flux.io[22] has created a data exchange and collaboration platform for architects and urban designers that is used by many of the largest design firms in the world, including Gensler and Arup. The team, led by CEO Jaime Roche, a former architect, is comprised of a combination of software developers (some of whom are former architects and urban designers) and building industry professionals. The product itself is a series of plug-ins for existing design software programs such as AutoCAD, Rhino, and Revit that allow data and models to be synced and updated between platforms. The data itself is stored on Flux's cloud, which allows for automatic backup and web viewing—especially useful for contractors and clients who do not have software licenses!

If this then that: code as planning and decision tool

While the projects in the previous section represent tools that facilitate site design— whether at the scale of streets, sites, or entire cities—the following case studies follow the approach laid forth by Ian McHarg in his "Ecological Method for Landscape Architecture,"[23] concentrating on prioritizing site selection and allocating land use rather

than designing specific site elements. Just as McHarg's method devised a systematic methodology to determine ideal land uses for preservation, development, agriculture, etc., the following case studies also rely on systematic workflows to suggest recommended land uses or recommended sites for previously identified land uses.

The project Fluxscape: Landscape Infrastructure Strategies for Deindustrializing Cities was originally developed by the author as a graduate thesis project at the University of Pennsylvania. The central aim of the project was to develop a methodology for suggesting remediative landscape practices for vacant lots— particularly vacant industrial lots—in Philadelphia. The end product took the format of an interactive website on which users click on a vacant lot via a map interface to view suggested remediation strategies and case studies such as biocontrol, phytoremediation, and stormwater management. These case studies are determined using both objective parameters about the site such as square footage, adjacent uses, impervious surface coverage, as well as subjective parameters such as the user's predilection toward using more or less intensive remediation strategies.

A similar approach was applied to a real-life vacant lot remediation project in Philadelphia for the 2015 Knight Cities Challenge winning project, Urban Arboreta, which creates nurseries on vacant lots to provide plant material for the city's Parks and Recreation Department. The author teamed with landscape architects Tim Baird and Deenah Loeb on this project to create a systematic approach to selecting sites for the nurseries. The team began by brainstorming a list of criteria that would determine if a site had high potential for becoming a nursery. These criteria included the site's size (greater than 1.5 acres), permeability, proximity to

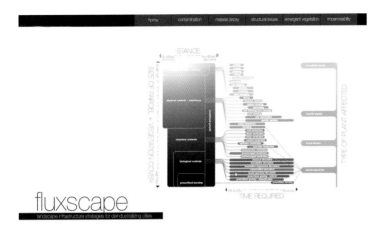

FIGURE 3.3.3 **Screenshots from the Fluxscape web interface, where users can select an appropriate precedent from a number of landscape remediation case studies**

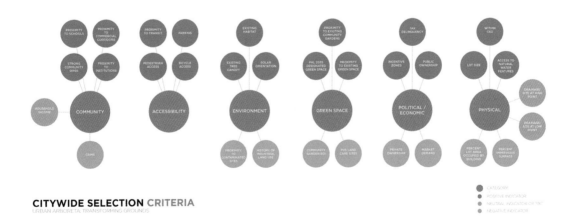

FIGURE 3.3.4 **A diagram showing the beneficial and detrimental site selection criteria inputted into the Urban Arboreta site selection model**

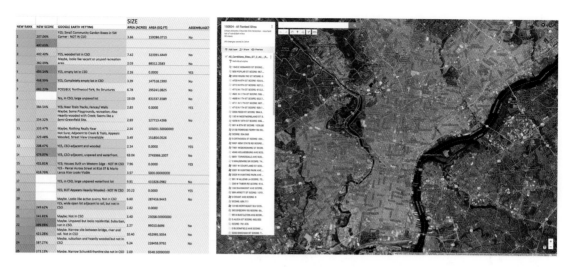

FIGURE 3.3.5 **Color-coded table view and map view of the Urban Arboreta site selection model**

community resources such as churches and schools (to promote partnerships), and location within the city's Combined Sewer Service Area (a requirement so that the city's Water Department would provide support). These criteria were mapped in GIS and then assigned a weight, with the top 100 sites being color-coded in both Excel and Google Maps.

Recently, landscape architecture students and faculty at North Carolina State University have worked to take the interactive planning and decision tool into 3D with their project Tangible Landscape. Tangible Landscape projects GIS map data, and in some cases data from drone mapping, onto a CNC-milled 3D site model. The team of students, led by landscape architect Brendan Harmon, associate director of geovisualization Helena Mitasova, and statistician and GIS programmer Francisco Tonini, is using this modeling technique to simulate various scenarios for tree density, water flow, wildfire paths, and more, with small wooden pegs representing interventions. Most recently, the team used the Tangible Landscape methodology to model a section of trees in Sonoma Valley, California,

that might be susceptible to sudden oak death. Beginning by mapping out locations of bay laurel trees, which are a known host to the disease, the team then simulated removing those trees at different rates to account for factors such as budget, time, and rate of disease spread. Tangible Landscape is now being demoed at various industry conferences, and in the future the team hopes to incorporate Tangible Landscape into afterschool programs for school-age children.[24]

Hack your city: code as community participation tool

Alongside its many positive benefits, the Internet has had the unfortunate side effect of substantially reducing participation in civic life. Voter turnout and participation in the United States, for instance, ranks thirty-first out of 35 countries in the OECD, with a measly 53 percent of the voting age population voting in the 2012 presidential election and far fewer voting in the average midterm election.[25] This apathy has an impact on the community participation process for landscape architecture and urban design projects as well. This process—typically confined in public projects to a series of sparsely attended community meetings—is sorely inadequate because it fails to gather a representative sampling of citizens. While some potential stakeholders may miss meetings because they did not see an announcement (or they ignored it), others who actually do wish to attend are unable to owing to work or personal conflicts, disabilities, lack of transportation, etc. Digital and web-based community participation tools remove time and access constraints and scheduling issues by being accessible 24/7; they also help to reach younger individuals by targeting them where many already spend the bulk of their time—online. Granted, these online engagement tools aren't perfect—there is still a small but not insignificant portion of the population who does not have regular Internet access—

but they represent an improvement over the status quo.

A number of landscape architects have tried their hand at building web tools for community participation. Douglas Meehan, founder of the digital media firm Test/Plot, created the project Possible City to match vacant lots in Philadelphia to people who are interested in revamping them. The project, which was a semi-finalist in the 2013 Knight News Challenge, used the JavaScript mapping library Leaflet.js to map the city's 40,000 vacant lots. Upon clicking on one of the lots, users could find more information on the lot's ownership, as well as citizen proposals for new projects that could help to revitalize the vacant land.[26]

Landscape architects Nico Koff and Marissa Bernstein are the founders of Projexity (projexity.com), a Canadian technology company that offers community engagement

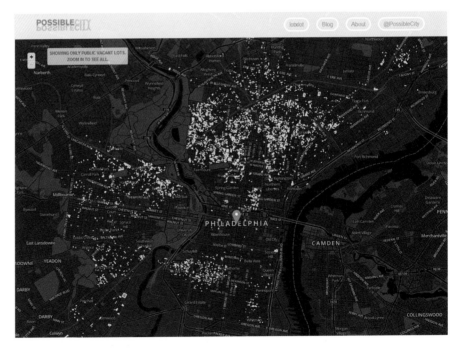

FIGURE 3.3.6 **The Possible City project, created by Douglas Meehan**
Image: Douglas Meehan

FIGURE 3.3.7 **The original Community How-To Guides were a series of colorful printed brochures created by Ceara O'Leary at the Detroit Collaborative Design Center. Now on the web, a screenshot above shows the guide creation interface for the Community How-To Guides website, www.communityhowtoguides.org**

tools designed for organizations and municipalities. These tools, which have been used by the University of Toronto and the David Suzuki Foundation, provide intuitive, easy-to-use interfaces called embeddables, which allow citizens to submit content such as events and initiatives through Facebook or their own websites. Prior to its current focus on online engagement tools, Projexity had

been a platform crowdfunding urban improvement projects, in which users could post their own projects or vote on their favorites.

The project Community How-To Guides (www.communityhowtoguides.org) was developed by the author for the Detroit Collaborative Design Center (DCDC),

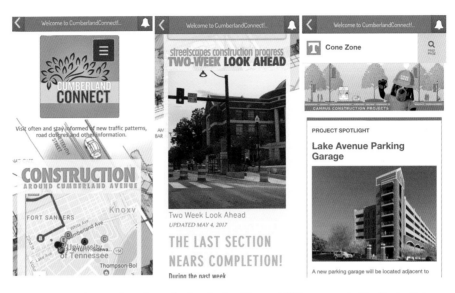

FIGURE 3.3.8 **Screenshots from the CumberlandConnect iOS app, created by Becky Rehorn**

with funding from Enterprise Community Partners and the Surdna Foundation.

This project was inspired by a set of printable guides for community building in Detroit that DCDC developed in 2014. The guides were so popular that DCDC wanted to build a web-based tool so that community builders in other cities and countries could create their own guides and then either share them via social media or email or print them. In addition to an interactive interface for creating guides (built using PHP, MySQL, and JavaScript), the site also includes a library of guides created by others, which can also be viewed and shared to allow for knowledge sharing across communities.

While the Internet continues to be a rich resource for landscape architects and urban designers, mobile is quickly surpassing desktop applications—indeed, mobile Internet usage surpassed desktop for the first time in November 2016.[27] Landscape architects Vaughn & Melton out of Knoxville, Tennessee, have capitalized on this trend with their project Cumberland Connect. The project involves both physical landscape

design and community engagement. For the former, Vaughn & Melton created streetscape designs for the revitalization of Cumberland Avenue, one of the main streets in Knoxville and the central retail corridor for the University of Tennessee. For the former, Vaughn & Melton's Becky Rehorn developed an iOS app called CumberlandConnect that allows community members to receive notifications of street closures, upcoming events, and construction progress.[28]

Performance (para)metrics: code as assessment tool

To introduce the 1999 exhibition and accompanying publication *Metacity/Datatown*, Winy Maas of the architecture firm MVRDV wrote: "Imagine a city that is described only by data, a city that wants to be explored only as information. A city that knows no given topography, no prescribed ideology, no representation and no context: only huge pure data."[29] The case studies in this final group imagine landscapes themselves as data, data to be quantified in order to create a system in which different landscapes, by different landscape architects, can be stacked up against one another and compared across different metrics. These tools, some of which are discipline-focused and others that are more publicly accessible, help to establish a profession-wide "standard of practice" and a growing library of successful built projects that can be used for analysis and teaching purposes.

The Landscape Architecture Foundation's (LAF) Landscape Performance Series[30] was launched in 2010 as an online portal and set of initiatives to document innovations in landscape architecture. Currently standing at 100 case study briefs—a searchable database of exemplary projects—and 120 "Fast Facts," the series also includes a handy set of benefits toolkit calculators. With these calculators, LAF has brought together a number of national, industry-standard metrics, recommendations, and regulations that can be used in the design phase to compare projected landscape performance benefits among various options. These benefits toolkit calculators include US EPA's National Stormwater Calculator, USDA Forest Service's i-Tree, the State of Washington Department of Ecology's Rainwater Harvesting Calculator, and many more. The Landscape Performance Series website was developed by TOKY,[31] a St. Louis-based branding and digital services firm specializing in work with arts and architecture clients.

The nonprofit organization Conservation International has developed an assessment system called the Landscape Accounting Framework[32] (also shortened to LAF, though not to be confused with the Landscape Architecture Foundation). This tool is being

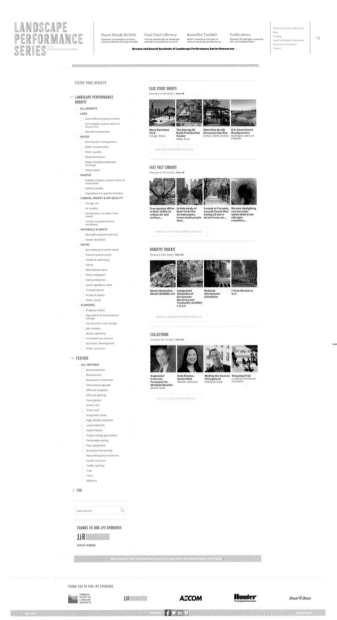

FIGURE 3.3.9 **Screenshot of the Landscape Performance Series website created by TOKY for the Landscape Architecture Foundation, https://landscapeperformance.org/browse**

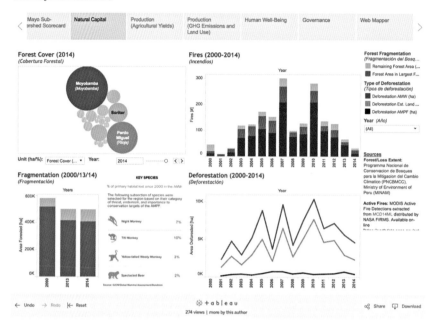

Alto Mayo Sub-Watershed Landscape Accounting Framework

Alto Mayo Sub-Watershed Landscape Accounting Framework (In Progress)

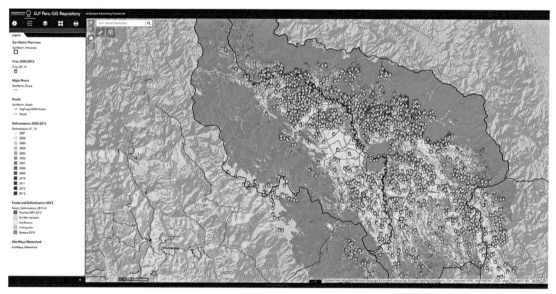

FIGURE 3.3.10 **Conservation International's Landscape Accounting Framework (LAF) includes both quantitative and spatial views of many different kinds of green development indicators. These are shown through both interactive charts and graphs created in Tableau (top) and an in an interactive web map (bottom)**

Source: https://public.tableau.com/profile/carbon.fund via www.conservation.org/projects/Pages/Landscape-Accounting-Framework.aspx

FIGURE 3.3.11 **The 2016 ParkScore® rankings. Users can click on individual cities to learn more about how the rankings were calculated**

Source: http://parkscore.tpl.org/rankings.php

used in green development projects in North Sumatra, Indonesia, and San Martin, Peru, which collectively comprise 8 million hectares (~20 million acres) of land. The LAF framework uses quantifiable indicators of sustainability such as range of natural capital, rate of production, and level of human well-being, and monitors those data using an interactive dashboard built in the data visualization platform Tableau. In addition to the Tableau dashboard, the LAF also includes an interactive GIS repository that allows for the data to be used and viewed spatially, and broken down into individual administrative units such as provinces, states, etc.

Another nonprofit organization, the Trust for Public Land, has developed the ParkScore index,[33] which is a comprehensive rating system designed to measure how well the 100 largest cities in the United States are meeting the need for parks. ParkScore uses GIS data for these cities to identify which neighborhoods and demographics are underserved by parks. Another metric determines how many people are able to walk to a park in 10 minutes or less. The ParkScore rankings are documented on a website, which is updated annually to determine new rankings. As of 2016, Minneapolis ranks number one in the U.S., with St. Paul, MN, Washington, DC, Arlington, VA, and San Francisco, CA, rounding out the top five. The website itself includes an overview of the rankings, and upon clicking on an individual city in the rankings users can see much more information about how that city's ranking was determined, including charts showing access to parks by age and income, total acreage of parks, and relative municipal spending on parks. The detail page also includes a link to view an interactive map of that city's parks and areas where park need is moderate to very high. In addition to this map, the ParkScore website includes a link to the ParkEvaluator tool,[34] which is an interactive map-based tool where users can draw a

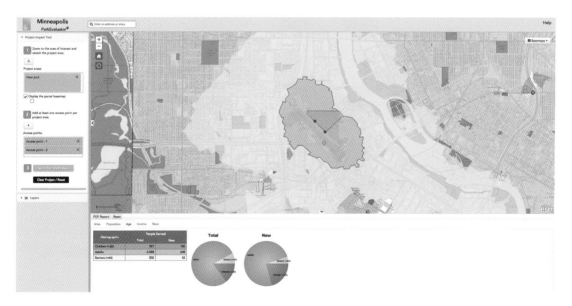

FIGURE 3.3.12 **The ParkEvaluator is an interactive map that lets users test out locations for new parks to see how the ParkScore would change**

Source: http://parkscore.tpl.org/evaluator/evaluator.html?city=Minneapolis

new park and run an analysis to see how the proposed park affects the surrounding community in terms of additional residents served broken down by age, income, and race.

Conclusion

Robert Pirsings wrote in *Zen and the Art of Motorcycle Maintenance* (1975):

> "What's new?" is an interesting and broadening eternal question, but one which, if pursued exclusively, results only in an endless parade of trivia and fashion, the silt of tomorrow. I would like, instead, to be concerned with the question, "What is best?"

Landscape architects have just begun to face the possibilities of how technology can substantially change the face of the profession as we know it, and with the breadth of new technologies at our disposal it is more important than ever to continually consider "what is best" rather than simply "what is new."

In determining which computational technologies are best to add to the landscape architect's toolkit, it is important to first consider purpose-built technologies—those designed by and for the landscape architecture industry—such as those outlined in this essay. However, at present the vast majority of landscape architects do not have the computer programming knowledge to be able to develop these tools, and it is arguably not economically viable for the software industry to develop commercial software exclusively for landscape architects since the field is comparatively small, with only 21,000 landscape architects employed in the United States as of 2012 and a total market share representing less than 0.1 percent of GDP (for architectural and design services as a whole).[35] Thus, it is now more important than ever that landscape

architecture pedagogy becomes more proactive in in teaching students how to code.

Coding is beginning to be taught in elective courses in many MLA programs; however, as programming languages are constantly changing (and it is inefficient if not impossible to teach all of the programming languages that have applicability to landscape architecture), it is more important that students learn the fundamentals behind computer programming—those principles that are common to all programming languages, such as functions, loops, and conditional logic. One model for how this might be done is the Master of Advanced Studies in Landscape Architecture (MAS LA) program at ETH in Zurich, which is organized as a series of workshops and modules that teach programming incrementally. Beginning with a workshop introducing computational software such as Rhino and Grasshopper, the program gradually introduces more challenging concepts and coding languages including Processing and Rhinoscript. However, in addition to the hands-on training, the program also includes a three-day intensive workshop entitled "Theoretical Programming," which introduces the theoretical fundamentals of computer programming in general and as it relates to landscape architecture, covering more advanced concepts such as genetic algorithms and agent-based systems by using interactive demonstrations and role-play.[36,37,38]

Equipped with more robust and comprehensive training in both the theoretical and practical applications of computer programming, the next generation of landscape architects has vast potential to affect change both inside and outside the profession. Within the profession, individuals such as Adam Mekies, computational design lead at Design

Workshop in Colorado,[39] and Chris Landau, Manager of Design Technology at Olin in Philadelphia,[40] are developing custom technology in house and serving as design technology consultants for a range of landscape projects. The aforementioned firm Fletcher Studio, led by David Fletcher, has expanded the definition of the landscape architecture project to include digital, virtual landscapes, having designed environments for the video game the Witness, a 3D puzzle video game developed by Thekla, Inc.[41]

Individuals trained in landscape architecture, architecture, planning, and urban design are also bringing their training in spatial design and complex problem-solving to various technology companies as designers and engineers outside the profession. Some examples of these individuals are Xiaowei Wang, who received her MLA from the GSD in 2013 and is now a platform engineer at Mapbox;[42] Lou Huang, who received a master's in city planning from the University of Pennsylvania in 2010 and is now a user interface engineer at Mapzen;[43] and Patrick Stowe Jones, who trained as an architect at the University of Michigan and the GSD and is now a User Experience (UX) and interaction designer at IA Collaborative in Chicago.[44] Others have formed their own technology companies. Sha Hwang received his architecture degree from the University of California, Berkeley, in 2007 and subsequently worked for the mapping and data visualization firm Stamen and the real estate website Trulia before founding Nava, a software company dedicated to creating software for government services.[45] Nadia Amoroso, a lecturer at the University of Toronto and the University of Guelph, founded the software company DataAppeal, which creates compelling 3D maps.[46] The author's own practice, Datum Digital Studio, meanwhile, creates websites, applications, and decision tools geared toward landscape architecture and urban

design projects, some of which are described in this essay.

There are many benefits to increased emphasis on coding and scripting in landscape architecture, and few downsides. When landscape architects, architects, and urban designers take it into their own hands to create design tools, they are able to create greater functionality for the kinds of work these disciplines do on a day-to-day basis. These advancements have the potential to profoundly change the profession, expand its purview, and improve its ability to integrate community input, advocate for ecological and sustainable best practices, and create dynamic site designs that utilize real-time data to adapt to changing urban and natural environments.

Notes

1. Bentley, C. "Follow the Script: Computation Reshapes Landscapes—And Thinking," Landscape Architecture Magazine, July 2016, 70.

2. Internet Usage Statistics: The Internet Big Picture. World Internet User and 2017 Population Stats, Internet World Stats: Usage and Population Statistics, www.internet worldstats.com/stats.htm, last modified March 25, 2017, accessed May 3, 2017.

3. Cosmos: A Personal Voyage, episode 2, "One Voice in the Cosmic Fugue," produced by Adrian Malone. Written by Carl Sagan, Ann Druyan and Steven Soter. Public Broadcasting Service, October 5, 1980.

4. "Computer-aided design/History, Present and Future," Wikiversity, https://en.wikiversity. org/wiki/Computer-aided_design/History,_ Present_and_Future, last modified January 13, 2017, accessed April 7, 2017.

5. Piecre, T.W. and Neville Ward, E. "Canada Land Inventory," The Canadian Encyclopedia, www.thecanadianencyclopedia.ca/en/article/can ada-land-inventory, last modified December 16, 2013, accessed April 7, 2017.

6. "The Remarkable History of GIS," GISGeography, http://gisgeography.com/history- of-gis, last modified January 26, 2017, accessed April 7, 2017.

7. "The Remarkable History of GIS."

8. Chrisman, N. *Charting the Unknown: How Computer Mapping at Harvard Became GIS*, ESRI, 2006, p. 4.

9. Chrisman, *Charting the Unknown*, p. 4.

10. Artz, M. "C. Dana Tomlin to be Inducted into URISA's GIS Hall of Fame," *GIS and Science*, https://gisandscience.com/2010/09/07/c-dana-tomlin-to-be-inducted-into-urisas-gis-hall-of-fame, last modified September 7, 2010, accessed June 16, 2017.

11. "Jack Dangermond," *Wikipedia: The Free Encyclopedia*, https://en.wikipedia.org/wiki/Jack_Dangermond, last modified March 8, 2017, accessed April 7, 2017.

12. *International Directory of Company Histories*, Vol. 62, St. James Press, 2004.

13. "Esri," *Wikipedia: The Free Encyclopedia*, https://en.wikipedia.org/wiki/Esri, last modified March 13, 2017, accessed April 7, 2017.

14. Wallis, J. and Rahmann, H. *Landscape Architecture and Digital Technologies: Re-conceptualising Design and Making*, Routledge, 2016, p. 65.

15. Mode Lab, *The Grasshopper Primer*, Gitbook, 3rd ed., 2015, http://grasshopper primer.com/en/0-about/1-grasshopper-an-overview.html, accessed April 7, 2017. From this volume on the origins of Grasshopper:

The origins of Grasshopper can be traced to the functionality of Rhino3d Version 4's "Record History" button. This built-in feature enabled users to store modeling procedures implicitly in the background as you go. If you lofted four curves with the recording on and then edited the control points of one of these curves, the surface geometry would update. Back in 2008, David posed the question: "what if you could have more explicit control over this history?" and the precursor to Grasshopper, Explicit History, was born. This exposed the history tree to editing in detail and empowered the user to develop logical sequences beyond the existing capabilities of Rhino3D's built-in features. Six years later, Grasshopper is now a robust visual programming editor that can be extended by suites of externally developed add-ons. Furthermore, it has fundamentally altered the workflows of professionals across multiple industries and fostered an active global community of users.

16. Bentley, "Follow the Script: Computation Reshapes Landscapes—And Thinking," p. 66.

17. Bentley, "Follow the Script: Computation Reshapes Landscapes—And Thinking," p. 67.

18. Project Credits: Design Director: Enriqueta Llabres. Design Team: Giorgio Ponzo, Jung Hyun Woo, Juan Carpio, Javier Serrano, Giulia Grassi. Coding Direction: Immanuel Koh. Coding Assistant: Tessa Steenkamp. For Arup: Eduardo Rico. Peer Review: Charles Waldheim.

19. Tessa Steenkamp, "Relational Urban Model," http://cargocollective.com/tessa steenkamp/Relational-Urban-Model, accessed May 3, 2017.

20. Cantrell, B. and Holzman, J. *Responsive Landscapes: Strategies for Responsive Technologies in Landscape Architecture*, Routledge, 2016, pp. 147–150.

21. Code for America, "Contributing to Streetmix," Streetmix, 2013–2017, Github repository, https://github.com/streetmix/streetmix/blob/master/CONTRIBUTING.md, accessed May 4, 2017.

22. Flux.io, https://flux.io, accessed May 4, 2017.

23. McHarg, I. "An Ecological Method for Landscape Architecture," *Landscape Architecture*, January 1967, 105–107.

24. Rae, H. "Using RPGs to Solve Environmental Problems," *PC Mag*, April 21, 2017, www.pcmag.com/news/353149/using-rpgs-to-solve-environmental-problems, accessed May 6, 2017.

25. DeSilver, D. *U.S. Voter Turnout Trails Most Developed Countries*, Pew Research Center, August 2, 2016, www.pewresearch.org/fact-tank/2016/08/02/u-s-voter-turnout-trails-most-developed-countries, accessed April 7, 2017.

26. Cary Betagole, "Possible City Wants to Match Uses with Philly's 40k Vacant Lots," *Technical.ly*, May 13, 2013, https://technical.ly/philly/2013/05/13/possible-city-vacant-land, accessed May 5, 2017.

27. *Mobile and tablet internet usage exceeds desktop for first time worldwide*, StatCounter, November 1, 2016, http://gs.statcounter.com/press/mobile-and-tablet-internet-usage-exceeds-desktop-for-first-time-worldwide, accessed May 5, 2017.

28. Rehorn, B. "CumberlandConnect," iOS application, https://appsto.re/us/JXG36.i, downloaded May 7, 2017.

29. Maas, W. and MVRDV, *Metacity Datatown*, Stroom Centre for the Visual Arts and 010 Publishers, 1999.

30. "Landscape Performance Series," Landscape Architecture Foundation, https://landscapeperformance.org, accessed May 8, 2017.

31. TOKY, https://toky.com, accessed May 8, 2017.

32. "The Landscape Accounting Framework," Conservation International, www.conservation.org/projects/Pages/Landscape-Accounting-Framework.aspx, accessed May 8, 2017.

33. ParkScore 2016, The Trust for Public Land, http://parkscore.tpl.org, accessed May 8, 2017.

34. ParkEvaluator, The Trust for Public Land, http://parkscore.tpl.org/evaluator/evaluator.html, accessed May 8, 2017.

35. "ACPSA Issue Brief #8: Value Added by Architectural and Design Services," Office of Research and Analysis, National Endowment for the Arts, January 2015, www.arts.gov/sites/default/files/ADP6–8_ValueAddedArchitectural Design.pdf, accessed April 7, 2017.

36. *ETH: Master of Advanced Studies in Landscape Architecture 2013/2014*, http://girot.arch.ethz.ch/wp-content/uploads/2012/10/MASLA_2013_module_Girot.pdf, accessed April 7, 2017.

37. Fricker, P. "How to Teach 'New Tools' in Landscape Architecture in the Digital Overload: Developing Emergent Design Methodologies," *eCAADe Curriculum*, 2 (Computation and Performance), September 18–20, 2013, http://papers.cumincad.org/data/works/att/ecaade2013_028.content.pdf

38. Wallis and Rahmann, *Landscape Architecture and Digital Technologies*, p. 67.

39. Bentley, "Follow the Script: Computation Reshapes Landscapes—And Thinking," p. 70.

40. Chris Landau, LinkedIn profile, www.linkedin.com/in/chrislandau, accessed April 7, 2017.

41. Blow, J. "Architecture in the Witness," December 23, 2011, http://the-witness.net/news/2011/12/architecture-in-the-witness, accessed April 7, 2017.

42. Wang, X. LinkedIn profile, www.linkedin.com/in/xiaoweirwang, accessed April 7, 2017.

43. Huang, L. LinkedIn profile, www.linkedin.com/in/louhuang, accessed April 7, 2017.

44. Stowe Jones, P. LinkedIn profile, www.linkedin.com/in/patrickstowejones, accessed April 7, 2017.

45. Hwang, S. LinkedIn profile, www.linkedin.com/in/shashashasha, accessed April 7, 2017.

46. Schwartz, A. "How To Turn Your Data Into Beautiful 3-D Maps," *Fast Company*, August 29, 2013, www.fastcompany.com/3016379/how-to-turn-your-data-into-beautiful-3-d-maps, accessed April 7, 2017.

03.04
Code matters

Consequent digital tool making in landscape architecture

Contributors

Luis E. Fraguada
Director, Master of Advanced Interaction Program, Institute for Advanced Architecture of Catalonia; Rhinoceros 3d Plug-in Development, Robert McNeel and Associates; Research Director, Built by Associative Data

James Melsom
Coordinator of the Landscape Visualisation and Modeling Lab LVML, ETH, Swiss Federal Institute of Technology, Zurich; Landscape Architect, BSLA, Switzerland

The relatively young discipline of landscape architecture has been fundamentally shaped by its tools and typical means of representation, which have not evolved markedly since its inception, only developing substantially in the last decade. As a discipline, its predecessors could be seen to include not only architecture and garden design but also surveying, geography, cartography, geology, botany and the other earth and climate sciences. The adoption of the term by practitioners such as Olmstead coincided with the realization of New York's Central Park, an exceptionally modern conceptual project that could be seen as a taxonomy of the natural sciences. As such, and despite its diversity of scope and varied vocabulary, it is somewhat surprising to note that the techniques and tools of such parallel disciplines have influenced landscape architecture so little, particularly in technique and method.

In contemporary discussions of spatial understanding and landscape design, the key factor driving the process has remained the perception and sensation of the environment by its inhabitants in regards to aesthetics, programmatic and physical comfort implications (Reiter and De Herde, 2011; Moonen et al., 2012).

While such intuitive approaches remain relevant, demands have increased on the designer to work holistically, incorporating non-visual understanding of the complex systems behind a dynamic landscape environment.

In the book *Thinking with Objects* it was demonstrated through various examples that the development in the seventeenth century of many of the governing laws of physics and the natural world occurred principally through the instrumentalization of these fundamental principles, often generating discrete tools in parallel, or as a direct product (Meli, 2006). The development of organized human computation, the precursor to modern computing, is generally agreed to occur around the start of the nineteenth century (Grier, 2005), coincidentally around the time the term landscape architecture was first used. It is at this time that the concept of garden design was deemed insufficient, as entire cities became conceptualized and catalogued in terms of their open space organization, design and construction, as perhaps best characterized in the 1867 publication of *Les Promenades de Paris* by Adolphe Alphand. While not directly connected, such impulses reflected a shift towards intellectual rigor and organization, which was nevertheless conducted within the contemporary restrictions and methods of practice.

The current contemporary spatial design field places increasing demands on the profession to integrate interdisciplinary processes, massive data sets, analysis and regulatory constraints. There are a multitude of issues associated with such 'big data' sets in fidelity, scale, resolution, and type, which must be overcome (Peralta, 2006; Koolhaas, 2014; Ekbia et al., 2014), requiring specialized tools and approaches. The discipline of landscape architecture is faced with entirely new demands in order to deal with the big data external to and generated by a given project. These demands have long since rendered traditional tools and workflows inadequate, and often obsolete, as symptomatically demonstrated by the lag behind the field of architecture in areas such as (landscape) BIM. Recent research in the field of landscape architecture has marked a shift towards the crafting of the physical and digital tools that mediate our interaction with built and unbuilt environment. This shift is symptomatic of a fundamental transformation in the manner and potential of our ability to shape the environment, and our fundamental relationship with it.

Seeing things differently

Consider how much we rely on our senses to guide our understanding of the space around us. Specifically, our sense of sight is paramount to how we navigate, how we socialize with others; many times, it is the sense by which we first evaluate a scenario in front of us so that we may act accordingly. Sight has evolved as a sense to help us navigate the physical world around us, but reality is much more nuanced. While we can successfully react to a variety of scenarios based on what we see, how does that

compare to our ability to gauge the necessities of a site with regards to a project brief? If we compare, for example, how the human eye responds to wavelengths in the light spectrum versus the wavelengths useful for active plant photosynthesis, we'll see that the domain of the wavelength spectrum are similar for a variety of human eyes and a variety of plants (400–700nm). There is, however, a significant difference in the spectral sensitivity of a human eye to that of a plant's photosynthetic cells. The human eye is sensitive to wavelengths in the middle of the visible spectrum, whereas plant photosynthesis will be activated by the wavelengths at the ends of the spectrum. Of course, plants use light radiation for a different purpose than human eyes, which begs the question: why should a decision on appropriate light levels for plants be made by human eyes when the instrument can't properly sense the light wavelengths that a plant may need?

This last rhetorical question could be abstracted to inquire about almost any decision made during the landscape design process. Some answers will come from a more pragmatic point of view: decisions in a design process cannot be made by human intuition alone. Some decisions must be evaluated based on third-party empirical knowledge acquired after repeatable, documented experiments related to phenomena that we are not equipped to detect. As a case in point, a significant territorial intervention by a landscape architect will require a topographical and geological survey on which they will base some of the design decisions and project planning. There are instruments and methods in place that not only extend our ability to understand a space; oftentimes the application of this technology in practice is a legal requirement. This should not be seen as an imposition on the creative design process, because, really, why limit our understanding to one that is derived from

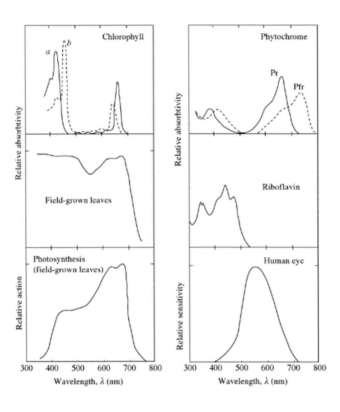

FIGURE 3.4.1
Plants and microclimate – finite data of complex systems (Jones, 1992)

our built-in senses when there is really so much more going on around us? Can technology be the medium by which we engage a deeper understanding of a territory and its fluctuations over time?

The toolmaking process has been enabled through various recent developments, notably open-source coding, hardware production, WYSIWYG/nodal interfaces, cloud connectivity, bandwidth and standardization. These developments have resulted in a transparent, streamlined approach to tool crafting, which allows the designer to craft tools seamlessly within the design process. Several recent software and hardware developments, such as multi-platform visual programming, accessible electronics, cloud database and open data platforms (e.g. Processing, Grasshopper, Arduino, GeoJSON, OSM, WU etc.) have further enabled this shift, leading to a more inclusive, transparent network of possible applications.

Digital toolmaking

The authors have explored the questions posed previously both in professional practice and academia, beginning with explorations in data acquisition, and later linking that with developments in specific hardware and software tools (Melsom, 2015). Common to these areas of research and application is an approach that is composed of digital tools written and built in a variety of programming languages and evolved iteratively with each new project. These digital tools started out as individual hypotheses; a simple, early example: can the data from this sensor give us a different way of seeing a site? This parallel development of toolmaking and site-focused enquiry develops into a combination of hardware (the sensor and the components to enable sensing), firmware (the software responsible for controlling the hardware) and software (the necessary logic to read the data and

FIGURE 3.4.2 **Sensor preparation, on-site application and analysis on the Zurich lakeshore**
Photos: ETHZ

programs that take the data as inputs), and feedback from the applied data analyses, in a process of digital toolmaking. The term 'digital toolmaking' is utilized here to describe bespoke software and hardware development in response to a project brief or specific functional necessity otherwise not satisfied by existing software and hardware platforms (see Figure 3.4.2) (Moonen et al., 2012). Digital toolmaking can be at once a methodology to describe a process applied in a professional context as well as a pedagogical method where students learn problem-solving through the creation of novel software and hardware tools.

Exploring new modes of sensing the site was a fundamental step in our research, and has become fundamental to the teaching method of each site-based student workshop. First, the ability and desire to acquire data called into question the nature of data as a concept. A cursory understanding of data collection

processes, statistical refinement and error reduction reveals that the data we trust implicitly and empirically is by its nature a blurred, generalization of environment and site conditions. Instead, the potential of data for a designer becomes the attentive recording of the response of the site, via sensor or other means, instead of a referenced set of averaged and standardized numbers from a document downloaded from a government source. Such an act exposes the person acquiring the data to a whole new set of issues, including calibration of sensors and eventually calling into question the very validity of the values being recorded, yet also the true nature of microclimate, and nuances that vegetation, terrain, exposure and material effect on the environment and its inhabitants.

The technical hardware issues often faced by amateurs in the implementation of sensors have been all but eradicated and thus made accessible through abstracted programming (Arduino-compatible). Thanks to many developments in this field being open-source, the sensors will often come with a source code library that greatly facilitates the programming necessary to read the values from the sensor in question. Therefore going from one sensor to a combination of sensors and their interconnection becomes a trivial programming task, often requiring only the customization of values and example code.

After the novelty of acquiring your own data wears off, and the implications of data collection and quality control are understood, one must mine the data for meaningful signals. This process at first was a manual one: looking through the numbers to see if there were any obviously erroneous entries into the data record. This process often

reveals patterns or behaviours inherent in the sensor that must be ameliorated if of any use; quantitative comparison is to be carried out. This in the end is the point: quantifying these signals is the basis for augmenting our understanding of the phenomenon in question. Additional statistical processes can be integrated to automate this laborious process within complex research projects. Nevertheless, we consider it a crucial didactic step for the designers to get their hands 'dirty' in the raw data, to become familiar with its often unpredictable and pattern-filled nature, and to gain a critical and discerning eye. After recognizing certain aberrations in the data acquisition process, we could begin automating the scrubbing of the data into a set that is free of anomalies, presenting trends, exceptions and correlations. As a process, this data verification phase is also relevant to

FIGURE 3.4.3 **Synthesis of Zurich lakeshore TLS scan site data with current iteration of design project to form navigable high detail pointcloud**
Source: ETHZ

microclimatic processes – a microclimate is also a microcosm, with its own local variations and extremes. Beyond a literal reading of the data, even a vague indication or confirmation of difference from the norm or larger site relevant within a design process.

Comparison of two sets of data from two different sites could be the basis for several design options, but the data can only be compared if sensors are calibrated and data is free of anomalies. In practice, this is often a luxury, requiring more expensive sensors capable of self-calibration and reporting results in SI units. Nevertheless, low-cost sensors, while not benefiting from features present in higher cost counterparts, can give us useful information that can often offer great insight in spite of their diminished precision (Fraguada et al., 2012).

As an ongoing case study, the postgraduate semester design theme of the Zurich lakeshore is an excellent example of a large-scale urban landscape site with a substantial framework of existing infrastructure, built fabric and vegetation, lacking an open space strategy. The shoreline has undergone constant shifts over the last 150 years, bearing no resemblance to its pre-settled form. As such, it is a perfect test bed for a studio of projects varying from subtle interventions to substantial re-engineering of the entire shore. While the quality and quantity of available data are perhaps atypically substantial, it also provides a perfect test case scenario in data management and building efficient workflows. This project contrasts with a glimpse of a second case study – the four-day intensive workshop in landscape scanning and analysis in the forested hills of Barcelona, Spain. The implementation and development of various landscape tools went through specific phases, from mining of site data to scanning/sensing, and iterative analysis and design.

Data mining tools

The concept of data mining lends itself to an iterative, critical process, where the available data is not simply imported and applied but sampled in a controlled manner (Fry, 2009). Through the maintenance of a link to the original data sets, data of all types may be filtered, referenced, replaced, supplemented and additionally categorized based on its accuracy, age and source. The tooling process begins at the large scale, mining and applying available site data. This particular Swiss site is data-rich, including detailed historical maps, GIS layers and CAD data of the city and landscape elements. The typical 'Swisstopo' filtered LIDAR laser scan data, detailing terrain and infrastructure features at a 2m resolution, was combined with a detailed bathymetry point cloud of Lake Zurich at.5m resolution. The resulting surface model forms an ideal base from which to begin the analysis and design process, as well as apply other abstract data sources. It forms the iterative topographical base which is revisited and readjusted throughout the design process (see Figure 3.4.3). By keeping a live link to the original data, the shifting focus of the design site area can be resampled for large-scale analysis or supplemented with additional topographical data as the project progresses through its development.

Additional open data sources such as environmental data (compiled from government/weather underground data), serve as a key first understanding of the site's performance. This process relies on the ability of the designer to build discrete tools to scan through the available data and apply seasonal statistical analysis in wind, sunshine, humidity and temperature.

Such open data specific to the city of Zurich includes extensive open space data, such as built structures, exact tree positions/types/ages, accurate urban lighting locations,

FIGURE 3.4.4 **The entire geo-referenced lighting network**
Source: From the Open-Data project of the City of Zurich (data.stadtzuerich.ch, 2016)

transportation nodes and local demographic data (see Figure 3.4.4). Tools that combine this data along project-specific corridors and design-critical areas form a holistic model of the site under study, and justification for design decisions. The synthesis of terrain, vegetation, structures and urban lighting, for example, provides a detailed insight into the current performance of public space on a large scale, and potential for reuse and transformation (lighting image). Analysis of complex, multi-scale sites based on synthesized data types from various sources requires by definition a flexible tool set and workflow-crafting capabilities.

Scanning/sensing tools

As the first analysis and design concepts coalesce, the initially sourced data invariably reveals its limits, especially in terms of resolution and focus. Proprietary and openly sourced data, however valuable, are generated with external criteria, tolerance and resolution and are by their nature not project-specific.

The development of specific tools, whether on-site hardware and on-/off-site software arm the landscape architect with possibilities to supplement their site-specific approach with additional data, analysis techniques and resulting design potential (see Figure 3.4.5).

The first rescanning of the site involves a strategic densification of the terrain, vegetation and built structures, through the application of UAV photogrammetry and where appropriate, terrestrial laser scanning (Girot and Melsom, 2014). These tools and associated software apply techniques from the disciplines of surveying, geomatics and remote sensing and can be adapted and applied with a landscape sensibility, adding additional data only where it is required and efficient, at varied density, capturing materiality, texture and colour information. The topographical surface meshes are

FIGURE 3.4.5 **Student project presentation using a web-based interactive browser – IRIS – to demonstrate an interactive mobile tree catalogue for the site and surroundings, including various data including species, size and age. Interactive model of soil moisture and infiltration rates, based on interim project terrain, adjusted for long-term moisture content and typical rainfall events; visualization of speed of water runoff based on interim project terrain, adjusted for slope and materiality**

Source: ETHZ

supplemented with missing and additional detail data, resulting in multi-resolution terrain data, which can be sampled in various resolutions across one site, gradually shifting between resolutions, rather than sudden shifts in detail level. Through focusing on the tool for sampling multiple data sets rather than the definition of a finite surface data set, the terrain, vegetation and built structure data can be supplemented and augmented throughout the development of the project, and be scalable to the scale of analysis and design, from territory to construction detail, where required. The crucial existing pier, jetty, bridge and infrastructure details filtered from the original high-resolution terrain data could be resampled on a project by project basis, adding spatial fidelity and accuracy to the decision-making process.

Sensing tools have become a core part of the design process, both in the design education process and in the flexible generation of additional detailed site microclimatic data, such as specific characteristics of the soil, air quality, temperature, humidity, light and sound. Drawing upon the years of combined research of the authors at IAAC and the ETHZ discrete sensor deployment on site, whether static, carried or UAV mounted, have allowed project-specific refinement of the site data and project-specific design research (Fraguada et al., 2013; Dubor et al., 2013; Fraguada and Melsom, 2014).

The sampling of the resulting sensor results can add nuance to larger-scale open data and develop patterns for the microclimatic and ambient performance of the site, invisible to the landscape architect. In the case of the Zurich lakeshore site, specific feedback centred on soil conditions, water infiltration, temperature and humidity gradients across the site, and the sound impact of neighbouring transportation infrastructures. While user- and designer-based sensing is well documented in research circles (Fraguada and Melsom, 2014), the nature, assembly and deployment by the designer themselves on a discrete site allows new potential for relevant data collection (Cambell et al., 2008).

Iterative analysis and design

The implementation of the acquired and filtered data into the project brief allow the simultaneous design and analysis of the site. Rather than separating the two processes, the assembly of tools that allow simultaneous site/concept analysis can quickly confirm or negate early design concepts, facilitating a truly iterative design process.

From the large-scale sketch concept through design development, impact assessments in hydrology, ecology, cultural potential and the spatial potential of the project are addressed and refined. In the case of the Zurich site, simultaneous terrain generation, dredging/earth moving, volume analysis, runoff, infiltration and existing vegetation were linked to the bathymetry, terrain and sensor data. This cohesive set of design

FIGURE 3.4.6 **Resulting visualization of the interim landscape project and surrounding city and territorial model, without additional retouching or editing. Site data above demonstrate characteristics and design performance of the current project iteration. Interactive volumetric analysis of site terrain, bathymetry and required project dredging and earthworks, and impact on existing tree positions, including potential to relocate**

Source: ETHZ

analyses, generated in response to specific site phenomena from the design concept, required the development of several software and data handling tools.

The resulting decision-making process was then synthesized and visually simplified for communication and dissemination, whether for presentations or in a mobile format to be taken on site visits for reference and spatial testing (see Figure 3.4.6). The potential for large-scale visualization, when connected to a database of landscape features, vegetation, historical water levels and environmental characteristics, transcends typical visual impact and aesthetic considerations. The annual, seasonal and daily cyclical performance of the site can be assessed and iteratively refined (see Figure 3.4.7). Such results, when overlaid with extra-sensory site data and analysis, facilitate entirely novel directions for project development, interdisciplinary collaboration and dissemination of landscape site impacts and potential to the public (Melsom, 2015).

Crafting tools and landscape perception

In order to understand the potential of such techniques, it is also necessary to prove their accessibility and deployment capability. To this end, the landscape analysis workshop held over four contact days at the Collserola Natural Park in the hills above Barcelona serves as a compelling case study. In contrast to the Zurich site, rudimentary landscape data sources had restricted the scope of landscape intervention projects in the area, relying only on outdated analogue sources such as printed maps and aerial images. The student workshop involved the UAV scanning of a heavily forested post-agricultural site, and detailed landscape analysis, with students with rudimentary

landscape architecture knowledge, yet elementary scripting and tool-building skills.

The landscape and architectural analysis tools were adapted from both academic and professional applications, developed within the ETHZ, the IAAC and the authors' research offices of Built by Associative Data and LANDSKIP Lab. Within the workshop scope, and in addition to the landscape analysis tasks, supervisors and students built tools that allowed the students to dictate the movement and scan paths of the various UAV platforms used, adapting to the physical and atmospheric site conditions, as well as the density and fidelity of the scan results (see Figure 3.4.7).

With a research colleague supervising the flight planning and execution, the student groups were rotated to facilitate on-site scanning as well as digital analysis roles for all participants. The high-resolution full-colour point clouds enabled a broad variety of landscape analysis to appear, from detailed terrain and slope analysis, water flow direction and speed to lighting analysis of canopy and forest floor, to vegetation detection and diversity. Cultural and landscape morphological traces are clearly rendered in the results, whether in the deteriorating yet sharply visible terraces or the patterns of planned and spontaneous vegetation. At the end of four contact days, the students made their first tentative yet informed statements on the future development and evolution of the site, and take with them a swathe of adaptable landscape analysis tools (see Figure 3.4.8). These have since been adapted to be tablet-compatible, running suitably on a small tablet (Win/Intel/Wifi/BT/7{doubleprime}), improving not only physical but also resource accessibility (the tablet purchase cost around that of a single one-hour train ticket between Zurich and Basel), greatly increasing the flexibility and distribution potential of sensing and analyses platforms, not to

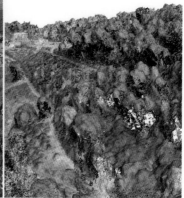

FIGURE 3.4.7 **Image series showing the historical, contemporary and scanned sites of the Valldaura site in Collserola National Park**
Source: ETHZ/IAAC

mention UAV control and dynamic site characteristic surveillance. While only the start of a true landscape design process, the workshop presentations demonstrated an empowering of the designers through tool building and adaptation, engendering process thinking and finally a certain curiosity for a site and acknowledgement of its unique and largely hidden characteristics (Girot and Melsom, 2015).

The implications of these methods for the discipline of landscape architecture are best demonstrated through the lens of a complex landscape design task. A project developed by Landskip Lab, a landscape architecture research platform partnership of Ilmar Hurkxkens and James Melsom, in collaboration with Luis Fraguada of Built by Associative Data, demonstrates well this potential within an open landscape competition, working within a data-rich project environment, within a compressed timeline, on an openly accessible site, with heavy existing uses and phasing challenges,

as well as a design brief which combines ambitious programmatic, budget and environmental restrictions.

The landscape architecture competition Lausanne Ecuméne, launched by the city of Lausanne, Switzerland, for the redevelopment of the Swiss Expo '64 site on the Lac Léman, demonstrates well the practical implementation of such tools in professional practice. Various data sources were available including detailed geolocated tree-inventory, high-resolution terrain data, and detailed information on the hydrology management of the site, including drainage channel organization, historical locations of the Expo ponds, and underground location and depth of the Flon river.

The compressed competition timeline meant that a collapsing of the traditional linear project development and production process was necessary. The analysis, concept design, vegetation management, terrain displacement, hydrological concept and

FIGURE 3.4.8 **Collserola National Park analysis and interpretation through intensive workshops and collaborative design discussions, demonstrating forest light daylight access, vegetation variation analyses, and an application of tablet-based (7{doubleprime}) Rhino/Grasshopper simulation**
Source: ETHZ/IAAC

quantity surveying documentation and visualization phases were tackled simultaneously, combining competition, open and aerial data collected by UAV on site. These various diverse yet overlapping topics were tackled within a two-person team, with heavy reliance on custom tools developed previous to and within the production phase of the competition.

In the case of the Lausanne waterfront competition these custom tools were developed to connect these project phases with a strong iterative potential, which allowed the vegetation and terrain displacement phases to be assessed from the sketch design phase through to final detailed project development, quantity surveying, and accurate visualization phases – within one evolving digital site model that evolved from conceptual through to a high

precision synthesis of terrain, hydrology, vegetation and built structures.

The final aerial visualization and sections demonstrate the culmination in this process, a model that was developed iteratively and contains all of the processes and products of the design and analysis processes. Each tree is linked to the original database that controls species and scale; the terrain model contains both original and shifted terrain information, allowing volume data calculations for both the displacement of earth and substrate and the calculation of water retention volumes and the fluctuation of the Lac Léman and peak flow of the Flon river. The visualizations, whether resulting sections of the model or aerial views, are dynamically linked to the analysis and design data, with no retouching beyond image filters and colour correction. This allowed both

FIGURE 3.4.9 **Aerial views of the Lausanne Ecuméne site, demonstrating UAV footage, terrain displacement, aerial visualization and sectional perspectives**
Source: LANDSKIP LAB

early appraisal and confirmation of the impact of the project within its context and constant adjustments in collaboration with the engineers and architects collaborating on the project, whether with technical terrain and hydrological sections or viewshed and shading analysis of the key public program and movement infrastructures. Since the design, computational, documentation and visualization models are one and the same, a consistent synthesis of constructional, functional, ecology and cultural impact logics becomes possible.

Synopsis: crafting the discipline

A deeper understanding of the direct and indirect implications of our actions as designers is forming a key part of our discipline in what has come to be known as the Anthropocene era (Sijmons, 2015). Beyond the inherent responsibility of the designer comes the potential of an informed design process that can design within performance models, sketching with data itself, to test the potential of the site. This role of iteration in landscape architecture,

an enduring and essential part of site analysis, design development, execution and site development, has been further empowered through the capabilities of the digitally empowered designer.

As dynamic, cyclical systems the landscape site is inherently an iterative apparatus, the simplest intervention generating a broad matrix of potential impacts. These adaptive tools should form design and perceptive prostheses, synthetic extensions of the intuitive design process and method. Ultimately, CAD and documentation should further become a by-product of the design process, as the potential of a landscape BIM (LIM) method may promise, although we are some way from a synthetic implementation of such a system.

This essay has discussed several techniques surrounding the concept of digital toolmaking that are accessible and applicable extensions of existing design tools. The application of these techniques is not without its consequences: dealing with mass quantities of data, ensuring sensors are calibrated, and making sense of the results are all skills that perhaps inhibit the limit of the accepted tasks for a landscape architect and associated disciplines of spatial design.

It is at these necessary limits of the discipline, in scale and specialization, at which the overlap with other scientific and engineering disciplines constantly provide new potential for the development of the discipline. In this shared zone of disciplinary limits lies the greatest potential for novel hybrid design processes, tool capabilities and resulting landscape morphologies to emerge. For this reason, the nature of the interdisciplinary research work of the authors often attempts to work beyond what is directly applicable or even practicable to the discipline. The resulting tools, their applications are often pushed beyond their limits, before being reduced back to a synthesized state, integrated into an applied design workflow by the students that co-develop them.

In contemporary design practice we now confront scenarios where data and equipment are abundant and accessible, but abstract and not project or site-specific. In a context where data becomes ever more abundant and diverse, the means to filter, re-create, replace and refine shall become a key aspect of site appraisal and understanding. This paradigm shift is one of fundamental accessibility, whether in cultural terms of uptake, cost and availability or spatially, miniaturization and UAV integration allowing remote sites and entirely new scales to be addressed by the discipline.

As has been discussed, accepted expectations of the landscape architecture discipline were perhaps ill-defined to begin with, lacking the ambition to wield the tools and methods of its sister disciplines and forge entirely new processes. It is through the critical and continuing reinvention of our methods and approach to landscape systems

and their potential that the role of landscape architecture can be strengthened and can retain its essential role in the built and dynamic environment. It is clear to the authors that the natural sciences and related specialist disciplines have much to gain through a renewed and deeper association with landscape architecture and its methods, approach to digital tooling, iterative modes and heterogeneous view of terrestrial systems.

References

Cambell A., Eisenmann, S., Lane, N., Miluzzo, E. and Peterson, R. 'The Rise of People-Centric Sensing', *IEEE Internet Computing: Mesh Networking*, v (July/August), 30–39, 2008.

Dubor, A., Fraguada, L. and Melsom, J. 'Asynchronous Streams (Workshop Cluster Leader)' in *SmartGeometry 2013 Conference*, Bartlett, 2013, smartgeometry.org

Ekbia, H., Mattioli, M., Kouper, I., Arave, G., Ghazinejad, A., Bowman, T., Suri, V.R., Tsou, A., Weingart, S. and Sugimoto, C.R. 'Big Data, Bigger Dilemmas: A Critical Review', *Journal of the Association for Information Science and Technology*, 66(8), 1523–1545, 2015.

Fraguada, L., Girot, C. and Melsom, J. 'Synchronous Horizons: Redefining Spatial Design in Landscape Architecture through Ambient Data Collection and Volumetric Manipulation', in *Peer-Reviewed Proceedings ACADIA 2012: Synthetic Digital Ecologies*, 2012, p. 3.

Fraguada, L., Girot, C. and Melsom, J. 'Ambient Terrain: The Generation of Large-Scale Landscape Site Data for Design Applications', in *Proceedings eCAADe 2013: Computation and Performance*, 2013, pp. 433–438.

Fraguada, L. and Melsom, J. 'Urban Pulse: The Application of Moving Sensor Networks in the Urban Environment: Strategies for Implementation and Implications for Landscape Design in *Peer-Reviewed Proceedings Digital Landscape Architecture 2014*, ETH Zurich, Wichmann Verlag, 2014, p. 222.

Fry, B. *Visualising Data*. O'Reilly, 2009.

Girot, C. and Melsom, J. 'The Return of the Aviators: The Transformed Understanding of Site through Flight and Associated Implications for Landscape Architecture', *Topos Magazine*, 86, 102–107, 2014.

Girot, C. and Melsom, J. 'Chapter 20: Case Study – Recasting Jakarta: Processing the Plastic River', in Amoroso, N. (ed.), *Landscape Visualisation: Digital*, Routledge, 2015, pp. 227–238.

Grier, D.A. *When Computers Were Human*, Princeton University Press, 2005, p. 152.

Jones, H.G. *Plants and Microclimate : A Quantitative Approach to Environmental Plant Physiology*, Cambridge University Press, 1992.

Koolhaas, R. *Keynote Speech*, United Nations Group Meeting on Smart Cities, Brussels, 24 September 2014, http://ec.europa.eu/archives/commission_2010–2014/kroes/en/content/digital-minds-new-europe.html

Meli, D.B. Thinking with Objects: The Transformation of Mechanics in the Seventeenth Century, Johns Hopkins University Press, 2006, p. 220.

Melsom, J. 'The Apparatus of the Invisible Landscape: Sensing Beyond Sight', in Girot, C., Hurkxkens, I., Melsom, J., Konzett, J. and ILA ETH Zürich (eds.), *Field Instruments of Design, Pamphlet 18*. GTA Verlag, Zurich, 2015.

Melsom, J. 'Chapter 4: Mapping and Refining the Site', in Amoroso, N. (ed.), *Landscape Visualisation: Digital*, Routledge, 2015, pp. 47–57.

Moonen, P., Defreye, T., Dorer, V., Blocket, B. and Carmiliet, J. 'Urban Physics: Effect of the Microclimate on Comfort, Health and Energy Demand', *Frontiers of Architectural Research*, 1(3), 215, 2012.

Peralta, V. *Data Freshness and Data Accuracy: A State of the Art*, Instituto de Computacion, Facultad de Ingenieria, Universidad de la Republica, Uruguay, Tech. Rep. TR0613., 2006, p. 3.

Reiter, S. and De Herde, A. 'Qualitative and Quantitative Criteria for Comfortable Urban Public Spaces', in *Proceedings of the 2nd International Conference on Building Physics*, ORBi, 2011.

Sijmons, D. 'Resilient Urbanisation as a Landscape Architectural Question', *Resilient Cities and Landscapes*, 90, 30–37, 2015.

Prospective 04

As within any nascent series of technologies, the prospective quality of the tools requires deep experimentation, prototyping, and speculation. Computation must take on this task, not reconstituting existing media but instead reforming the environment through complex models that enhance rather than dull biological and material systems.

04.00

Technology, evolution, and an ecology of cities

Contributor:

Kurt Culbertson,
FASLA
*Chairman and CEO,
Design Workshop*

While technology is described as revolutionary, it is in many ways also evolutionary, gradually, through the centuries advancing from stone to steel, to silicon and, in the process, shaping human evolution and perhaps even our DNA. The use of parametric and computational design processes and techniques are not only avant-garde, enhancing our ability to understand and mold our environment, but, on another dimension, are also evolutionary, shaping the way we think, communicate, and see ourselves and our world.

Technology now allows for the exponentially rapid testing of ideas, experimentation, failure, quick recovery, and success upon which progress depends. The equally rapid growth in social media makes us more aware of our need for human interaction, offering an opportunity to further understand the relationship between social and environmental issues.

Social ecologists would suggest that there is a strong correlation between social issues and ecological ones. Ecological problems cannot be earnestly addressed without considering social issues. In this sense, environmentalism (and by extension much of the work of landscape architects) is concerned with the symptoms of our problems rather than the causes.

A modern definition of social ecology understands it as the interactions within the social, institutional, and cultural contexts of people–environment relations that make up the well-being of humans and the planet.

This approach adopts an explicitly systemic approach by focusing on the interdependencies of social systems and on the possibility that the foundations of ecological crises can lie in social structures, or that war can originate from environmental scarcity. These phenomena call for approaches that are cognizant of system complexity. Ecological problems cannot be understood, much less resolved, without facing social issues.

Social ecologists suggest that the most persistent ills of society (sprawl, malnutrition, deforestation, urban violence, waterborne disease, obesity, housing insecurity, and many others) resist the prescriptions emerging from uni-disciplinary research. Social ecology focuses on the centrality of context or place in understanding these phenomena.

As landscape architects, we must address not questions of ecology *in* the city but of an ecology *of* the city. We must begin to view humans not as apart from nature but as part of nature, and in turn to view cities as human habitat rather than view urbanization as a threat to nature. We must understand the social-environmental factors that contribute to our well-being. Such an understanding will require interdisciplinary teams of researchers and practitioners leveraging a collaborative emergence of data-centric and responsive design systems, built on the expanding realm of computational tool sets. Aspects of design, or human perception of design, that up to now seemed purely qualitative, presently lie at the cusp of a seamless human to computer interactions with data analytics not only facilitating the restructuring our urban environment but also reshaping our vision of urbanization.

In this regard, there is a growing movement redefining our understanding of our environment. That movement, led by Steward Pickett and the members of the Baltimore

School of Urban Ecology, suggests that environment as a matrix of habitat patches that are in dynamic relationship to one another (Grove et al., 2015). These patches are formed by natural features but also by political, legal, and economic constructs. Resources such as flows of capital, or proximity to employment, transportation, arts, and culture, attract human habitation. The principles of the spatial economy have been outlined by Masahisa Fujita, Paul Krugman, and Anthony Venables (1999). Disturbances such as Hurricanes Katrina and Sandy can lead to vacancy and set these patches into motion, changing the health and viability of habitat patches and their scale and relationship.

Similarly, a wide range of other "disturbances" including changes in transportation technology and systems, economic investments or the decline of key industries, immigration and emigration, social relationships, legal and governmental frameworks, and even design interventions can lead to modifications of this patch matrix. Such impacts cannot be viewed strictly from an environmental perspective as the dynamic relationships between the patches of habitat are impacted by social, economic, and even aesthetic concerns as environmental factors impact society, the economy, and the beauty of the places we create.

In my recent dissertation research, I have sought to develop a habitat quality model for *Homo sapiens* based upon these principles. This research suggests that high-quality habitat supports occupancy and poor-quality habitat, such as that found in the shrinking cities of New Orleans, St. Louis, and Detroit, vacancy. Computational modeling will someday allow us to predict the movement of these patches in the landscape over time.

With the commitment by landscape architects to engage in these computational questions of not only form but social, environmental, and economic city structure, we will increasingly see a greater reach and understanding of our potential design impacts. One can, today, imagine the ability to develop parametric models for the design of an entire city that provide the ability to adjust the mix of opportunities and risks in response to specific site constraints and to optimize habitat for human settlement.

While these "virtual cities" already exist in response to and documentation of our physical environments, we are seeing an increasing presence of "smart city" models, the first steps in wrapping this technology full circle within its impacts on the built environment in real time. Is it preposterous to suggest that cities may already be defined by algorithm? Who will the creators of such an algorithmic city be? Is landscape architecture poised to engage productively in this computational realm of future cities?

Given the complexity of these factors, modeling and understanding of our dynamic environment can be greatly aided by parametric and computational design. Ecosystems are defined by flows of nutrients (including information), energy, and waste. One can envision a future in which designers can model geophysical risks such as hurricanes, tornadoes, earthquakes, storm surges, and the rise of sea level as determinants of the designed form of the city.

Can designers plan for the resiliency of coastal cities such as New Orleans by modeling the influence of and developing responses to the powerful winds that frequently batter the city? Soon, we will be able to model surface water movement through networks of green infrastructure on a citywide scale to create cities that do not merely respond to hydrological concerns but are also truly shaped by the movement of water. It is imperative that landscape

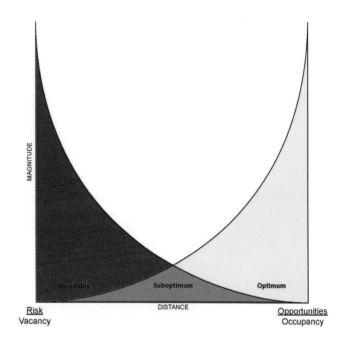

FIGURE 4.0.1 **Habitat quality model and land vacancy**

architects begin to understand this potential for sensor or responsive technology integration. The static constructs of ecological benefit in urban storm water, or tree canopy/root growth, are certainly valid and critical movements in physical infrastructure. However, how do these constructs adapt over time?

Our cities already feature apps for notification of elements needing repair. We have sewer and electrical systems that can notify us of a pressure or power loss. At what point can we breed trees capable of "requesting" irrigation through flow levels of photo-synthetics transfer? With the rapid and impending approach of automated vehicle technology, the algorithmically controlled city, the city of the future, poses a plethora of new baselines from which to judge and craft collaboratively through numerous disciplines.

Researchers such as Bettencourt and West have suggested that the growth of cities follows power laws allowing prediction of change in land cover, employment, energy flows, and a host of other factors through the evolution of a city (West, 2017). My own work has examined the inverse of these relationships – how do power laws apply to shrinking cities? Such mathematical models will allow planners and designers to anticipate the needs of cities as their population grows or contracts over time. British researchers Nelson and Rae (2016) used data from 4,000,000 commuter flows to define economic megaregions within the United States. With West's algorithm for city scale, and Nelson and Rae's algorithm for defining regional boundaries, can an algorithm for city form be far behind?

The use of cellular data allowed researchers at the AT&T Research Labs to map the mobility patterns of the residents of Los Angeles, New York, and San Francisco, and to compare the range and pattern of movement among these residents (Isaacman et al., 2010). Such research, in turn, suggests the ability to define a human "home range." Home range is the area in which an animal lives and moves on a daily or periodic basis. It is related to the concept of an animal's territory, which is the area that is actively defended. Biologists often use radio collars and other devices to map the movements of animals, utilizing this data to define the home range of populations and species and to understand the impact of particular habitat characteristics upon a given home range. The species *Homo sapiens* greatly simplified this task by the ubiquitous use of the cellular telephone and its GPS locational features. Such information may radically change our understanding of neighborhoods.

Through the analysis of such data we will be able to model and test the impact of alternative urban forms to improve mobility, enhance human health, and strengthen

social relationships. Current route and network analysis, utilizing geographic information systems, will be supplanted by more sophisticated analysis that will model human movement three-dimensionally in response to design changes.

Similarly, a Four Square designer utilized Processing, a processing and visualization environment, and data from Four Square "check ins" to map and animate the intensity of activity in Tokyo, Istanbul, and New York (Gelli et al., 2015). The potential for analysis and modeling is enormous. Urban designers have long theorized and speculated on the ability of urban form to strengthen social relationships. Through data mining and computational techniques, we may at last be about to understand empirically and predictively the implications of design interventions of community health and vitality. How do the arrangements of services and attractions, and transportation routes within a city, impact social activity? Like William Whyte in the digital age, future landscape architects and planners will be able to develop algorithms from our observation of human behavior and model designed landscapes that contribute to social interaction.

Firms providing market segmentation data such as Claritas, Nielsen, comScore, Quantcast, Webtrends, and Amazon are using algorithms to improve their methods. One can imagine a future in which such market data is utilized to simulate consumer response and to tailor designs to the psychographic profile of the audience. This will particularly be true of the design of retail spaces, where firms such as Placemeter are using video surveillance and algorithms to understand the movement of pedestrians and automobiles in shopping environments and other urban settings.

Smart kiosks, already installed in New York, Miami, Kansas City, and Chicago, and smart benches, such as Soofa, will connect citizens to the Internet but also gather data on user movement and preferences. Georgia Tech has developed a tablet-based application for wheelchairs that assesses sidewalk conditions utilizing video, GPS, gyroscopes, and accelerometer.

While these new technologies may raise privacy and security concerns, they may also contribute to the creation of a more balanced society. The Trust for Public Land's ParkScore and the University of California, Berkeley, have demonstrated the potential of big data to impact governance at an urban scale level, and to challenge historic patterns of civic investment to create spatial equity. Algorithms will soon model the flows of capital through a city in much the same way as we model traffic and water in the landscape today. Equity mapping offers a tool for creation of a more balanced planning, as we understand the distribution of capital expenditures and maintenance dollars across the urban landscape.

In a like manner, researchers in London utilized data mined from Four Square to predict, on a micro basis, the business success of retailers based on visitations to the London Olympic Games (Rodionova, 2016). One can extrapolate from such efforts the ability to create predictive models to forecast the economic impact of public investments in public parks, brownfield reclamation, or transportation improvements and to spatially target those investments for maximum impact. Nobel economist Paul Krugman has developed models of the spatial economy that offer valuable lessons to planners, urban designers, and landscape architects who are willing to address not only the environmental health of our cities and regions but their economic health as well (Huiskes et al., 2010).

Researchers at the University of Cambridge have also used Twitter and Four Square data to build a model that they believe can predict gentrification, utilizing the United Kingdom's Index of Multiple Deprivations (Rodionova, 2016). Colleagues at Northwestern University have similarly utilized social media to predict and track disease outbreaks (Xie et al., 2013).

Parametric modeling will also impact aesthetic decisions. A team of American and Chinese researchers have utilized geo-tagged photographs from Flickr to identify urban areas of interest: those areas within the urban environment that attract people's attention (Murphy, 2010). A team of French and Spanish researchers have created a predictive model for visual preference analysis of photographic images utilizing 250,000 digital photos (International Projects, 2012). Other researchers are utilizing data mining of information from Pinterest and Instagram for a variety of purposes (Wilson, 2013). Danish researchers are extracting information from Pinterest to understand color preferences by room of a home (Bakker, 2015).

Surely landscape architects will soon be extracting similar information regarding color, material, form, and compositional preferences of site designs as well. These efforts suggest that we will someday predictively model the characteristics of the urban environment, including aesthetic attributes that contribute to the success of design landscapes and to gather public feedback on our proposals through social media.

Parametric design will impact our environment at a regional, city, and site scale. Our ability to model and analyze sun, shade, wind, views, and other measures of human comfort has already created a design environment in which proposals can be simulated and adjusted in real time to create landscapes digitally shaped by these forces.

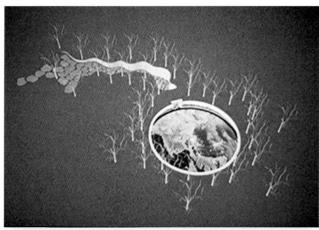

FIGURE 4.0.2 **Garden of Virtual Reality, created in 1983 on Silicon Graphics Iris computer**

Image: Design Workshop

Reflections on the profession

What do these advances mean for continued learning in the landscape architecture profession as it relates to the shifting spectrum of landscape architecture?

First, as human knowledge grows exponentially our own thinking must be expansive as well. The value of parametric design will only be limited by our imagination. Ironically, the growth of the Internet and of big data may bring diverse professions together as each seeks to interpret and manipulate common sets of data in new and innovative ways.

In 40 years of practice, I have observed that the profession does not change in its totality as much as shift its emphasis over time in response to changing societal needs or challenges. Issues such as environmental justice or social equity are ever present but rise or fall in relative importance to other issues as our entire society evolves. These shifts are also a product of our inability to address complex issues comprehensively and synthetically. Computation design will increasingly facilitate our understanding of complex urban, social, environmental, and economic sciences. This continual evolution suggests that landscape architects must be adaptive and resilient and possess the skills to address a wide range of issues. As with technology, humans must develop the personal bandwidth to deal with diverse and complex issues.

When we consider the impact of parametric and computation design on the profession of landscape architecture, this evolution suggests a need to be able to model the fourth dimension of time. Just as Google Earth Timelapse provides a way of viewing the historic development of a city over time, parametric modeling will provide predictive models of land cover and the three-dimensional form of a city into the future, based upon a range of design parameters. Our analysis of time, as a design parameter, will include the perception and resilience of landscape-based changes through the day, the seasons, year upon year, the centuries, and the millennium.

In 1983, Kurosh Valenejad and I produced an entry for an imaginary landscapes competition sponsored by *Landscape Architecture* magazine. Inspired in part by the video for Michael Jackson's hit 'Billie Jean', our scheme rendering, utilizing a Silicon Graphics Iris computer, envisioned a circular space open to the sky. As in Jackson's video, the pavement surface would be activated by stepping on paving squares. Each paver activated a remote video camera, placed within a distant landscape. The video image was projected over 360 degrees, surrounding the viewer, immersing the viewer in the distant landscape. The scheme, which drew no recognition from the jury, challenged the boundaries between technology and landscape. Is parametric design the application of mathematics and computing technology to the modeling and illustration of landscapes that will be constructed of traditional materials of stone, wood, and plant materials? Or can a technological environment itself be a landscape?

A year later, we pitched the idea to a Denver television station, convinced that this technology could connect their viewers to the landscape of the state in real time. Imagine watching the morning news from your home in Denver as sun rose on a snow-capped peak along the Continental Divide. But, again, no traction!

In 2017, Adam Mekies, at Design Workshop, and I again explored this possibility as part of the design of a coastal promenade in Dubai.

In the United Arab Emirates, the work force is comprised of expatriates from almost every country in the world. Imagine the ability of a visitor to the park to immerse themselves within a virtual reality pod and to be transported to their distance homeland – to stand in digital space along the banks of the Ganges, or to stroll below Big Ben in London.

Are such design proposals landscapes or technological environments? Where are the boundaries between the two? Time will tell, but 34 years later it appears that a version of the Garden of Virtual Reality may at last be built, suggesting that the possibilities are only limited by our imagination and our power of persuasion.

The importance of computation design emphasizes once again the critical importance of STEM (science, technology, engineering, mathematics) education. It also highlights the challenge of fitting this needed knowledge into an already jam-packed curriculum. Undoubtedly, the user interface will increasingly make such tools accessible to a wider range of users, although not every landscape architect will have the interest and aptitude to embrace the mathematical or programming skills necessary for parametric design.

Progressive firms will need a wide range of understanding of parametric design among their staff, as well as specialists who find their passion for this type of work. Just as many firms have CADD and BIM managers today, one can envision the position of "Director of Parametric Design" within landscape architecture firms, a position that already exists within some product design companies, such as Nike, and a growing number of architecture firms.

A new kind of landscape design practitioner, one with degrees in landscape architecture and computer science or computational

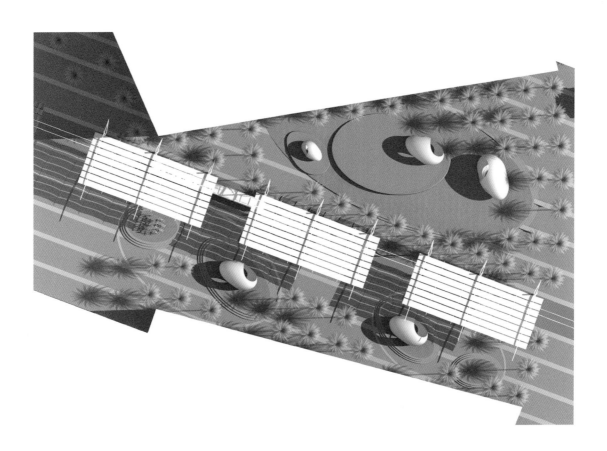

FIGURE 4.0.3 **Virtual Reality Plaza, created in 2017 on Dell Ultrabook Laptop**

Image: Design Workshop

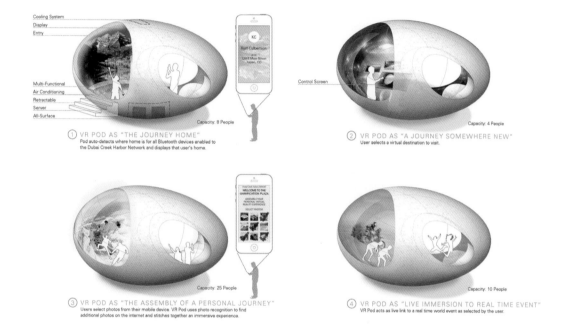

① VR POD AS "THE JOURNEY HOME"
Pod auto-detects where home is for all Bluetooth devices enabled to
the Dubai Creek Harbor Network and displays that user's home.

② VR POD AS "A JOURNEY SOMEWHERE NEW"
User selects a virtual destination to visit.

③ VR POD AS "THE ASSEMBLY OF A PERSONAL JOURNEY"
Users select photos from their mobile device. VR Pod uses photo recognition to find
additional photos on the internet and stitches together an immersive experience.

④ VR POD AS "LIVE IMMERSION TO REAL TIME EVENT"
VR Pod acts as live link to a real time world event as selected by the user.

FIGURE 4.0.3 **Virtual Reality Plaza, created in 2017 on Dell Ultrabook Laptop** (*continued*)
Image: Design Workshop

design, will emerge. All staff, however, must have a sense of the capabilities and limits of the technology. The challenge of how to make productive use of all the data at our fingertips will require the creative contribution of all of us.

What do these advances suggest for the future of landscape architecture?

While individuals may continue to choose to specialize in narrow bands of the subject matter of landscape architecture, the profession must develop a more comprehensive and integrative view. As a profession we must decide what we want our role in society to be. One of leadership or of support to other professions? The world is not going to "ask" us to lead.

The master planning of suburban communities on large tracts of open land is a shifting endeavor. The critical relationship between ecological, economic, formal, and social systems are a delicate balance demanding ever-higher consideration for preservation, efficiency, and artistic expression in the stewardship of our rural and urban ecologies.

Leadership is a role we must seize. New ways of thinking can create a new integrated syntax of the profession, leading into a

systemic whole. I know of no professionals more suited for this role than landscape architects, but it means we must commit to a lifetime of learning to stay abreast of the exponential growth of human knowledge. When we consider the implication of this view on parametric and computation design on the profession, it suggests the need to create models that consider environmental, economic, social, and aesthetic factors in an integrative manner to better understand the relationships between these four areas of inquiry.

How will these emerging technologies influence our profession's approach to provide guidance and mentorship for young landscape architects?

I believe that changes brought by technology will place very high expectations upon the profession. In turn, we must have high expectations of ourselves and for those whose set of mentorship and education is entrusted to our care. We must encourage a diversity of training and experiences for young professionals. Cross-disciplinary education in the form of multiple degrees in diverse fields is one way to achieve the required intellectual bandwidth. We must encourage both specialists and generalists and, better yet, individuals with the comprehensive view of a generalist and the

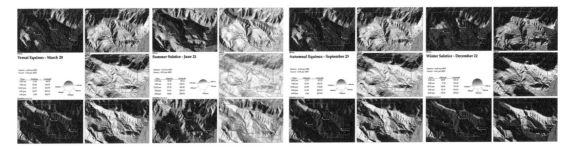

FIGURE 4.0.4 **Ameya Preserve – solar analysis of terrain and mountain topography**
Image: Design Workshop

deep knowledge of a specialist. We must encourage the development of that "bandwidth" in practice, in a nutshell: individuals who can both draw and code.

As we continue to develop a comprehensive view of landscape architecture that embraces environmental, community, economic, and aesthetic considerations, computational design will allow us to assemble the complex relationships between these factors and resolve what may currently appear to be conflicting interests.

References

Bakker, I., Van Der Voordt, T., Vink, P., De Boon, J., and Bazley, C. "Color Preferences for Different Topics in Connection to Personal Characteristics," *Color Research & Application*, 40(1), 62–71, 2015.

Fujita, M, Krugman, P., and Venables, A.J. *The Spatial Economy: Cities, Regions and International Trade*, Vol. 213, MIT Press, 1999.

Gelli, F., Uricchio, T., Bertini, M., Del Bimbo, A., and Chang, S.-F., "Image Popularity Prediction in Social Media Using Sentiment and Context Features," in *Proceedings of the 23rd ACM International Conference on Multimedia*, Brisbane, Australia, 2015.

Grove, J.M., Morgan, M., Cadenasso, M., Pickett, S., and Machlis, G. *The Baltimore School of Urban Ecology: Space, Scale, and Time for the Study of Cities*, Yale University Press, 2015.

Huiskes, M.J., Thomee, B., and Lew, M.S. "New Trends and Ideas in Visual Concept Detection," in *Proceedings of the 10th MIR*, Philadelphia, Pennsylvania, 2010.

International Projects, *1988–2012*, Institut Cartogràfic de Catalunya 10, 2012.

Isaacman, S., Becker, R., Cáceres, R., Kobourov, S., Rowland, J., and Vasharsvky, A. "A Tale of Two Cities," in *Proceedings of the Eleventh Workshop on Mobile Computing Systems & Applications*, ACM, 2010.

Murphy, K. "Web Photos That Reveal Secrets, Like Where You Live," *New York Times*, August 11, 2010.

Nelson, G.D. and Rae, A.. "An Economic Geography of the United States: From Commutes to Megaregions," *PloS one*, 11(11), e0166083, 2016.

Rodionova, Z. "London Gentrification Can Be Predicted by Twitter and Foursquare, say Cambridge Researchers," *Independent*, April 15, 2016.

West, G. *Scale*, Penguin Press, 2017.

Wilson, M. "Infographic: Mining Pinterest To Discover Our Color Preferences, By Room," *Fast Company* Digital, January 16, 2013, www.fastcodesign.com/1671629/infographic-mining-pinterest-to-discover-our-color-preferences-by-room, accessed May 14, 2017.

Xie, Y., Chen, Z., Agrawal, A., Choudhary, A., and Liu, L. "Random Walk-Based Graphical Sampling in Unbalanced Heterogeneous Bipartite Social Graphs," in *Proceedings of the 22nd ACM International Conference on Information & Knowledge Management*, October 27–November 1, 2013, San Francisco, California, USA.

Contributor:

David Fletcher
*Founding Principal,
Fletcher Studio*

04.01

The Witness

FIGURE 4.1.1 **The Witness island at the time of game publishing**
Source: Thekla, 2014

FIGURE 4.1.2 **Evolution of the island through time**
Source: Fletcher Studio/Thekla, 2010–2014

You wake up in a dark circular tunnel and walk up to a door. With a series of simple gestures, you solve a puzzle and gain access outside. Your avatar is now free outside, in an open world environment. The world is familiar, but a bit off-kilter. It is rendered in bright hues, dappled and almost pointillist in texture. You hear the sounds of nature, birds, wind, running water, and your own footsteps. You move through ruins, modern adaptations of ancient buildings, and diverse landscapes. One minute you are in a scarlet red autumn forest; the next you are in snow atop a volcanic cinder cone. You are in a place of wonder.

As a video game, the Witness is an intellectually challenging work of art. It is an adventure puzzle, set on a complex and mysterious abandoned island, populated with a multitude of biomes, geologies, cultures, and seasons. It expresses the overlaid palimpsests of fictional civilizations that have been planned and designed using the media of time and entropy. There are no guns. There is no high score. You do not compete with anyone. It is simply you and your brain solving puzzles, exploring a fictional world with a larger narrative that unfolds as you progress.

Jonathan Blow, and his independent video game company Thekla developed The Witness. Jonathan sought to create a game that would encourage users to become sensitive to their environment and to achieve a sense of accomplishment and enlightenment. Having a rich and engaging environment was crucial to gameplay and in 2008, Jonathan approached Fletcher Studio to help develop a geographical and spatiotemporal framework for the various teams to work within. Our studio worked full-time for three of the game's seven years of development, designing and modeling spaces, structures, geography, geology, environmental puzzles, and biomes. Designing the Island requires temporal thinking across many scales, and the blending of science and artistic expression. It is a task for which landscape architecture is uniquely qualified.

For clarity, I will refer to the Thekla team as the game development team and the landscape architecture/architecture team as the design team. The Thekla team was partly made up of programmers, who worked on the technical practicalities of the game engine, the game coding, and user interface. This team also included talented illustrators, programmers, and modelers. Jonathan is the ultimate producer and art director of The Witness.

In order to understand the planning and design of The Witness's island, it is important to understand the mechanics of gameplay. It should be noted that there are greater meanings and stories that unfold as the game progresses, which will not be disclosed in this writing. Gameplay progresses as you solve approximately 650 maze-based puzzles, each with their own mechanics and symbols. The game takes between 60 and 80 hours to complete. Players discover solutions through environmental clues, prior puzzle solutions, and listening to audio recordings found in the environment. The game requires and inspires heightened perception, balancing gameplay with environmental sensitivity. Reviewer Chloi Rad described it best: "The Witness does more than equip you with the tools needed to find the right answers – it teaches you how to ask the right questions." Unlike other games, a sense of accomplishment is not rewarded with points, tokens, or "achievements." "I feel like unearned rewards are false and meaningless, yet so many people spend their lives chasing [them]," Johnathan states in an early interview about progression incentives.[1] The many epiphanies offered in The Witness are motivation enough. He was also committed to creating a world that was quiet, without visual clutter, where every object has a purpose and where everything is interconnected.

The island is separated into roughly 19 zones and an undisclosed number of subterranean spaces and tunnels. The puzzles are maze-based, and are mostly located on flat panels that vary in material, transparency, and technology. The player simply solves them by drawing within the maze presented on the panels. A given area may contain puzzle arrays (a bank of connected puzzles) and puzzle groups (separate, but in the same area). All must be solved in sequence and they become progressively more challenging. When a puzzle group is solved, a turret emerges from a box and projects a white beam to the top of a mountain. Seven of these beams must be focused on the mountain in order to gain access to the underworld, where the "Endgame" exists. Clues to puzzle group solutions are often hidden in the environment and can be discovered through body positioning and careful anamorphic alignment, relative to natural and man-made objects. From a certain vantage point, a tree or rock formation might geometrically convey the symbolic language to solve a given puzzle group. Certain arrays and groups also serve to teach the mechanics and the symbolic language needed to solve future puzzle. They might also trigger access to hidden areas. Also embedded in the environment are hidden 3D illusions, which are known in the industry as "Easter eggs." These illusions are sometimes tied to puzzles but more often they relate to the greater game narrative. Often anamorphic, they require one to position oneself just so, and a figure or symbol is revealed.

Jonathan's team worked for the first three years, coding a custom and their own streamlined game engine. During that time, they developed concept puzzles, rudimentary structures, and a rough island form. He hired Fletcher Studio to design the island and Forum Design Studio to design the buildings. During this initial period, most of the development team's time was spent in refining the game engine, and in further developing puzzles, which were continuously added to the island. Buildings and spaces

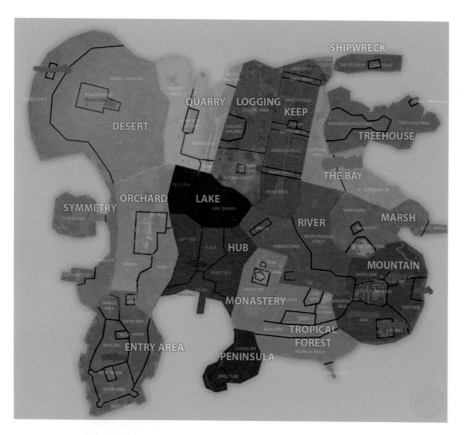

FIGURE 4.1.3 **Map of island zones**
Source: Thekla, 2014

were placeholders, which had only enough development to support basic gameplay and testing. Aesthetics and geographical rules were not important. In terms of the landscape, we viewed the island as a tourist experience. We sought out to create an engaging, beautiful, strange, and memorable experience for the player, independent of the gameplay experience. The experience of the island should be one enriched by wonder, even if one never solves a single puzzle.

Designing environments for video games should be a relatively easy undertaking. A designer is given a context, such as "You are designing a first-person shooter, in an abandoned Russian research laboratory on Mars . . . " For that scenario, one might

already know what the constraints may be, what it may look like, what materials might be used, what the feeling and atmosphere might be. Unlike Mars, The Witness island began as a green blob, with eight randomly placed test puzzles and structures that included a windmill, towers, a forest, and a few docks. Many of the familiar considerations that might guide a designer's work were nonexistent. Cultural history, climate, ecology, geology, boundaries, spaces, buildings, boundaries, rule sets, and constraints had to be created from scratch.

We first set out to reverse-engineer the island, as it might have existed before Civilization. Hundreds of islands were identified and studied, in the search for

FIGURE 4.1.4 **Puzzle group tied to environmental cues**

Source: Fletcher Studio, 2012

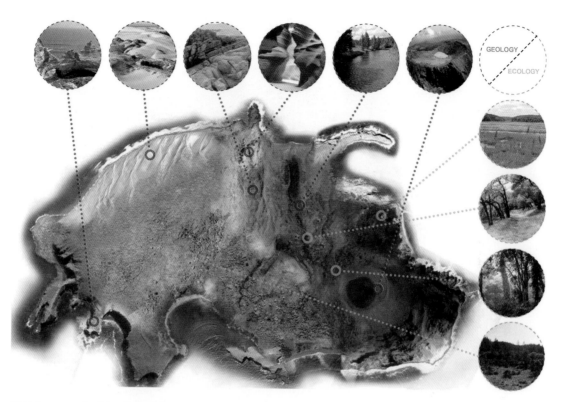

FIGURE 4.1.5 **Aerial collage and early geology and landscape studies**
Source: Fletcher Studio, 2011

small, temperate islands that have a rich
history of isolated civilizations. Known as
Europe's secret islands, the archipelago of
the Azores offered the most material to
work with. The layers of different cultures,
from ancient civilizations to the Portuguese
monarchy, to present-day fishing villages,
proved to be the most fitting precedents.
Available aerial imagery was collected
from the Azores and then collaged
together to create a fictional island in
plan, now with topography, beaches,
water bodies, etc.

We also wrote an environmental narrative for
the island, which formed the basis for design
in subsequent phases. Through
determination of solar orientation and
dominant winds, the studio was able to

establish the crucial gradients of wet and
dry, windward and leeward. We then
diagrammed the underlying geology,
establishing assumptions regarding rock
types, soils, and substrates. The resultant
mash-up of granite, basalt cinder cones,
limestone and loose sandstones were
located in specific zones and guided
building materiality, soil types, and
subsequent biomes. Using these
fundamental climate and geological
assumptions, we began to develop a set of
simple ecological rules that established the
makeup of the island's ecologies and their
bordering ecotones.

With the island geography adopted, both the
development team and the design team had
an agreed common context, into which

FIGURE 4.1.6 **Geology**
Source: Fletcher Studio, 2011

emerging puzzle groups could be placed. The development team had conceived of a few existing buildings and their associated spaces that needed to be "designed." The design team needed to provide these immediate design services, while also addressing the new structures and spaces that were appearing rapidly and randomly. Spaces no longer needed to be built around existing puzzle groups. Rather, puzzle groups could be sorted and located in areas with which they were geographically compatible. Certain puzzles might need to be located in a forest; others might require bright sun or water reflections to be solved.

At that time, our office had few billable projects. To intellectually supplement this work, we entered into "ideas competitions" and explored the world of academic exhibition-based practice. The research that was conducted during this period helped us learn and develop methods that later proved invaluable to our work on The Witness. Especially useful were competitions that required both large- and small-scale planning and design solutions, set in near and at times far-off futures. The most compelling challenges we found related to emerging economic and environmental anxieties that required projective and temporal thinking, competitions such as "Out of Water," "A New Infrastructure: Transit Solutions for the Future," and "WPA 2.0."[2] Planning for the future of Los Angeles regional infrastructures in the year 2125 required our studio to develop projective temporal matrices. The "future" needed to be subdivided into 25-year time increments. Assumptions about the future, and also about societal or technological responses, needed to be plugged into the matrix in order to provide a projective succession, for the future of the megaregion. The Witness island was not about the future but about the past and present. Game critic Ian Bogost calls the game player "the archaeologist of the lost civilization, that is a game's creator."[3] The player moves through environments and they piece together their own narrative of the civilizations who might have inhabited them.

In the beginning, the island was a cultural tabula rasa. In order to make sense of the existing and constantly introduced structures and spaces, its cultural history had to be designed. The projective methods that we had developed were applied to the island in reverse. The past was divided into three successive epochs, which we termed Civilizations (CIVs) One, Two and Three. A simple description of each was developed, and then a larger matrix was produced that

related to each in terms of infrastructure, architecture, and landscape. Each of these three categories had its technologies, agriculture, religion, and cultures. Materially, each epoch had its own techniques of building, based on assigned resources and technologies, with each CIV methodologies and products growing more refined over time.

Existing and emerging structures, spaces, and puzzle groups could now be plugged into spatiotemporal context. The windmill, for example, served gameplay as a kinetic puzzle, but was perplexing in terms of cultural or geographical logic. This structure, and ones like it, could now be placed in time and be subject to that time's governing rule sets. In our narrative, the windmill began as a CIV One sacred mound, whose rock was reused to construct the foundation for a watchtower in CIV Two. Civilization Three then adapted the tower as a means to

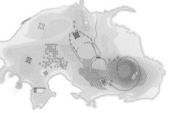

CIVILIZATION I

Though little evidence remains, there appears to have been a technologically primitive yet complex society founded upon the worship of ancestral and geographical deities on the island. Evidence of a settlement is found at the watercourse divergence at the center of the island. There is also evidence of an adjacent grazing pasture for limited domesticated animals. Their primary source of nutrition came from two highly productive fishing bays on either end of the island. The economic axis between these two bays lay perpendicular to a spiritual axis that lead from the volcanic crater to an aberrant lava rock on the other side of the island, both of which contain evidence of spiritual activities and numerous tomb sites.

CIVILIZATION 2

Later, the island's culture and tectonics development rapidly, through the introduction of new technologies and exposure to foreign intellectual societies, by way of naval maritime trade. The economic and substantive heart of the island moved inland where an elaborate water management system came to reform the land with dams, reservoirs, irrigation channels, and agricultural terraces. The primary settlement transformed into a feudal state with a walled town and keep that oversaw the society. The focus of the islanders' spiritual practices transitioned towards a management of life giving resources such as water, and as gatekeeper to the mystic powers of the volcano.

CIVILIZATION 3

The current state of the island speaks to a destruction event which lead to the abandonment of the previous civilization and a recent reoccupation of the island by a much smaller, modern population that brought with them a high technological sophistication. Many of the surviving structures of the previous civilization lie in ruin though have been reappropriated by contemporary inhabitants who have grafted new constructs onto these remnants. Recent uses include a factory for the production of high quality goods as well as a scientific observatory on the rim of the volcanic crater. A lone house has been constructed on a bluff that seems to have been the primary residence of an important actor on the island who oversaw much of its recent development.

FIGURE 4.1.7 **Three fictional civilizations**
Source: Fletcher Studio, 2011

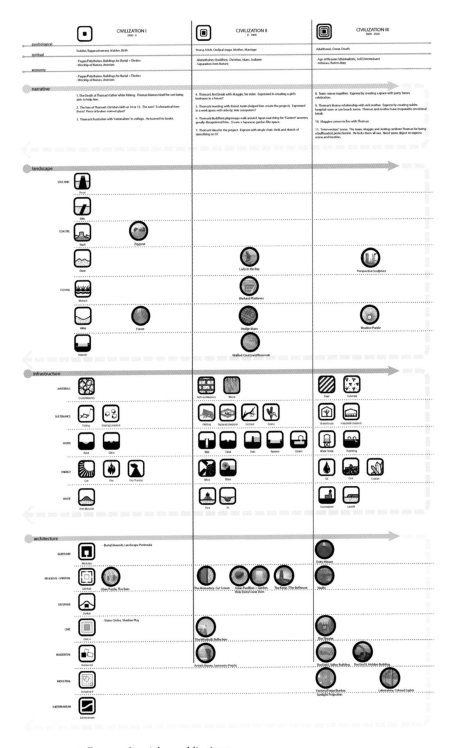

FIGURE 4.1.8 **Temporal matrix: architecture**

Source: Fletcher Studio/Forum Studio, 2011

pump freshwater from the reservoir to the rest of the island. Often, once a structure had been given meaning it then inspired the addition of other landscapes and infrastructures.

There was a growing reciprocity between the gameplay, architecture, and landscape with the island environment and story. For example, the presence of a given building material led to the creation of a logged forest, a rock quarry, and a glass factory. Puzzles were added to support the resource extraction and manufacturing narratives: for example a partly sunken shipping freighter was added to justify the use of steel on the island. This ship was perhaps the source of something that could not be easily made on the island, and much of its iron had been harvested and can be seen in various states of reuse throughout.

The island became increasingly more complex and required a great deal of physical, invisible, and behavioral analysis to understand the multitudes of structures, ecologies, and puzzles, and their interconnectivity. The programmers also employed many constraints to control and limit circulation. Visible objects (structures, terrain, rocks, etc.) are, in gameplay, solid. Edges of water and cliff faces must have invisible barriers, termed collision maps, which keep the player from walking out into the ocean or falling to their peril. Within those barriers, one is free to roam within a given area.

The first and simplest design challenge was in how to locate and design for the puzzle arrays. A certain array needs to be positioned in a logical place or conversely, hidden from view. Often, though, the solution is tied to something else in the environment. The limbs of an apple tree or the pattern of its apples, from the vantage point, may reveal a solution. In the second, separate puzzles or "puzzle groups" might be

physically connected with wires, cables, or environmental effects such as light and shadow. In the third tier, whole puzzle arrays and groups were connected to each other or to other structures, such as the beams that all concentrate on the mountain. In short, a single puzzle may be symbolically or mathematically tied to objects within its space while also being interconnected with other puzzles. The design team had to learn the mechanics of the puzzle groups, how they worked, and how they interrelated. They also would need to anticipate player behavior, in order to improve clarity and to minimize frustration. The programmers often used algorithms, to record, anticipate, and analyze user behavior. The design team had to use diagramming, modeling, and sketching to sort out this complex, invisible, and ever-changing network of connections.

With an understanding of puzzle mechanics, and with the planning and geographical framework in place, the hard work of designing the individual spaces began. The space around every building and structure needed to be designed, either as a present-day, historic or retrofitted space. At the height of development, the team was designing over 70 simultaneous "projects" and also receiving new structures and areas on a weekly basis. Each project had a series of reviews and each had deadlines. Initially, projects were worked on iteratively and were tracked through architectural phasing and conceptual design through to design development. Though helpful at the beginning, the sheer number of projects and their interdependence made this working model impossible. During the final year of planning and design, our team was sharing images and 2D design proposals online, and also working directly in the game engine, placing models and making adjustments. At the height of production, our offices collaborated on dedicated and networked computers in real time.

FIGURE 4.1.9 **Three temple and two desert options, parked in ocean for gameplay trial**
Source: Fletcher Studio, 2012

Often, we would create on three alternative models for a space, which we would park in the ocean. The development team would then test them in the island and evaluate them relative to gameplay.

Sorting through the multitudes of project types became a live mapping exercise. Each structure and space was sorted into a typology, assigned an icon, and then plugged into the CIV temporal matrix. Newly created buildings and puzzle areas would be placed in appropriate geographical and ecological context. They would then be run through the matrix, to fix assumptions as to how it has evolved, what purpose it serves, and its aesthetic, materials, etc. As noted previously, at times new landscapes were created for new structures or to support narratives relative to resource extraction and materiality. Maps were then presented to the development team that allowed different associations to be tested relative to gameplay.

The design team worked simultaneously at many different scales. On a given day, the design team might be working on detailing an ornamental gate for a hidden map room, modeling complex ritual stairs and perimeter walls for a temple, and designing a desert. Each would typically have two to three alternatives for review. Initially site design began with the collection of concept images to support loose analog drawings and studies. Often overlay perspectives were used to convey complex ideas. Analytical gameplay diagrams were created to help ensure that the proposed design did not "break" a puzzle.

Once a concept was approved, it was modeled in Rhino and alternatives were developed. Certain design challenges required pragmatic problem-solving such as grading, access, containment, ornament, etc. The design team would work on rock arrangements, pits, ridges, and other landforms to support the immediate needs of gameplay. Other design challenges were more conceptual in nature and would require a great deal of precedent research to build up a compelling and complete concept. In spatial conceptual development, our studio had free rein to invent new spaces, to incorporate references to some of our favorite landscapes, natural, man-made, and infrastructural. The only rules were that everything had to have a purpose, spaces had to work with gameplay, and that there could be "no circles," because the circle always signifies gameplay. To that end, there are no round rocks; even stumps and the ends of logs are deliberately misshapen.

There were some spaces that were impossible to design, because they were too open-ended. These spaces often did not fit neatly often into the matrix or were where gameplay demanded random walls or subdivided gardens. In these areas, we employed entropic design techniques. Whole defensive buildings, with ramparts and whole towns, were designed, developed, and then destroyed to provide armatures for puzzle spaces. What may at times look like random garden walls can be, from a distance, understood as the walls and foundations of ancient civilizations.

Eventually, all of the landscapes and spaces had been roughed in and the final six months of our work involved constantly refining and clarifying them. Key perspectival points were chosen. These were often at important symbolic moments, or at thresholds between one puzzle space and another. These views also needed to be carefully composed in order to clearly show a symbolic subject, but also to mask or screen out parts of other puzzles, hidden paths, etc. In this way, the exercise was not unlike Humphrey Repton's picturesque visualization techniques. We would prepare boards that include a current screenshot of the area in question and then would reference its biome and geology type. We would then prepare a collage, that expresses vegetation character and materials and plant massing. Often, anomalies and exceptions were often deliberately added to subtly influence behavior. A strangely shaped stone or plant might be placed in a certain location, to encourage a player to desire one path over

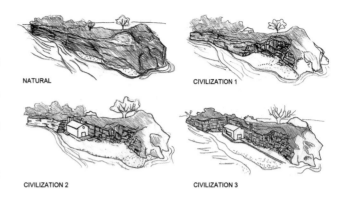

FIGURE 4.1.10 **The successive stages of the quarry through time**
Source: Fletcher Studio, 2013

another or draw them to an area in order to view a symbolically significant object. Near the entry, for example, a red bush was placed so that the player would be drawn toward a knoll. From that view, framed with stone, the player sees the mountain, which represents the "End" and more specifically death. The development team modelers

FIGURE 4.1.11 **The quarry at the time of publishing**
Source: Thekla, 2017

would then create plant palettes to match the scenes. Each scene would go through a few iterations and be constantly evaluated in the shared master model. After a time, the design team would make refinements within the model.

We filled The Witness with our favorite landscapes. Often, these were pulled from personal experience or to celebrate cherished landscapes and habitats. The game has heather fields, orchards, an invasive weed garden, deciduous forests, flower gardens, a tropical rainforest, cypress groves, dwarf manzanita, brutally pollarded sycamores, swamps, pine forests, palm groves, a bamboo forest, and one ancient and sacred fig tree. Concepts were borrowed from landscape ecology, and simple systematic thinking was applied to each with special sensitivity to how they might interact. With so many different landscape types, it was critical to develop simple rules that govern how the edges overlap and interact. One or two dominant species from one landscape can be seen overlapping another, to soften transitions and blend them. The plant materials were modeled and placed by the development team, with adjustments by the design team. Field guides to each landscape type, such as the ecological stratification of the jungle, were provided to them to help them understand the hidden rules that determine the landscape structure.

The landscapes also included references to pop culture, landscape history, and ecological theory. There is an engineered logging flume, which has failed and overflowed its banks, crazing dendritic forms across the mudflats. This is a miniature homage to the Los Angeles River, a commentary on entropy, and a juxtaposition of the engineered and the "natural." The weed garden is overtaken by pampas grass, eucalyptus, phragmites, Spanish moss. To the average user, it is serene and peaceful;

to the restoration ecologist it is terrifying. The faceted treehouses relate to a lecture on "The Oblique" by Hashim Sarkis. His courses on "Construction Vision" contributed greatly to the thinking behind the spaces. The Monastery is a representation of a winning competition entry, in which a tree provided the structural armature for a sacred building. Like the living mortars and walls of Angkor Wat, the tree both holds the structure together and tears it apart. These are a few details of certain themes and concepts that gave secret meaning to the spaces we worked on, most of which the development team is unaware of. There are many more . . .

A typical game might cycle through many different environments, or variations upon a theme. To my knowledge, no game has so many interrelated and diverse spaces in one area simultaneously. My thought is that The Witness is a one off. I do not think we will ever work on another video game. I do not expect that such a complex challenge will present itself again. The experience has changed how our office designs. We now use video game engines to represent and evaluate every project we do.

The game was published in January of 2016, to resounding critical[4] and commercial success. Thekla broke even on their six-million-dollar investment during the first week of sales. During that time, more individuals and groups explored landscapes and spaces (legally or illegally) that we designed than will ever explore our built landscapes in my lifetime.

Notes

1. A Higher Standard, www.mtv.com/news/2455935/a-higher-standard-game-designer-jonathan-blow-challenges-super-marios-gold-coins-unethical-mmo-design-and-everything-else-you-may-hold-dear-about-video-games

2 Chloi Rad, C. "The Witness Review," IGN, January 25, 2016, http://za.ign.com/the-

witness/97309/review/the-witness-review,
accessed November 28, 2017.

2. Chloi Rad, C. "The Witness Review," IGN,
January 25, 2016, http://za.ign.com/the-
witness/97309/review/the-witness-review,
accessed November 28, 2017.

3. GDC Lecture, "Play with US,"
http://bogost.com/writing/play_with_us

4. PC Gamer: "The landscape is also more than
it appears. As time goes on, you'll pick up on a
delicate negotiation between the screen puzzles
and the geography and architecture that
surrounds them," www.pcgamer.com/the-
witness-review

IGN:

Best Puzzle Game of the Year: IGN, PC Gamer,

Best Game of the Year: PCGamer

Experimental fast matter

Contributor:

Craig Reschke
*Co-founder, Future
Firm*

04.02

From documents to directives

FIGURE 4.2.1 **Installation of Geofoam at Maggie Daley Park**
Photo: Lynn Becker

In 1871, debris from a catastrophic landscape change, the Chicago Fire, was dumped into Lake Michigan to expand what was known then as Lake Park. One hundred years later, parts of Grant Park had still not been developed and much of the ground at the northern edge was used for rail yards and parking lots.

Daley Bicentennial Plaza, built on top of a parking garage that, itself, was built to replace a surface parking lot, finally connected Grant Park to its planned northern edge at Randolph Street. For little more than 40 years, Daley Bicentennial Plaza served as a quiet formal garden in the northeast corner of the park, especially after its much more flamboyant neighbor, Millennium Park, was built in 2007. In that same year, the deterioration of the waterproof membrane between Bicentennial Plaza and the garage below became untenable and the park was designated for redevelopment.

Maggie Daley Park, the replacement that would be named for another member of the Daley family, was conceived of, by Michael Van Valkenburgh, as a collection of highly programmed spaces along, what he calls, both an active axis and a passive axis. These programs were to be nestled between rolling hills that would stand in sharp contrast to Chicago's flat landscape. The hills were formed by a layer of 150,000 cubic yards of Geofoam,[1] some of which was recovered from beneath Daley Bicentennial Plaza and reused in the new park.[2]

In addition to the Geofoam, mature trees were harvested and reused in the new park as parts of the play garden and benches, but the Geofoam was the only material that was reused without modification. Considering the history of this corner of Grant Park, one can only imagine that in a few decades the park will need to be replaced again, its programs and facilities updated, and the parking garage membrane reapplied.

In *Re-Placing Process*, Anita Berrizbeitia calls for parks to "require a process driven approach that does not intend to provide a definitive plan for the site as much as it seeks to guide its transformation into public recreation space."[3] In fact, one could even conceive of places, such as Maggie Daley Park, as ongoing design projects, not only with no definitive plan but also with no definitive end to the design process.

In the age of parametrics, when no parameter is ever final, the idea that design happens before construction is outrageous—as are design phases, construction schedules, paper sets and as-built drawings. In the profession, we already see these norms eroding. On "Fast Track" projects, many decisions are finalized before others are designed. The Nestle Chocolate Museum in Mexico City was designed with architects on site designing just days ahead of construction.[4] During contract negotiations, savvy clients are beginning to request a copy of BIM models for future tasks, which has resulted in whole new set of AIA Contract Documents.[5]

Landscape architects have consistently addressed the evolving landscape: water flow, plant growth, seasonal temperature variations and more. Yet the flow of the design process, the feedback loop that is generated from a completed project, is only considered the next time a landscape architect is hired. Postoccupancy studies within a landscape architect's own offices are rare. The "parametric landscape" promises more than a method to quickly iterate through options only to settle on a single solution, as Grasshopper is often used today, or to handle the complex data in sets of construction documents, as in the current state of BIM software. The parametric landscape wants to be an open system that self-organizes in

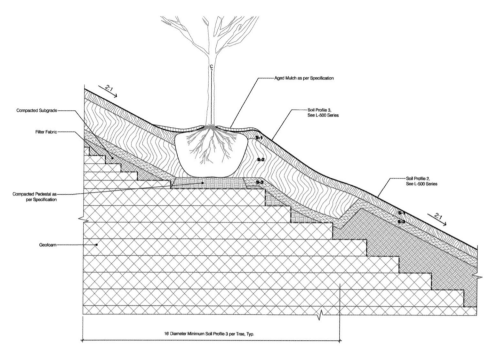

Aged Mulch as per Specification

Compacted Subgrade

Filter Fabric

Soil Profile 3,
See L-500 Series

Compacted Pedestal as
per Specification

Soil Profile 2,
See L-500 Series

Geofoam

16' Diameter Minimum Soil Profile 3 per Tree, Typ.

③ **Deciduous Tree Planting on Geofoam Slopes Steeper Than or Equal to 3:1** Section
Scale: 1/2"=1'-0"

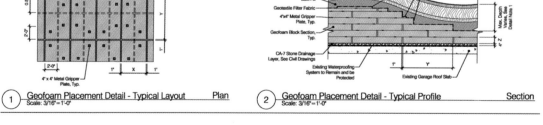

0.5 X

Edge of Geofoam Block below

Top Geofoam Layer

0.5 Y

Y

2'-0"

1"   X   1"

2'-0"

4" x 4" Metal Gripper
Plate, Typ.

① **Geofoam Placement Detail - Typical Layout** Plan
Scale: 3/16"=1'-0"

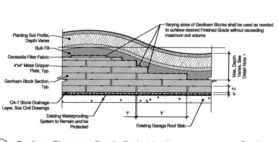

Varying sizes of Geofoam Blocks shall be used as needed
to achieve desired Finished Grade without exceeding
maximum soil volume

Planting Soil Profile,
Depth Varies

Bulk Fill

Geotextile Filter Fabric

4"x4" Metal Gripper
Plate, Typ.

Geofoam Block Section,
Typ.

CA-7 Stone Drainage
Layer, See Civil Drawings

Existing Waterproofing
System to Remain and be
Protected

Existing Garage Roof Slab

Max. Depth
Varies, See
Detail Note 1

4" Z

1"   Y

② **Geofoam Placement Detail - Typical Profile** Section
Scale: 3/16"=1'-0"

FIGURES 4.2.2 AND 4.2.3 **Geofoam as installed at Maggie Daley Park**

Images: Michael Van Valkenburgh Associates

order to, with every feedback loop, consistently arrange itself to meet the complex and changing parameters set forth by a landscape architect. In this effort the landscape architect becomes the author of an algorithm rather than designer of a specific, even if flexible, site solution.

This work is also beginning to take shape within the design professions. Andrew Heumann developed a Grasshopper plug-in named Human UI that allows users to create an easy-to-use interface that references specific Grasshopper components. Human UI allows clients to take control of specific elements within a digital model and see, in real time, what happens if they increase the height of the building or change the cut and fill balance of a landscape.

What once would have required several meetings and hours of revisions on the part of designers can now be communicated in a matter of minutes. These methods are fundamentally changing the current design process for designers. As the easily accessible parameter expands into construction, maintenance, and deconstruction tasks, one can begin to imagine the continuous design process and resulting fast-matter landscape.[6]

The difficulty with operating a landscape that responds to feedback at the speed of an algorithm is that the actual matter used to create landscapes—such as rock, soil, and vegetation—are not easily rearranged at the speed of electricity, the speed at which sensors deliver updated data sets. With the exception of water flows, or sand dunes, there are few landscape changes that alter our spatial experience of a site within 24 hours, or even seven days.

In *Landscape Ecology*, by Richard T.T. Forman and Michel Godron, Chapter 12 opens with catastrophes: the 1906 San Francisco earthquake, the Chicago Fire,

Second World War bombings, and the inundation of Dutch dikes in 1953.[7] These are the given examples of high-speed landscape changes, before the chapter moves into more familiar topics such as seasonal changes and vegetal succession. This leaves landscape architects to wonder if there are forms of fast matter that can encourage high-speed landscape change without calamity.

Since the 1990s, in the same decades that the word parametric infiltrated the landscape architect's lexicon, the use of a lightweight fill material, Geofoam, has also exploded. Geofoam is an expanded polystyrene product marketed specifically for terrain alterations. Since the 1960s, it has been used for projects such as road and rail construction, retaining wall fill, and public parks. In spite of the name lightweight fill, the product is able to bear heavy loads at a low cost. At only 2.85 pounds per cubic foot, EPS Geofoam is able to bear 18.6 pounds per square inch, similar to that of sand or gravel.[8] The product is in high demand: some estimates put US production alone at 1.3 billion cubic yards per year, enough volume to cover the island of Manhattan in 36 feet of Geofoam.

Generally we are conditioned to think of EPS, Styrofoam,[9] as something that is environmentally disastrous because it lasts forever. Geofoam, as fast matter, will change our thinking about materials like EPS, as it's incredibly useful for matter that is intended to spend most of its life under a layer of soil and to have the tendency not to rot or otherwise degrade. It is the exact reason EPS is thought of negatively that gives it the potential to be a high-quality fast-matter aggregate.

Fast matter in landscape architecture will realign both the cultural and physical productions of landscape architects toward a parametric landscape based in computation.[10] Using Geofoam as a potent case study, this argument is made in three parts. First, that materials like Geofoam fit into existing conversations on aggregates, or easily rearranged materials that can be programmed. Second, that the alignment of modeling methods and construction techniques sets up a feedback loop that compresses the steps between design and construction. Third, that a parametric series of instructions ultimately serves as a better translation and index of construction directives than the documents typically called for in professional practice.

Geofoam as landscape aggregate

In 2015, a group of architects, led by Ryan John King and Ekaterina Zavyalova under the name Foamspace, won the New Museum's Ideas City Competition with an entry that reimagined funding strategies for architecture competitions. The Foamspace project utilized the $20,000 fabrication funding to buy standard-size[11] blocks of Geofoam that were arranged along the street for the day of the festival. At the end of the day the manufacturer picked up the blocks and a percentage of their cost was refunded. These blocks went on to be resold for other projects and uses, and the competition monies, rather than being exhausted for one festival, were rolled over into a fund for future projects.[12] While the arrangement of the blocks was more "building" than "landscape," the project demonstrated how aggregated Geofoam can act as fast matter.[13]

Landscape architecture is familiar with aggregates in design, from the movement of sand dunes to the angle of repose of a pile of gravel. Geofoam opens up a conversation about designing synthetic aggregates. The form of each Geofoam block could have a function, which manifests itself as a specific form, designed into the aggregate, whether it be to direct water flow, or encourage a particular type of vegetal growth, in addition to its role as lightweight fill. These functions would be more complex versions of the functions we already assign to other aggregates: coarse stone for easy drainage, or peagravel to create a level surface. These Geofoam aggregates could be made using a subtractive method that removes parts of a large block of EPS, or they could be formed in molds like EPS in packing materials, an additive process. In both cases the Geofoam would function structurally as a part of the ground section, just like any other subsurface material.

As an aggregate, Geofoam taps into a timely conversation in (landscape) architecture discourse on the design of granular systems and their structural characteristics. This discourse includes the work of Achim Menges, Skylar Tibbits, and Heinrich Jaeger.

At the Institute for Computational Design at the University of Stuttgart, Achim Menges is working on what he has titled "aggregate architecture." He describes the aggregates as programmable matter that can be reconfigured rapidly, not by downcycling but by simple reuse in a new arrangement, much the same way the Geofoam from Daley Bicentennial Plaza was reused or the foam from the Foamspace installation at New Museum was also reused.[14]

In his research, Menges and his team are focused on highly designed aggregates that are intended to affect the possibilities of a whole made from thousands of individual pieces. According to Menges, these aggregate systems

FIGURE 4.2.4 "Foamspace" by SecondMedia. Design team: Ryan John King, Ekaterina Zavyalova, Bettty Fan, and Nikolay Martynov. Project Documentation: Varvara Domnenko

challenge conventional architectural design principles: whereas an architect precisely defines the local and global geometry of a structure, in a designed granular system he can only calibrate the particle geometry in order to tune the overall behavior of the aggregate formation.[15]

In Maggie Daley Park, the desired ground surface of the park was designed first and the Geofoam was simply a means to create that surface with a minimum amount of soil between the top of the foam and the park's grassy surface, while keeping minimal weight on the parking garage below.

In order to harness the potential of fast matter, Geofoam landscape architects need to design the entire thickness of the foam, not just the soil surface: how each piece interlocks, the form of the foam, and its function or program. In Menges's work, each aggregate is categorized as either nonconvex, double nonconvex (hooks), or actuated materials. Convex materials (ball shapes) won't interlock to form a stable construction. The typical rectilinear volumes of Geofoam already function as an interlocking aggregate, but greater formal diversity could move Geofoam past a purely structural function.

At the 2015 Chicago Architecture Biennial, Skylar Tibbits, working alongside Gramazio Kohler, developed a project titled Rock Print. The project used a robotic arm to lay down a continuous string within a wooden formwork. A lightweight rock was then poured into the form one layer at a time.[16] Eventually the formwork was removed and those rocks not held in place by the textile filament fell away to reveal a designed form. While the "in-person" experience of the project was stunning, the truly remarkable part of the project was a later published video of the project's disassembly. As the string was pulled from the top of the print onto a motorized spool, the rocks are projected into the air before falling back to the floor. Finally, the rocks are swept up and placed back into the bags from which they came months earlier at the beginning of the Biennial.

The disassembly of aggregates allows them to be moved directly from one project to the next as part of an open system. The unused aggregates from one generation of a landscape that are not used in the next do not become waste but are simply moved to another site, or set aside for a future, more populated generation of the landscape. These aggregates would become part of their own economy, bought, sold, and traded as needed. Like a highway Jersey barrier, or a returnable milk bottle, the aggregate is a component in a much larger system that can be used over and over again with minimal processing between uses.

Aligning systems of feedback

In architectural practice, SHoP Architects is already working on reinventing construction documents and eliminating paper documents with its work on the Barclay's Center Façade and B2 modular towers at Atlantic Yards. At Barclay's Center, SHoP was brought on as façade consultants to design a new wrapper for an already-designed building. Politics, land acquisition schedules, two architects, and a multiplicity of contractors were some of the site's myriad challenges. The contractor had already assigned the foundations and steel work to a subcontractor when SHoP came on board to redesign the façade.[17] The availability to work with the contractors and architects across a single model allowed the changes to be made quickly in a series of short feedback loops.

Pushing the model integration further, SHoP designed a system of barcoding so that each of the 12,000 pieces of the complex façade could move directly from the firm's digital model to the fabricator, to its installed location on site. All the while, each piece was tracked like a FedEx package. No paper documents were ever produced. One can imagine some affinities between the 12,000 complex steel façade pieces and the many rectilinear pieces of Geofoam beneath Maggie Daley Park. The same feedback loops used for complex facades could be engaged for complex ground surfaces.

Philip Bernstein, the vice-president of Autodesk, relates the move from hand drafting to two-dimensional drawing in CAD to modeling in the BIM environment as analogous to Nicolas Negroponte's argument in *The Architecture Machine* that "digital technologies first mimic the processes that they are designed to replace, then extend them, and eventually disrupt them completely."[18] While Bernstein believes we are still in the "mimicking" phase in architecture, the SHoP approach begins to disrupt a one-way flow of information with feedback loops. Landscape architecture is also at a critical juncture at which the relationship between design modeling and construction execution can merge into an evolving, but always active, system.

In studios across professional landscape architecture programs, students download digital elevation models in ArcGIS, create surfaces in Rhino, manipulate those surfaces with Grasshopper "scripts," and then contour those surfaces at even intervals to create two-dimensional drawings that represent a three-dimensional landscape. This workflow uses extraordinary computational power to create a representational device that has been used for hundreds of years: the contour line. Those same students will then import that surface into a software program, such as MasterCAM, to create tool paths, which in turn will generate NC code for a CNC router to excavate material that creates a physical manifestation of the designed surface, often in an expanded polystyrene material. These workflows result in many steps of unnecessary translation.

Outside of academia, professional surveyors, civil engineers, and excavators have all started to use GPS-enabled hardware and software to guide their workflow. In 2005, *Engineering News-Record* published the cover story, "3D grade control puts designers right in the operator's seat; automation is rocking traditional earthmoving and project teams have to make changes." The early complaints from contractors who were utilizing these systems were centered on the time it took to translate two-dimensional drawings into three-dimensional models that the grade control systems could understand.

As digital modeling becomes the standard in design offices, replacing two-dimensional representations, one can imagine that soon the contractor will not be building the model at all but instead will simply execute it, like SHoP's panels on the Barclay's Center. It is the compression of model information into two-dimensional paper documents that interrupts the feedback loop.[19]

Autodesk is also starting to deliver products such as Autodesk BIM 360, which integrates with Topcon (one of the leaders in producing GPS-based automation systems for excavation equipment) products. Autodesk allows equipment operators and installers to understand exactly where they are in the model and on site, closing the feedback loop between design and construction with a commercial product.[20]

While commercial software is changing the way the construction industry thinks about manipulating the Earth's surface, it is not the technological advancements that contribute to faster landscape change. Instead, the evolution of techniques are simply the symptoms of an ideological shift, one in which we move from thinking about the construction process as a series of linear steps or the passing of a baton to an open flow of three-dimensional information that is accessible by all agents involved in the project.

Directives instead of documents

In 1970, John Horton Conway created the Game of Life, a program that is represented by an infinite two-dimensional grid in which each cell can be either "on" or "off." The game has four simple rules: a live cell with fewer than two live neighbors dies; a live cell with two or three live neighbors lives; a live cell with three or more neighbors dies; and a dead cell with three neighbors comes to life. The system, given these four initial directives plus an initial seed layout of live and dead cells, runs for generation after generation. Depending on the seed layout, the system could die, grow, or reach a state of equilibrium.

An algorithm is a set of rules or tasks that can be executed over and over again until a particular state is reached. In data sets, we use algorithms such as Bubble Sort, which sorts numeric values one after the other until all values are in ascending order. As new data sets arrive, they too can be sorted. If we think of the landscape architect as the author of an algorithm and the feedback loop consistently moving through that algorithm, then the possibilities of fast matter exponentially increases. If the landscape design process is continuous, and the algorithm is periodically updated in response to the feedback loop, then fast matter has even more potential to respond to specific site conditions, such as changing water flows, poor growth areas, or programming. With directives, the role of the landscape architect is to observe and direct, rather than create a final product. Kostas Terzidis calls algorithms a "vehicle for exploration."[21] Like the Game of Life, the designer must set the system into motion, watch it evolve, and then make adjustments or restart the game, as necessary.

Parametric design software, such as Grasshopper, is already allowing designers to think in terms of logical questions and commands: copy this; scale according to the distance from X, etc. While Grasshopper is not iterative the way an algorithm is, it does begin to make designers respond in code, observe the results, and enact a response. Once the process is iterative, the exploration is amplified. Graphic-based coding, such as Grasshopper, also places design firmly in the realm of directives instead of documents.

With Grasshopper, the design work is in creating the process. The drawing, a representation of the process, can be created again and again.

By positioning Geofoam as "fast matter," we can begin to see the emergence of a new paradigm for landscape design and construction in three territories: first, the possibility of a system for providing feedback in aligned construction and design tools; second, a material of the proper size and design that functions as an "aggregate"; and, third, a method for delivering instructions, "the algorithm."

The methods by which we are already interacting with Geofoam have eliminated the need to think of construction as a specific time that is between design phases and a finished landscape. This opens the possibility for landscape architects to eliminate the oppositional ideas of model and reality. Instead, in this new mode, the model is always forming the reality and the reality is always influencing the model, so they are both "real" parts of a feedback system.

The idea of aggregates gives us a way to think about Geofoam (or other materials) that is not based on achieving a specific surface (or form) but instead provides a way to design and tune landscape qualities. And, finally, the feedback system can be controlled by algorithms designed by landscape architects that set out the necessary rules for both the feedback system and aggregate design.

Geofoam is the critical example for the potentials of fast matter in landscape architecture because it is readily available for scale modeling in design contexts and widely used in existing construction processes. It is lightweight and almost ubiquitous in both academic and professional settings. But the list of fast-matter materials could be much longer. The salvaged beams of demolished barns, precast concrete soakways and culverts, or the ubiquitous stone paver are all materials that could be harnessed as fast matter.

Why does fast matter, in fact, matter? It represents a potential for the design profession to stop making the wrong decisions at high speed. Since the computerization of many architectural tasks began in earnest in the 1990s, huge amounts of readily accessible data have inundated the design process.

Parametric design software such as Grasshopper seems to have allowed an endless number of options, yet the options do not necessarily improve our current condition. As the project to create open systems of infrastructure that responds to natural processes continues we must rely on feedback from the materials in these systems to inform the next generation of ideas.

Notes

1. www.architecture.org/architecture-chicago/topics-news/chicagos-playscapes/six-things-you-need-to-know-maggie-daley-park, accessed February 2017.

2. www.dnainfo.com/chicago/20140401/downtown/maggie-daley-park-development-update-tree-planting-follow-geofoam, accessed February 2017.

3. Berrizbeitia, A. "Large Parks," in Czerniak, J. and Hargreaves, G. (eds.), *Re-Placing Process*, 2007, p. 175.

4. Rojkind, M. "Building on Speed," in Ruby, I. and Ruby, A. (eds.), *Re-Inventing Construction*, Ruby Press, 2010.

5. See AIA Document E203–2013 section 4.9: Post Construction Model.

6. Andrew Heumann in discussion with the author, October 2016.

7. Forman, R.T.T. and Wilson, E.O. *Land Mosaics: The Ecology of Landscapes and Regions*, Cambridge University Press, 1st ed., 1995, p. 427.

8. Arellano, D., Bartlett, S., and Stark, T.D. *Expanded Polystyrene (EPS) Geofoam Application & Technical Data*, The EPS Industry Alliance, 2012.

9. Styrofoam is a brand name trademarked by Dow Chemical Company that covers Dow's expanded polystyrene products, as well as extruded polystyrene products and other foams.

10. For more on the differences between computation and computerization see Kwinter, S. "The Computational Fallacy," *Thresholds*, 26, 90–92, 2003.

11. There are not actually standard sizes of Geofoam. Block sizing depends on the capabilities of individual manufactures, but is usually around 4' x 3' x 10'.

12. The agenda of Foamspace is based in financial, not material systems, so the aggregate could be considered the funding, but project is relevant here because of the materials and the way they were used. You can read more about Foamspace, which is now part of a larger project called the decentralized architecture office, online at foamdao.space

13. www.newmuseum.org/ideascity/view/foamspace, accessed February 2017.

14. Dierichs, K. and Menges, A. "Towards an Aggregate Architecture: Designing Granular Systems as Programmable Matter in Architecture," *Granular Matter*, 18(25), 1–14, 2016.

15. Ibid., p. 1.

16. Aejmelaeus-Lindström, P, Willmann, J., Tibbits, S., Gramazio, F., and Kohler, M. "Jammed Architectural Structures: Towards Large-Scale Reversible Construction," *Granular Matter*, 18(2), 1–12, 2016.

17. Post, N. "Complexity on the Face of It," *Engineering News-Record*, July 16, 2012.

18. Bernstein, P. "Parameter Value," in Poole, M. and Shvartzberg, M. (eds.), *The Politics of Parametricism*, Bloomsbury, 2015, p. 205.

19. Of the standard contract documents used by the AIA, those that specifically address digital practice were not released until 2013. Generally they do not yet address the legal repercussions

of sharing a live model, so in some cases it is not a methodology that needs to change to achieve a feedback loop but a legal structure.

20. This is not an argument for technological determinism. These commercial software packages are examples of the way the design industry is engaging a feedback loop, not implying that the software's feedback loop is providing a "solution." See Kludge, K.M. *Models of Models* from Actar's UrbanNext project for an in depth analysis of the role of simulation in design.

21. Terzidis, K. "Algorithmic Form," in Menges, A. and Ahlquist, S. (eds.), *Computational Design Thinking*, John Wiley & Sons, 2011, p. 96.

04.03

Towards sentience

Contributor:

Leif Estrada
Designer,
Kuth Ranieri Architects

1. Introduction— addressing complexities

Complexities and indeterminacies are some of the issues that designers must confront when dealing with landscape phenomena— and the foremost concerns when engaging with fluid dynamics that affect a landscape's geomorphology. While it is possible to design infrastructures and interventions that alter such landscapes, responsive technologies provide a method of real-time adaptive management, creating methods that curate and choreograph evolving ecological relationships. The result is a design methodology that has the ability to engage the inconsistency and spontaneity that exists between ecology and infrastructure that does not require precision in modeling and simulation.

Historically, when the son of the father of relativity, Hans Einstein, approached his father about his keen interest in leaving structural engineering to study and research sediment transport, he was dissuaded, citing the very study as intractable and that he should do something less complex (Einstein, 1937–1972).

Towards Sentience, a graduate design thesis, and other various research experiments, sponsored by the basement laboratory of the Responsive Environments and Artifacts Lab (REAL) at Harvard University's Graduate School of Design incorporates the design of responsive systems to test adaptive infrastructures within a geomorphology table (see Figure 4.3.1). These experimental tests aim to simulate the potential of responsive infrastructures to modify the behaviors of riverine landscapes and their fluvial morphologies—including land accretion, vegetal proliferation, and species colonization.

The precision required to precisely compute the complexity of fluid dynamics in real time may be outside the grasp of current scientific knowledge and computing power; however, the utilization of a physical hydrological model can capture the essence of a river's alluvial processes. The physical model provides a tangible model that simulates sediment transport through analog interactions between synthetic sediment densities and rates of water flow. Using real-time sensing, the indeterminate becomes latent (see Figure 4.3.2) and becomes enmeshed through the introduction of technology as a new form of ecology, and eventually a nascent form of *nature*.

The addition of real-time sensing and response creates new layers of perception that are immediately acquired and understood in relation to a specific moment or occurrence of change. However, despite this heightened level of observation, sensing is limited to fully perceive the projective morphology of riverine landscapes, as every moment is infinitely iterative, as it is asymptotic (see Figure 4.3.3). Despite this, the complexities of a hyper-real feedback loop (see Figure 4.3.4) produces new understandings of the immediate context, such as new directions of water flow as observed in an early study model, the *Depositor* (see Figure 4.3.5) or the emergence of temporal landforms that is in constant flux with the *Attuner* (the responsive model of *Towards Sentience*) (see Figure 4.3.6). These manifested forms are usually not latent to human understanding or even through the nature of delayed analyses brought upon by postprocessing. In turn, delayed understanding becomes a hindrance to the potential manifestation of unseen landforms and land types.

Though lacking the precision of data, real-time sensing and monitoring enable the facilitation of the emergence of new morphological forms across a constantly shifting landscape, specifically those of riverine systems, which at the same time is brought upon by the epoch of anthropogenic processes and the already-seemingly technology-augmented hyper-reality we are in.

2. Theoretical—mergence of nature and technology

As the machine's senses are different from that of a human, its perception is modulated by the translation of such perceived phenomena happening in the *natural* realm of reality into the realm of the virtual through sensing and actuated response (see Figure 4.3.7). The infinitely iterative process is eventually reapplied back into the initial state of *nature* to create a neo-incarnate.

The compounding process is as follows:

Nature (Reality) → Virtual → Neo-nature (new reality) → Virtual → (Neo)Neo-nature . . .

For some this transformative process creates an image of a degrading environment and produces the perceived notion that nature is in danger owing to technological augmentations. This problematizes and undermines the undiscovered value of such emerging neo-natures, hybrids that are produced through technology. It further oversimplifies the complexities produced co-dependently by ecological processes and technology—where the proliferating ubiquity of novel systems are immediately deemed bad, without consideration that its existence is an indication of a productive and sustaining system.

However, one can argue that technological advancement has always been in dialectic with nature. Framing the processes of nature through a Marxian perspective, it can be deduced that production is a continuing process, which alters the forms of nature by humans aided by technology. As such, the producer

can work only as *Nature* does, that is by changing the form of the matter . . . he is constantly helped by natural forces . . . the producer changes the forms of the materials furnished by *Nature*, in such a way as to make them useful to him.

Marx and Engels, 1845/1947

Humans have altered objects from nature through labor to produce useful things in order to facilitate and fulfill our needs to thrive as species, whether or not we are conscious of the ecological impact we are causing and altering. The shift is inevitable, as we continue to create new technologies in order to mitigate landscape phenomena for our benefit.

Today, new technologies, specifically those that augment the environment with its mergence with the virtual realm, have become an extension of our being. Digital connectivity is more and more becoming a part of our own neo-nature. A disconnection from this phenomenological and responsive infrastructure brings upon a new sense of anxiety, which can be disabling. Though created by man, it can be unsettling when these creations become uncontrolled and informalities begin to occur. The idea of man's inability to tame his own creation reverts our perception of these neo-natures as "unnatural" and exoticizes their existence as being the "other."

3. Experimentation and projection— toward neo-nature

Towards Sentience incorporates the design of a responsive infrastructural model, which attunes the projective alluvium of the geomorphology table through a series of real-time sensing and responsive manipulations as a way to curate successive sediment accretion—constantly altering and modifying the riverine landscape, privileging the evolution of ecological processes over static constructions.

When deployed in the one-to-one landscape, the machine intends to learn from initial site conditions of typically degrading engineered channels (the LA River, as explored in the thesis), but also from the modifications it will produce independently with its sensor systems, and co-dependently with sensed data of environmental phenomena. The responsive infrastructure aims to become sentient, learning from its environments, iteratively honing in on specific operational processes, as an opportunistic ecological agent, which strives to:

erode existing concrete lining, and understand the new material as part of the sedimentation process (see Figure 4.3.8 and 4.3.9);

attenuate flows of water and sediment in order to accrete new temporal landforms;

infiltrate the subterranean landscape to potentially recharge existing aquifers and create new ones (see Figures 4.3.10 and 4.3.11); and

seed the potential successive planting that would endure the projective new nature of such channels (see Figure 4.3.12).

Sentient-*ly*, it will attune the fluvial landscape—to a level of degree that man is incapable of processing in order to respond and modify the landscape in real time. Projective-*ly*, responsive infrastructures could be created by landscape architects and designers to aid themselves to address human incapabilities in order to negotiate complexities that occur in real time, which necessitates immediate responses. These necessitated responses are usually slowed down or hindered by subjective policies that govern landscape processes. This new ability also enables our relationships with nonhuman agents throughout all terrestrial landscapes.

FIGURE 4.3.1 **Image of the geomorphology table—utilized as the site of intervention for multiple experiments**

Photograph: Bradley Cantrell

FIGURE 4.3.2 **Temporal 3D-printed soil samplings scanned from the geomorphology table, which were produced at an instant creating a neo-nature**

Models: Leif Estrada; photograph: Robert Tangstrom

FIGURE 4.3.3 **A conceptual diagram, based upon the idea of an *asymptote*, showing the resolution of phenomenal predictability in relation to time (the development of technological precision and a responsive infrastructure's understanding of its context)**

Diagram: Leif Estrada

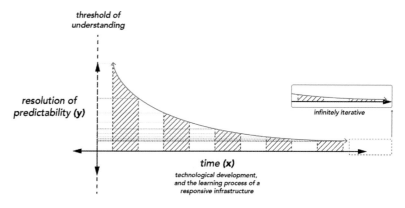

threshold of understanding

resolution of predictability **(y)**

infinitely iterative

time **(x)**
technological development, and the learning process of a responsive infrastructure

FIGURE 4.3.4 **Feedback loop diagram showing the machine's learning, narrowing the gap between intentionality and indeterminacy**

Diagram: Leif Estrada

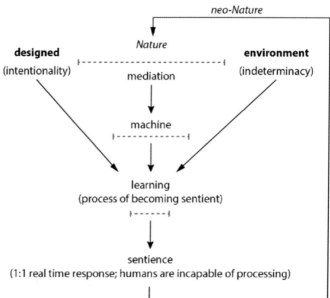

neo-Nature

designed
(intentionality)

Nature

environment
(indeterminacy)

mediation

machine

learning
(process of becoming sentient)

sentience
(1:1 real time response; humans are incapable of processing)

Through the introduction of new imagined sensor systems the emergence of new forms of construction and maintenance within the landscape are enabled, which has never been possible without the machine's new dimensions of sentience. Such manifested forms created by the compounding process of the neo-nature would further bring upon a disorientation as to what was once natural. This phenomenon would cause the rejection of the current dichotomy created by "man-made" technologies and "idealized" notions of idealized and untouched natural processes.

Our ability to conceptualize and create hybrids of biotic and abiotic systems facilitates the evolution of neo-natures. Technological design is consistently introduced to "tame" biologic systems to human will. To legitimize these interventions, humans find and extract any economic and practical capacities. However, despite levels of human control, there is always a moment in which a system will reach its limitations. As such, these limitations will produce our new perceptions of nature. A shift concerning ecology and nature in what has been the accepted norm is inevitably upon us.

FIGURE 4.3.5 **Depositor, an experimental real-time responsive model programmed to interrupt the flow of water, instantaneously redirecting it to percolate down a new fluvial direction, affecting its geomorphology**

Model and temporal images: Leif Estrada, https://vimeo.com/152837202

FIGURE 4.3.6 **Attuner, a real-time responsive model that monitors and modifies the alluvial morphology of sedimentation based on the fluvial flux of water, resulting in land accretion. It constantly learns from its environment and context through a feedback loop**

Model: Leif Estrada; photograph: Robert Tangstrom, https://vimeo.com/166623512

FIGURE 4.3.7 **An imagined machinic-sensory of the Attuner, modulated by the translation of the perceived phenomena happening in the natural realm of reality into the realm of the virtual**

Drawing: Leif Estrada

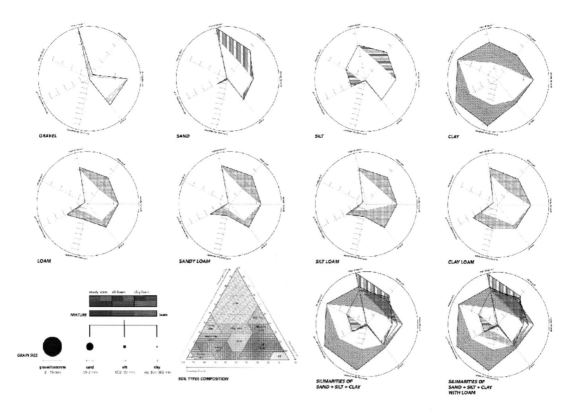

FIGURE 4.3.8 **Soil analyses presented as an attribute matrix, analyzing the varying soil compositions that would potentially accrete in the projective succession of the LA River as the concrete substrate is degraded**

Drawing: Leif Estrada

FIGURE 4.3.9 **Engineered soil samples. The following "sediments" were used in the live-modeling of the fluvial morphology of riverine systems, which are based upon the weights of the corresponding compositions of varying soils that were analyzed: gravel, sand, silt, clay, loam, sandy loam, silt loam, and clay loam**

Soil mixtures: Bradley Cantrell and Leif Estrada; photograph: Robert Tangstrom, https://vimeo.com/166623512

FIGURE 4.3.10

Attuner, imagined as real-time responsive injection piles charging existing and new aquifers seen from below the water table as a swaziometric perspective

Rendering: Leif Estrada

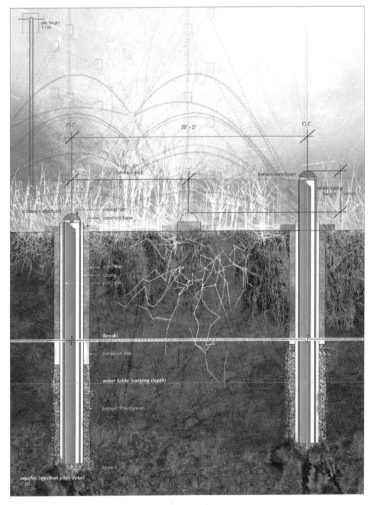

FIGURE 4.3.11

Attuner, injection piles detail shown in multiple conditions

Drawing: Leif Estrada

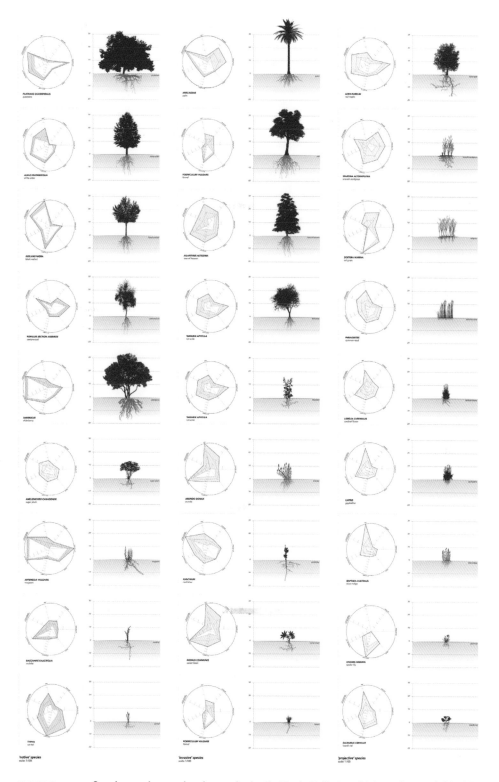

FIGURE 4.3.12 **Species analyses, showing each plant's ideal attribute, which can be overlaid with the soils analyses**

Drawing: Leif Estrada

References

Bryant, L. *Onto-Cartography: An Ontology of Machines and Media*, Edinburgh University Press, 2013.

Benjamin, W. *The Work of Art in the Age of Mechanical Reproduction*, Penguin Books, limited reprint, 2009.

Cantrell, B. and Holzman, J. *Responsive Landscapes: Strategies for Responsive Technologies in Landscape Architecture*, Routledge, 2015.

Einstein, H.A. MS 80/8. Inventory of the Hans Albert Einstein Papers, 1937–1972. The Water Resources Collections and Archives, University of California-Riverside, Riverside, California.

Holmes, R. and Holzman, J. "Material Failure and Entropy in the Salton Sink," in *Landscape Research Record*, No, 4. Presented at the Cela Conference Proceedings, Incite Change, Change Insight, 2015, pp. 95–110.

Marx, K. and Engels, F. "Part I: Feuerbach. Opposition of the Materials and Idealist Outlook," in *The German Ideology*, Parts I & III,. Vol. 6, International, 1947 [1845].

Waldheim, C. "Strategies of Indeterminacy in Recent Landscape Practice," in *Public 33: Errata*, Public, 2006, pp. 80–86.

04.04

Design for a mind with many bodies

Contributor:

Ricardo Jnani Gonzalez
*Interaction Designer,
Project Aerial*

Cybernetic design

Historically, designs that function within the realm of ecological interventions have heavily gravitated toward attempting to gain full authority and control over the particular ecosystem in order to reform it. This approach is seen far more often than that of working in tandem with the ecosystem through an adaptive and autopoietic manner (Pickering, 2013). According to Pickering, this predominant, hegemonic, and static mode of operations "ignores emergence [and] assumes that we know all the chains of cause and effect." The thesis proposed here instead suggests that through a cybernetic approach of aggregated micro-interventions a higher degree of adaptability and autopoiesis could be attained within the realm of interventions in natural ecosystems. This essay explores a methodology of embedding the iterative process of design into the design itself. It acknowledges that relationships *become*;

they are born, they grow, and they develop over time through a back-and-forth evolution. The logic behind micro-interventions is that the design is not a single large-scale intervention but rather an aggregate, dispersed, and flexible network that generates the necessary influence through incremental accruement. In designing the system of cybernetic micro-interventions, I similarly argue that it is necessary to consider both the logic and the processes of operations, the mind, and the methods of physically interacting with the environment, the many bodies. The work culminates in a step toward the design of one mind with many bodies: a network of soft robotic agents functioning through a responsive and iterative organizational system. This essay will focus on the cybernetic logic designed to self-regulate and adapt.

In order to investigate this hypothesis, the ongoing degradation of the ice caps in the cryosphere is examined as the setting.

The increasing speed at which melting is taking place, and will continue to take place (Frieler et al.,2016), calls for a focused exploration of intervening directly at such remote and fragile ecosystem in order to mitigate its ongoing atrophy. A wide range of current analysis into the dynamics of the cryosphere are beginning to show distinct methods of inherent self-regulation embedded in the materiality of ice and the flux of the ecosystem, and a relationship between form and performance. Recent research shows direct correlations between the subsurface structures of a glacier and the activity observed on its surface, as well as how it decays and moves through time (Phillips et al., 2013). Likewise, structural glaciology investigations highlight relationships between atmospheric conditions and the formation of ice masses (Hambrey, 2011; "Structural Glaciology," n.d.).

The work developed here investigates the potential of cybernetic micro-interventions as the approach to monitor, mediate, and activate the evolving needs of a dynamic equilibrium within various ice formation in the cryosphere. The thesis is composed of four elements. First, an extensive survey maps the flux between elements of the ecosystem and their relationship to self-regulating performance. This survey serves as the foundation by which the mind and the bodies are organized through, which is the focus of this essay. Second, a series of ice experiments explore methods of strategic melting and snow capturing. Third, a series of design studies suggest utilizing tessellated folding surfaces as a potential method of pneumatically activating the agents. Last, a catalog of speculative scenarios illustrates strategic melting on glaciers as a method to facilitate self-regulation through increasing snow retention while decreasing mass and relieving stress.

Self-regulation and classification method

Through analyzing a series of structural glaciology principles (Hambrey, 2011), as well as different cycles in the dynamics of the cryosphere (Frieler et al., 2016; Schulson, 1999), a pattern of self-regulation among the ice masses emerges. This theme of self-regulation can be observed both at the minute scale of snow crystal composition, and the global scale of the overall glacier. For example, a crevasse can only be so deep owing to the lateral pressure of the ice as the crevasse travels downward (Hambrey, 2011). However this maximum depth changes as soon as water is introduced to the crevasse, or moreover if there is flow that begins to erode the ice away. The following diagrams illustrate several key mechanism inherent to the way of life of glaciers as they emerge from, decay into, and change within the dynamic states of the cryosphere.

Given the incredibly dynamic and complex ecosystem that the cryosphere proves to be, any system that aims to interact with it at a multidimensional level of monitoring, mediating, and activating, should begin with a basic classification method of the relationships between the various elements. Through the lens of early cybernetics, one key part of this process is to first categorize these components into *variables internal* to the system, and *external parameters* that affect or influence the system. Ashby proposes defining the *operator*, the *operand*, and the *transform* (Ashby, 1979). To ground these terms, he gives the example of pale skin turning dark with light from the sun. In this scenario, the sunlight is the operator (the force that induces change), the pale skin is the operand (that which the force is applied to), and the darker skin is transform (the change state of the operand). Through a slight reinterpretation of these categorization techniques, this thesis classifies the cryosphere and methods of intervention as follows. First, the many different *states of material* are grouped as variables internal to the system, i.e., the operand. Second, *atmospheric conditions* are set up as the external parameters that affect the system, i.e., the operator. A third category I add here is *methods of activation*. This category aims to place itself between the operator and operand and strategically mediate the effect one has on the other, as a catalog of possible hylozoistic intervention techniques. These methods serve as a mechanism to enable the system to further self-regulate and maintain within its defined limits of dynamic equilibrium.

Logic of interventions

Given the vast array of atmospheric conditions and states of material introduced in the previous essay, which of those would influence it the most? Which one would influence it the least? How would its mind decide the hierarchy by which it operates, by what it responds to first, second, third, etc.? And, if we have an answer, how can we be sure that this hierarchy will prove befitting of the cyclical variation inherent to the cryosphere? Is hierarchy even important?

Since the core focus of this design strategy is the ability to repeatedly reassess its interactions, to reinvent its function, and to recharacterize its role, what type of hierarchy would befit this autopoietic mind? It appears that it would be crucial for the mind to be entirely malleable and capable of adapting to any situation, however this is not entirely the case. Structure, a framework of sorts that binds the soft and flexible, is

required. This mind has two governing segments: a root hierarchy and a fluid hierarchy.

The root hierarchy is the decision-making process division that serves as the foundation on which to apply the fluid hierarchy. It is composed of elements that affect the ecosystem at the largest and slowest scales. For example, the Earth's cycle of precession, which plays a key role on whether we are in an ice age or not, is approximately 26,000 years long. Similarly, the Earth's obliquity, which is key to the Milankovich Cycle, is a roughly 41,000-year cycle. As you can see in the table, the Milankovich Cycle components are the first portion to the root hierarchy. An oversimplified example of a possible result of this portion would tell you that you are currently not in the middle of an ice age. From this, the second tier of factors relate to the glacial mass balance of an ice mass, indicating location on the glacier either in a state of growth or recession. The final tier of the root is the shift in annual seasons. This short periodic turnaround is a similarly anticipated cycle. The result of root segment is a condition set that captures an array of atmospheric and periodic assumptions from which to test.

The hierarchy of the second division, the fluid hierarchy, will depend on which condition set is arrived to as active. For example, in the case of a wintertime operation on the accumulation zone of a glacier in recession, the UV index level would be considered an earlier priority to calculate than the current atmospheric temperature, the assumption being that, since you are in the accumulation zone during a winter on a glacier, the atmospheric temperature is likely below freezing but the mass might be gaining heat through light. Therefore, that's the factor with a stronger hierarchy. Through the evaluation method the system might realize,

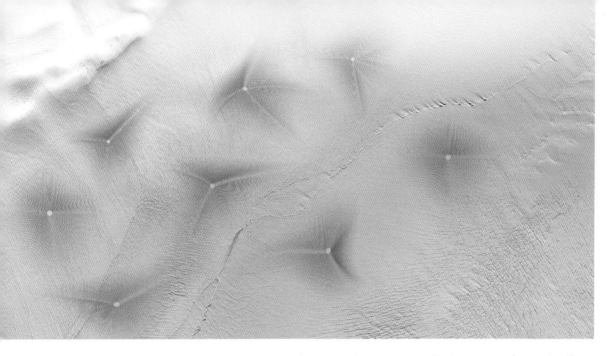

FIGURE 4.4.1 **Cybernetic ice forms. Impact through incremental accruement and enhancement of natural self-regulation methods**

FIGURE 4.4.2 **Surface geometry computationally generated through incremental accruement and enhancement of natural self-regulation methods**

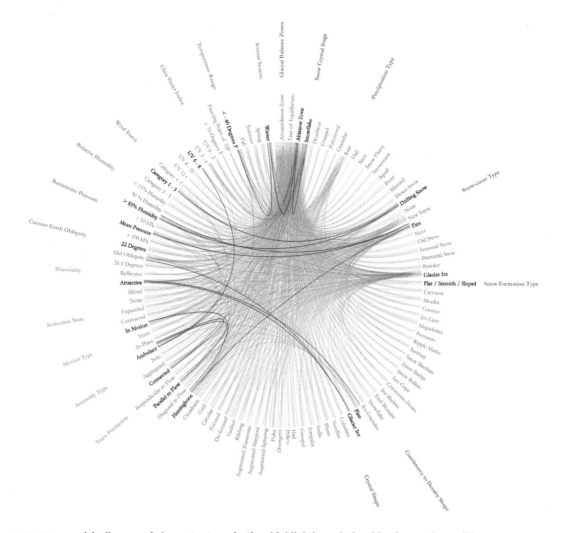

FIGURE 4.4.3 **Iris diagram of element categorization, highlighting relationship of scenario conditions**

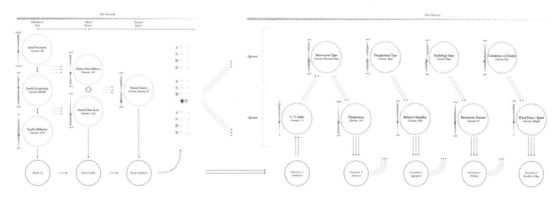

FIGURE 4.4.4 **Decision-making process tree, starting with root hierarchy and continuing to fluid hierarchy**

through the aggregation of its micro-interventions, that such assumption was not accurate. In that case, that item would get bumped to a lesser priority. Hence, the hierarchy of this second division is fluid in two ways. First, it is dependent on which state the root arrives to. Second, it is able to reevaluate the priority levels assessing the environment's response to its interaction. Here, note the importance of routinely reevaluating the importance and relevance of the contextual elements, especially while experiencing how the environment responds to the intervention.

As the design interacts with its *Umwelt*, it assesses both its procedure of mediation and the subsequent response of the environment. Through utilizing the categories introduced earlier, the system comparatively evaluates the changes through time of: atmospheric conditions, states of material, and methods of activation. It compares the previous states to current conditions and projects an anticipated scenario based on previous iterations. Depending on the accuracy of its projection to the actual response of the environment, the mind evaluates likely reasons for discrepancies. These likely reasons are based on observed relationships, i.e., degrees of influence, between internal values and external parameters. After this assessment it adjusts its strategy and tests once again. Given the advantage of micro-interventions, the mind is able to cast a variety of activation strategies across different bodies. Depending on which strategy yields the closest outcome to its projection, it informs the others and embeds that experience into their next iteration. If after distributing the new logic to the rest of the bodies there continues to be some with discrepancies, the system picks out the variations of atmospheric and material conditions in order to fine-tune the reason for the deviation.

References

"Structural Glaciology," *AntarcticGlaciers.org.*, n.d.

Ashby, W.R. *An Introduction to Cybernetics*, Methuen, 1979.

Frieler, K., Mengel, M., and Levermann, A. "Delaying Future Sea-Level Rise by Storing Water in Antarctica," *Earth System Dynamics*, 7(1), 203–210, 2016.

Hambrey, M.J. "Structural Glaciology," in Singh, V.P., Singh, P., and Haritashya, U.K. (eds.), *Encyclopedia of Snow, Ice and Glaciers*, Springer Netherlands, 2011, pp. 1089–1091.

Phillips, E., Finlayson, A., and Jones, L. "Fracturing, Block Faulting, and Moulin Development Associated with Progressive Collapse and Retreat of a Maritime Glacier: Falljökull, SE Iceland," *Journal of Geophysical Research: Earth Surface*, 118(3), 1545–1561, 2013

Pickering, A. "Being in an Environment: A Performative Perspective," *Natural Sciences Sociétés*, 21, 77–83, 2013.

Schulson, E.M. "The Structure and Mechanical Behavior of Ice," in *The Structure and Mechanical Behavior of Ice*, JOM, 1999.

Von Uexkull, J. "A Stroll Through the Worlds of Animals and Men," in Schiller, C. (ed.), *Instinctive Behavior; the Development of a Modern Concept*, International University Press, 1934.

Index

fractal recursion 106
future of landscape architecture 252–253

Game of Life 275–276
Generate and Test 97
generative modeling 50–62
genetic algorithms 97
geo-design, emergence of 9
Geofoam 268, 269, 270–274, 276–277
GIS (geographic information systems) 7, 206–207
Googleplex campus 18
Grasshopper software 20, 25, 75, 208
"Greetings from Owens Lake" 158, 160–161, 163
GUI interface 20, 99

heat waves 137–140
high-tech campus 17–18, 31
history of computation 6–10, 91, 94, 206–208
human body scale (generative modeling) 51–52
human-technology relation 157
humanities, big data in 134
"humanness", incorporating 156

IBM 3270 mainframe computer 1
ice caps 289–294
imperative language 95–96
infrastructure, in Turing landscape 111
Ingels, Bjarke 25
innovation for innovation's sake 9, 11, 28
input-output translation 78, 96
interaction see interface; mode of interaction
interface: using play 163–165
Internet of Things (IoT) 90, 101–104

Jacquard loom 105

Kara, Hanif 42
Koren, Benjamin 42

Laboratory for Computer Graphics and Spatial Analysis, Harvard University 1, 7
LAG bench 189–193
landform, in Turing landscape 111
Landscape Accounting Framework 217–218, 220
landscape Turing test 108–110
language: code as a 89–90, 99–101; design acts as 93; imperative 95–96;

natural vs. artificial 5; procedural 95–96
learning: and C21st workforce 64; curricula of programming 69; forward learning reality 69–70; SEE and MAKE tools 65–70; theory 68–69; virtual reality 65–67, 92, 104
levels of programming 23–24
Lifelong Kindergarten (MIT Media Lab) 26
Local Code project 210
Los Angeles River Integrated Design Lab (LA-RIDL) 156–158, 161–162
Loxahatchee Impoundment Landscape Assessment (LILA) 127–129
L-systems 106
Lucas Films 10
Lucas, George 9

McHargian Analysis 7
machine language 95
MAKE tools 65–70
manifesto 46–47
mapping, open-source 149–154
Marionette algorithmic scripting 173–177
marketing 43
materials, coding behavior of 187–194
materials-first design methodologies 182–187
mathematics 22, 26, 94
mental models 68
meteorology 180–181
Milankovich Cycle 291, 293
MIT Media Lab 26
mode of interaction: code as a language 89–90, 99–101; software as a tool 89, 98; via Internet of Things (IoT) 90, 101–104
modeling, scientific: Arnold Arboretum 121–123; atmospheric behavior 135–137; Experimental Lakes Area, Ontario 125–126; Loxahatchee Impoundment Landscape Assessment (LILA) 127–129; overview of 120; Seine Estuary model 123–125
motion through representation 103–104
multi-disciplinary practice 87–88
multiple design iterations 41, 50, 73–75

natural language 5
navigation, spatial 139
needs-driven projects 44–45
neo-nature 280–287
neurology 68

next-generation tool sets 171–179
NSA Cryptology magazine 7, 8

object-oriented systems 100
Olmsted landscapes 90, 109
open-data 197, 230–231
open-source mapping 149–154
"open space" concept 19
opportunity-driven projects 44–45
optioneering 41, 50, 73–75
Orchard Road, Singapore 135–136
Owens Lake Dust Control Project 158–161, 164–165

Paralabs (interviews) 41–49
parallel processing 94, 107–108
parametric design: Arcadia 2014 exhibition 72; multiple design iterations 41, 50, 73–75; South Park, San Francisco 71–76
parametric generation 105–106
ParkScore index 219–221
participatory design 150
particle systems 106–108
pattern generation by repetition 105
perception, of the landscape 149–150
Performance Series (LAF) 198, 217
perspective, agency of 159–161
photorealism 108–109
play 163–165
Possible City project 214
postdigital practice 77–80
postoccupancy evaluation (POE) 198, 269
precipitation tool 177
prediction see modeling, scientific
procedural language 95–96
procedural programming 100
productivity, and abstraction 23–26
programming, levels of 23–24
Projexity 214–215

query pursuit 172–173

radiation and environmental analysis 40
randomness 97
reality, sense data and 119
Relational Urban Model (RUM) 209–210
relationship: between innovations and physical urban environment 18; between synthetic models 16
repetition, pattern generation by 105
Rhinoceros software 20
risk-taking 21
route mapping 150–154
rule-based generation 106